Grammar and Christianity
in the
Late Roman World

DIVINATIONS:
REREADING LATE ANCIENT RELIGION

Series Editors

Daniel Boyarin
Virginia Burrus
Derek Krueger

A complete list of books in the series
is available from the publisher.

Grammar and Christianity in the Late Roman World

Catherine M. Chin

PENN

UNIVERSITY OF PENNSYLVANIA PRESS

Philadelphia

Published by
University of Pennsylvania Press
Philadelphia, Pennsylvania 19104-4112

Printed in the United States of America on acid-free paper

10   9   8   7   6   5   4   3   2   1

Library of Congress Cataloging-in-Publication Data

Chin, Catherine M.
   Grammar and Christianity in the late Roman world / Catherine M. Chin.
     p. cm.—(Divinations)
   Includes bibliographical references and index.
   ISBN-13: 978-0-8122-4035-1 (hardcover : alk. paper)
   ISBN-10: 0-8122-4035-9 (hardcover : alk. paper)
     1. Grammar, Comparative and general—History. 2. Christianity and culture—History.
3. Rome—History—Empire, 284–476. I. Title.
   P63.C49 2007
   415.0937—dc22   2007023273

For my parents

Contents

I

Introduction
Toward Tyranny

THIS BOOK IS A VERY LONG ANSWER to a very short question: How did literate Romans of the fourth and fifth centuries come to the idea that there was such a thing as Christianity? On its face the question seems naïve. There was, in this period, a dramatic growth in the numbers of people, buildings, books, and public events that were called, at least in some contexts, Christian; historians now conventionally refer to this period as one in which the Roman Empire was Christianized. The question that this book attempts to answer, however, is not whether people or places called Christian existed in the later Roman Empire. Instead, the book addresses the question of how some later Roman readers and writers went about transforming those people, places, texts, and events into a generality, and how they summoned that generality into conceptual existence. My basic argument is that a movement from the description of various people or things as Christian to the concept of a free-standing religious and cultural entity that could be named Christianity did take place in this period, but took place in a series of quite tenuous intellectual movements, under very specific educational conditions, and with no immediate guarantee that the notion of Christianity would become an enduring component of the Western cultural imagination. *Christianitas* is a decidedly uncommon formulation in the early centuries of Christian history; its conceptual fragility is worth examining.

Because this is a book about the conceptual consequences of names and naming, it is about language as much as it is about religion. Specifically it is about how the teaching of language in late antiquity shaped the ability of late ancient readers and writers to have concepts that we call religious. This language teaching was primarily in the hands of grammarians, and so texts surrounding the discipline of grammar, in both Christian and traditional contexts, form the evidentiary core of this study. The modest premise of this work is that the discipline of grammar, which in late antiquity encompassed both language analysis and literary criticism, had fundamental effects in religious as well as literary discourse; less modestly, I argue that the conventions of the discipline of grammar transformed linguistic work into incipient religious practice. The conflation of literature and religion was not without precedent. The rise of formal grammatical study from the fourth century to the sixth coincides not only with the growth in numbers of identifiably Christian texts and people but also with a rich period of text-based magical practices, divination through books, and the like.[1] While such practices are not directly the concern of this book, they testify in a particularly clear fashion to the numinous power that could at the time be attributed to linguistic acts. The licit religious ideations of grammar, I suggest, were more diffuse but no less potent.

Since this book is about the potency of language in late antiquity, it is also very much about the texts in which such potent language was taken to reside, texts that we can still meaningfully describe under the disciplinary rubric of "classics." The Latin grammarians of the fourth and fifth centuries were among the most important agents who defined the canon of Latin authors that would be studied, copied, imitated, and so passed on into the Middle Ages and up to our own time. Part of the imaginative work that grammarians accomplished, then, was the construction of an authoritative literary tradition whose strengths lay primarily in the language of the late republic and early empire. Henri-Irénée Marrou, in his magisterial *Histoire de l'Education dans l'Antiquité*, described this production as follows:

On the whole, despite the new tendencies, grammar was still essentially theoretical, analytical, and, so to speak, contemplative. The grammarian did not teach people how to use a living language; he took stock of the material that had been used by the great classic writers, the language which in their masterpieces had been hallowed for all eternity. A tyrannical classical ideal dominated this teaching. . . . Latin *was*—it was there for all time in the great writers; the science of correct speaking—*recte loquendi scientia*—was based in the last analysis on *auctoritas*.[2]

Despite the appearance in recent years of revealing work on the status of grammarians in late antiquity, on the types and transmission of grammatical treatises, and on the material conditions of ancient education,[3] the general picture of late ancient grammar and its tyrannical ideal has not changed much in the decades since Marrou.[4] The reader will see in what follows that I agree with Marrou on many points; what interests me here, however, is not a condemnation of grammatical tyranny but a description of that tyranny's difficult birth, and of the conditions of its reproduction. The classical and the Christian are thus presented here as simultaneous constructions: in investigating the notion of Christianity in the late Roman world, it is impossible to avoid the construction of its apparent opposite, the pre-Christian, pagan, classical world. These two categories are phantoms that haunt narratives of the Western tradition to this day. In this book, I examine the words that conjure them.

Roman grammar began, if we are to believe Suetonius, accidentally, absurdly, and with a certain nostalgia: "In my view, therefore, the first person to introduce the study of grammar to the city was Crates of Mallos, a contemporary of Aristarchus. Sent to the senate by King Attalus between the Second and Third Punic Wars, at just about the time of Ennius' death, Crates fell down and broke his leg in a sewer-hole in the neighborhood of the Palatine and spent the whole time of the embassy and of his recuperation constantly giving a host of lectures and holding frequent discussions, thereby providing an example for our countrymen to imitate."[5] This unglamorous foundational narrative dramatizes one of the undercurrents that run through the works of the *grammatici Latini*, the sense that grammatical work salvages what it can from disaster. The common idea that linguistic work is a kind of rearguard action against the advances of time, opinion, or contrary social interest helps explain some of the productivity of the discipline.[6] Understanding grammar as a practice that makes the best of adverse conditions, ancient grammarians operated within a conceptual framework that allowed for the simultaneous construction and negotiation of opposed entities, both that which needed to be salvaged and that which worked against such saving. A few examples from Roman accounts of grammar before late antiquity will provide the disciplinary context for the production of religious, temporal, and social generalities in the later grammatical treatises and grammar-related works that form the core of this book.

Quintilian's account of rhetorical education places grammar at the outset of a process of subject formation that fits into a specific ideological framework, one based on predictable divisions between elites and non-elites, Romans and non-Romans, masculinity and its lack. Quintilian argues in the first book of his *Institutio Oratoria* that proper language usage, the province of the grammarian and the foundation of the orator's professional skill, is "the agreed practice of educated men,"[7] noting that this is not the usage "of the majority. . . . For where is so much good to be found that what is right should please the majority?"[8] Throughout the *Institutio*, he is careful to argue that the correct performance of one's educated status is dependent on conformity to the consensus of the correctly educated minority.[9] The parameters of this community are regulated in part through the ideologies of masculinity and Romanness promoted in Quintilian's configuration of the ideal educated individual.[10] Not only does Quintilian frame his entire discussion of grammatical education in terms of the responsibilities of fathers toward their sons,[11] he also warns fathers against those primary teachers who might educate boys to become "soft,"[12] and he derides bad grammarians as "groomed and fat."[13] Barbarisms may be dependent on the *gens* either of the word or of the speaker,[14] and in this context even the otherwise admirable Greeks find it more difficult than Romans to follow the "ancient law of language."[15] Quintilian's construction of correct Roman linguistic behavior, beginning with proper grammatical instruction in the necessary *auctores*,[16] is clearly engaged in more than the task of promoting literacy—it also uses literacy as a site at which to call into being an ideal Roman person.

In a similar vein, Suetonius' *De grammaticis et rhetoribus* paints a far from neutral picture of the entry of grammar as a discipline into Rome, dwelling instead on the foreign or lower-class status of grammar's practitioners. One of the striking features of Suetonius' *De grammaticis* is the extent to which the grammarians represented seem to have been members of the Roman lower classes. Fourteen of the twenty grammarians whom Suetonius lists are said to be freedmen;[17] one was a boxer;[18] one an unsuccessful centurion;[19] and two more, although freeborn, are said to have been quite poor.[20] Most scholars take this as evidence that the profession of grammarian, or the knowledge of grammar, could have served as a means of social mobility in the republic and early empire.[21] Robert Kaster, although he accepts the premise of the first-century grammarians' relatively low status, warns against taking Suetonius' characterizations too literally: he describes Suetonius' biography of the grammarian Palaemon, who "was notorious for every sort of vice,"[22] as "the standard picture of the arrogant and depraved parvenu."[23] While there is no substantial reason to doubt Suetonius' information on the social standing of first-century grammarians at Rome, it is clear that his emphasis on their status owes more than a little to the broader tradition of invective.[24] In short, grammar and grammarians allow Suetonius to articulate a hierarchy of status in Roman society, and to map that hierarchy onto specific cultural practitioners. Notably, where Quintilian straightforwardly narrates grammar as saving elite

Roman masculine language from outside incursions or corruptions, Suetonius' picture is more complex: on the one hand, grammar allows for the valuation of Roman literature, on the other, grammar's professionalization comes along with social decline.

The double function of grammar in the Roman social imagination is historicized in Suetonius by the implicit narrative of grammar's rise through social decline. This historicizing or periodizing effect, and the implication of decline, may also be found in more technical linguistic works. Varro's *De lingua latina* ties the historical effects of grammatical work not merely to its practitioners but to the techniques of the discipline itself. Grammar's usefulness in preserving a past and representing a decline is particularly well illustrated in Varro's comments on the limits of etymological knowledge. At *De lingua latina* 6.39, he compares the formation of words to the formation of the world according to the atomic theory of Democritus:

Democritus, Epicurus and likewise others who have pronounced the original elements to be unlimited in number, though they do not tell us whence the elements are, but only of what sort they are, still perform a great service: they show us the things which in the world consist of these elements. Therefore if the etymologist should postulate one thousand original elements [*principia*] of words, about which an interpretation is not to be asked of him, and show the nature of the rest [*reliqua*], about which he does not make [this] postulation, the number of words which he would explain would still be enormous.[25]

The etymologist's task is twofold. He is to postulate *principia* and demonstrate *reliqua*: the things to which originality is and is not to be attributed. Varro's etymologist is a historian of language, and the historical mode is based on a conceptual break between origin and derivation. The origins of the *principia* are, moreover, explicitly characterized as beyond the scope of investigation, while the postulation of such original elements allows for the multiplication of the amount of knowledge derived from them. This historical narrative of language is common in Hellenistic and Roman linguistics; what is notable here is how the narrative insists on a temporal framework for the understanding of language, postulating a deliberately vague, but unadulterated, "then" in contrast to the complex and derivative "now." Varro's apparently simple description of etymology is heavy with ideological import, and it locates that ideology within the techniques of linguistic analysis itself.

Grammatical education cannot, then, be taken as a simple fact of Roman cultural life but deserves examination as a forum for cultural production in its own right. This is no less the case in the later Roman

Empire, during the period in which the majority of the grammatical treatises surviving from antiquity were composed. During this period, ideological gestures and clashes began to include the perceived rise of Christianity as an imperial religion. Here, too, grammatical education became an arena in which cultural ideals could be articulated and subjects could be produced within specific frameworks of identity. Much of the debate as to the meaning of adopting a Christian identity in this period presupposed that the act of reading "pagan" or "Christian" texts marked the reader's cultural and religious status. Most famous, perhaps, are the accounts of Augustine lamenting in the *Confessions* his childhood spent in reading Virgil,[26] or of Jerome, chastised in a dream for attending more to the writings of Cicero than to the Bible.[27] These accounts are more than mere tropes of the dangers of classical literature; they also reveal the ways in which reading was understood as a cultural practice and an articulation of subjectivity. This book therefore focuses on how basic reading practices were construed in this period as determining religious and cultural affiliation. It examines the historical event generally described as the rise of Christianity in the Roman Empire as part of the history of reading and of literate education.

The works that provide this book with its basic hermeneutic for approaching late ancient reading are the surviving Latin *artes grammaticae* that date from around 350 to around 500, particularly the almost entirely complete *artes* of Donatus, Charisius, Servius, Diomedes, Pompeius, and Priscian.[28] These educational texts, outlining the study of Latin grammar and attempting a systematic discussion of correctness in Latin usage, have long been studied as documents in the history of linguistic theory and in the history of literary scholarship.[29] Here I consider the ways in which they both promote a classical ideal and construct late ancient subjects in relation to that ideal. For instance, when the grammarian Diomedes quotes a passage of Virgil to illustrate a possible use of the accusative,[30] he is on one level simply demonstrating a view of the place of the accusative in late ancient grammatical theory. He is also, however, placing his reader into a system in which the citation of Virgil is a culturally and historically significant act, one that uses an exemplary mode to exhort the reader to take a certain cultural and linguistic position in relation to Virgil, be that position imitative or not.[31] This study thus places the *artes* in their context not only as texts revealing the content of late ancient Latin schooling but also as texts that reflect the cultural investments that such schooling could entail.

My consideration of grammatical method and its effects is organized as follows: Chapter 2, "Imagining Classics," first examines the Latin *ars grammatica* as a genre of late ancient educational literature. I argue that the two primary linguistic practices that the *ars* promotes, fragmentation of texts and the juxtaposition of verbal fragments in lists, encouraged readers to envision language, and literary texts, as classifiable into two temporally defined corpora, that of the "ancients" and that of themselves. Much like the etymologizing described by Varro, reading practices as presented in grammatical literature produced larger ideological structures and implicit narratives, particularly the idea of a homogeneous authoritative past, manifested in literary objects. The theoretical basis of my analysis in this chapter lies in poststructuralist approaches to language teaching, particularly in the work of sociologist Pierre Bourdieu on the ideological uses of education and on the teaching of legitimate language.[32] I use Bourdieu's basic insight, that standardized language teaching tends to produce and reproduce group and class boundaries, to illuminate the production of imaginative boundaries through language teaching in the Roman Empire. The practice of grammar formed a technology of the imagination that allowed its users to understand themselves as part of a coherent cultural system, one specifically oriented toward the valorization of an idealized past.

Chapter 3, "From Grammar to Piety," considers the relationship produced by the grammars between the idea of the literary past and the present linguistic actor. The first part of the chapter argues that this relationship was construed in the *artes* as one of obligation, that is, that the present linguistic subject was construed as under obligation to an authoritative past in all of his or her linguistic acts. This was an obligation not necessarily to imitate past linguistic practices but to acknowledge that past textual objects were valid symbols of cultural authority. Thus linguistic actors could, for example, recognize a line of Cicero as culturally potent on one level, while categorizing it as grammatically inimitable on another. The promotion of this recognition placed the linguistic actor into a temporal and cultural framework in which he or she could only be understood to exist as a linguistic subject through the articulation of a subject-position under obligation. The second part of the chapter examines the way in which this linguistic obligation could be understood as a form of piety, and ultimately of religious obligation, in literature dealing with grammar but outside the formal *artes*. The texts on which I focus in this part of the chapter are Macrobius' *Saturnalia*, Ausonius' *Parentalia*, Julian the Apostate's letter 36, on Christian teachers, and Augustine's *Confessions*, book 8, on the conversion of Marius Victorinus. Each of these texts claims that linguistic acts, and especially grammatical acts, place the linguistic actor in a specifically religious framework of obligation. In other words, literary obligation is transformed here into religious affiliation. Throughout this chapter, I supplement Bourdieu's theoretical analysis of educational systems with the work of Judith Butler on the performative and linguistic nature of subject formation.[33]

The following chapter, "Displacement and Excess: Christianizing Grammar," shifts focus to the ways in which writers who identified themselves as Christian made use of grammatical techniques in order to produce two mutually exclusive ideological bodies of literature, *litteratura apud gentes* and *litteratura Christiana*. In the first part of the chapter, I consider some of the more theoretical approaches to classifying literature, as found in Rufinus' *Apology Against Jerome*, Jerome's *Apology Against Rufinus* and letters 21 and 70, and Augustine's *On Christian Doctrine*. These works theorize the practice of quotation in terms similar to those used by the grammarians to discuss textual fragmentation in the *artes*, and indeed rely on the technical framework of the *artes* to conceive of quotation as a literary and ideological practice. After considering the ways in which quotation is understood as a textual practice, I turn in the second part of the chapter to some of the more technical grammatical works of Christian writers. I focus on Origen's *Hexapla*, Jerome's *Book of Hebrew Names*, and Augustine's *Locutions in the Heptateuch*, and consider how these works promote the idea of a freestanding literary Christianity, using techniques that in the *artes* create an equally freestanding classical past.

The fifth chapter, "Fear, Boredom, and Amusement: Emotion and Grammar," returns to the grammarian's schoolroom to examine the production of "Christian" and "Roman" subjects in the process of elementary schooling, as it was retrospectively imagined by adult writers. It considers this production as related to experiential and affective tropes common to late ancient descriptions of education under a grammarian. These tropes are: that the grammarian is boring, that the grammarian is frightening to pupils (because he beats them), and that the classroom situation, especially involving the boring or beating of children, is an amusing spectacle. I argue that these tropes were useful to educational writers in imagining the pedagogical situation as one that required the adoption of a fixed identity. The main texts used in this chapter are Martianus Capella's *Marriage of Philology and Mercury*, book 3 (on grammar), Augustine's *Confessions*, book 1, Jerome's letter 22.30, and John Chrysostom's *On Vainglory*. In analyzing these texts, I complicate Bourdieu's discussion of the symbolic power of education by drawing on the work of Gilles Deleuze and his interlocutors; this work structures my consideration of the connections between affective experiences, varieties of linguistic fragmentation, and the production of both multiform subjects and multivalent ideological entities.[34]

The final chapter, "Grammar and Utopia," places literature about grammarians and grammatical practice within the larger context of Christianization in the Latin West, using especially the critical work of Louis Marin to situate the late ancient idea of Christian space within the Western tradition of utopian writing.[35] I examine grammatical literature's use of spatial language to support the idea that Christian or classical bodies of literature were manifestations of a broader Christian or classical culture, with physical presence in the geographic reaches of the Roman Empire. It also considers the ways in which readers were imagined to inhabit classical or Christian space in the process of reading. In order to explore this concept of the spatialization of abstract ideological entities, I have focused on three sets of texts: first, Ausonius' *Professors of Bordeaux*, which locates grammatical education within the physical "cohort" of the educators who move in and out of Bordeaux; second, the correspondence between Ausonius and his former pupil Paulinus of Nola, which has as its two themes Ausonius' desire for Paulinus to visit him, and Paulinus' argument that Ausonius' literary acts bind Ausonius too closely to a "pagan past." Finally, I consider Jerome's letters to Paulinus, which, like Ausonius', combine the themes of travel and literary activity, this time with these acts configured as acts of scriptural interpretation and of pilgrimage. Examination of spatial language in the literature of the later Roman Empire thus returns the study in a very concrete way to its broader goal, a description of the relationship between language and the imagination of substantive religious realities.

Traditional Marxist accounts of ideology and its productive force have generally focused on the structural inequities produced and sustained by different ideological formations. In one sense, this book stands in the same tradition, for it is obviously the case that grammatical education in late antiquity helped to maintain the hierarchy of the literate in the administrative ranks of Roman governance.[36] Yet the tyranny with which Marrou charges late ancient education is of a different kind, although it relies on some of the same social imbalances. For Marrou, the tyranny of the classical is ultimately misguided, a failure to recognize the strengths of later Latin as a language system in its own right.[37] I would like to suggest, however, that it is precisely the vitality of the ideal, rather than the real, that allowed late ancient readers to form narratives of themselves as agents within a cultural and historical matrix, that is, as individuals who could choose to determine in what ideological or temporal relation they might stand vis-à-vis the cultural objects with which they were continually presented in any linguistic action. It is possible, in other words, that late ancient literary education was indeed subject to a tyrannical ideal, that of the classical past. It is equally the case, if this is so, that this subjection created a framework in which those who saw themselves as voluntarily submitting to it could also understand themselves as setting the conditions for their own reformulation as new subjects. Such subjects, the products of an ideal, would be capable of actions in violation or support of the ideal's tyrannical law, and perhaps in support of hegemonies, like Christianity, whose articulation would lead to further expansions, however painful or revolutionary, of the late ancient cultural imagination.

2

Imagining Classics

LEARNING TO READ IS ALWAYS a matter of learning to read *something*. Late ancient grammarians formed their discipline by teaching their students how to read the classics—or rather, by teaching their students how to read in a way that created classics. A wealth of material survives from late ancient grammatical culture, and the reading practices described in this material had a profound effect on late ancient ideologies of literacy and literature. Although the specific connection between these practices and ideologies is seldom studied,[1] the idea of a shared literary culture was constructed and maintained in the technologies of language that grammarians produced.[2] In this chapter, I consider how late ancient modes of reading Latin contributed to the imagination of unified sets of linguistic acts and *mores*, sets that not only positioned readers within a social network but also placed these readers within a temporal progression from the republican past to the late ancient present. I am interested in how grammatical education set the conditions for late ancient Latin readers to think of themselves in relation to a supposedly unified cultural tradition, and in how nonnarrative technical texts made it possible for these readers to think narratively about their imagined selves and their communities.[3] Thus I take the surviving *artes grammaticae*, the body of technical treatises defining correct Latin grammar, as examples of a specific and relatively consistent genre of educational writing in late antiquity.[4] These *artes* span easily 150 years of grammatical writing, from the mid-fourth century to the early sixth, and I do not claim to do them justice as individual works situated in individual historical contexts; for the purposes of this discussion, it is more important to be able to examine the characteristics that they have in common.[5] The persistence of such characteristics reveals, I think, the persistence of certain habits of reading, or at least certain habits of thinking about reading, that were in place for readers of the *artes* throughout this period.

Despite differences in many aspects of the *artes*, there are two familiar verbal gestures that are fundamental to the teaching of reading, as it is configured in each of them. The first is the quotation of earlier texts as exempla. The second is the making of lists. Both of these gestures are at once destructive and productive, in that they tend to break up narrative sequence, or interrupt flows of argument, and to introduce expansion.[6] Illustrating a grammatical point with a line of Virgil both interrupts the grammarian's voice and expands the point into another text; the quoted line is likewise interrupted and expanded to include grammatical meaning. Lists of words, for example of verb conjugations, similarly both interrupt the flow of grammatical argument and expand it through illustration. These are techniques that have important effects, as they are deployed by late ancient grammarians in the construction of a Latin literary tradition. In the first part of this chapter, I consider the uses to which quotation is put in the formulation of a literary past; in the second, I consider the uses to which lists are put in the articulation of a relationship between that imagined past and the grammarian's imagined present.

Grammatica dividit

It would be difficult to trace out a history, either on an individual or a cultural level, of how people physically perceive words and their component parts, but the *artes grammaticae* of the mid-fourth to early sixth centuries provide one essential, and consistent, piece of information in this regard.[7] The basic technique for approaching Latin reading in late antiquity was verbal fragmentation: *grammatica*, as Sidonius Apollinaris tells us, *dividit*.[8] One of the typical arrangements of the *ars grammatica* begins with sound and pronunciation, moving on to letters, combinations of letters, and syllables, before considering whole words as parts of speech. So, for example, Donatus' *Ars Maior* opens with the following six sections: *de voce, de litteris, de syllaba, de pedibus, de tonis,* and *de posituris,* and then the parts of speech.[9] This is the arrangement as early as Dionysius Thrax, and it is observed by Charisius, Donatus' *Ars Maior* (and hence "Sergius" and Pompeius, who follow Donatus), Priscian's *Institutiones,* and Asper. The other typical arrangement of the *ars* begins with the parts of speech, analyzing each separately, and then moving to letters and their subsequent formation into syllables. Remmius Palaemon may have followed this order, and Donatus' *Ars Minor,* Diomedes, Cledonius, and Consentius do the same.[10] Probus' *Instituta Artium* combines the two forms, beginning with letters and then moving to parts of speech. While the *Instituta* do not have a separate consideration of syllables,[11] Probus considers word endings of various kinds throughout the work. For example, he organizes his discussion of the ablative around the possible endings of nouns: *De a.* [. . .] *De ia.* [. . .] *De as.* [. . .] *De es.*[12] The differences between these types of organization notwithstanding, the reader's attention in the *artes* is consistently drawn to individual units and letter combinations rather than whole texts or even complete sentences. To take another example, Charisius' discussion of the adverb begins with a definition ("an adverb is a part of speech that, when added to a verb, adds to or explains its meaning")[13] but quickly moves into the ways in which different noun endings transform into different adverbs ("nouns that end in the letter *a* . . . nouns that end in the letter *e* . . . nouns that end in the letter *r* . . . nouns that end with the letters *or*," and so on).[14] Similar examples could be adduced from other *artes*. As a discipline, then, grammar is first imagined to be a discipline of word division. This is naturally consistent with the principle of word division in ancient reading more generally, as most texts were produced with little or no punctuation, but the principle of division extends further. The grammarians' interest in letters and syllables independent of words makes clear that word division was an active analytic technique rather than a simple necessity.

For this reason, the genre of the *ars*, based on the partitioning of speech, dictates that individual units at the verbal level also be taken in isolation. Each part of speech is treated as a single item, and lists of examples given by individual grammarians tend to remove these items from any syntactical setting in order to analyze them as singularities. So, for example, Diomedes' discussion of appellative nouns begins as follows: "Appellatives are nouns that are said to be general or common. These are divided into two types, one of which is comprised of corporal things that can be seen and touched, like man, tree; the other is comprised of incorporal things, which are perceived in a way by the intellect, but cannot in truth be seen or touched, like god piety justice dignity wisdom learning fluency."[15] Man tree god piety may share some conceptual connections, of course, but they are not here used to make up coherent sentences. Rather, each is taken out of one signifying context (e.g., one whose subject is particular men or gods) and moved as an individual unit into another context. This is very much the point of grammatical work: larger units of thought are continually broken down into smaller units as part of the grammarian's approach to literacy. Priscian's *Partitiones* offers an idealized example of this kind of advanced classroom training in reading *Aeneid* 1.1:

Scan the verse. Arma vi rumque ca no Tro iae qui primus ab oris. How many caesuras does it have? Two. What are they? A penthemimera and a hephthemimera. Explain. The penthemimera is arma virumque cano, and the hephthemimera is arma virumque cano Troiae. How many figures does it have? Ten. Why so? Because it consists of three dactyls and two spondees. How many parts of speech does the line contain? Nine. How many nouns? Six: arma, virum, Troiae, qui, primus, oris. How many verbs? One: cano. How many prepositions? One: ab. How many conjunctions? One: que.[16]

The line is first removed from its context in the *Aeneid* proper and then broken into individual syllables, feet, and words. Whether or not readers invariably read with this dissecting technique as their overt *modus*,[17] it seems clear that high-level comprehension of a text was largely based on the observation, and thus production, of singularities.

Priscian's use of the question-and-answer format further suggests that his work is modeled on actual classroom practice, so that this type of reading appears to have been one of the primary reading methods taught in schools.[18] Priscian's work is of course only one example of this technique and not itself a formal *ars*, but there is substantial conceptual and social overlap, apparently throughout the Roman Mediterranean, between the work of the grammarian and the work of the elementary *magister*. The breakdown of language as a means of teaching literacy is evident both in Quintilian's instruction and in the school papyri: Quintilian suggests that teachers require students to recognize alphabetical letters placed in random orders,[19] and he likewise insists on the learning of all possible syllabic combinations;[20] school papyri attest to the commonality of alphabetic rearrangement and syllabic practice.[21] Although reading and writing were separate skills, they worked in some ways along similar lines, in that literary texts were often broken down syllabically in the teaching of both.[22] Part of the method found in the papyri for teaching writing was the copying of exemplary lines or *sententiae*, which were often quotations from canonical literary texts.[23] The emphasis in the *artes* on letters, syllables, and exemplary quotations should thus be construed not as the rarified product of grammarians' thought exercises but as part of a technique that ancient readers learned early in their reading careers to apply to the texts that they approached. The fundamental process of reading involved the singling out of individual units of comprehension, from letters to entire lines.

DIVISION AND AUTHORITY

One of the effects of this method is clearly visible in the *artes*. When not generating their own examples of parts of speech (man tree god piety), the grammarians provide examples from numerous earlier authors, who stand as authoritative figures in the construction of Latinity. The idea of *auctoritas* is complex, and the authority of the grammarians was very much bound up in that of the *auctores* whose texts they quoted and taught.[24] At the same time, however, the authority of the *auctores* can be attributed in part to the uses to which the grammarian put them.[25] To return to Priscian's *Partitiones*: the text of the *Aeneid* is broken first into individual lines, then into individual words and syllables. Priscian's authority is produced in part by his mastery of the text, in that he is the figure dividing it and offering analyses.[26] His authority is further suggested by the question-and-answer format that replicates classroom practice, so that he is also the figure asking the questions and issuing the imperatives (*tracta singulas partes*).[27] In formally gesturing toward the classroom, the *Partitiones* create the figure of Priscian as a reader to be taken seriously.[28] Nor is Priscian the only figure whose authority is being produced. Virgil, too, benefits from being taken apart. The division of the *Aeneid* into *singulas partes* allows a number of important interventions to occur. Priscian's discussion of *que* in *arma virumque*, for example, is as follows:

What part of speech is *que*? A conjunction. What is a conjunction? A part of speech that connects a sentence, and that sets it in order. How many characteristics does a conjunction have? Three, significance, position, figure. What is its significance? Copulative. What is its position? Postpositive. What is its figure? Simple. What accent does it have? This and two other conjunctions, that is *ve* and *ne*, are "inclinatives" in Latin, which the Greeks call *enklitikas*. They generally have their accent on the last syllable of the preceding word, as in *virumque, subiectisve, tantone*. But *ne* very often loses its *e* and is noted by an apostrophe, not only when there is a vowel, but even with a consonant following it, as in the tenth book of the *Aeneid*: *tanton me crimine dignum*? Form composites of it, that is, *que. Atque, neque, quoque. nec quoque* is formed from *neque* through the apocope of the final letters; and because one cannot write *q* at the end of a syllable, it becomes *c*.[29]

Here, what might at first seem to be a minor part of the opening of the *Aeneid* becomes an occasion to demonstrate a very wide range of knowledge: the uses and forms of conjunctions, morphology of final syllables, a fragment of *Aeneid* 10.668, even a bit of Greek. Priscian's insertion of this knowledge into the reading of the first line of the *Aeneid* transforms the poem into a repository of information, in which each syllable carries much more significance than a connected reading of the poem might suggest. Virgil thus becomes a locus of educatedness far beyond his status as a poet.[30] The dissection of texts thus provides readers with the opportunity to enhance not only the reader's status as educated but also the status of the text that is read.

This enhancement is not limited to the genre of the *Partitiones* or to commentary, although it is particularly clear in that branch of grammatical work. The effects of reading by division are also visible in the *artes*, which are not text specific. It is usual in these texts for examples of grammatical points to be drawn from writers from diverse periods of Latin literary history, most of them from before the second century C.E.,[31] although quotation practices vary both according to grammatical topic and according to grammarian.[32] To mention two examples of quotation practices, at one point in his discussion of the noun, Pompeius provides four quotations, from Virgil, Persius, Terence, and Plautus, in the space of about twenty lines;[33] and Priscian, a copious quoter, quotes Horace (twice), Terence (twice), Accius, Cato the Elder, Cinna, Virgil (three times), Laevius, Gracchus, Ovid, Statius, and Nonius Marcellinus, all within the space of one forty-four-line passage, as part of his discussion of feminine nouns in the *Institutiones*.[34] By virtue of becoming didactic tools, these quoted texts take on a certain cultural potency: they are the authoritative texts for cultural interchange. They do not all necessarily possess precisely the same degree of *auctoritas*,[35] since the preponderance of quotations from Virgil, Cicero, Plautus, and Terence ensures that these specific figures will have primacy. By being inserted into the pedagogical situation, however, even the less often quoted authors also become objects in the cultural economy; that is, they are marked for the grammarian's audience as legitimate points of reference in the construction of Latinity, to be inserted into discussions of literate culture as markers of cultural competence.[36] The ability to quote Laevius in part reinforces the quoter's literate status, and in part reinforces the status of Laevius as a "quotable" poet, even if not an "imitable" one.

Such texts are understood to mark the boundaries of acceptable Latin.[37] Both Donatus and Pompeius, typically for the *artes*, use far more quotations from exemplary texts when dealing with the categories of "barbarism" and "solecism" than with simple nouns and verbs.[38] This use of examples reinforces the authority of the quoted *auctores*: examples of barbarism are not simply marked as "wrong," but as something the *auctores* could do but students cannot. As Donatus defines barbarism, it is "a single part of speech that is incorrect in common discourse. In poetry it is called metaplasm,"[39] and although metaplasm may occur "for the sake of meter or ornament,"[40] barbarism, which occurs in *nostra loquella*, is simply to be avoided.[41] The exemplary text, then, is allowed to remain exemplary, even if it is not to be imitated. The boundary created between what the poets can do and what students are expected to do further reinforces the canonicity of the texts from which the grammarian draws examples: they are a *corpus* whose function is to represent authoritative Latinity. This representative function of the *auctores* should be emphasized. Quotations do not necessarily present the reader with usages to be followed; instead, they serve as points of reference to a style of educated discourse.[42] Even authorial usages that are not to be imitated, then, come to represent the act of speaking well, by virtue of their inclusion in the discourse of correctness.

Literary fragmentation plays a further role in generating the cultural authority of the quoted texts. In the same way that the insertion of grammatical knowledge around the syllables of the *Aeneid* makes the *Aeneid* (and perhaps more fundamentally the figure of Virgil) a repository of knowledge, so the use of literary fragments to generate a representational field of acceptable Latin endows these fragments with a particular potency. The *auctoritas* of, for example, Lucan may be "less" than that of Terence,[43] but the entry of Lucan into the idea of *auctoritas* is itself significant. This is the case because the fragments become icons of literary meaningfulness apart from their meaning in their originary verbal contexts.[44] This is particularly clear in the conservatism of grammarians in the use of specific literary exempla.[45] The most immediately recognizable quotation from Ennius may be the somewhat outré *o Tite tute Tati tibi tanta tyranni tulisti*.[46] This line is used repeatedly in the *artes* to illustrate principles of alliteration. Similarly, the Virgilian line *itur in antiquam silvam* is frequently used in the *artes* to illustrate variously the use of the impersonal, the length of vowels, or the use of the accusative.[47] These lines have been removed from their original signifying contexts and placed into a new didactic context; their primary significations are no longer to Titus or to an *antiqua silva* but to the linguistic points that they illustrate. They have thereby become symbols of grammatical knowledgeability.[48] The repetition of these and other lines across the *artes* suggests both the mobility of literary fragments and the productivity of that mobility. It is specifically the removal of the exemplum from its context and its repositioning that allows this transformation to take place.[49] The technique of quotation, then—that is, of breaking down literary texts and of recontextualizing the resulting fragments—is a kind of signifying technology, producing both literary knowledge and the objects of that knowledge, namely, the fragments that make it visible.

The *artes* promote this kind of signification on a large scale, to the extent that the idea of literary knowledge and the idea of authoritative texts, as categories, take on a greater prominence than any individual literary work. The literary examples given for grammatical points are removed and repositioned, but they are also frequently set in relation to other, equally decontextualized quotations, so that the reader is presented with rapid movement from fragment to fragment, the order being determined by the new grammatical context. For example, in Diomedes' discussion of metaplasm, the reader is given examples drawn primarily from the *Aeneid* but in the following order: *Aeneid* 11.178, 3.409, 8.630, 9.231, 4.493, 12.454, 6.620, 10.68, 4.682, and so on, with a few lines from other authors also used.[50] Diomedes, of course, has his own linear order with which to organize, as he progresses through the various types of metaplasm, but with respect to the *Aeneid*, the reader is expected to read in a nonlinear fashion.[51] The nonlinearity of the exempla is reinforced when they are taken from different authors, for example when Priscian illustrates the accusative singular of the first declension, first with three lines from the *Aeneid* (5.850, 6.684, 3.179), then a passage from Horace (*serm.* 2.1.16–17), a line from Terence (*Andr.* prol.1), a line from Lucan (*Phars.* 3.94–95), four more lines from Terence (*Adelph.* 3.1.4 and 3.4.33, *Andr.* 2.1.33, *Eun.* 5.1.7–8), a line from Juvenal (*sat.* 3.9.2), another passage from Horace (*carm.* 1.8.1), a final bit of Virgil (*Aen.* 5.38–39), and two lines from Statius (*Theb.* 5.44 and 7.319).[52] Priscian is admittedly one of the grammarians who is most fond of juxtaposing multiple examples (Donatus shows much greater restraint),[53] but his perhaps extreme example is useful in uncovering a basic generic approach to earlier texts in the *artes*. Earlier works can be read and appropriated in a profoundly nonlinear manner while being used to construct a linear grammatical argument.[54] The original literary text is thus subordinated to the production of the knowledge of which it is the object.

Nonlinear reading in the *artes* produces not only objects of literary knowledge but also an idea of literary knowledge, that is, of a unified literary tradition to be mastered. The juxtapositioning of quotations from diverse authors and contexts has a homogenizing effect. The placement of these authors into a single conceptual group (texts to which one should refer), as if they were self-evidently "the same," ought, obviously, to come as something of a surprise. Yet in the *artes*, and hence in the basic education of late ancient Latin speakers, the chronological and stylistic differences between writers like Plautus, Terence, Virgil, and Cicero are effectively collapsed. Textual fragmentation introduces a certain interchangeability between the fragments used. Donatus can introduce nearly any quotation with the homogenizing *ut*; Pompeius, more precise with names, nonetheless at one point runs through quotations from Virgil, Persius, Terence, and Plautus in the space of about twenty lines,[55] without distinguishing the authors by anything *other* than name. In a particularly dense twenty-five lines on prepositions, Cledonius moves back and forth between three quotations of Sallust, four of Virgil, two of Cicero, and one of Terence, with no indication that the authors are not interchangeable.[56] For the purposes of grammatical explication, the exemplary texts are simply not differentiated.[57]

These individual phrases are ultimately unified by the broad idea of *auctoritas*.[58] Diomedes refers to Varro as his source for the four elements of good Latin: *natura, analogia, consuetudo,* and *auctoritas*.[59] *Auctoritas* in this context is suggested specifically by the quotation of *auctores* and is, according to Diomedes, the most inexplicable criterion, based solely on received texts.[60] *Auctoritas* thus functions as "that which is handed down through the opinion of the orators,"[61] that is, as strictly literary knowledge. Practices of author citation are fundamental to the construction of *auctoritas* in the *artes*. Pompeius, for example, will occasionally elide an *auctor* with *auctoritas*, as he does in the progression *in auctoritate . . . ab auctoribus . . . Persius*, where a line from Persius is the only example given.[62] Cledonius, Consentius, and Servius speak of *auctoritas* as a quality possessed by specific writers whom they quote.[63] Donatus' few references to *auctoritas* refer to it as the combined product of many readings: "*Auctoritas* has often taken precedence against this rule"; "some deny that adverbs can be formed from participles, but the *auctoritas* of wide reading proves them wrong."[64] These constructions of *auctoritas* are created out of the generalized representation of *auctores* who can be cited or quoted in defense of particular turns of phrase. The joining of *auctores* into *auctoritas* is significant. The movement from plural to singular is an imaginative unification of the *auctores*, despite their evident differences. The idea of using multiple, nonlinear quotations in forming the basis for *auctoritas* both unifies the field of literary knowledge (many different authors become symbols of *auctoritas*) and expands it (*auctoritas* is derived from the reading of many *auctores*). *Auctoritas* represents more than a symbol of potency; it is the conceptual unification of a field of diverse textual elements.

Division and Antiquity

It is not surprising, perhaps, that an abstract noun should come to be used as an abbreviation for many singularities similarly deployed. This kind of unification, however, lays the foundation for another imaginative unification, namely, that of the Roman past.[65] The appeal to *auctoritas*, that is, to strictly literary precedent, when it is overtly signaled, is rarely formulated as a straightforward appeal simply to *auctoritas*. Rather, it is formulated either in terms of the "authority of the ancients" (*auctoritas veterum*)[66] or, most frequently, in terms of usage *apud veteres, apud maiores,* or *apud antiquos.* The idea of the *auctoritas veterum* obviously indicates the overlap between the idea of *auctoritas* as literary knowledge and the idea of the past, as does the fact that the *auctores* cited by grammarians of the fourth to sixth centuries tend to be writers from the second century and earlier.[67] There are significant differences between the Latin of Plautus and the Latin of Juvenal, however, and it is notable that professional readers whose expertise lay in linguistic differentiation nonetheless conflate these kinds of Latin in a schematic temporal division between "the ancients" and themselves. Their ability to do so reveals one of the ways in which grammar contributed to a homogenization of both literature and the past in Latin antiquity, and to the idea of a unified "classical" culture.

This unification is the product of a prior fragmenting. The quotation of earlier authors is of course a de facto gesture toward the past, in that it relies on past linguistic artifacts to construe grammatical knowledge. The introduction of such exemplary fragments with the words *ut apud antiquos,* or a similar reference to the past, pushes this practice further toward the active construction of the past as well. The fragment then becomes not just a unit and object of knowledge but specifically a unit of knowledge about the past and a past object.[68] The locution adds another dimension to the fragment's productivity, that of temporality.[69] This dimension, like that of *auctoritas*, is produced by the overt removal of the quoted text from its original context.[70] The juxtaposition of "ancient" locutions with the grammarian's prose creates a temporal relation, an imaginative break, and a site for the multiplication of units of knowledge as such. In this case, it is knowledge about the *auctores* as representatives of antiquity, and conversely about antiquity as the producer of the *auctores*.[71]

The two most common words used in the *artes* to describe past figures are *antiqui* and *veteres*, with some use of *maiores*.[72] Each of the grammarians uses the terms slightly differently. Donatus, the grammarian most sparing with exemplary texts, uses them least. When he does refer, once, to the practice of the *antiqui*, this practice is illustrated with an unattributed phrase from Virgil: "The ancients used prepositions also with the genitive case, as in *crurum tenus*."[73] On the other hand, the three times Donatus refers to the *veteres*,[74] he adduces no examples from earlier literature, describing earlier usage in more general terms. Charisius provides much more evidence, as might be expected in a much longer work. Charisius both uses the terms *antiqui* and *veteres* more often and uses many more exemplary authors to illustrate ancient usage. As examples of the practice of the *antiqui*, he appeals to Plautus, Terence, Pacuvius, Titinius, Virgil, Lucilius, Ennius, and Cicero.[75] As examples of the practices of the *veteres*, he appeals to Terence, Sallust, Varro, Propertius, Virgil, Ennius, Plautus, Pacuvius, Cato, Lucretius, Lucilius, Aemilius Macer, and Accius.[76] Charisius also uses the terms *antiqui* and *veteres* frequently as generalities, for example referring simply to how language was used *apud veteres* or *apud antiquos* without assigning specific literary examples to these references, just as Donatus does with the term *veteres*.[77] The authors here are for the most part republican, but it is important to note the distinction between chronological position and ancient usage. If Charisius and Donatus can be taken as evidence for broader mid-fourth-century grammatical teaching, it seems likely that literary *antiquitas* was not strictly defined by the chronological periods of the different *auctores*. Propertius, for example, is not writing the Latin of the much earlier Accius, but to the extent that he archaizes, Propertius can be used as an example of *antiquitas*. Virgil, too, although he is the most often quoted *auctor*, is temporally problematic. His work is used to illustrate both "antiquity" and current practice, as well as current practice that is archaizing.[78] Thus Charisius' or Donatus' introductory *ut* clause should not be read as assimilating an *auctor* into antiquity absolutely: that Virgil or Propertius provides the reader with an ancient reading does not entail that Virgil or Propertius is an ancient author. Charisius' and Donatus' references to a generic antiquity, without examples, perhaps more helpfully convey the idea of antiquity as a general, unmarked category. Quotations of specific authors, then, reinforce the presence and importance of antiquity without themselves being the substance of it: antiquity is transmitted through Plautus, Virgil, or Propertius but is not confined to them or to any nameable set of *auctores*.[79]

Uses of *antiqui*, *veteres*, and *maiores* in later fourth- and fifth-century grammars seem to bear this idea out. Servius' Virgil commentaries contain explanations of Virgil that refer frequently to earlier custom or history but more often to earlier, "ancient" language usage;[80] constructions of antiquity in Servius' Donatus commentary tend also to concentrate on linguistic markers of *antiquitas*, as is natural, given the grammatical bias of the work. When Servius refers to writers who demonstrate usage *apud maiores*, he includes the following figures: Virgil, Horace, Juvenal, Cicero, Lucretius, Sallust, and Cato.[81] The list of authors whom Servius cites as illustrating usage *apud antiquos* include all of the above and add Terence, Pacuvius, Ennius, Plautus, Lucilius, Livy, and Sisenna.[82] Usage *apud veteres* is illustrated in an overlapping group of authors: Virgil, Terence, Sallust, Ennius, Juvenal, Plautus, Lucilius, Calvus, Pacuvius, Titinius, Cicero, Coelius, Lucan, and Statius.[83] Servius is not unaware of chronological differences between Terence and Juvenal, or Plautus and Statius;[84] the fact that these authors can be used equally to illustrate ancient usage indicates that antiquity is a much more complex category than simple chronological position. There are points at which Servius signals what he takes to be conscious archaizing on the part of an author:[85] in his commentary on *Bucolics* 5.5 Servius notes that Virgil will sometimes follow ancient precedent, and sometimes *nostram consuetudinem*.[86] Likewise, Servius suggests in his *Aeneid* commentary that Virgil "departed" from "antiquity" at *Aeneid* 9.641.[87] This need not imply, of course, that Virgil was not a venerable and ancient author for Servius,[88] but it does indicate that Servius' concept of literary antiquity is more nuanced than a listing of authors from the republican to early imperial periods might suggest. Rather, like Charisius and Donatus, Servius' conception of literary age is much more circumstantial; it is primarily an articulation of difference between a linguistic "then" and a linguistic "now."[89]

Diomedes and Priscian have similar, if slightly longer, lists of authors whom they cite as conveyors of literary *antiquitas*,[90] but like Servius they also create antiquity as a generality out of which specific examples are drawn. Thus, for example, Diomedes: "The ancients [*veteres*] also used *amo* in the inchoative mode, *amasco*, and therefore they also called *amatores amasios*, as Plautus does in *Truculens*: *stos mundulos amasios*; and Naevius has *nunc primulum amasco*."[91] Perhaps the most important addition to the rhetoric of antiquity in the *artes*, however, is a different phrase, found in Diomedes and Servius, and later in Priscian, but not present in Donatus or Charisius, namely, the "custom of the ancients" (*mos veterum* or *mos antiquorum*).[92] This verbal generalizing suggests the creative relationship between the idea of antiquity and examples of ancient usage. The idea of a *mos antiquorum* is not limited to language use[93] but is used primarily in that sense in Diomedes and Servius, at times with examples from specific authors attached, as when Diomedes cites Virgil on the use of imperatives that end in *o*, which he says follows ancient custom (*more veterum*),[94] but more often without examples. The generalization of usages into a *mos* is conceptually important to the homogenization of the past: by suggesting an infinite number of similar examples of a particular usage,[95] the idea of the *mos veterum* creates both an expansive and a one-dimensional "past," one full of linguistic events, but whose linguistic events are all in some sense the same. The idea of the *mos veterum*, moreover, solidifies the authority of the past as separate from the authority of individual authors. Unlike the individual examples of, for example, the "authority of Virgil" (*auctoritas Virgilii*), the totalizing *mos veterum* brooks no exceptions: where Sallust may be persuaded by the *auctoritas* of Plautus to use a particular construction,[96] leaving open the possibility that he might not, the nameless *veteres* invariably follow *morem suum*. The introduction of the language of ancient custom thus allows for a more homogeneous, more authoritative, and less clearly defined conception of the past. Following the use of the idea of *mos veterum*, Priscian, too, refers occasionally to the *auctoritas veterum* as a generality, in the same way as he refers to the notion of *auctoritas poetica*.[97] "Antiquity" serves a function similar to "poetry," using a real referent as an imaginative category. Priscian also frequently describes certain passages as having been written "in the ancient manner" (*more antiquo*),[98] or simply "archaically" (*antique*).[99] The adverbial sense further consolidates the conception of the past as a single essentializable entity, reducible, at least in terms of its representation, to linguistic gesture.

By creating a corpus of *veteres* from whom to quote, and by then generalizing certain linguistic acts as representative of the *mos veterum*, grammatical training clearly encouraged a particular kind of thinking about the past as part of the act of reading, facilitated by the practice of reading via fragmentation. The combination of generality and the proliferation of textual fragments in the construction of the past serves as a framework for the positing of a gap between the past and the present, as the consistent contrast between the *antiqui* and *nos* throughout the *artes* demonstrates. Charisius, typically, writes such passages as "the ancients said *naviter, duriter*, and *humaniter*, which we [form as] *nave, dure, humane*"; Cledonius tells his readers, "We should now say *iugerorum*; the ancients used to say *iugerum*, like *tuberum*."[100] The repetition of this contrast in the many quotations of earlier texts creates a body of linguistic acts that can be labeled temporally as "ancient" or "contemporary"; the generalization of this temporal scheme naturalizes the labeling and reifies the two temporal periods.[101] The gap between the two, while posited simply, is less simple to negotiate. The authors who represent ancient usage in one context may represent current usage in another. Virgil, for example, serves as a representative of three different kinds of Latin: ancient, standard, and "poetic."[102] At times he is introduced along with earlier, republican authors as an example of ancient usage, which might suggest that late ancient grammarians saw him as indeed an ancient figure, but at other times he is called a "lover of antiquity" (*amator antiquitatis*),[103] deliberately archaizing from a "post-ancient" position. Yet at other times he is said to "depart" from ancient practice entirely.[104] The changing position of Virgil with respect to the past suggests the usefulness of past linguistic objects in shaping multiple lines of interaction with texts into a single, apparently linear relationship.[105] Confrontation and identification with particular linguistic acts can be negotiated temporally, in that similarity can be seen as "received" and therefore synchronous with the actor, while difference can be located in a general past.[106] The simultaneous presence of multiple linguistic usages—some allowed, others not—is made more comprehensible by locating them in an imagined temporal framework.

The ways in which grammarians fragment texts and frame these fragmentations is thus not merely a matter of taking wholes apart. Rather, it is a technique that allows for the production and perpetuation of much larger categories of thought, in this case the categories of authority and temporality, into which the quoted texts and the reader are both placed, but in a certain tension.[107] The quoted text functions on two levels, as an object and marker of knowledge, and as an object and marker of temporality. These functions create a matrix into which the reader is inserted, as more or less knowledgeable and more or less distant in time.[108] In forming a working model of correct language, the practice of quotation invokes two fields of multiples, multiples of authority and multiples of temporality, and the reader's position within these fields at any given time is made up of his or her understood difference or similarity to the individual instances culled from these fields. For example, when Pompeius quotes a fragment of Cicero in which Cicero is guilty of homoteleuton,[109] he adds the comment "this is completely archaic, no one does this now; if anyone were to do it, he would be laughed at" (*antiquum est hoc totum, hodie nemo facit; siqui fecerit, ridetur*).[110] Pompeius is simultaneously positing a knowledge of Cicero as exemplary, Cicero as *antiquus*, and the reader as necessarily distant from Cicero's practice both temporally and stylistically. The reader, in turn, is expected to recognize and acknowledge the Ciceronian text and name as an appropriate exemplum, retain it as a unit of knowledge about language and about the past, and distance himself or herself from the usage that it exemplifies.[111] On the other hand, after offering only the decontextualized fragment, Pompeius' statement that "this is completely archaic" (*antiquum hoc est totum*) becomes an extrapolation of an entire, distant, *antiquitas* from a single line and name; and his assurance that "no one does this now" (*hodie nemo facit*) conjures an equally large but vague idea of contemporary knowledgeability and intellectual exchange to which the reader must conform.[112] The repetition of such exempla reinforces the idea of *antiquitas* and knowledge as general fields from which singular examples can be drawn; the accumulation of singularities and their conjured positions defines the reader as a figure in relation to these larger fields. Part of the task of textuality, following this grammatical technique, is the imagination of contexts and the building of contextualized selves out of multiple parts.

Lists

Where fragmentation as a general textual practice works to produce broad, prolific categories like *auctoritas* and *antiquitas*, the list as an organizing technique in the *artes* promotes the redirection of fragments into new kinds of linearity.[113] It thereby begins to articulate a new conceptual category, the relation of *auctoritas* and *antiquitas* to "us" (*nos*).[114] Juxtaposition as a literary technology has, as we have seen in the case of the *auctores*, a certain homogenizing effect. The list, as an extreme technique of fragmentation and juxtaposition, both reinforces the homogenization necessary to the creation of *auctoritas* and *antiquitas* and relocates textual fragments into yet another homogeneous context, that of the *ars grammatica* itself, and its rhetoric of contemporary education. The list thus brings forward to an even greater degree the temporal tension between the ancients and ourselves found in a phrase like Pompeius' *maiores nostri*.[115] The mechanism of the list has a particular function in pedagogical texts: the conceit of the text is that it conveys knowledge from one figure or group of figures to another figure or group. The list in this context configures its knowledge as pure conveyable knowledge, that is, as completely decontextualized, but it also assumes a clear relation between the authoritative source of knowledge generating the list and the consumer of knowledge reading it.[116]

I would like to focus here on Charisius, and on his use of lists as a technology of temporal dissonance and homogenization.[117] Charisius is an

exemplary generator of lists: where other grammarians use rather clearly
defined lists throughout their works, especially with traditional lists of parts
of speech, conjugations and declensions, types of locution or meter, and so
on, Charisius takes this tendency to an extreme. He inserts long alphabetical lists of words into his discussions of nouns and adverbs in books 1 and
2; his treatment of the principal parts and forms of verbs in book 3 is primarily made up of verb lists; book 4, more conventionally, lists the different kinds of barbarisms, solecisms, and figures; and book 5, to the extent
that its contents can be described at all, seems to consist primarily of lists of
idioms and synonyms, some alphabetical and others not.[118] While Charisius
is extreme, however, the tendency to use lists as a means of organizing and
defining grammatical information is consistent in all the *artes*. It may therefore be helpful to examine what is stressed in one extraordinary grammar
in order to shed light on the practices of the more conventional others.

One of the more conspicuous lists in Charisius' grammar, the list
de analogia in book 1, is itself temporally problematic, being a lengthy extract from the third-century grammarian C. Julius Romanus.[119] Charisius'
acknowledgement of Romanus is in part a gesture toward past grammatical activity and in part a consolidation of all grammarians as acting in the
same temporal position, opposite the *veteres*.[120] In this Charisius is not
unique, since it is rare for a grammarian, when citing another grammarian,
even one from a significantly earlier period, to refer to that grammarian as
vetus or *antiquus*.[121] The list itself further eschews clear temporal boundaries in being organized more or less alphabetically, that is, sequentially,
but not according to either a narrative scheme or a chronology of historical
usages.[122] Charisius' use of Romanus' list, illustrating the use of analogy
in the declension of nouns, ignores temporality in its larger structure, on
the one hand conflating the knowledge of the third-century Romanus and
the fourth-century Charisius, and on the other refusing a chronological
sequence or account of its contents. Yet the list itself is deeply historicizing. Some of the items on the list, for example, are names of historical or
quasi-historical figures (including, interestingly, Adam and Abraham, both
of which Romanus/Charisius classifies as indeclinable).[123] More importantly,
however, nearly all of the items on the list are given with examples of
authoritative past usage, as in the following two entries, on the declensions
of *clavis* and *diligens*:

> Tibullus uses *clavim*: "*hinc clavim ianua sensit*" and Lucilius uses *strigilim*. Varro, in
> the second book *de poematis*, uses *lentim*, since the ablative singular of these nouns
> ends in *i*. However, [the accusatives of *avis* and *navis* are] *avem* and *navem*, since

they become [in the ablative] *ab hac ave* and *nave*, so the accusative cannot be formed with *i*. *Diligente*. Pliny says that Verrius Flaccus [says that] for those nouns that end in *ns* in the nominative, the ablative should end in *e*. Thus Caesar, in letters to Cicero, says, "*neque pro cauto ac diligente se castris continuit.*"[124]

Although there is no narrative connection or logic to the sequence *clavim*, *diligente*, within each entry an implied narrative about past usage informing present correctness is clear: these authoritative figures used these forms, therefore these are the forms in use.

This combination of narrative sequence and nonnarrative sequence also informs the lists in books 2 and 3, especially the list *de adverbio* and the lists of verb forms. The list *de adverbio* in book 2 is structured very much like the list *de analogia* in book 1, unsurprisingly, as it too owes much to Romanus.[125] The list is introduced as follows: "But for the readers' accessibility [*facilitas*], so that they need not ask further, it is fitting to arrange the material in alphabetical order and thoroughly, not in individual characteristics and examples of this part of speech, with its divisions numbered and connected by rules. For the Stoics, as I said elsewhere, call the adverb *pandecten*, since it receives all things as if they were all collected together in a mixture, and power over all sorts of things were granted to it."[126] The target of the information is clear: the reader, who desires *facilitas* in covering the material; the list is a mechanism for conveying it. The list is, moreover, associated with thoroughness, justified by Stoic precedent, and with a totalizing goal. Although Charisius does not by any means list all Latin adverbs, the function of the list (especially the alphabetical list) is to suggest a totality. That this totality is both temporal and atemporal can be seen in the entries, of which these are the first three:

Aliter for *alias*. Sallust in book 1 of his history has *sanctus alias et ingenio validus*, and in the same work *insanum aliter sua sententia atque aliarum mulierum*.

Actutum for *cito*. Virgil, book 9: *tum cetera reddent / actutum pius Aeneas atque integer aevi / Ascanius*.

Alias for *aliter*. Terence in *Andria*: *quid alias malim quam hodie istas fieri nuptias?* Fl. Caper, in his work On Latinity, says, "I would not dare assert that *alias* is said for *aliter*, since it is neither a pronoun nor an adverb of time." But we might say it is nearer the truth that it is said for *aliter*.[127]

Again, like the words in the list *de analogia*, the arrangement is overtly atemporal, with no necessary narrative logic or connection between the terms. At the same time, it is fundamentally historicizing, with *exempla* from Sallust, Virgil, and Terence given a prominent place.

The tension between timelessness and the historical impulse is even more clearly illustrated in entries like the following, on *ampliter*: "Plautus has *ampliter* for *ample* in the *Bacchides*. For all nouns, no matter what their quality or quantity, if they end in *o* in the dative, they form their adverbs with *e*, as in *doctus docte, amplus ample*. But the ancients did not follow this."[128] On the one hand Charisius offers a rule for adverb formation that appears universal and timeless ("every noun behaves this way"), but this rule is surrounded by contradiction. Plautus, the exemplar, does not follow it. After the rule is stated, the original contradiction is reasserted (*sed veteres non observaverunt*). The tension is lessened by the arrangement of figures in a temporal line: the fact that the rule is timeless, and yet has been violated, is made comprehensible[129] by the notion of a "difference in times,"[130] in which the ancients were free not to observe the rule. Thus the list, while eschewing standard narrative, reorients its fragments into new implied narratives. The first is a narrative from the *antiqui* to the reader;[131] the second is one from the reader to the potential deployment of the knowledge unit in the future.[132] Hence Charisius' comment correcting Caper, which implies an ongoing usage and exchange of linguistic units.

The same combination of suppressed and implied narrative occurs in lists with no quotation of earlier material. Here, for example, is an extract from book 3, on defective verbs:

There are some verbs that, since they do not have their own perfect tense, take over the perfect from verbs of the same meaning, as when *vescor* becomes *pastus sum*, although that comes from *pascor*, since no one says *vescitus sum*. Likewise *arguor* becomes *convictus sum*, from that verb, that is, *convincor*, although in ancient times it had the perfect *argutus sum*. Likewise *angor, anxius sum*; although *anxius* is a noun that means [someone] worried. Likewise *fero, tuli*, which is from the verb *tollo*. Likewise *reminiscor* becomes *recordatus sum*. No-one says *rementus sum*, nor *opperior, oppertus sum*. These are also called defective, because they change their form.[133]

This is rather conventional list-making. Like the previous lists, however, these lists are situated between the historical and the ahistorical, and between narrative and nonnarrative. The list of verbs that take a principal part from another verb stem (*vescor, arguor, fero, reminiscor, opperior*) is again used to suggest totality, the whole of the category of verbs that lack a unique perfect tense. The list is also a nonnarrative sequence, and the totality is thereby presented as if timeless. Yet here again a historical narrative is set in motion, based on the pedagogical function of the text. Not every list contains the tag "in ancient times" (*apud antiquos*) to demonstrate linguistic change over time, as this one does (*habet tamen apud antiquos argutus sum*), but the reminder that these constructions are for present use ("no one says," *nemo dicit*) introduces a narrative situation. In a hypothetical state of affairs calling for articulation, the reader, the target of the grammatical knowledge, will presumably use one or another word in a particular construction, perhaps the grammatically "correct" one.[134] That is, Charisius imagines the reader as an actor, conditioned by education, and placed in a linguistic situation.[135] He thus imposes a narrative logic on word choice. By removing his exemplary words from a more conventional narrative context, Charisius can redirect the narrative line toward the reader, implicating him or her in the new temporal situation.[136] Two narrative lines are thus drawn in this passage: one from the *antiqui* to the present reader, and another from the present reader to the reader's future statements. These lines remove contradictions, in the first case the contradiction between the fact that certain verbs change their *figurae*, although one finds them unchanged in certain texts *apud antiquos*, and in the second case the contradiction between the reader's role as recipient of knowledge and as user or reproducer of it. These simultaneities are arranged along a temporal line from past to future.[137]

The list format can also function temporally without overt reference to the *antiqui* or to earlier literary texts. Donatus' *Ars Minor* uses remarkably few quotations from earlier literary texts, but it does contain many lists.[138] The famous opening sequence is "How many parts of speech are there? Eight. What are they? Noun pronoun verb adverb participle conjunction preposition interjection."[139] Even without the question-and-answer format, the invocation of an imagined context and an imagined reader would be clear: Donatus' lists represent the decontextualization of linguistic knowledge (in that none of the parts of speech is placed in a context, although they are assumed to belong to one),[140] and its recontextualization in the *ars grammatica*. The temporal implication is that prior units of knowledge are here being transferred to a later reader. The conjured reader, moreover, is expected to contextualize gradually, with each answer providing incrementally more surrounding or exemplary information: "What is a noun? A part of speech having a case, and signifying a body or a specific or general thing. How many attributes does a noun have? Six. What are they? Quality comparison gender number figure case."[141] Here Donatus returns to the first item on his first list and begins to place it into a new context of linguistic information, which in turn generates another list of information that, according to the conceit of the *ars grammatica*, the reader is expected to master.[142] Although the lists themselves are not narratively organized, there is a narrative logic in which the imagined reader is implicated, from the prior existence of units of knowledge in an originary context to their mastery in another.[143] The list thus calls into being a narrative of readerly activity.[144]

In the context of the *artes* as pedagogical works, the repetition of the micronarratives that the list generates functions like the juxtaposition of quotations elsewhere. Where the repeated quotation of *auctores* homogenizes earlier writing into the general categories of *auctoritas* and *antiquitas*, the repeated movement from *auctor* to reader produces a third general category, based on the hypostatization of that movement. This third category is perhaps best expressed in the somewhat fluid concept of Latinity (*latinitas*), or what Charisius calls "Latin eloquence" (*Latina facundia*).[145] The reification of the relationship between the imagined reader and the exemplary text lies at the heart of the cultural work that the *artes* do.[146] As pedagogical texts (or texts that use the tropes of pedagogy), one of their tasks is to implicate their audiences in a specific cultural system, in this case a system of literacy. One of the concepts in which this reification occurs is that of *latinitas*, although the process should not be restricted to that term.[147] Quintilian cites age (*vetustas*) and authority (*auctoritas*) as two of the criteria for Latinity, thus establishing it as a temporal and textual relation at the outset.[148] Diomedes and Charisius use *latinitas* following Varro, although Varro's definition is known only from Diomedes: "Latinity is the practice of speaking correctly according to the language of the Romans. Varro tells us that it consists of these four things: nature, analogy, usage, and authority."[149] Charisius offers a similar definition, without using the word *latinitas*: "The freedom of Latin eloquence is restrained by nature, or analogy, or by the logic of careful observation, or by usage, which is strengthened by the consensus of many, or of course by authority, which is received in the opinion of the wisest men."[150] In each of these formulations there is an attempt to define *latinitas* as in part a relation between elements classified as temporally different, here overtly in the relation between *consuetudo/usus* and *auctoritas*. Other definitions of Latinity delineate similar relations, as when Probus says that "all *latinitas* consists of two parts, either analogy or anomaly."[151] Here Latinity is strictly a relation abstracted from strings of examples, with the reader expected to master the logic behind the division. Probus' examples of analogy and anomaly are given to the reader as data already compiled (analogy: *ut puta hic Catilina, haec lupa, hoc scrinium et cetera talia*;[152] anomaly: *ut puta ab hoc altero, huic alteri. . . . sic et cetera talia . . . anomala sunt appellanda*).[153] This listing of examples again appeals to the narrative scheme whereby a connection is drawn between a prior linguistic datum and the reader. The unifying concept of *latinitas* thus covers a number of possible, and possibly conflicting, relations between exemplary words and readers, formulated in terms of past and present.[154] The concept is given substance by the repetition of narratives of relation between exemplum and reader. The list format invokes the participation of the imagined reader and thus sets up the relation in a singularly direct manner. The idea of Latinity as the abstraction of a relationship between a conjured reader and a conjured exemplar ultimately becomes clear through the pedagogical mechanism of the list.

The quality of *latinitas*, at once hypostatizable into an individual entity and imaginable as Latin eloquence, that is, dependent on a contemporary user, thus contains its own temporal and narrative movement. I would like to use this movement as a hermeneutic for reading two of the more conventional lists in Charisius and in other grammarians, that is, lists of the virtues and vices of speech. For Charisius, these lists make up most of book 4 of his grammar, and, typically, quotations from earlier authors are frequent.[155] The ostensible purpose of these lists is to define and illustrate for the reader the boundaries and possibilities of Latin usage, so that, for example, the section *de vitiis ceteris* offers the reader the following definitions:

On tapinosis. Tapinosis is the presentation of a great matter in a low style, as in Horace, *Pelidae stomachum cedere nescii*. He uses *stomachum* in the low style, rather than using *ira*.
On cacosyntheton. Cacosyntheton is a certain inappropriate placement of words, such as *verasque iuvencum / terga fatigamus hasta*.
On amphibole. Amphibole is a locution or phrase with an ambivalent meaning: a locution like *ut vadatur Cato*; a phrase like *aio te, Aeacida, Romanos vincere posse*.[156]

On one level, this is information that exists in a timeless present. Definitions are offered unconditionally and without clear contexts. The persistent use of examples from the *auctores*, however, inserts two temporal aspects. First, knowledge of these vices immediately becomes knowledge about the past.[157] The association between a single Latin idiosyncracy and a single author becomes a unit of knowledge about that author, and, especially when names are not given, about the *auctores* more generally. The past is the time when this locution was used. Second, as in the lists previously discussed, a temporal sequence is created from conjured *auctor* to imagined reader, or rather from *auctor* to exemplum to present, with the reader implicated in that present, and indeed in a possible future. The "present" then is the point in the sequence at which the past is recognized as such and at which the imagined reader can demonstrate his or her mastery (or lack thereof) of units of knowledge marked by "pastness."[158] Charisius' configurations of Latinity, as found in his discussion of virtues and vices of speech, like other lists, promote a redirection of narrative from the narrative within texts like the *Aeneid* to narrative specifically about the relation of the imagined reader to the cultural past.

To the extent that the same device is found in other grammarians, it is reasonable to expect that it has similar effects. Donatus' *Ars Maior*, as I noted earlier, also quotes much more frequently from earlier authors in his treatments of the tropes, virtues, and vices of Latin speech. His list of *vitiae ceterae* runs partly as follows:

Tapinosis is the setting low of a great thing with a sentence that does not indicate [its greatness], such as *penitusque cavernas / ingentes uterumque armato milite complent*, and *Dulichias vexasse rates* and *Pelidae stomachum cedere nescii*.

Cacosyntheton is a faulty construction of speech, such as *versaque iuvencum / terga fatigamus hasta*.

Amphibole is an ambiguity in speech, which may occur through the use of the accusative, if someone were to say, *audio secutorem retirium superasse*; or through common verbs, if someone were to say, *criminatur Cato, vadatur Tullius*, without adding whom or by whom; or through [unclear] differentiation, as in, *vidi statuam auream hastam tenentem*.[159]

Again, the decontextualized quotations (some the same as in Charisius) are both removed from their original narrative contexts and inserted into new narratives of readership and knowledgeability. Likewise, the examples that Donatus generates without quotation, not differentiated from the others, invoke an imagined context from which they have been taken in order to promote a new imagined context of pedagogical progression.[160] The repetition of these new narratives reinforces the idea that the individually constituted relationship between earlier narrative and contemporary reader is part of a larger abstraction, *latinitas*, that is instantiated in each example, rather than being conjured by the homogenizing accumulation of examples.

The same pattern is found in book 2 of Diomedes' grammar, whose subsections on the virtues and vices of speech are introduced by the definition of *latinitas* quoted earlier. Diomedes' list of the same virtues and vices as Charisius and Donatus, although not given in the same order, is otherwise very similar:

On amphibole. Amphibole is a fault in composition in which a sentence is structured ambiguously, such as *aio te, Aeacida, Romanos vincere posse*; likewise *certum est Antonium praecedere eloquentia Crassum*. These two sentences lack correctness because of the problem of ambiguity, since it is unclear whether the Romans can be defeated by Aeacida or Aeacida by the Romans; similarly it is unclear whether Crassus is outdone by Antony in eloquence, or Antony is outdone by Crassus. . . . The problem can also arise through the use of common verbs, as in *vadatur in foro Cato, criminatur Cicero*. . . . Likewise it can occur through [unclear] differentiation, as in *vidi statuam auream hastam tenentem*. . . .

On tapinosis. Tapinosis is the low presentation of something great, contrary to its dignity, as in *marcido dies sole pallet*, when *marcere* is properly used of earthly, rather than immortal, things; also in Horace *Pelidae stomachum*, instead of *ira*; and in Virgil *multa malus simulans*, instead of *scelestus*. . . .On cacosyntheton. Cacosyntheton is an inappropriate arrangement of words, such as *versaque iuvencum / terga fatigamus hasta*.[161]

The repetition of quotations and exempla indicates both the conservatism of the genre and the transformation of these fragments into newly contextualized units of knowledge implicating the imagined reader in a relationship with the exemplary texts, representatives of both an authorial and a grammatical "past." The use and reuse of such units provides substance for Diomedes' invoked *latinitas*, or Charisius' *latina facundia*, both in the very literal sense that they are the content of the discourse marked as "about Latinity" and in the ideological sense that they provide the imagination with exemplary matter in its reification of Latinity.[162]

I do not mean to suggest by my choice of examples that this relationship is reified only in lists of virtues and vices, although the reification is particularly clear in such lists. Several of the *artes* do not address the virtues and vices of speech, Priscian perhaps most prominently, or Donatus' *Ars Minor*.[163] Nonetheless they construct a relationship between the reader and the exemplary text through the medium of the list. To return to Priscian's fragmenting list of syllables: book 6 of Priscian's *Institutiones* deals with the correct function of genitives, depending on the syllables with which the nominative forms of the nouns end. The book is structured as a list of different ending syllables, each of which is then supplemented by a list of exemplary words, and often (but not in all cases) with a subsequent list of examples from the *auctores*. Here, for example, is part of Priscian's discussion of words ending in *es*:

Latin words ending in a short *es*, when they are masculine or common in gender change *e* to *i*, with the *s* removed and *tis* added to form the genitive, as in *hic miles huius militis, trames tramitis, termes termitis, merges mergitis, hic* and *haec sospes sospitis, pedes peditis, eques equitis*. . . . The exceptions are those that have a penultimate diphthong *ae* or that are derived from verbs that have a short *e* as their penultimate. These retain the *e* in the genitive, as in *hic* and *haec* and *hoc praepes praepetis, tero teris, hic* and *haec* and *hoc teres teretis* . . . *impeto, impes impetis*—Ovid in the third book of the *Metamorphoses* has *Impete nunc vasto* instead of *impetu*. Likewise Statius in the seventh book of the *Thebaid* has *aurigamque impete vasto, / Amphiarae tuum.*[164]

The didactic nature of the lists is clear: the reader is imagined as the recipient of the grammarian's teaching. This didacticism conjures the reader in relation to the imagined sources of the grammarian's doctrine, first the apparently atemporal rules of noun formation, then the appeal to prior linguistic examples, and finally the overtly historicizing list of examples from the *auctores*. Like Pompeius' *maiores nostri*, the combination of past and present in this passage, as in the work more broadly, emphasizes the relation between the two that creates the notion of educatedness. Priscian's educated readers will know when to follow ancient precedent and when to diverge from it, and will know, more fundamentally, how precedents can be invoked or bypassed.[165] They will then possess *latina facundia*.

There are, then, two functions that the list serves in the pedagogical context of the *ars grammatica*. The first is to suggest a relationship (in this case a temporal relationship) between the exemplary material used in the list, especially the *antiqui* and *auctores*, and the reader of the grammar. This is done through the removal of the exemplary material from one context and its placement into a specifically pedagogical one. The material thus removed is redirected into the more general narrative of pedagogy. The second function of the list is to reify the suggested relationship and the negotiations that it entails into a single conceptual entity. The reification is accomplished through the repetition of repositioned units and their accompanying pedagogical narratives; these repeated units become the corpus of knowledge that is imagined as the single, relational, entity *latinitas*. Both the practices involved in this grammatical activity and the rhetoric surrounding them involve their participants in a certain basic structuring of what might be called the grammatical imagination. The most fundamental characteristic of this structure is the use of fragmented texts and their juxtaposition to create large categories of thought. In the case of the *artes*, this is most clear in the construction of a seamless literary past populated by *antiqui* and *maiores*, and in the construction of a relationship between that past and the reader, in the abstract *latinitas*. In addition, the production of these homogeneous categories allows for the creation of a temporal scheme moving from one "imagined community" to another, here from the *antiqui* to *nos*. Put simply, late ancient reading practices required a constant invocation of an imagined past and a constant reproduction of an abstract relationship between the reader and that past. I would like to emphasize the imaginative level at which this process worked. While it is undoubtedly true that cited authors existed before the writers who cited them, and that individual readers develop relationships to knowledge generally as part of the process of education, particular formulations of the past and of the relation that readers bear to it should not be seen as natural outworkings of the mere existence of texts and of reading. Instead, the idea of a consistent Roman literary tradition, a definable *latinitas*, and an elite Latinate reader are products of a constellation of rhetorics and linguistic gestures concentrated on the idea of grammatical education.

Conclusion

The ideological products of the *artes grammaticae* (the literary past, the linguistic present, and Latinity) thus evolve from the "raw material" of grammar to more imaginatively developed, and ideologically engaged, forms. Laevius and Ennius, for example, were undeniably important figures in the Roman literary past; they wrote the works the grammarians attribute to them; and grammarians read these works (or at least parts of them) before quoting them.[166] Yet there is a significant difference between these historical conditions and the existence of a seamless, homogeneous past peopled by interchangeable literary greats. Likewise, it would be hard to deny that the Latin language was understood by its speakers, hearers, writers, and readers to possess certain contours of intelligibility, although those contours might shift from speaker to speaker and from occasion to occasion.[167] The existence of Latin, however, need not entail the imagination of "Latinity," a hypostatized relation between the boundaries of a linguistic past and the boundaries of a linguistic present. The production of these latter forms is what I attribute, at least in part, to the techniques of grammatical education. Grammatical education, whose practice is division, is also fundamentally a practice of expansion.

The transformative power of grammatical techniques is perhaps most clearly visible in the marking and homogenization of past textual fragments. As we have seen, the classification of certain textual units as representative of a past and the homogenization of that past through the language of *auctoritas*, *vetustas*, or the *mos veterum* is to a large extent the result of the ways in which grammarians frame those textual units and deploy them in the supposed pedagogical situation. The simple fact of this deployment is itself also significant. Up to this point, I have been speaking of these verbal fragments as "objects," but although they are physical marks and sounds,[168] the fact that they are not tangible "objects" in the conventional sense leads to the question of iterability, and of repetition more generally.[169] That quotation is repetition is so obvious that it is easy to overlook. Likewise, that repetition is basic to the construction of the *ars grammatica* is clear not only from the repetitions of form (e.g., lists) but also from the repetitions of content in and across the *artes* (quotation, and the use of the same quotations in different grammarians). As numerous theorists of modern mass production have suggested, however, the possibility of such repetitions may entail the idea of an ontological displacement from "originality," and an emphasis on the deployment of the repeated object or image in various social contexts.[170] While the *grammatici* are not involved in a modern cultural economy, the obvious iterability of textual fragments may also entail a kind of displacement, in this case articulated in the temporal terms of past and present. Although Ennius existed in a temporal past with respect to the fourth-century grammarian, his function as a representative or manifestation of the past does not arise until his name is attached to a repeatable (and repeated) textual unit. The force of this temporal displacement is twofold. In conjunction with the homogenization of "the past," it lends itself to the homogenization of that which is displaced from that past—the ubiquitous "us" (*nos*) of the *artes*.[171] It further augments the *auctoritas* of the past in relation to the later linguistic actor by construing the deployed text as a representative of the past only in, as it were, reproduced form, and not in an accessible "originality," that is, by ensuring that the present by definition cannot participate in the past.[172] Iterability contributes to the cultural value of these past objects by ensuring that they are continually viewed as accessible manifestations of the inaccessible. Thus even when Charisius, Donatus, and Diomedes are listing the vices of speech, their repetition of the same textual exempla reinforces the canonical status of the texts and their associated *auctores*, not merely by signaling the *auctores'* presence in educated discourse but also by appealing to the repeatability that marks off the texts as past.

That which is imagined to negotiate the gap between a past and a present is, as I have argued, Latinity in its reified form as a relation between exemplary language and nonexemplary linguistic activity.[173] Latinity comprehends the temporal and narrative movement between the *antiqui* and *nos*, both in the sense that it suggests the persistence of textual units from "then" to "now" and in the sense that it suggests the turning of the linguistic actor to the past in order properly to become a Latinate actor. Latinity is thus the category that structures the interaction between text unit and linguistic actor, or more broadly the interaction between past and present. We have already considered how this interaction is reified in the *artes grammaticae*; I would like to consider briefly how it is also reified by the *ars grammatica* itself. The standard definition of the *ars* given by the grammarians is that it is "the science of a specific thing" (*rei cuiusque scientia*), derived from the Greek word *aretê* ("that is, from 'virtue,'" *id est a virtute*);[174] the *ars grammatica* is thus a *scientia* of a certain *res*, variously defined as letters or parts of speech. The works *de arte grammatica* themselves are therefore positioned as instantiations of an abstract *scientia* that requires both a *res*, a thing, as a discrete entity and a practitioner to approach that entity.[175] The existence of the *artes* as educational texts necessitates the double narrative of the past's persistence (the existence of the *res*) and the present's interaction with it (the possession of *scientia*).[176] The *artes* thus promote in their content the idea of a past and a present separated by a temporal break,[177] and promote in their existence the negotiation of that break as an entity in itself, Latinity, physically manifest in the *artes*.

These three entities and their relations constitute the imaginative apparatus of late ancient grammar,[178] constructed through the technologies of fragmentation and listing. The art of grammar helped to set the ideological conditions for the production of subjects who could be understood as participants in a narrative of educated relation to an idealized past, a past defined especially in literary terms. It is important to remember, however, that this sort of apparatus tends to be self-erasing,[179] and to be seen, when it is visible at all, as not more than a naturally existing state. This fact undoubtedly contributed to the "liminality" of the grammarian in late antiquity: despite the necessity of grammatical education for the ideas of *auctoritas* and *latinitas*, the professional grammarian remained for the most part a relatively obscure figure, as Robert Kaster has amply demonstrated.[180] The partial erasure of the means by which a temporal break was posited between the *antiqui* and *nos* in late ancient literary culture may also contribute, however, to a more fundamental historiographical narrative, namely, that of the lateness of late antiquity itself.[181] Given the scarcity of Latin grammatical texts from any period earlier than the fourth century, it would be foolish to suggest that fourth- to sixth-century grammars were the first educational texts to posit such a break in Latin cultural history; what I would suggest instead is that the techniques of grammar themselves contribute to a narrative of grammar as a postclassical phenomenon, even when the periodization is problematic. The invention of grammar during the Hellenistic period fits in well with this narrative,[182] as does Suetonius' account of early Roman grammatical practice as taken over from Greece.[183] Grammar is consistently positioned as a cultural epiphenomenon. This does not mean that grammar did not arise as a discipline in the Hellenistic period, or that early Roman grammarians did not follow Hellenistic models. What is important, however, is that these narratives are not historically transparent, and that they rely on the works of the grammarians themselves—works that, as we have seen, produce significant ideological effects. To take the fourth-century *artes* as evidence for the literary culture of "late" antiquity, then, may be to underestimate the extent to which the *artes* themselves are generically responsible for the reader's perception of that lateness, at least in literary terms.

It is ultimately difficult not to submit to the grammarians' claims and take the *artes* as both generative and reflective of particular cultural moments. The moments are not, however, points on a naturally existing temporal continuum. They are moments in which that continuum is invoked in the linguistic actor, in which it becomes possible for that actor to become, like Virgil, an *amator antiquitatis*.[184] Diomedes and Servius describe Virgil as such in moments when Virgil appears to be imitating an "ancient" usage: again the practice of repetition represents the distance of the imitator from the imitated, as well as the desirability of the supposed original. The *artes* on a larger scale create a forum in which "we" become de facto lovers of antiquity;[185] that is, the immediate undefined movement around textual fragments is crystallized into a temporally and culturally charged narrative scenario,[186] precipitating a present, a past, and an engagement between them. The *artes* record and produce such moments of crystallization—which become, in turn, the materials for the writing of late ancient literary history.

3

From Grammar to Piety

MODERN DISCIPLINARY BOUNDARIES separate literary history from religious history, and the study of language from the study of belief. For premodern readers, these distinctions did not apply. We have already seen that ancient linguistic practice took literature as both its beginning and its end. It did the same, we will see, with religion. The grammarian's practices of breaking down texts and of listing performed two complementary tasks: first, the creation of abstract bodies of knowledge and, second, the implication of subjects in relation to those bodies. In the previous chapter I examined the primary relationship between the projected subjects and bodies of knowledge as a relationship of time, the relationship between the grammarians' *antiqui* and *nos*. In this chapter, I consider the ways in which grammatical texts, and more prominently texts about grammarians,[1] construed this relationship as one of obligation. The two crucial imaginative movements that follow from this construction are the movement from obligation to piety, and the movement from piety to religion.[2] The construction of temporal lines in late ancient grammatical work, I argue, entailed a discourse of obligation that was "ethical" both in the traditional sense, in that it related to virtuous or vicious behavior, and in the sense that it called into being an ethos for the linguistic actor by virtue of her or his linguistic acts. In writings about grammar outside of technical grammatical literature, this discourse of obligation became aligned with literary, and ultimately religious, *pietas*. The texts I have found most useful for considering this alignment are Ausonius' *Parentalia*, Macrobius' *Saturnalia*, particularly book 3, and two of the texts surrounding the literary career of Marius Victorinus, namely, Julian the Apostate's letter 36, against Christian teachers, and Augustine's account of Victorinus' conversion in the eighth book of the *Confessions*.[3] In these texts, narratives about the relation between a homogenized past and a readerly present ultimately become narratives about piety, conversion, and Christianization.

Duty and the Art of Grammar

In very general terms grammatical education in late antiquity, as in earlier periods, was understood to produce a particular kind of social and cultural actor, or more broadly, to contribute to the maintenance of a subject's educated ethos.[4] Literary knowledge was construed as (and was, in many cases) the standard accompaniment to elite social standing, as is clear from Diomedes' comment describing grammar as "work by which we are known to surpass the unlearned . . . as much as the unlearned surpass their flocks."[5] Other grammarians voiced similar opinions on the relation between literacy and social status, and the sentiment is clear from nontechnical grammatical sources as well.[6] Beyond the marking of social levels, however, these notions implicate the grammatically trained reader in a certain ethos: the literate person ought to be urbane, selfless, knowledgeable, and virtuous.[7] This picture is the same as that promoted in rhetorical education, and it seems to have been common at earlier stages of literacy training as well, if the copying of moral maxims by schoolchildren is any indication.[8] Grammatical ethics are part of an established trope of the values that educated persons more generally were supposed to hold.

The characters produced by literary education are also inserted into a temporal framework that is particularly clear in writing about grammar and grammatical activities. Most obviously, readers are learning from earlier writers, as Priscian's patron Julianus is said to do, "whose mind [Priscian holds] consists as much of the spirit of Homer as of Virgil."[9] In addition, students of grammar are commonly configured as children who are to receive the learning of their elders. While it is true that students sent to a grammarian were typically children,[10] there is also a specific rhetoric of childhood at work here. The practice of fathers dedicating educational treatises to sons was not new to late antiquity, but it continued as a trope throughout this period, with figures like Macrobius, Martianus Capella, and Charisius dedicating their works to their sons.[11] Sons might act as their fathers' literary executors, as Symmachus' sons did,[12] or textual work might be passed down within a family, as was notably the case with Macrobius' commentary on the dream of Scipio, edited in the fifth century by a later Symmachus and a Macrobius Plotinus Eudoxius.[13] That a generational literary connection might be expected is made clear in, for example, Symmachus' letters to his father,[14] or Ausonius' use of father-son rhetoric in his correspondence with Paulinus of Nola.[15] Literary learning is imagined as placing the practitioners into a temporal, often familial, progression.

Grammatical education, then, contributed not only to the production of a particular ethos but also to the insertion of that ethos into a framework of temporal progression, so that part of the virtue of being educated was participating in the progression of learning from elder to younger.[16]

The idea of readerly virtue and of its place in a progression of learning leads to the question of readerly piety. This is not an issue that is addressed in any direct way in the *artes* themselves.[17] The *artes*, however, as a technical pedagogical literature, do supply a framework for understanding how reading could be tied to piety, and especially how the self-conscious reading of "ancient" literature could be tied to the maintenance of traditional religious custom, in the context of less technical writing about literary practice. The idea of "paganism" is a problematic one, formulated in late antiquity primarily in opposition to "Christianity."[18] The existence of a militant, self-conscious "pagan revival" in the late fourth century has rightly been called into question.[19] I would like to suggest, however, that the "ancient custom" (*mos veterum*) of the grammarians, coupled with the idea of readers as ethical figures in a temporal framework leading from the ancients to themselves, was instrumental in the merging of literary activity and "paganism" in the minds of some late ancient readers, both Christian and non-Christian. Whether or not non-Jewish non-Christians living in the Roman Empire in late antiquity would necessarily have called themselves by a single name, "pagan," the use of the temporal and ethical narrative implied in reading allowed bodies of literature to take on broad religious significance, while also allowing differences in religious practice to be construed in individual narrative terms.[20] This construction is beyond the bounds of the *artes* proper but occurs nonetheless in literature with strong ties to the grammatical tradition. As a first step in considering the grammatical contribution to a religious ethos, however, it is necessary to understand how the notion of obligation, and specifically the notion of the linguistic actor as a subject under obligation, is promoted in the *artes*.

That the *grammatici* themselves construe grammatical correctness as obligatory will hardly be surprising. It is worth emphasizing, however, that this obligation is set within an overt discourse of temporality: "correct" speech is not merely timelessly correct (although it may also be that) but, as it were, temporally correct. In being temporally correct, such speech either replicates the gap between the *antiqui* and *nos* or, by archaizing, closes that gap (and thereby of course also replicates it, but differently).[21] To return to an example quoted in the previous chapter: when Pompeius criticizes a line of Cicero for the fault of homoteleuton by saying, "This is completely archaic, no one does this now; if anyone were to do it, he would be laughed at,"[22] Pompeius is construing the passage as problematic on two related grounds: first, on the ground of homoteleuton without regard to context and, second, on the ground of temporal impropriety. The first ground seems at first timeless. Homoteleuton, Pompeius seems to say, simply *is* homoteleuton, in Cicero's time as in Pompeius', but the condemnation on temporal grounds raises a new issue, namely, the extent to which correct usage is itself bound to the discourse of temporality that Pompeius introduces. Pompeius' comment occurs in his discussion of figures, and he is using Cicero's line to define what homoteleuton is (timelessly): "Homoteleuton is when the endings of words have the same sound. For example, we have a very clear instance in Cicero."[23] After quoting the example, Pompeius ends with *antiquum hoc est totum*, "but this is completely archaic." The line thus exists on at least three different temporal levels. On one level, it is presented as a timeless definition of homoteleuton. On another level, it is an authorized ancient statement, by attachment to the figure of "Cicero."[24] On a third level, it is, for the implied reader, a present formal statement with no validity ("if anyone were to do it, he would be laughed at").[25] The establishment of obligation on these temporal levels, and their relationship to each other, should now be considered.

Grammatical obligation in a present sense, with present statements, is readily understandable, and relatively clear in the *artes*. Donatus' *Ars Minor* suggests present obligation in what may be its purest form through its use of the question-and-answer format and its persistent use of imperatives directed at an imagined student.[26] By presenting grammatical knowledge as the product of interlocution, not to say interrogation, Donatus establishes the necessity of the interlocutor/reader's participation in correctness: "What is a noun?" (*Nomen quid est?*) and "How many kinds of nouns are there?" (*Nomini quot accidunt?*)[27] interpellate the imagined reader into a system in which correct knowledge of current linguistic practice can simply be demanded, as well as repeatedly produced, in an ongoing contemporary context.[28] To the extent that other grammarians use similar interrogatives and imperatives, a similar interpellation may be observed in their work. Obligation is not, however, tied only to these forms. Present obligation is also construed in more overtly social forms, as in Pompeius' "if anyone were to do it, he would be laughed at." The obligatory nature of grammatical correctness is established in part in the *artes* with respect to the imagined reader's ongoing subjection to both positive and negative social sanctions. Thus when Pompeius argues for the propriety of placing the verb and adverb in proximity to one another, he does so with reference to their intelligibility to a present audience: "The adverb rightly follows the verb, since it cannot be separated from the verb. When I say 'tomorrow,' can this have any meaning unless you add a verb? For example, 'I shall do it tomorrow,' 'I shall speak tomorrow,' 'I shall come tomorrow.' Therefore, it follows from the verb, since it cannot be separated from the verb."[29] The argument, despite its inelegance, is perfectly clear: the need to be understood by others obliges the speaker to speak properly, just as the wish to avoid being ridiculed obliges the speaker to do the same.[30] Larger-scale social sanctions encouraging the speaker to correctness are also relatively easy to find in the *artes*. Diomedes' insistence that grammar clearly marks the separation between urban elites and "rustics" indicates the well-established connection between correct speech and class distinction, and implies the importance of correct speech to the maintenance of social order.[31] Again, the imagined reader is implicated in a system of ongoing social obligation that requires the use of a particular kind of speech; for Diomedes, as for other grammarians, this kind of speech is construed as correct in a context contemporaneous with the speaker, that is, a projected present.[32] The need to use correct speech is tied to obligations toward those with whom the potential speaker is imagined to be interacting in a currently existing setting.

The same act of speaking, however, also includes obligations that are tied to configurations of a past. In the last chapter I described the temporal dimensions of *auctoritas*. These dimensions entail the configuration of the reader as under a certain compulsion generated by the fact of past textual fragments, that is, by the presence of the fragments and their construction as representative of a past. This does not, in the *artes*, take the form of an obligation to imitate past *auctores* or the past textual objects that represent them, as Pompeius' criticism of the Ciceronian line clearly shows. Instead, the obligation is to remain within the linguistic parameters that *auctoritas* marks.[33] In temporal terms, this entails an obligation both to know what parameters have been set by past textual objects and to recognize those supposedly past objects as active and continuing interventions in present language.[34] Just as ties to present interlocutors are imagined, through the rhetoric of intelligibility, to constrain speech, past textual objects are imagined to have ties to the potential speaker that constrain speech; this imagination occurs in rhetorics of temporal propriety. This does not in every (or, necessarily, in any) case entail simple imitation of locutions identified as past; it does entail the placement of the potential speaker within a temporal framework understood to be indebted to the past.[35]

The compelling force of past textual objects on this projected reader is clear at one of the most basic levels of the *artes*, the definition of grammar itself.

Grammar is the science specifically concerned with reading and with the exposition of what is said in the poets and other writers: in the poets, that their proper arrangement may be preserved, and in writers, that their proper arrangement may be free of faults. There are two parts of grammar, one that is called exegetic and one that is called horistic. The exegetic is explanatory, and has to do with the matter of reading; the horistic is delimiting, and demonstrates principles such as the parts of speech, and the virtues and vices of speech. The whole art of grammar consists above all in the understanding of the poets, writers, and historians, in ready exposition, and in the logic of speaking and writing correctly.[36]

To take Diomedes' definition at face value,[37] grammar is the science used in reading and in the exposition of past textual objects. This use of the past has present consequences; indeed, it is undertaken precisely for the sake of those consequences, namely, the deduction of the *ratio* of speaking and writing from the *ordines* of the past objects. Diomedes' conclusion is not simply that the educated person will understand past textual objects and will be able to speak and write, but that the student's speaking and writing correctly is directly derived from the parameters set by earlier texts. In other words, present correct action places the present reader or potential speaker in a position of indebtedness to past textual objects; they are objects by virtue of which correctness is recognized, and they are also objects the recognition of which is the condition of correctness.[38] They are understood to have a certain temporal momentum: the reader is understood to be that which *ought* to be acted upon by their movement.[39]

A few examples may help to clarify the temporal status of these objects and of the subjects that are imagined to encounter them. Part of Charisius' account of the verb ends with a discussion of "ancient" as opposed to "contemporary" verb forms.[40] Charisius notes here that the third person plural is often given as ending in *–re* rather than *–nt* in earlier authors: "Additionally, in the historians, Sallust and Livy, [we see] *parare arcere facere adire* instead of *parabant arcebant faciebant adibant*, as can be seen in these readings."[41] Farther on in the same passage, Charisius contrasts ancient (*veteres*) and more recent (*posteriores*) conjugation of the passive infinitive: "The ancients were accustomed to end the passive infinitive verb as follows: *agitarier docerier legier audirier*, while later writers use the letter *–i*, as in: *agitari doceri legi audiri*."[42] In neither case is fault found with ancient or contemporary usage, but the explicit marking of usages as time-bound

(*Praeterea apud auctores historicos, velut Sallustium Livium*; or *ita solitos veteres*) creates a discursive framework in which linguistic difference is contained by an implicit temporal narrative. Thus Sallust and Livy are "allowed" to write in one way, while the grammarian's contemporaries are aligned with a different normative usage. The obligatory nature of these norms becomes even clearer at the end of Charisius' discussion of the passive imperative: "But this entire construction seems so absurd that it is extremely rare even in the *auctores*."[43] Here the *auctores* form a limit to contemporary speech and display their double function of prohibition and prescription: they can use the "absurd" locution (if rarely) because of their status as *auctores*, but precisely because they do use it rarely, the imagined reader is to understand that its use is not licit any more.[44] The contemporary speaker is thus urged into correctness by an appeal to *auctoritas* that assumes a need to know the *auctores* and to recognize them as limiting figures. This binds the construction of contemporary correctness by obligation to textual objects construed as originating in the past.[45]

Priscian uses the *auctores* similarly, for example, when he is disputing the claim that *equidem* is a contraction of *ego quidem* (GL 3.103.5–15):

> It should be noted that some people consider *equidem* to be a contraction composed [*compositam*] of *ego* and *quidem*; but they are mistaken, since it is simple [i.e., not composite], and we can recognize this primarily from the locution itself. For we say, *equidem facio, equidem facis, equidem facit*, and the construction can be carried over to first and second and third person, which could hardly happen if it were a composite of *ego* and *quidem*. For no one says, *ego quidem facis, ego quidem facit*, but only *ego quidem facio* in the first person. And the usage of the *auctores* supports this, since they joined *equidem* as a prepositive to *ego*, as Sallust does in the Catiline history: *equidem ego sic existimo, patres conscripti, omnes cruciatus*; but if *equidem* were composed of *ego* and *quidem*, he would hardly have added *ego* to it.

Here the combination of current and past usage dictates correctness, although in fact the usages cited by Priscian are different: current usage pairs *equidem* with first, second, and third person (which Priscian argues is incorrect if the first person is implied); past usage pairs *equidem* with *ego* (which Priscian argues is redundant if the first person is implied). That is, Priscian presents two different arguments for his basic point, basing one on contemporary use and the other on "ancient" use. The different arguments work in tandem to make Priscian's point, engaging the imagined reader on the one hand with contemporary interlocution and on the other hand with authoritative precedent. The engagement is successful, however, only to the extent that the reader is positioned as existing in a state of obligation with respect to both present interlocution and textual objects construed as exempla of a linguistic past.[46] That is, Priscian can only carry his point if the reader is understood as bound by the parameters that contemporary use and precedent set forth.

The foundation of the linguistic subject here lies within the grammarian's matrices of temporality and obligation.[47] The grammarians consistently construe the linguistic actor as both necessarily acting in and being formed by the combination of temporal placement (*antiqui/nos*) and linguistic obligation. Without this construction, there is in the *grammatici* no continuously existing subject,[48] since the subject is only called upon in moments of speech conditioned by precedent and obligation (e.g., *dicimus, nemo dicit, siqui fecerit*). This is the force of Priscian's striking dedication of his work to the consul Julian: "Nonetheless, I make you, who encouraged this work, also the judge of its fate, Julian, consul and patrician, in whom the splendor [*claritudo*] of genius in every inquiry also acquires the highest rank of honor . . . whose mind I think consists as much of the soul of Homer as of the soul of Virgil, each of which possessed the summit of music; I affirm that you are a third, composed of each of them, excelling no less in every sort of Greek learning than in every sort of Latin."[49] On one level, of course, this is simply a rather florid conceit, but I would like to suggest that there is a great deal of consistency between this conceit and the actual construction of subjectivity in the *artes*. That is, linguistic subjects in the *artes* are understood to exist primarily in moments of locution; and the typical mode of locution in the *artes* is the reproduction of past language.

One of the points at which this becomes clear is in the series of interrogatives that form Donatus' *Ars Minor*. Here, the grammatical interlocutors, as temporally continuous subjects, are effectively nonexistent outside the exchange of linguistic singularities used to construct larger abstractions like Latinity itself. The conventions of the dialogue form and the model of typical classroom practice suggest, of course, that there is one questioner and one respondent, but this is itself an imposition of the idea of temporally continuous subjects on individual verbal acts.[50] Consider, for example, the *Ars Minor* on the pronoun:

What is a pronoun? A part of speech that, in the place of a noun, signifies to almost the same extent, and that at times is declined according to person. How many characteristics does the pronoun have? Six. What are they? Quality, gender, number, figure, person, case. In what does the quality of a pronoun consist? It is twofold: pronouns are either definite or indefinite. Which are definite? Those which are declined according to person, such as *ego tu ille*. Which are indefinite? Those which are not declined according to person, such as *quis quae quod*.[51]

There is in principle no reason why this sequence cannot be read as attributable to a series of questioners and respondents, but it is a strain on the imagination to do so. One reason why this alternative scenario is difficult to imagine, I suggest, is because the subjects are here placed within a context of temporal and linguistic obligation, a context that interpellates them as continuously existing.[52] The first level of obligation is that supposed between the fictive questioner and the fictive respondent. The setting out of grammatical information is here construed as an exercise in which demands are made and met. They are, further, made and met sequentially, so that each element in the sequence of answers (both the answers themselves and their constituent parts, in list form) is understood as both required by the questioner and required by linguistic usage. The respondent is in this way imagined to exist both in the time that the question is being asked (i.e., immediately prior to the response), and in a time in which the usage that is the subject of the question has been established in some authoritative manner (i.e., in an indeterminate prior period). Moreover, the respondent is also supposed to be about to exist in the time in which the question is answered. The obligatory force of the interrogatives thus posits a subject existing over time.[53] Thus when the question is "Which [pronouns] are definite?" the answer, "Those which are declined according to person, such as *ego tu ille*," reflects both the immediate requirement of the question and the broader requirements of knowledge and usage, requirements that, as we saw in the last chapter, place the linguistic actor in a specific temporal context. The scenario of obligation is then repeated in the next question and answer, and so on. As with the repetition involved in lists generally, the repetition of the scenario of obligation, and its formal similarity to its predecessor and successor, implies that these obligations have a certain sameness.[54] This conjured sameness may on the one hand be used to produce imagined bodies of knowledge, but it also extends to the sameness of more concrete bodies, here those of the conjured questioner and respondent. The foundations are here laid for a continuously existing linguistic subject, existing necessarily in a state of obligation and continuous because the obligations laid upon this subject are formally repeated and therefore understood as repeatable.[55]

Donatus' *Ars Minor*, however, is not one of the *artes* that engages most explicitly with the idea of *antiquitas*. It will help to consider the temporal

dimension of linguistic obligation by moving to a text with a clearer engagement. One such text is Diomedes' *ars grammatica*, especially its sections on the virtues and vices of speech. These sections are, as is common
in the *grammatici*, thick with quotations of earlier texts as exempla, both
exempla to be imitated and exempla to be avoided. For example, in his
section *de vitiis orationis*, Diomedes discusses the following problems:

Pleonasm: A pleonasm is a sentence full of more words than necessary, such as *sic ore
locutus est*, when it would have sufficed to say *sic locutus est*. . . . Ellipsis: An ellipsis
is a sentence that is deprived of a necessary locution, when something is missing
that a more accurate sentence would demand, such as *terris iactatus et alto*, where the
preposition *in* is lacking; or *Italiam fato profugus*, that is, *ad Italiam*.[56]

The hortatory function of these passages is relatively clear; in theory the
same exhortation, to avoid pleonasm and ellipsis, could be given without
recourse to the *auctores*. By tying the observance of correctness to authoritative units of pastness, however, Diomedes places the reader into simultaneous relations of time and of obligation, so that the force of obligation
is directly connected to the conjured reader's recognition of the *auctoritas*
of past objects.[57] The use of examples from figures defined as "past" inserts
the conjured reader into a framework in which linguistic acts are predicated on a temporal and ethical position in relation to that imagined past.
In order for linguistic actors to exist as such, they must therefore exist in
a state of obligation.[58] Thus, when Priscian describes Julianus as "made
up" of Homer and Virgil, he is not only paying an extravagant compli-
ment, he is also revealing the constitutive nature of grammatical discourse:
Julianus is recognizable as a linguistic actor precisely because of his relation
to units of past linguistic knowledge.[59]

   That language has a constitutive function, and that this function is tied
to understandings of past and present usage, is not a particularly new idea.
I would like to emphasize the explicitly hortatory aspects of the function,
and its discourse of obligation and relation, for a simple reason: it is this
"ethical" discourse that is used in texts surrounding grammatical learning
to connect literary activity with the concept of piety. The connection is not
made in the *artes* themselves, but it is consistently made in and about the
work of late ancient grammarians and grammatical education, outside the
genre of the *ars*. In the remainder of this chapter, I would like to consider
four examples of the connection between linguistic obligation and literary
piety, found in the work of Ausonius, Macrobius, the emperor Julian, and
Augustine.

Ausonius, Macrobius, and Literary *Pietas*

AUSONIUS

Decimus Magnus Ausonius was born into the lower strata of the Gallo-Roman aristocracy some time around the year 310, and by the mid-330s he was teaching as a professional grammarian at Bordeaux.[60] Ausonius became a professor of rhetoric at Bordeaux around 360, and from that position he was appointed tutor to the young emperor-to-be, Gratian, in the mid-360s.[61] On Gratian's accession in 375, Ausonius rose as well, ultimately being made consul in 379. With the movement of Gratian's court from Trier to Milan, however, followed by the usurpation of Magnus Maximus and the death of Gratian in 383, Ausonius' political influence rapidly declined, and he spent his final years in literary pursuits at Bordeaux.[62]

Although it is now generally agreed that Ausonius was a Christian,[63] one of the most striking late ancient texts that combines grammatical literary pursuit and traditional piety is Ausonius' textual enactment of familial ritual, the *Parentalia*. The *Parentalia* is not, in the most obvious modern sense, a set of "religious" texts, at least not in the sense that "religion" must have to do with "theology," but it is clearly a set of texts whose theme and framework is piety.[64] Ausonius declares as much in the prose preface, when he explains that "this little work . . . is mournfully religious" (*hoc opusculum . . . habet maestam religionem*), and "the respect of the living has no holier task than to memorialize the departed with reverence" (*nec quicquam sanctius habet reverentia superstitum quam ut amissos venerabiliter recordetur*).[65] Both the prose preface and the verse preface of the work note the pre-Christian origins of the ritual of the *parentalia*, supposedly from the time of Numa,[66] in which, traditionally, portrait busts of deceased family members were displayed and offerings made to the dead.[67] The presence here of the pre-Christian past might be read as evidence for Ausonius' lack of devotion to Christianity,[68] but regardless of the Christian or non-Christian aspects of Ausonius' piety, what is most notable is the overt confluence of the themes of piety, obligation, literary culture, and temporal positioning, all of which contribute to the constitution of a very particular literary and religious subject, the speaker of the poems himself.[69] In this respect, the opening of the *Parentalia* resembles the opening of Ausonius' *Epicedion in Patrem*, in which Ausonius explains that "after God, I have always revered my father, and have owed secondary respect to my parent. . . . The title [*Epicedion*] is taken from Greek authors, dedicated to the honor of the dead, not pretentiously, but piously" (*post deum semper patrem colui secundamque reverentiam genitori meo debui. . . . titulus a Graecis auctoribus, defunctorum honori dicatus, non ambitiosus sed religiosus*).[70] Again, the themes of piety, obligation, literary culture, and genealogy are the components entering into the construction of the literary figure of the elder Ausonius, who is, of course, a picture of Ausonius *iunior* as well (*nomen ego Ausonius*).[71] The recurrence of this constellation in the *Parentalia* suggests the important ideological role of the combination of literary culture and piety in the work of at least one late ancient grammarian, Ausonius himself. The *Parentalia* thus establishes at the outset the link between literature and piety in nontechnical literature by and about grammarians.

The theme of obligation in the *Parentalia* is developed especially in its prefaces and in its first and third poems, and the connection between literature and obligation is discussed most explicitly in the third poem, to Ausonius' uncle, Aemilius Magnus Arborius.[72] The first poem, to Ausonius' father, opens as follows: "First of all, my father Ausonius, whom / order urges [*iubet*] me to place first, although Ausonius the son might hesitate."[73] The use of *iubet* clearly conveys the obligatory sense, taking up the obligation to commemorate the dead established in the verse preface: "The undisturbed ashes rejoice when their names are spoken; / even the monuments urge [*iubent*] this, with their inscribed faces."[74] The third poem opens with an even more strongly worded claim that the poet is following the dictates of *pietas*: "I have kept *pietas* by speaking of my father and mother first; / the third (but this is awful) is Arborius, / whom it would be blasphemous [*nefas*] to commemorate first, with my father second, / but whom it is practically blasphemous [*paene nefas*] not to place first."[75] The reason that it is "practically blasphemous" to place Arborius third is then given: Arborius, who was "father and mother"[76] to the poet, deserves a more prominent place because of his help in training Ausonius in the liberal arts.[77] Arborius is praised especially for his fine Latin (*Latio sermone*),[78] and this is, according to Ausonius, the key to Arborius' reputation (*fama*).[79] In *Parentalia* 3, the element that is intertwined with genealogy as that which places the poet under pious obligation is literary education. The specific importance of verbal fragments of a past to the establishment of pious duties is further suggested by Ausonius' praise of Arborius as "learned in a thousand ways and a thousand precepts of speaking, / eloquent, quick, and never forgetful" (*tu per mille modos, per mille oracula fandi / doctus, facundus, tu celer atque memor*).[80] *Doctus* and *memor* imply that the key to Arborius' facility was at least in part the learning (i.e., memorizing) of established literary precedents (*modi* and *oracula*), hardly a surprising task for a student to undertake, given the techniques of grammatical education already discussed. Arborius, then, is a figure to be revered because of his literary skill and participation in literary tradition, both as recipient and as transmitter.

The position of obligation in which the poet places himself is likewise negotiated through literary practice. A reliance on verbal fragments in the carrying out of one's pious duties is established in the prefaces: in the prose preface, Ausonius appeals to the word *parentalia*, an "ancient title," suitable as the conveyor of "reverence";[81] in the verse preface, Ausonius lays stress on the importance of verbal reminiscences by claiming, as already noted, that the dead wish their names to be spoken and that funerary inscriptions order such speaking.[82] In both prefaces, the references to Numa as the founder of the *parentalia* enact the use of verbal fragments (i.e., the name "Numa") to represent the past, precisely to argue for the propriety, and piety, of the verbal acts in the poems as a whole. The poem to Arborius promotes the concept of verbal piety by taking this enactment one step further and insisting that verbal acts, and training in verbal action (constituted in part by the reproduction of past verbal acts), are themselves worthy of pious respect.[83] Literary activity thus entails a certain *pietas*, here established in the context of familial ritual.

The use of the familial line, moreover, embeds Ausonius' literary piety in an explicit scheme of temporal progression. Much scholarship on the *Parentalia* has focused on the biographical and prosopographical information available in the poems, and it is true that readers are better informed about Ausonius' family than about the families of many late Roman figures. By shifting this focus slightly, however, it is possible to consider instead the ideological role played by the sequential, temporal, notations in the poems.[84] On the one hand, as with any other grammatical list, one of the products of the set of poems is an imagined wholeness or completion, even if in fact that completion is never quite reached. Thus Ausonius' language in these poems often refers to duties fulfilled, or at least fulfilled "enough": for example, at 23.19, "so this is sufficient, father Paulinus" (*sic satis hoc, Pauline pater*), which echoes the verse preface's "this is enough for the tombs, enough for those who want earth" (*hoc satis est tumulis, satis et telluris egenis*).[85] In this sense, the list format supports an imaginative construction of Ausonius' "whole" family as well as of an *officium* "completely" discharged. Yet the list, like other lists, also appeals to a temporal movement and narrative element. Each poem not only suggests a temporal line from the birth to the death of each figure but also construes the surviving poet as a figure within a temporal sequence, from Numa, through his familial line, to the narrative present.[86] It is this temporal placement that is understood to place the subject under obligation.[87] That is, the temporal and narrative function that we have seen in the lists in grammatical texts is here extrapolated into the construction not only of a temporally defined subject but of a subject under specifically "pious" obligation. Thus in the prose preface the poet claims that "the reverence of those still remaining has no more holy task than respectfully to memorialize the departed."[88] As has already been discussed, this obligation can be construed as simultaneously "literary" and "religious." In other words, the appeal to temporal position in the *Parentalia* plays a supplementary role in the configuring of the literary exercise as a "pious" activity. By construing the poems as the fulfillment of a duty that temporal placement imposes, the more general grammarian's obligation of literary correctness takes on, in the new poetic context, a religious cast, and piety in turn is construed as having a literary dimension.

Perhaps not surprisingly, then, piety in this context is understood as the discharging of obligations toward an imagined past, and further, as the discharging of those obligations in a literary fashion. The construction of piety in this form necessarily has implications for the concomitant construction of the pious subject, and it is clear that in many ways the *Parentalia* is as much, or more, about the presentation of Ausonius the poet as it is about the presentation of the *gens Ausonii* in the abstract.[89] Thus the subject of each poem is situated in relation to the poet in an imagined familial relation: mother, father, uncle, son, grandfather, and so on, a situation that requires the conjuring of the central figure of the poet in order for the sequence to cohere.[90] It also requires the conjuring of the poet specifically as a composite of temporal relationships and movements, from parents to children to siblings on the one hand, and from the living to the dead and back to the living, on the other. These complex temporal movements and relations are remarked upon several times in the poems themselves, for example in poem 13 on Ausonius' brother Avitianus: "Younger than I by birth, but greater in intelligence / he drank in the paternal arts";[91] Avitianus' untimely death is lamented, and the poem closes: "Brother by virtue of the flesh and by familial birth, / almost my son by love."[92] Here several different temporal positions are suggested, those of older and younger sibling, student and teacher, father and son. The poet himself is a combination of older and younger, brother and father. Similarly, poem 10, to the poet's son, also named Ausonius, joins the poet and his child by name[93] and collapses the sequence of generations in the line "You are buried in a common grave, in the lap of your great-grandfather."[94] Here again the poet Ausonius exists in a plurality of temporal situations, as father, as child, as grandson, and as the persistently present.[95] The specific temporal location of the poet is ambiguous; what is consistent is the positioning of the subject as a composite temporal figure.

These temporal gestures are fundamental to the construction of piety in this set of poems; thus the construction of the poet as a temporal figure is basic to his construction as pious. More tellingly, each poem also returns, in this context, to the theme of the poet's discharging of his literary and pious duty. Indeed, the poems themselves are repeatedly said to be pious acts, taking the place of the traditional ritual, as suggested in the verse preface.[96] Poem 3, to Arborius, ends with this sentiment: "I pour out this poem to you from your Muses" (*haec tibi de Musis carmina libo tuis*).[97] Poem 4, to Caecilius Argicius Arborius, opens: "Dutiful page, do not lack a pious gift" (*pium . . . munus*);[98] poem 5, to Aemilia Corinthia Maura, ends: "Restful shades, if I speak pious words [*si pia verba loquor*], keep the ashes of my grandmother forever undisturbed";[99] poem 8, likewise, is called "these . . . pious gifts" (*haec . . . pia munera*).[100] Notably, the *pietas* of the poems is not an accompaniment to any prior piety; the words themselves are what constitute the pious gifts.[101] That is, Ausonius is not describing himself as a pious person who also happens to be writing poems but is describing himself as pious precisely to the extent that he has written the poems as a fulfillment of the obligations of piety. The verbal gifts themselves are the locus of *pietas* (*pia verba, pia munera*), and Ausonius as the bearer of these gifts merely participates in the display of *pietas*. In this context, then, literary activity simply is piety, when that activity is placed within a specific temporal and hence obligatory matrix. Hence the temporal location of the poems is tied to the efficacy of the pious act: poem 3 is "poured out" to Ausonius' uncle, an act that only makes sense after the uncle's life is over.[102] Similarly, the shades are to bring rest to his grandmother's ashes if Ausonius speaks *pia verba*.[103] These verbal acts are, in other words, positioned as present responses to the past, in the same way that Ausonius is configured as part of a temporal continuum. Literary piety, like the obligation of literary correctness, is understood to occur in specific temporal situations as a response to past and present demands.

That Ausonius' poems are in some sense literary acts of piety has, of course, never been widely doubted; my interest is in how that piety is construed as specifically literary or, better, how literary acts can be seen as pious gestures in themselves. The relationship between late ancient grammatical practice and late ancient religious identity hinges in part on the construction of literary work as having religious meaning. Ausonius' poems offer one example of how literary obligation is transformed into pious debt. Ausonius' transformation of those to whom he is indebted into literary objects, moreover, results in the poet's configuration as a product of literary and temporal interactions.[104] The acts that constitute these interactions (i.e., the poems) are the locus of *pietas*, and the subject whom the acts imply becomes a necessarily pious subject.[105] Fundamentally, then, literary acts that construct a relationship between past and present in the late ancient period rely on ideas of literary obligation that can be, and here are, extrapolated into much broader concepts of piety and the pious subject. The fact that this imagined relationship is basic to grammatical training in late antiquity should lead to a clear instantiation of "piety" as a concept in works surrounding the grammatical tradition, as here in Ausonius. Nor is Ausonius an isolated case. It will be helpful next to consider the relationship between literature and piety as it is created in the much more ambitious *Saturnalia* of Macrobius.

MACROBIUS

Perhaps the most obvious extended example of the conflation of grammar and religion in a late ancient literary text is in the books of Virgilian criticism in Macrobius' *Saturnalia*. Although not a professional grammarian, Macrobius' grammatical activities are well known. In addition to the Virgilian material in the *Saturnalia*, he also composed a treatise comparing Latin and Greek words,[106] which draws on earlier grammatical doctrine. Similarly, the *Saturnalia* itself, while not an *ars grammatica*, is nonetheless an educational treatise with grammatical concerns at its core. These concerns are voiced, like those of the *Parentalia*, in the context of traditional religious ritual, and the best means of observing the ritual are considered to be literary: "Why should it not be considered a religious task to offer the sacred study of literature to these sacred days?" (*cur non religionis honor putetur dicare sacris diebus sacrum studium litterarum?*)[107] As in the case of Ausonius, Macrobius' literary participation in traditional ritual is often taken as evidence for Macrobius' "paganism," although, unlike in the works of Ausonius, there is no counterbalancing evidence in the extant corpus of "Macrobius" to suggest an interest in Christian ritual as well. Macrobius' literary characters in the *Saturnalia* and his speakers and commentator in the *Commentary on the Dream of Scipio* seem predominantly interested in a later Platonic version of solar cult, or at least in late Platonic cosmology.[108] Not surprisingly, the *Saturnalia* has also been claimed as one of the primary documents in the pagan revival of the fourth century.[109] Book 3.1–12 is set in the house of Nicomachus Flavianus and is dominated by the figure of Praetextatus, both prominent pagan aristocrats in fourth-century Rome, with Flavianus deeply involved in the usurpation of Eugenius in 394, an event also frequently understood as a pagan movement.[110] As with a purely prosopographical reading of the *Parentalia*, however, reading the *Saturnalia* primarily for its informative content with regard to late ancient philosophical monotheism obscures the productive ideological relationship between literary practices and the construction of *pietas* as a broader category. The now generally accepted dating of the *Saturnalia* to the 430s[111] obviously removes some of its relevance as a historical record of Rome in the 390s, but as Charles Hedrick points out, the text should not be relegated to the ranks of the merely nostalgic.[112] On the contrary, it is precisely because of its discourse about literature, piety, and the past that the text is so ideologically potent.

Like the *artes*, the *Saturnalia* positions itself as an educational text, in this case in dialogue form, and it explicitly enjoins the decontextualization and recontextualization of literary fragments as the best method of creating an ideal whole. In his prefatory explanation of his working method, Macrobius says:

The disparity of various matters, taken from different authors and varying time periods, is organized into a single body, so that whatever I have noted in a disordered and confused fashion, as a memory aid, will come together as its members. Nor should you blame me if I borrow some things from my various readings and often set matters out using the same words as were used by these authors. This work is not, after all, meant as a display of oratory, but as the collection of knowledge, and you should think it a good thing to become acquainted with ancient knowledge both in my own clear style and through the faithful use of the very words of the ancients, just as they supply themselves, either for explanation or for transcription.[113]

Macrobius then goes on to use the standard educational metaphor of the bee taking pollen from various flowers to justify his copious quotation of earlier sources: "We should, after a fashion, imitate the bees" (*apes enim quodammodo debemus imitari*).[114] The hortatory function of the passage is clear and sets up the framework of obligation at the outset. It is, moreover, a specifically literary obligation that is expressed, to be fulfilled in the

learning of verbal units attached to the *antiqui* (*ipsis antiquorum . . . verbis*).
Macrobius' addressee, his son Eustachius, is placed under obligation both
to his father and to the *antiqui* simultaneously, as an effect of being summoned into the literary-pedagogical situation. At the same time, Macrobius expresses his work as a fulfillment of his own obligation to bring up
his son correctly: "But [nature] vanquished us with nothing greater than
the love of those whom we have fathered, and wished our concern to be
with their upbringing and education."[115] Literary activity is thus construed
in the *Saturnalia* as fundamentally obligatory, the result of temporal and
familial debts that must be discharged, and that can only be discharged in
a literary fashion. After this opening emphasis on ancient words and their
reuse, it is not surprising to find much of the work (books 3–6) focusing on
literary criticism. As in the *artes*, Macrobius' primary method of argument
is to set out a basic informational argument (e.g., in book 5, that Virgil
borrows from Homer), and Macrobius expands and supports that argument with short quotations from earlier literary sources. This literary work,
however, must be seen in this context as both religious and obligatory.

One of the first topics of the Virgil criticism, in fact, is Virgil's knowledge of religious practice, specifically pontifical law, and the speaker who
expounds on the subject is Praetextatus, whose multiple religious offices
are well known.[116] Notably, it is not Virgil's overarching narratives that
are taken to represent the poet's religious knowledge but his choice of
specific words, genders, or phrasings. As in the *artes*, such singularities
receive expansive treatment, for example at 3.8.1–3, Macrobius' discussion
of *Aeneid* 2.632: "It often happens that we corrupt through poor readings
lines that have been set down with great erudition, as when some read
discedo ac ducente dea [i.e., Venus] *flammam inter et hostes expedior*, although
he learnedly wrote *ducente deo*, not *dea*. Aterianus asserts that, in Calvus,
one ought to read *pollentemque deum Venerem*, not *deam*. On Cyprus there
is a statue of the deity that is bearded but dressed in feminine clothing,
with male genitalia, and they consider her both male and female." Macrobius goes on to quote further supporting passages in Aristophanes, Laev-
inus, and Philochoros, indicating that Venus is to be considered both a
masculine and a feminine deity. Religious knowledge is here produced in
a manner very similar to the production of linguistic knowledge in the
artes: first a right and a wrong reading are defined, then an earlier literary
precedent is invoked; the right reading is even naturalized by appeal to a
state of affairs existing prior to the reading (i.e., the statue). Thus the units
of religious knowledge to which Praetextatus appeals when he claims that

Virgil "preserved pontifical law, most learnedly, in many different parts of his work" (*doctissime jus pontificium . . . in multa et varia operis sui parte servavit*)[117] are suggested in overtly grammatical terms. Here religious knowledge falls under the heading of literary knowledge: Praetextatus, in order to demonstrate Virgil's literary ability, demonstrates Virgil's grasp of cultic particulars, and it is this grasp that confirms Virgil's status as not only a poet but also pontifex maximus.[118] Thus, Praetextatus concludes, "it is not possible to understand the depths of Virgil without a knowledge of divine and human law."[119] Again, the exhortation is both literary and "religious," in that in order to carry out one's literary obligations, it is necessary to carry out religious ones as well. In combination with Macrobius' suggestion that the *Saturnalia*'s characters are fulfilling religious duties through literary discussion, it seems clear that religious and literary practice are fundamentally inseparable in the *Saturnalia*: each entails the other, and both are obligatory. The linguistic subject is construed as religious, and the religious subject as literary.

Grammatical techniques also produce the idea of religious knowledge more broadly: Macrobius does not focus on Virgil's knowledge of any individual cult; he is given credit for knowledge (*doctrina*) "about both our own religious matters and the religious matters of other nations" (*et circa nostra et circa externa sacra*).[120] Virgil's knowledge is construed as general within this specific category, and the existence of a general object of knowledge, *doctrina circa sacra*, is the clear implication. The homogenizing process is an extrapolation from a series of fragmentary examples (the gender of Venus; proper purification rites; which animals can be sacrificed to which deities; on which days sheep may be dipped)[121] to an entire *doctrina*. As in the *artes*, we have in the *Saturnalia* the imagination of a very broad field of knowledge, conjured from juxtaposed particulars. In this case, however, the field of knowledge is both linguistic and religious, that is, it is religious knowledge that is imagined as manifest in literary terms, and linguistic knowledge that entails cultic facility.[122] This *doctrina* must be understood as arising within a matrix of temporal and pious obligations, all of which are articulated in literary terms. The *doctrina* is the sum total of knowledge *circa sacra*, which is illustrated, but not exhausted, in the Virgilian passages that Macrobius cites.[123] Thus the manifestation of *doctrina* occurs only as Praetextatus is discharging his duty to Virgil as his literary predecessor, on the occasion of the religious festival of the *Saturnalia*. This *doctrina* is given further substance as that which Macrobius is attempting to hand on to his son, in further discharge of his literary and familial duties. *Doctrina circa sacra* as an imagined entity in the *Saturnalia* is in part the effect of the framework and movements earlier described as temporal and pious obligations. The matrices of obligation allow the field of religious "doctrine" to become imaginable as such.

All of this is accomplished within a clear temporal framework. The dedication of the work from father to son[124] establishes the progression in time, as does the dramatic setting of 384 for a work written some decades later.[125] Indeed, Macrobius calls attention to his manipulation of time and its progression at 1.1.4–5, in which he claims to be copying the dialogues of Cicero and Plato by including participants whose "real" ages would have been different from those presented in the dialogue. This claim neatly historicizes both the action of the dialogue and the dialogue itself, while at the same time making clear the literary construction of time as the reader is supposed to experience it.[126] Perhaps equally telling is Macrobius' use of the same temporal language as contemporary grammarians to describe Virgil's relation to religious practice. Virgil is persistently described as having "preserved," "followed," or "remembered" earlier practices,[127] much as he is said to do in Servius, and in Charisius and Diomedes.[128] Virgil is construed as a medium between the *veteres* and Macrobius' fifth-century reader, here in terms not only of language but also of religious practice. The idea of Roman custom, the *mos Romanorum*, here becomes extremely useful for the ideation of a literary-religious "culture" in late antiquity, and Macrobius examines this notion within the Virgilian context, here *Aeneid* 7.601: "We cannot overlook another of his observations. He says: *Mos erat / Hesperio in Latio, quem protinus urbes / Albanae coluere sacrum, nunc maxima rerum / Roma colit.* Varro in *On Customs* says that a *mos* is an intellectual decision that common usage ought to follow. Pompeius Festus, in book 13 of *On the Meanings of Words*, says that '*Mos* is an institution of our forebears having to do with the religion and ritual of our predecessors.' Virgil has followed both authors."[129] While this passage need not imply that either Virgil or Macrobius understood *mos* as having a solely religious meaning,[130] the overlap between religious *mos* and literary *mos* is suggestive of the way that the homogenizing tendency of grammatical practices enters the broader cultural sphere. Virgil's observation of the "most ancient custom of the Romans" (*vetustissimum Romanorum morem*)[131] refers, first, to his knowledge of earlier religious practice and, second, to the incorporation of that knowledge, and its vocabulary, into his literary work, of which Macrobius' readers are consumers. To the extent that "custom" entailed the construction of a past both literary and religious, late ancient readers could easily conflate the two in the reading of Virgil.

The conflation also implies, as in the other grammatical narratives discussed thus far, a constitutive ethical component. Macrobius' discussion creates a temporal sequence from the *veteres* to the reader of Virgil, a sequence that becomes a narrative of continuity in the character of Praetextatus.[132] Macrobius' Praetextatus, as is well known, is an ideal portrait, not a strictly historical one,[133] and the memory of the historical Praetextatus could be used for many different purposes in the later fourth and fifth centuries.[134] Praetextatus' function in the *Saturnalia* is both that of host and that of religious expert.[135] He dominates books 1 and 3 of the work, and his discourses are consistently on the origins, nature, and observance of traditional religion. He thus adds traditional piety to the list of ideal characteristics that the grammarians espouse. These virtues (piety, nobility, generosity, learning, and moderation) are stereotypical traits of the good aristocrat in late antiquity, but it is notable that here, like the virtues in the *artes*, they are specifically tied to literary learning. Macrobius, in other words, is adding piety to the other educational virtues, and is using a similar narrative of the reader as a figure negotiating the movement from past to present in order to do so. Praetextatus' learning and piety are of a piece with his "respect for antiquity" (*reverentia antiquitatis*),[136] for the sake of which he defends the grammarian Servius' archaizing language.[137] Praetextatus' character in the *Saturnalia* is thus built around the combination of piety and learning, where learning means specifically learning about antiquity and piety is piety toward the objects of knowledge attributed to ancient sources. On the one hand, then, Praetextatus models the ethos generated by a narrative of continuity between past and present; on the other, Praetextatus, as a fantastic historical figure himself, mediates the movement from antiquity to Macrobius' reader.[138] Whatever the complexities of the historical Praetextatus' character, here he becomes a fixed figure embodying traditional piety as an actor in the apparently obligatory movement from past to present.[139]

There are, then, three products of the grammatical art as it appears in the *Saturnalia*. One is the field of *doctrina circa sacra*, which arises out of the same juxtapositions of singularities that produce the *mos veterum*. Another is the framework of temporality and obligation; that is, the idea that the *mos veterum* persists. Finally, there is the subject that is required to participate in the framework of obligation in order to be understood as a viable literary actor. Although these three products arise simultaneously, the subject is necessarily constructed as temporally secondary to the larger field of *mos/doctrina* into which she or he is interpellated. The field of *doctrina* is, in turn, construed as determinative for the subject within the frame of obligation. Praetextatus' status and Virgil's status are both reinforced by the idea of a general field of knowledge that their acts of obligation both produce and are thought to follow. Praetextatus' audience equates his knowledge with that of the poet (*doctrinam et poetae et ennarrantis*) at the close of Praetextatus' discourse.[140] In order to break into the discussion at this point, the dialogue's naysayer Evangelus must present himself as equally a subject under obligation and therefore also a possessor of *doctrina*: "I also put my hand under the teacher's cane; I also heard about pontifical law."[141] These acts, constituting a subject under obligation, are what Evangelus offers as his qualification to speak on the *disciplinam iuris*. Only as a participant in this field of knowledge/obligation is Evangelus' interjection possible. The field is on the one hand produced by acts discharging obligation and is on the other hand the ideological justification for placing the subject within the larger obligatory framework.[142] That is, the creation of the field is simultaneous with the creation of the duty to stay within the field.

Like Priscian's dedicatee Julianus, Macrobius' characters are made up of particular strands of knowledge—knowledge that places them under pious obligation. One of the ideological effects of the *Saturnalia*, then, is the same as the effect of the *Parentalia*, namely, the creation of the pious figure himself, whose piety is expressed as a relation between that figure and a body of knowledge that is manifested in verbal singularities. The pious figure is made up of verbal and temporal intersections that are configured as fulfilling a religious function. *Doctrina circa sacra* is also instantiated in the literary knowledge that is the justification for the *Saturnalia* as an educational treatise. The interpenetration of piety and literature is clear: it is not the case that linguistic activity determines a particular religious "affiliation" in either the *Saturnalia* or the *Parentalia*, but the field of literary activity is imagined to be, because of its temporal and ethical constitution, fundamentally pious in nature. The idea of pious action, in turn, is understood to be visible in literary acts that derive from basic grammatical practice. The reification of *pietas* and *doctrina circa sacra* is not in every case, however, free of religious particulars. It will be helpful to conclude this chapter by considering one pious figure in whom literary practices were considered to determine not just piety but a specific and exclusive religious affiliation: this figure is the grammarian and rhetor Marius Victorinus.

Marius Victorinus: From Literature to Religion

From the imagined figure of the pious and learned Praetextatus, we turn to the imagined figure of the pious and learned Victorinus. Unlike Praetextatus, his younger contemporary, Victorinus was a professional academic, a successful and celebrated rhetor who according to Jerome and Augustine was honored with a statue in the forum of Trajan as a tribute to his linguistic talent.[143] In this respect his career is more akin to that of Ausonius, since his literary acts raised him to prominence. Like Ausonius, at some point in his career, Victorinus identified himself as a Christian. Yet the most important similarity for purposes of this study is his likeness to Praetextatus in being best known through a later writer's portrayal of him in a work whose ambitions are simultaneously literary, protreptic, and religious. I refer of course to Augustine's narrative of Victorinus' conversion in *Confessions* 8. Victorinus' literary and grammatical output is relatively well known: an *ars grammatica*, perhaps two short works on meter, commentaries on Cicero and Virgil, translations and commentaries on Greek dialectical works and Platonist texts, anti-Arian works, and commentaries on the letters of Paul.[144] Presumably, from this list, Marius Victorinus took both literature and piety quite seriously, but the relation between the two in his work is difficult to chart. As a means of discovering one imagined relationship between the two, however, and the way in which that relationship could be understood to be embodied in the ethical figure of Victorinus, I would like to move away from Victorinus himself and concentrate on Victorinus as a literary and religious figure. There are two texts that "figure" Victorinus as both literary and religious, and that have largely determined the portrait of Victorinus that scholars of late antiquity have. One of these is, as I mentioned earlier, Augustine's account of Victorinus' conversion, and the other, although it does not mention Victorinus at all, is Julian's rescript against Christian teachers.

Augustine in *Confessions* 8.5.10 records that Victorinus resigned his public position in the wake of Julian's rescript, and while Augustine, as we will see, is not necessarily the most reliable source for Victorinus' attitudes, there seems no reason to doubt that this occurred. Jerome records that the same decision was made by the rhetor Prohairesius in Athens.[145] How, then, does Julian's measure interpellate teachers as religious figures, such that Victorinus might be understood to be affected by it?[146] As is well known, the edict directly connects the teaching of reading to the religious persona of the teacher: "Christians" ought to teach "Christian" texts; "pagans" ought to teach "pagan" texts. The phrasing of Julian's decision in his letter 36 frames the issue of education entirely in terms of the consistency and virtue of the teacher's character: "Whoever thinks one thing and teaches his students another seems to have abandoned the principle of education and to the same extent has ceased to be a virtuous man."[147] For this reason, Christians, who presumably "consider [earlier writers] to have been mistaken about what is most venerable,"[148] should refrain from teaching them, and teach only Christian books, "going off to the churches of the Galilaeans to interpret Matthew and Luke."[149] Here the character of the teacher is construed as directly correlated to the texts that the teacher uses. There are two imaginative tasks that this correlation presupposes: first, that a body of texts can be generalized into a *doctrina circa sacra* and, second, that knowledge of this *doctrina*, in its literary manifestations, is necessarily determinative of the character of a reader. In short, Julian's letter shares two of its presuppositions about literature and piety with the *Saturnalia*. In the same way that Julianus and Praetextatus are construed as "made up" of earlier literature, Julian's teachers are constituted by their reading of the *antiqui*. This requires them, in this framework, to be pious.

Where Julian differs from Macrobius and the grammarians is in his portrayal of piety as primarily imitative, a portrayal tied to his construction of the teacher as being in a very specific temporal position. What is notable here is the way in which Julian ties literary ethos to a particular movement from past to present. "I think it all the more necessary for those who spend time with the young, for the sake of their literary education [*epi logois*] to be of such [good] character, those who are interpreters of ancient literature, whether they are rhetors or grammarians, and especially philosophers."[150] The ancients, on the one hand, are homogenized through a list: "Homer and Hesiod and Demosthenes and Herodotus and Thucydides and Isocrates and Lysias,"[151] and the teacher is here set into a fixed role as a mediator between the ancients and the young. As part of this temporal progression the teacher is required to maintain a particular unified ethos: "But if they think [those writers] were wise, whose interpreters they are and for whom they are in the position of spokespersons, they should first imitate their reverence toward the gods."[152] Interpreting ancient writing is here understood as taking on the persona of the ancient writer, or rather a composite persona attributable to a collectivity of ancient writers—that is, interpreting is a matter of modeling an imagined (past) ethos in order to instruct the (present) young. The interpreter of the text is thus construed as an ancient and as a contemporary figure, required to make the two time periods agree through the adoption of a consistent readerly ethos. [153] The constitutive nature of literature for the linguistic subject here takes a rather dramatic turn. The ethos of the author and the ethos of the reader are both conjured from the textual object and are imagined to be necessarily the same in the act of invoking that object. The ideal end result is the continuance of the progression from antiquity to the present, so that willing children will eventually be led into the ancestral traditions, that is, they will be able to adopt this conjured, composite persona themselves, and will become viable linguistic subjects. [154] Julian thus assumes a homogeneity among past authors and appeals to the idea of temporal continuity to insist on a particular religious ethos, thus further collapsing readers (rhetors, grammarians, philosophers, and ultimately their pupils) into a single body unified by the adoption of that imagined religious character. Reading strategies here become points at which broad religious characterizations are articulated.

Writing more than thirty years later, Augustine in *Confessions* 8 famously recounts the conversion of Marius Victorinus in terms very similar to those used by Julian, and he in fact ends his account of Victorinus' conversion with Victorinus' resignation as a result of Julian's edict. "Afterward [Simplicianus] also told me that during the reign of the Emperor Julian, Christians were prohibited by law from teaching grammar and rhetoric. [155] [Victorinus] welcomed this law, preferring to abandon the chattering of the schoolroom rather than your word, by which you instruct the mouths of babes." [156] In Augustine's account, again, literary activity is used as a way of unifying a particular ethos in a narrative of movement from past to present. Augustine introduces Victorinus as "an extremely learned old man, well-versed in all the liberal arts," [157] and so famous for his learning that he has been honored with a statue in the Roman forum. For Augustine, Victorinus' reading is of importance primarily for the religious character it produces. Immediately after his introduction, Augustine pairs Victorinus' knowledge of the liberal arts and philosophy with the fact that he was "up to that time a worshiper of idols and participant in the impious rituals with which almost the entire Roman nobility was at that time taken up." [158] Augustine elaborates with a reference to *Aeneid* 8.698–700 to describe the varieties of gods and "monsters" worshiped at Rome, in addition to the traditional Roman pantheon, and then notes Victorinus' longstanding (*tot annos*) defense of these gods. Victorinus' conversion is accompanied, in turn, by a quotation from the Psalms, [159] and Augustine claims that it was the result of reading: "How did you make your way into his

breast? He read, Simplicianus said, the holy scriptures, and studiously re-
searched and examined all the Christian writings, and he said to Simplicianus—not openly, but secretly and in private—'You should know that I
am now a Christian.'"[160] After a period in which Augustine describes him
as "afraid to offend his friends, proud worshipers of demons,"[161] Victorinus decides to be baptized, again as the product of reading: "But afterwards, through his reading and observation, he drank in courage, afraid to
be denied by Christ before the holy angels, if he feared to confess Christ
before men."[162] Like Julian's grammarian, Augustine's Victorinus is reli-
giously constituted by the texts that he is understood to read.[163] Indeed,
Augustine's description of Victorinus' decision to be baptized places Victorinus within the biblical text entirely, with its use of Luke 9.26. Victorinus
is further placed under an ethical obligation by his reading: he is required
to act mimetically in order to be a literate actor at all. Julian's law certainly
applies to Augustine's Victorinus; they are constructed according to the
same standards of literary piety.

Yet Victorinus in Augustine's narrative is not entirely the same as
Julian's grammarians, who are either pious or hypocritical. Augustine's
Victorinus is placed in two different temporal situations, one conjured by
Virgil and entailing "idolatry" as its literary piety, and another conjured by
the Psalms and gospels and entailing baptism. For both Victorinus' pre-
Christian persona and his Christian persona, Augustine creates narratives
of temporal progression marked by unity of ethos. Victorinus is first a "worshiper of idols"—indeed, is a statue himself[164]—continuing for "many years"
in the course of Roman religion as Augustine, using Virgil, describes its
development. Victorinus is among those who worship "all sorts of mon-
strous gods, even the barking Anubis, monsters who once had taken arms
against Neptune and Venus and Minerva; and now Rome, conquered by
them, prayed to them."[165] Victorinus here becomes part of a timeline of
religious culture evoked by a list of gods in a literary text. He is a product
of a lengthy period of religious time. Upon becoming part of a new narrative, however, now one of Christian religious practice, his character immediately changes and becomes a consistently Christian character. Time does
not here progress, it starts over: "This old man Victorinus . . . did not
blush to become a child of your Christ and an infant at your font."[166]
Augustine thus does not describe the time Victorinus spends reading the
Bible while not baptized as a period in which Victorinus is both pagan
and Christian, he describes it as a period in which Victorinus is a Christian, albeit a "fearful" one. Readings of Virgil disappear and are replaced

with readings of the Bible. Like Julian, Augustine's narrative understanding of the readerly ethos does not posit a time when the reader can be both an "idolater" and a "Christian." The reader is simply conflated with the texts that she or he reads, and is inserted into a single narrative around that text.[167] Victorinus' resignation after Julian's edict is therefore "fortunate,"[168] in that it allows Victorinus "the opportunity to be free of everything but [God]."[169] Augustine's belief in the singularity of the readerly ethos is no less firm than Julian's.

Augustine's Marius Victorinus and Julian's grammarian, of whom Augustine's Victorinus is one, are, of course, no more accurate portrayals of the historical Marius Victorinus than Macrobius' Praetextatus is the real Praetextatus, or than Ausonius' *gens Ausoniana* is transparently the fourth-century Gallic house. What Augustine and Julian share, however, is the figure of the pious linguistic actor, whose literary obligations require him to negotiate the gap between the *antiqui* and *nos* by co-creating those two groups as necessarily ethically the same.[170] Difference is an ethical violation. The Marius Victorinus of Augustine's, or Julian's, fantasy thus serves an important purpose in the imagination of late ancient piety and its relation to literature. It allows the linguistic actor to be understood (and to understand herself or himself) as fulfilling a particular ethical, pious obligation through linguistic acts, and to understand the fulfillment as indicative of a fixed religious "identity."[171] Identity here is fundamentally a byproduct of the construction of literary obligation as both temporal and mimetic.

I have not chosen these three figures and their literary representations, spanning some seventy years, because I believe that grammatical reading practices universally required late ancient Romans to choose whether they would be pagans or Christians. That is far from the case. These texts do all demonstrate the imaginative ties between reading, the readerly persona, and the notion of time passing, as well as how these ties could be deployed in some religious contexts, both Christian and non-Christian.[172] These imaginative motions are, moreover, clearly connected to the practices and imagination of grammar as a discipline, with the former grammarian Ausonius revering his literary training, Praetextatus engaging in Virgil criticism, Julian investing in the grammarian as an educational figure, and Augustine, himself the author of an *ars grammatica*, portraying the occasional grammarian Marius Victorinus as the product of his reading practices. The *artes* do not address religion in any overt way but lay the foundation for such an address in their imposition of literary obligation on every linguistic subject. Outside the *artes*, however, the readerly ethos that the grammarians advocate could become a specifically religious ethos, especially when tied, as the grammarians tied it, to the idea of the *auctoritas* of the past, as transmitted through literary texts. To the extent that, outside the *artes*, this *auctoritas* could be understood as requiring continuity with that past, literary piety overlapped with traditional piety.[173] The conservatism of the *artes* lent itself to this conflation.

More important is the way in which narratives of the past, and imaginations of it, contributed to the imagining of religious entities as a whole and the personae of individuals who appear to support them. The practice of reading via fragmentation and disarticulation is a creative process, enabling the reader to imagine juxtaposed fragments as part of larger homogeneous wholes. In the *artes*, these wholes are imagined primarily in terms of time; they represent "the ancients" and "us." Fragments are then taken as symbols of a unified *mos veterum*, in relation to which the contemporary reader stands, at times in differentiation and at times in continuity.[174] This relation is itself reified in the idea of *latinitas*, and its cultivation is understood to produce a particular ethos and particular obligations. Within the generic constraints of the *artes*, this is not particularly controversial. When discourse about reading and grammar move beyond the *artes*, however, this imaginative technology takes on further productive possibilities. For Ausonius, Macrobius, Julian, and Augustine, the *mos veterum* includes cultic practice: there is no clear separation between literature and cult in their accounts. Thus Julian's list of ancient authors and Praetextatus' and Augustine's quotations of Virgil allow them to imagine an antiquity that is specifically cultic in nature, without differentiation between cults, deities, or specific authors' practices. Piety is imagined to be piety toward the homogeneous collectivity, not specific cultic devotion. In the same way as the *auctores* are listed and homogenized, deities here are rendered equivalent. Julian, for example, says of the *auctores*, "Did they not consider themselves priests, some of Hermes, and some of the Muses?"[175] He then, however, speaks of them simply as venerators of "the gods"[176] as a general category. When Macrobius speaks generally of Virgil's *doctrina circa sacra*, he illustrates it only with examples drawn from the cults of Apollo, Neptune, and Hercules.[177] The literary habit of decontextualizing, listing exemplary material, and homogenizing thus allows for the imagination of a unified religious corpus, a body that comes close to what modern scholars might call paganism. This body is simply part of the same *mos veterum* that the grammarians produce, as is made clear by its imagination in specifically literary contexts in these three texts. The ethos that grammatical education requires is also transformed into an ethos of piety. Augustine's Victorinus moves via reading from one monolithic religious identity to another; Julian's teachers are not virtuous unless they exhibit the same monolithic character. Just as Diomedes creates an ontological divide between civilized and rustic (it is impossible to be both), a divide is here marked between pagan and Christian, or, better, between pious and impious. As they are imagined, they are necessarily mutually exclusive. It is absolutely true to say that grammarians produced "the language and *mores* through which a social and political elite recognized its members,"[178] with the further understanding that they also provided late ancient elites with the linguistic technology for imagining language *as* custom, and both language and custom as ideal objects requiring an absolute allegiance.

Concluding Heterogeneity

As has been argued by many others, religious practice in late antiquity was never as clearly segregated in reality as religious entities could be in the imagination.[179] At least in linguistic terms, however, it is precisely a practical heterogeneity that makes the monolithic imagination possible, since without this heterogeneity there could be no list and no juxtaposition of fragments, the fundamental gestures of the grammatical technique of ideation. To conclude, then, it will be appropriate to consider this relation between heterogeneity and imagined unification as it plays out in grammatical writing. On the one hand, one can speak of late ancient reading practices that produce paganism or the *mos veterum*, but this is distinct from speaking of readers or texts as necessarily pagan, whatever the ethics of reading are assumed to be. I have argued that certain reading practices could be used for, as it were, "paganizing" purposes,[180] but I would like to close by noting that these purposes, as they are expressed by figures like Julian or Augustine, were not necessarily at any point concretely implemented.

To return to an exemplary passage to which I earlier gave little attention, Charisius' use of Romanus' list *de analogia* in book 1 of his *ars grammatica* provides an excellent illustration of the linguistically and culturally heterogeneous. Near the beginning of this list, an alphabetical catalogue of different noun declensions, the two names Adam and Abraham appear, both listed as indeclinable.[181] Adam is given the epithet *ho protoplastos*; Abraham is not given any descriptor. It is difficult to be certain whether these are insertions by Charisius or are in Romanus' original list, and although

no other biblical names appear in the *ars grammatica*, it has been suggested on the basis of these names that Charisius may have been a Christian.[182] Part of the logic behind this argument lies in the idea that "pagans
as a rule read only secular texts, while Christians (and especially Christian
intellectuals) read both secular and Christian works."[183] Although there is
certainly evidence for the idea that the reading of non-Christian texts projected a non-Christian ethos (and vice versa), as I have argued above, there
are two basic problems with this idea as a description of unfiltered historical reality. First, it supposes a fixed identity prior to, and consistent throughout, the act of reading.[184] Second, it supposes that texts and reading practices
tend to be homogeneous: although "Christians" may read "Christian" or
"pagan" (or "secular")[185] texts, these seem to be the only two possible textual categories. To take the second problem first, Charisius' list is nothing
if not heterogeneous. The varied sources of the list include Cicero, Varro,
Virgil, Terence, and of course the Bible.[186] It would be hard to characterize the list as Christian, Jewish, or pagan if what is meant by those categories is that the list requires a particular monolithic religious ethos of either
its readers or its writers. The entry immediately before "Adam" is "Apollo";
other non-Christian figures also people the list.[187] The heterogeneity that
makes up the list is, however, basic to the grammatical argument being
made, that is, that the morphology of some hard-to-decline words should
be extrapolated from other, morphologically similar, words.[188] Heterogeneity of signification and of literary source is thus basic to the postulation of
broad morphological principle, since the "sameness" of certain words only
becomes apparent through the juxtaposition of differences. The same principle holds true for the broader imagination of ethical unities: the presence
of multiple deities and time periods allows for their containment in an
imagined *mos veterum*; the insertion of biblical words allows for the containment of textual heterogeneity through the imagination of the homogenizing category "Christian."

Because heterogeneity is instrumental in the production of these unities, it is inadequate simply to oppose actual heterogeneity with imagined
paganism in describing the ideological production of a pagan literary tradition in late antiquity.[189] In order to avoid an uncritical labeling of late
Roman reading and cultic practices as necessarily either pagan or Christian,
the opposition of heterogeneity to homogeneity will not suffice. Instead
it may be helpful to reconsider the narrative, temporal aspect of these productive acts. As we saw in the previous chapter, the reification of Latinity
occurs in the repetition of temporal movement from a homogeneous past

to a homogeneous present. Likewise, the narrative of present relation to the *mos veterum* in Ausonius, Macrobius, Julian, and Augustine has a distinctly temporal aspect, which allows for the production of a present "custom" (*mos* or *consuetudo*) in the linguistic subject, that is, an interpellated continuity of ethos. By resisting the narrative aspect, however, it may be possible to intervene in the imagining of a homogeneous "paganism." That is, by considering reading acts outside a line of progression from past to present, the reification of this temporal relation—and hence the imagining of reading, or of the reader, as pagan or Christian—becomes unnecessary.[190] The shadowy figure of Charisius may not be Christian,[191] but he may equally not be pagan, if these terms are to be understood, as they conventionally are, in any exclusive sense.

We return to the issue of readerly ethos and its unity in the course of reading. Here it may be helpful to move from Charisius to Augustine's depiction of the reader Victorinus. Victorinus has an interest in the Bible, and in "Christian" texts,[192] and Augustine places this interest at the temporal beginning of a narrative of conversion.[193] If Augustine (or Simplicianus) is right to claim that Victorinus read the Bible and then adopted a Christian identity,[194] it is necessary to posit some length of time, even if only the time of reading, in which Victorinus' identity is suspended. Augustine partly suggests this: "He said to Simplicianus, 'You should know that I am now a Christian.' And Simplicianus answered, 'I will not believe it, nor will I count you among the Christians, until I see you in the church of Christ.' But Victorinus laughed at him, saying, 'So is it walls that make Christians?' And he often said that he was a Christian, and Simplicianus often responded with what he had previously said, and he would often repeat his joke about the walls."[195] Where Augustine portrays Victorinus as an incomplete Christian, however, I would like to see this notional period as one of heterogeneity comparable to that found in Charisius' list. Victorinus, on Augustine's account, continues to participate in the *mores veterum*, both literary and religious, but his reading also spurs Augustine to imagine a narrative of Christian conversion in which Victorinus participates by reading and speaking with Simplicianus. For Augustine, Victorinus can embody the negotiation of literary heterogeneity by being a Christian in the temporal process of conversion. That is, the heterogeneity is resolved into a simple homogeneous identity in a temporal progression. This identity is further used to consolidate the heterogeneities that constitute it into two single homogeneities, the "church of Christ" and the "worship of idols." The creation of an ethos-in-time that negotiates the heterogeneity

of words through the adoption of an imagined unity is, however, the same
imaginative process as that at work in the ethical productivity of the *artes*.
Readers of the *artes* are configured as persons negotiating the relation
between heterogeneous words through the acquisition of *latinitas*, an ideal
temporal relation between past and present language. The embodiment of
this negotiation is in the readers' ethical character as educated persons, persons under obligation to a literary past. With this narrative in place, the
docti can occupy various reading positions while retaining a unitary identity.[196] Likewise, Augustine's use of an ethos-in-time to contain heterogeneity allows Victorinus to read widely while remaining a Christian exemplar.
To interrupt this narrative is to see Victorinus as a heterogeneous reader,
and although Augustine's account presses for him to have been, through
reading, a "pagan" who became a "Christian," it is clear that at some point
neither of these categories could hold, precisely because of Victorinus' eclec-
tic reading.[197] The unified paganism that Augustine takes to be the core of
Victorinus' previous identity is, by the same token, largely a product of
narrative connecting past to present. Without that narrative, literary paganism vanishes, replaced, as it may have been for many later Romans, by a
heterogeneous field of possible verbal acts, leading to no ideological unity.

Fourth- and fifth-century uses of earlier Roman texts to configure a
unitary *mos veterum*, whether in positive or negative terms, should not therefore simply be dismissed as anachronistic.[198] While it is undoubtedly the
case that fourth-century citation of, for example, Varro or Livy might not
accurately reflect non-Christian cult in the later empire, appeal to the *veteres* was nonetheless necessary for the imagination of the *mos veterum*, or
what would come to be called paganism, as a whole. Relying on grammatical appeal to the linguistic uses of the *antiqui* and the imagination of a
homogeneous past, late ancient writers could formulate a coherent religious
tradition, exemplified in fragmentary texts, that negotiated the difference
between past and present, and that determined the apparently continuous
identities of their contemporaries. Moreover, this formulation was not
purely the product of Christian polemic.[199] While the concept of paganism is fundamental to the formulation of Christianity, the notion of a single, unified Roman religious tradition must be seen as partly the product
of specific reading practices that both cut across and produce religious lines.
The practice of breaking down texts and reordering their fragments is the
most basic of these: this practice homogenized the texts and allowed for
their placement within a broad temporal opposition between past and
present; it further generated a reification of the relation between past and

present in the fluid notion of Latinity. This productive ideological process is at work in the construction of paganism in its literary aspect, especially in the work of writers with a clear connection to the grammatical tradition. At the same time, the pervasiveness of these reading practices should not be seen as necessarily entailing a broad acceptance of imagined cultural unities. Without the overt theorizing of *latinitas*, or rather without the construction of reading as itself part of a narrative progression, the construction of a unified paganism is much more problematic. In turn, the identification of readers as pagan is much more difficult. The grammarians of the *artes* may well have written texts with "paganizing" effects. They are not, however, narrative texts, or narratives in which their authors necessarily participate; to call them pagan texts, or their authors pagan, based on the ideological effects of the texts would be extremely misleading. Instead, it may be better to think of the literary construction of the *mos veterum* as occurring in specific narrative moments, not necessarily at the hands of pagans or in every non-Christian Roman text. Despite the usefulness of grammar in imagining a unitary Roman tradition, both literary and religious, it must be remembered that one of the main tasks of the grammarians was to take grand narratives apart.

4

Displacement and Excess
Christianizing Grammar

LITERATE CHRISTIAN ROMANS read Virgil and Homer. At least some literate non-Christian Romans read the Bible.[1] The idea that one body of texts was the exclusive possession of one religious group, and another body of texts the possession of another, should puzzle us, in a literary and social context that did not enforce the segregation of books or readers along religious lines. Yet this idea was promoted by a number of late ancient readers: we have seen it already in the writings of Augustine and Julian the Apostate, briefly examined in Chapter 3. I will now examine in greater detail how some grammatical practitioners who claimed a Christian identity created a division between Christian and pagan literature. The process of decontextualizing texts and homogenizing them, as in the *artes*, was also undertaken by these Christianizing writers, with the significant difference that the *maiores* and *antiqui* of the *artes* are spoken of as *gentes* and *saeculares* in the overtly Christianizing texts. The grammarians' use of *apud nos*, "among us," to indicate temporal proximity became an *apud nos* of religious unity. Further, where the proliferation of words and quotations in the *artes* allowed late ancient readers to conceptualize a united past of which they were the heirs, the proliferation of language was used in a Christianizing context to instantiate a unified body of *gentes* and a unified body of *Christiani*. The same techniques were used to very different ideological effects, so that one set of texts classicized its objects of study, and another set Christianized its objects.

In order to make it clear that the Christian status of various texts is not inherent, I have tried to use the term "Christianizing," rather than "Christian," when appropriate throughout this chapter. Many of the grammarians whose technical works have come down to us were likely to have been Christians, in the conventional sense of the term, although their works do not contain references to Christian doctrine.[2] Such Christians were not necessarily actively or intentionally "Christianizing" in their discipline, in the sense that they do not overtly signal a Christian religious identity or a notion of separate Christian literature in their work. I do not take this to mean that their adherence to Christian belief or practice was any less than that of the other figures discussed in this chapter, who actively use grammar to construct Christian identity. For the purposes of this chapter, then, a "Christianizing" writer is one whose work overtly projects a particular delineation of "Christianity" as a real and laudable entity. Naturally it is possible for an individual writer to Christianize in one work and not in another; one clear example of an individual who did so is Ausonius, whose traditionally pious *Parentalia* was described in Chapter 3, and whose correspondence with his former pupil Paulinus of Nola, in which questions of Christian affiliation are prominent, will be described in Chapter 6.

The texts on which I concentrate here are divided into two groups: the first group consists of texts that set out the decontextualizing theory behind Christianizing reading, beginning with a brief discussion of Origen's principles of reading but focusing primarily on the famous debate between Rufinus and Jerome on the uses of traditional Roman literature,[3] Jerome's letters 21 and 70,[4] in which Jerome elaborates his reading techniques, and Augustine's *De doctrina Christiana*, book 2,[5] which sets out some of Augustine's ideas on the uses of grammar. The second group of texts consists of two of the more technical grammatical works produced by Jerome and Augustine: after a short consideration of Origen's *Hexapla*,[6] I turn to Jerome's *Liber interpretationis Hebraicorum nominum*[7] and Augustine's *Locutiones in Heptateuchum*,[8] as instances of how Christianizing grammar makes use of the proliferation of language to produce the conceptual entity "Christianity." These groups of texts have techniques in common: like the *artes*, all rely on the practice of reading in a fragmentary manner. This allows them to generate lists of fragments (either in the form of quotations or in the form of authors' names), which become, in turn, signs of plenitude.[9] That is, beginning with the removal of fragments from their original contexts, their subsequent listing suggests an approximation of totality, giving the appearance of unity and completeness to the objects listed.[10] To the extent that these texts use literary fragments, the multiplication of those fragments is an invocation of unified bodies, as in the *artes*. The desire to invoke such bodies is, however, played out in different ways. In the first group of texts, there is a concentration on the physical, even erotic, nature of reading, as a means of both marking and overcoming an implied displacement arising between reader and decontextualized text.[11] Grammar is the medium for reading, in that it both enables reading to occur and, through fragmentation, comes between readers and texts.[12] It is also, however, a productive medium: in the second group of texts, displacement is negotiated by the generation of excess language, in which texts are susceptible to linguistic expansion via translation, transliteration, or etymologizing. The multiplication of texts and the expansion of language in the technical work under consideration is thus an outworking of the principle articulated in metaphorical terms in the more theoretical work: the marking and negotiating of literary dislocation becomes, in grammatical work, the multiplication of linguistic elements. I begin, then, with the establishment of displacement as a guiding principle of grammar in the work of Rufinus, Jerome, and Augustine.

Displacement: Theorizing Reading

In order to examine properly the formal grammatical works of later fourth and fifth-century authors it will be helpful to begin by noting the importance of Origen, who comes most obviously out of the later Alexandrian tradition of grammatical work, and who, especially through Jerome and Rufinus, becomes a presence in the work of Christianizing grammarians in the Latin West. Eusebius informs us that Origen was a professional grammarian for at least part of his adult life,[13] and Origen's text criticism and commentarial work fit clearly into the patterns of ancient grammatical endeavor.[14] As a third-century Greek grammarian, trained in Alexandria, Origen inherits the fusion of Alexandrian critical techniques and Stoic grammatical theory that is found already in the work of Dionysius Thrax.[15]

Origen's exegetical practice is complex and much studied, and I will not attempt to describe it in any full sense here;[16] at the same time, his influence on later readers should be noted. While it would probably be wrong to characterize Origen's exegetical theory as a simple theory of substituting allegorical for literal meaning, it is significant that Origen uses the language of decontextualization in his remarks on the most productive way of approaching texts.[17] In his account of scriptural reading in *De principiis* 4, Origen uses a few important metaphors to characterize good reading: reading the Bible, for someone who "knows how to examine words, . . . provide[s], as if through a window, a narrow opening leading to multitudes of the deepest thoughts."[18] Adapting the educational *topos* of learning as an act of gathering sustenance, like bees, from a field full of flowers, Origen claims that the best mode of scriptural reading finds what is buried underneath the flowers: "Now let us consider whether the outward aspect of scripture and its obvious and surface meaning does not correspond to the field as a whole, full of all kinds of plants, whereas the truths that are stored away in it and not seen by all, but lie as if buried beneath the visible plants, are the hidden 'treasures of wisdom and knowledge,' which the Spirit speaking through Isaiah calls 'dark and unseen and concealed.'"[19] For Origen, good reading means digging and climbing through windows, displacing the "surface" of the text and displacing the reader as well. Pursuing the vegetal metaphor, in his first Homily on Exodus, Origen sees the displacement and decontextualized treatment of scriptural texts as the key to productive reading: "I think each word of divine scripture is like a seed whose nature is to multiply diffusely, reborn into an ear of corn or whatever its species be, when it has been cast into the earth. Its increase is proportionate to the diligent labor of the skillful farmer or the fertility of the earth."[20] For Origen, skilled reading is a matter of producing a great deal of knowledge from individual words; it would be hard to differentiate this idea of reading from the goals of the grammarians we have already met.

For Origen, this displacing strategy is also of use when reading other, nonscriptural, texts. In his interpretation of Deuteronomy 21.10–13, describing the proper treatment of a non-Israelite woman taken captive in war (she can only be married to an Israelite after her hair has been shaved off and her nails have been cut), Origen suggests that this is the proper treatment of nonbiblical or unorthodox texts: "For whatever we find said well and reasonably among our enemies, or we read anything said among them wisely and knowingly, we must cleanse it also from the knowledge which is among them, remove and cut off all that is dead and worthless . . . and so at last make her your wife when she has nothing of the things which are called dead through infidelity."[21] As we will see, this scriptural text is of central importance to Jerome's articulation of reading in letters 21 and 70; for Origen it is an admonition to read with discrimination, separating the "understanding" from the "more common words."[22]

Where traditional grammarians' displacements construct a temporal progression, Origen's displacements construct a spiritual one, from body to soul to spirit: "For just as man consists of body, soul, and spirit, so in the same way does the scripture, which has been prepared by God to be given for man's salvation."[23] Like the locutions of the *veteres*, the "body" of the text is the basic point of reference, even though it is sometimes "absurd."[24] Readers must observe spiritual propriety in a spiritual progression just as they must observe temporal propriety in a temporal progression. The change in emphasis from temporal to spiritual progression, moreover, also makes revaluation of the different poles of the spectrum possible.[25] Origen does not repudiate corporal meaning, but he inclines toward spiritual meaning as higher, whereas the traditional grammatical progression idealizes the first pole, antiquity, even if departure from that ideal is sometimes necessary.[26] Following Origen, Christianizing grammatical reading continues the use of displacement, but it may characterize the results of that displacement differently from either Origen or traditional grammar: although the beginning and end points of the resulting progressions are always present, the moments at which they are either valorized or criticized become moments of uneasy contention.

RUFINUS AND JEROME

This contention and uneasiness in Christianizing grammar is clear in one of the most famous Latin literary quarrels of late antiquity, that between Rufinus of Aquileia and Jerome. The quarrel, not coincidentally, was very much about the quotation of earlier texts, both the Latin *antiqui* and the works of Origen.[27] I will concentrate here on the quotation of the *antiqui*.[28] Rufinus and Jerome, onetime friends and schoolfellows, broke their friendship during the Origenist controversy of the 390s, and despite their attempts, and those of others, to effect a reconciliation, the vicissitudes of the controversy determined that the break became permanent. Rufinus and Jerome's relationship, although it came to a theologically motivated end, nonetheless had its contours, both friendly and inimical, shaped by grammatical pursuits. Both men were sent by their families to Rome for their grammatical education, and while Rufinus may not have studied under the grammarian Aelius Donatus with Jerome,[29] Jerome credits him with receiving an education in grammar comparable to his own: "I imagine that when you were a boy you read Asper's commentaries on Virgil and Sallust, Vulcatius' on the orations of Cicero, Victorinus' on Cicero's dialogues and on the comedies of Terence; likewise my teacher Donatus' on Virgil, and others on writers like Plautus, Lucretius, Flaccus, Persius, and Lucan."[30] During the course of this education the friendship seems to have been established. Likewise, it was the work of Origen, whose commentaries and philology were rooted in the Alexandrian grammatical tradition, that directly influenced the course of the relationship. Both Rufinus and Jerome began as partisans of Origen's style of textual work, with Jerome modeling himself on Origen as a textual scholar,[31] and Jerome and Rufinus both becoming Origen's translators.[32] Jerome's rejection of Origen during the Origenist controversy, and the mutual recriminations on grammatical topics found in Rufinus' *Apology Against Jerome* and Jerome's *Apology Against Rufinus*, do not signal the repudiation by either writer of the grammatical techniques of quotation, fragmentation, and linguistic multiplication but instead suggest how these techniques could become an arena for the production of competing cultural identities. Theological concerns were obviously of great importance to the two writers,[33] but the structure of grammatical practice that supported those theological concerns set a framework for the interchange between them.

The grammatical habits of quotation and decontextualization become the centerpiece of their argument in the *Apology Against Jerome* 2.6–11 and in the *Apology Against Rufinus* 1.30–31. Partly in response to Rufinus' arguments on the implications of quoting non-Christian Roman authors, Jerome develops a position on the practice of quotation that illustrates another mode of identity production central to the literary development of fourth-century Christianity. Both Rufinus and Jerome take quotation to produce the same kinds of imaginative bodies, "pagans," or *gentes*, and "Christians," but they position the individual quoting very differently in relation to the quoted material. At issue is whether the creation of these imaginative bodies is also directly productive of individual identities or tends to erase them. Both accounts of quotation ultimately privilege the imagination over the individual reader, but each provides a different perspective on how such imaginations are instantiated in individuals, and it is this difference in instantiations that I would like to explore in the following section.

Rufinus' *Apology*, first publicly circulated in 401, though probably in preparation for some time,[34] attempts to demonstrate Jerome's fickleness toward Origen: Jerome claims not to be a follower of Origen; Rufinus argues against this claim, adducing as evidence passages from Jerome's works that indicate Jerome's knowledge and approval of Origen's textual strategies.[35] As part of this argument about Jerome's reading and writing habits, however, Rufinus takes the opportunity to attack Jerome for his use of techniques presumably learned from another grammarian, namely, Jerome's teacher Donatus. Rufinus takes Jerome to task at *Apology* 2.6–11 for two things: for quoting lines from non-Christian authors in his works, and for violating the oath that Jerome claims in his letter 22 to have sworn in a dream: "If I ever again possess or read worldly books, I have denied [Christ]."[36] The sequence of Rufinus' argument is as follows: at 2.6, Rufinus summarizes Jerome's famous dream, in which Jerome has a vision of Christ on the throne of judgment; Jerome professes his Christianity, but Christ rebukes him for being a "Ciceronian" rather than a Christian, because of Jerome's reading of *saeculares libros*; and Jerome swears never to read or own such books again. At 2.7–10, Rufinus cites examples of Jerome's quotations from non-Christian authors as proof that Jerome has violated his oath. At 2.11, Rufinus adds that Jerome has actually commissioned copies of Cicero's dialogues and has owned books containing dialogues of Cicero and Plato. Moreover, Jerome's willful violation of this oath went so far, Rufinus alleges, that Jerome even "carried out the role of a grammarian, and expounded his Virgil and the authors of comedy and lyric and history to little boys given over to him for instruction in the fear of God, so that he even became a teacher[37] of the gentile authors."[38] The foundation of Rufinus' charges in book 2 is that Jerome has engaged in illicit use of non-Christian texts; this is proved by Jerome's acts of quotation and possession.[39]

In order for these charges to bear weight, Rufinus must rely on a conception of quotation and of the use of texts that positions both quoted material and quoter in a particular ideological framework, in which there are clear divisions and likewise clear areas of affiliation. In this way, Rufinus can use the traditional association of grammatical proficiency with mastery of a body of texts, and hence with a particular social identity, against Jerome. By equating the identity conferred by traditional literature with knowledge of the *gentes* rather than knowledge of the *maiores*, Rufinus can place Jerome in the non-Christian camp. Rufinus' notion of quotation creates conceptual unities and divisions in the same way the quotations of the *antiqui* and *maiores* found in the *artes* do, that is, through the juxtaposition of authors and texts in order to homogenize them. Rufinus claims at 2.7 that there is not "one page of one work [of Jerome's] that does not proclaim him a Ciceronian, where he does not say, 'But our Tully, our Flaccus, and Maro.'"[40] This accusation performs two important functions for Rufinus, beyond that of succinctly describing Jerome's work: it collapses Cicero, Horace, and Virgil into a single conceptual unit and it identifies that unit with a "Ciceronianism" that is supposedly antithetical to Christianity. Rufinus also implies that these names are located en masse on every page of Jerome's writing, so that the juxtaposition is not just Rufinus' but Jerome's as well, which further consolidates the *auctores*' status as a conceptual unit. In his next sentence, Rufinus conflates, and implies that Jerome conflates, Greek authors into the same unit, when he describes Jerome as also continually referring to "Chrysippus and Aristides, and Empedocles, and other names of Greek authors."[41] Rufinus here performs in miniature what he claims Jerome is doing on a large scale: he lists names of Greek authors as interchangeable symbols of a particular kind of knowledge.

Part of the rhetorical effectiveness of the lists of names lies in their suggestion of numerical plenitude,[42] in that the "actual" writings of Horace and Chrysippus are not under discussion; rather, the list stands in for the idea of many repeatable units of knowledge, for which "Chrysippus" and "Horace" are only ciphers. The implied repeatability in turn creates the notion of an entire genre of knowledge,[43] to which Rufinus applies the terms *gentilis* and *saecularis*. *Gentilium libri*, *auctores gentilium*, *saeculares libri*, and *saeculares codices* are used throughout *Apology* 2.6–12 as collective labels for the group of authors that Rufinus imagines.[44] *Gentiles* and *saeculares* here take the place that the *antiqui* and *maiores* do in the *artes*, as names for a homogenized body of texts, created through the juxtaposition of authorial names. By claiming that these juxtapositions are found in the works of Jerome, Rufinus can both produce the imagined entity of "gentile" knowledge and suggest that Jerome's quotations of non-Christian authors each uniformly do the same. Rufinus uses lists of authors, then, to suggest what Jerome's method of quotation ought to imply to Jerome's readers, namely, that there exists a corpus of "gentile" learning, and that its potency can be measured, at least in part, by the frequency of its representatives' appearances. Hence Rufinus' damning assertion that "in nearly all his works he sets out many more and much longer quotations from these 'his own' authors [*de his suis*] than from our prophets [*de prophetis nostris*] or apostles."[45]

Rufinus' attack on Jerome for using the language of possession is also telling. This method of attack occurs three times in *Apology* 2.7–8, first when Rufinus repeats Jerome's *noster* as *sed Tullius noster, sed Flaccus noster*, next in the opposition of *de his suis . . . de prophetis nostris,* and finally in Rufinus' terse aside "this is an idea of our apostle, not his—he says 'his' is Horace or Cicero" (*illam apostoli nostri non sui sententiam—ille enim suum aut Flaccum dicit aut Tullium*). To the extent that Jerome does use such language (as he does in his response to Rufinus when, for example, he pointedly refers to Donatus as *praeceptor meus*),[46] it seems clear that he is appealing to the conventions of literary mastery and to the traditional differentiation that grammar and education created between the literate elite and those less fortunate.[47] Rufinus, however, uses Jerome's *noster* to create a different division, between Jerome, with his traditional *auctores*, and Rufinus and the orthodox, whom Rufinus calls *nos*. This usage of *nos/noster* appeals to a different divisive *nos* in the grammatical *artes*, namely, the temporal *nos* that divides the *antiqui* from Latin speakers and writers of the fourth and fifth centuries.[48] Rufinus conflates these two usages of *nos* (social differentiation and temporal differentiation) to create a new division, that between the readers of the traditional *auctores* and those who read the prophets and apostles, in Rufinus' scheme, the *gentes* and the *Christiani*.

The creation of these bodies of literature through quotation takes a physical turn as well. Rufinus claims that Jerome "spreads around [author's names] like smoke or clouds, in order to seem to his readers to be learned and widely read."[49] The simile is apt, as it conjures the appearance of solidity generated by small physical particles, which then take on some of the functions of large objects. Rufinus insists on the physical details of Jerome's acquaintance with the *libri gentiles*, and draws attention to Jerome's "copy-[ing]" and "collat[ing]";[50] Rufinus' main evidence against Jerome is, first, Jerome's commissioning of some of Rufinus' monks to copy for him some of the dialogues of Cicero, texts that, Rufinus says, "I held in my hands."[51] Second, Rufinus calls the reader's attention to a book, containing a dialogue of Cicero and a dialogue of Plato, that Jerome gave to him.[52] These physical objects become the traces that allow Rufinus to postulate a whole intangible body of learning in which Jerome participates. So potent is the imaginative link between these material instantiations and the appearance of "clouds" of learning that Rufinus can attack Jerome for overgenerating material based on the nebulous knowledge he possesses: in response to Jerome's claim to have read the works of Pythagoras, Rufinus tartly notes: "Learned men, indeed, hold that these do not exist. But this man, in order not to leave out any part of his oath about gentile authors, writes that he has even read those works which have never been written."[53] The supposed materiality of the "gentile" canon here takes a surreal turn, as Jerome is presented as so caught up in the cloud of classical learning that he attempts to make the unreal physically present. Rufinus does not, in fact, use abstract substantives to designate "paganism" but prefers to signal differences through the use of the adjectives *gentilis* and *saecularis*, usually appended to *libri* or *codices*. The physical manifestations of these qualities, then, appear first, in specific instances: there is not, for Rufinus, a *gentilitas* so much as there are "gentile" objects and persons. Rufinus' metaphor of Jerome's scattering a "cloud" of names, however, suggests the process by which these physical objects come to represent a larger conceptual body, that is, by quotation and juxtaposition. The force of citation and quotation is thus circular: material objects, such as names and works, generate an apparent corpus of knowledge, which in turn is supposed to be able to generate new material realities.

Rufinus can use this generative cycle as another part of his strategy for identifying Jerome with "gentile" learning. Rufinus persistently links Jerome to the material objects and physical acts that seem to produce non-Christian identity. Referring back to Jerome's letter 21, to Damasus, in which Jerome compares reading non-Christian literature to "lying in a temple to idols,"[54] Rufinus argues that Jerome's writings constitute that very act: "Here he makes himself guilty of idolatry, for if someone is made to stumble by seeing another reading [gentile books], how much more so if he sees someone writing them! But since someone who has fallen into idolatry does not become completely and utterly profane unless he first denies Christ, [Jerome] says before Christ himself, seated in judgment . . . , 'If I read or possess gentile books, I have denied you.'"[55] It is specifically the possession of objects and the production of writing that Rufinus uses to support his argument. The books of Cicero that Jerome requests, and the book that Jerome lends to Rufinus, are two instances; Jerome's "pages" on which he "scatters" the names of non-Christian writers are another. Jerome's use of possessive pronouns in quoting thus becomes part of Rufinus' attack:[56] Jerome's reference to "our" Cicero leads into Rufinus' accusation that Jerome possesses actual books of Cicero's dialogues and inserts their words into his own writings, and this in turn produces the claim that Jerome has become fundamentally *profanus*. Rufinus further materializes Jerome's literary possessions at 2.9, when he takes up Jerome's reading of Porphyry's introduction to Aristotle.[57] Rufinus calls Porphyry "your guide" (*introductor tuus*), and then asks, "Where did Porphyry guide you? If it was to the place where he is, that is where there is weeping and gnashing of teeth" (*Quo te introduxit Porphyrius? Si ad illum locum ubi ipse est, ibi et fletus et stridor dentium est*). Rufinus' equation of Porphyry's "introduction" with a literal "leading into" takes Jerome to the literal place to which Porphyry is supposed to be leading. The culmination of these physical acts leading to a shift in identity is Jerome's relocation to Bethlehem, where, Rufinus says, he "carried out a grammarian's role" and taught "his Virgil and the comedians and lyric poets and historians" to the boys under his supervision. Jerome here becomes an incarnation of "gentile" learning, specifically through the textual practices of copying, quoting, and expounding. Grammar, in turn, becomes both the vehicle by which this learning is instantiated and the symbol of its instantiation. Grammar is the "scattering" of author's names and the transmitting of texts from one body to another. For Rufinus, grammar is the mobility that enables the production and reproduction of "gentile" bodies.

Rufinus' notion of what quotation implies is, then, fundamentally tactile in nature. Quotation accomplishes the task of instantiation, so that to quote is to create a physical presence for the material quoted, and from that presence to extrapolate a body of knowledge. Notably, in this dense passage, Rufinus himself never quotes a non-Christian author but quotes Jerome at length. He is, in doing so, creating a "literary persona"[58] for Jerome himself, the *grammaticus profanus*. Jerome's tactile relationship with fragments of classical learning, as Rufinus construes it, both reinforces the existence of a specific "idolatry" and associates that idolatry with Jerome's own writing. Literary corpora, produced by material corpora, ultimately return to generate further instantiations of themselves.

JEROME ON FOREIGN BODIES

Jerome, partly independently of Rufinus' pressure and partly in response to it, likewise has recourse to a theory of quotation and fragmentation, one that shares a great deal with Rufinus' but that Jerome, not surprisingly, can deploy very differently. Jerome's wavering opinions on the question of reading and quoting non-Christian works are most explicitly set down in his letter 21 (of 383 or 384), to Damasus,[59] letter 70 (of 397 or 398), to Magnus,[60] and *Apology Against Rufinus* (401–2),[61] although his letter 22 (384), as Rufinus' quotations from it show, also famously expresses some of Jerome's thought on the issue. Letters 21 and 70 are of particular note because both use the metaphor of the "captive woman" of Deuteronomy, which we have already seen in Origen, to describe the uses of non-Christian literature. The two letters are traditionally taken to represent the two poles of Jerome's relationship with Roman literature,[62] the first advocating total avoidance of it ("We must beware lest we should desire to have this captive woman as a wife"),[63] and the second defending its use ("What great wonder is it, if I . . . desire to make this captive slave woman an Israelite?").[64] Rather than dwelling on the change in Jerome's mind, however, I would like to examine the conditions that Jerome lays down in both letters as necessary for the existence of non-Christian literature as such, and to consider how the agreement in the letters on what these conditions are informs Jerome's additional recommendations. Likewise, in the *Apology Against Rufinus*, where Jerome attempts more specifically to answer Rufinus' charges about the ideological implications of grammatical work, I would like to concentrate on the ideological ground that Jerome shares with Rufinus, due to common training in the grammatical foundations of literacy.

The most striking commonality between letters 21 and 70 is their use of the same biblical metaphor to describe the relation between the Christian reader and non-Christian literature. Referring to Deuteronomy 21.10–13, Jerome says in letter 21, "The type of this wisdom [viz., the 'songs of the poets, worldly wisdom, and the pomp of rhetors' words' (*carmina poetarum, saecularis sapientia, rhetoricum pompa verborum*)] is described in Deuteronomy in the figure of the captive woman, about whom the divine word teaches that if an Israelite wished to make her his wife, he should shave her head, cut her nails, and pluck her hair out; and when she has been made pure, then she may enter into the embrace of the victor."[65] In letter 70, he argues that the Christian "should read in Deuteronomy the teaching by the word of the Lord about the captive woman, that she is to be shaved, and her eyebrows plucked, and all the hair and nails of her body cut, and then she should be taken to wife."[66] The image is, of course, used for overt instruction in the need for selectivity in reading; but it is also an exhortation to fragmentary reading practices of the sort that grammatical training encouraged, in that every text is to be broken apart before being read, and only the "useful"[67] fragments are to be made objects of study. In both letters, importantly, the placing of some texts in the position of a captive woman establishes decontextualizing as the main technique of reading, by appealing to the idea of removing objects from their original contexts. The shaving of the captive's head, in turn, marks her both as having been removed from an original context and as being abbreviated herself.

This kind of fragmentation implies Jerome's conceptual framework for approaching texts more generally. By configuring reading as the union of two bodies, Jerome places the reader and the fragments to be read into the same unifying scheme. The *carmina poetarum, saecularis sapientia, rhetoricum pompa verborum* are all collapsed into a single body; Jerome thus asserts the existence of a foreign domain from which the woman/textual fragment has presumably been taken. Here, like Rufinus, Jerome does not postulate an abstract substantive *saeculum* or a *gentilitas* but uses the adjectives *saecularis* and *gentilis* to describe the literature to which he refers, and the noun *gentes* to describe those whose identity is determined by that literature.[68] The physical manifestation of "gentile" literature as a female body, however, again suggests the process by which the *saecularis* object comes to stand in for an imagined *saeculum*, as the captive woman is taken to be the singular, compound representation of multiple texts and words. This compound entity, like Rufinus' smoke and clouds, is produced through the gesture of listing and collecting *saecularis* units and imagining that collectivity as a substantive in its own right. The opposed entity, Israel, is posited in the same manner. In letter 70, after placing himself in the position of the Israelite captor, Jerome generates a list of similar Israelite figures, first Hosea, Isaiah, and Ezekiel, and then patristic authors.[69] This list functions in the same way as Rufinus' list of "gentile" authors: by offering names in list form, it collapses the differences between authors as diverse as Basil of Caesarea and the prophetic writers of the Hebrew Bible, and configures them all as belonging to the same imagined body. Jerome's metaphor thus does some of the same work as Rufinus' *Apology*, in that it homogenizes works that can be read and establishes truncation, or reading in a fragmentary manner, as the means of imposing conceptual unity.[70] The imagined precondition of reading, on both of these accounts, is the reader's situation in one or another of the imaginatively unified entities,[71] "Israel" or "the nations," which can, however, only be produced via a decontextualizing reading technique.

Unlike the use of fragmentation in Rufinus, however, Jerome's metaphor of reading introduces another theme, one that will prove useful to Jerome in his *Apology*, namely, the theme of separation. Where Rufinus emphasizes the tactile closeness of the reader and the fragmentary text, Jerome emphasizes their conceptual separateness. This is accomplished, for Jerome, primarily through the notion of bodily lack. The first way in which this lack is established is through the trope of desire.[72] The captive woman of Deuteronomy has as one of her main functions the signaling of desire:[73] in letter 21, Jerome admonishes the reader to "beware of wanting to have the captive as a wife . . . or, if we have been taken over by love for her [*eius amore*], we must purify her."[74] In letter 70, Jerome asks, "Is it surprising, then, if I too want to make the wisdom of the world a captive and servant to Israel, because of the charm [*venustatem*] of her eloquence, and the beauty of her parts [*membrorum pulchritudinem*]?"[75] Jerome's desire for the captive, expressed in frankly erotic terms, implies both that "secular" learning is embodied outside Jerome and that Jerome is fundamentally separate from the context in which the captive woman originates. Reading thus becomes, for Jerome, an attempt to negotiate this fundamental separation and to create out of it plenitude.[76] In letter 21 this attempt is expressed first in Jerome's exposition of the parable of the prodigal son, which precedes his excursus on the captive woman. Jerome argues that wanting to read the poets is like the prodigal son's hunger for the rusks that he feeds to swine after he has squandered his patrimony. The *carmina poetarum* are the "food of demons,"[77] in which there is no "fullness of truth, no nourishment of justice."[78] Reading is a hungry act: "Those who study [the poets] are in real hunger, and remain in a poverty of virtue."[79] The goal of reading is satiety; the state of reading is want. Similarly, in letter 70, Jerome, now more positive, claims that his union with the captive woman has, at least in part, overcome paucity: "My work profits the household of Christ; my adultery with a foreign woman increases the number of my fellow-servants."[80] There follows a list of fellow-servants, like Cyprian, who represent an admixture of "Israelite" and "foreign" writing. Where Rufinus stops at situating the reader in one or another imagined context, Jerome suggests that that situation necessitates an appropriation of material from outside in the process of reading. The important condition in Rufinus' account of quotation is the physical and hence conceptual conjunction of reader and text, marked by tactility; the important condition for Jerome is the separation that draws the reader to the text, marked by desire.

For Jerome, grammatical education is both the method by which this separation is overcome and that by which the separation becomes visible. At 1.16, he uses the example of grammarians' commentaries on Cicero, Sallust, and the poets (including the commentaries of Donatus, *praeceptoris mei Donati*, on Virgil and Terence) to argue that the point of their work is to present the reader with a multiplicity of interpretations of a given text, "so that the prudent reader, when he reads the various interpretations . . . can decide which is most true, and like a good money-changer, discern riches from adulterated coin." Grammar here offers the reader access to texts but also forces the reader to negotiate potentially false readings, underlining the reader's basic separation from the classical work. Jerome's sarcastic characterization of Rufinus' grammatical proficiency further emphasizes the dual role of grammar: on the one hand, Jerome claims that Rufinus has read the same grammarians as himself[81] and, like Aristarchus of Samothrace, the renowned Alexandrian grammarian,[82] concerns himself with the meanings of texts.[83] On the other hand, Jerome sneers that Rufinus' Latin style shows a lack of basic grammatical knowledge,[84] and that Rufinus would do better to return to the grammarian's school.[85] Grammar shows up Rufinus' separation from classical learning, but at the same time provides him access to it.

Jerome further pursues this theme through the idea of memory and dreaming, both of which imply, for Jerome, a removal from the physical world.[86] Memory is Jerome's main defense against Jerome's attack, although Rufinus attempts to disqualify this argument: "But it is natural that he would want to extricate himself from such a sacrilegious depth of perjury, and offer some sort of excuse, and say, 'I do not read them now, but since I have a tenacious memory, I can retain many things from various works that I learned as a child, and these are what I set down now.'"[87] This is, in fact, Jerome's primary argument: "An oath is about the future; it does not erase past memories. . . . Who does not remember his childhood?"[88] Memory is conflated with dreaming in letter 70: "After such a long period of inactivity I barely remember, as if it were a dream, what I learned as a child."[89] Dreaming is a way of remembering childhood education in the *Apology Against Rufinus*: "And, what will amaze you more, . . . I often see myself in dreams, curly-headed and wearing my toga, declaiming some exercise before a rhetor."[90] Dreaming is not an unproblematic mode of remembering, however, and since Rufinus' charges against Jerome are framed by the account in Jerome's letter 22, of his dream oath not to read non-Christian literature, Jerome's second line of defense is to discount the validity of dreams in general: "Whoever finds dreams incriminating should listen to the words of the prophets, that dreams are not to be believed."[91] The relegation of classical texts to the uncertain realms of dreaming and memory creates greater distance between Jerome and his books, by calling into question Rufinus' insistence on the physical proximity of reader and text.

The separation that Jerome posits via grammatical reading does not, however, diminish the potency of the imaginative construct of "gentile" literature. It has instead the opposite effect. Jerome's questioning of the proximity between reader and book is effected through an undermining of the ontological status of the reader, rather than of the book. Hence Jerome can say of his dream oath, "How often have I seen myself [in dreams] dead and laid in my tomb! How often have I seen myself flying over the earth, and crossing over mountains and seas by swimming through the air! [Rufinus] would force me to live no more, or to have wings at my sides, as often as my mind is fooled by vain images."[92] Jerome renders himself physically impossible, rather than questioning the status of the texts he reads; that is, the derivative figure of the "Ciceronian" disappears, but the projected category for which "Cicero" stands remains constant. Likewise, in letter 70 Jerome ends his defense, curiously, by suggesting that it is not really Magnus who is pressing him on the issue but Rufinus, whom Jerome calls by the name Calpurnius Lanarius.[93] The strange disappearance of Magnus, replaced by Rufinus, who is in turn replaced by a reference to the very literature that Jerome must defend using, and the shifting dream body of Jerome in the *Apology Against Rufinus*, introduce a level of uncertainty to the place of the individual reader with regard to the corpus of "gentile" literature. On the one hand, this allows Jerome to posit a fundamental separation between these existent texts and the sporadically existing reader; on the other, it reinforces the importance of the imagined literary corpus. Unlike the list of Israelites with which Jerome presents Magnus, Magnus himself becomes literally a non-entity. To the extent that the reader can become an "unreal," derivative Ciceronian, or Lanarius, the construct of "gentile" literature takes over the ideologically productive role of determining the status of particular subjectivities in relation to itself. The configuration of the reader as alienated from the text, in other words, foregrounds the potency of the imagined text at the expense of the imagined reader.[94] Reading as an act of hunger makes the canon a repository of fullness, enabling grammarians to posit multiple meanings for every text, and making the text the goal that overshadows the desire for which the reader stands.

The quarrel between Rufinus and Jerome, as might be expected, reveals more about their similarities than about their differences. Both writers base their approaches to reading on the idea of fragmentation and on the production of homogenizing lists of authors, in much the same way that reading is presented in the formal *artes*. Both Rufinus and Jerome predicate the notion of reading in relation to separation: Rufinus by emphasizing the tactile closeness that reading engenders between readers and texts, and Jerome by insisting that the act of reading is an attempt to overcome physical separation, that is, by defining separation as the motivation for reading. Finally, both writers use the technique of fragmentation and the idea of separation to delineate religious entities and identities. Fragmentation, as in the *artes*, suggests imagined wholes, either of *gentes* or of *nos*; and the reader must negotiate between them during the act of reading. The shared assumptions of Rufinus and Jerome, despite their opposition, indicates a commonality in their thinking about basic reading practices, a thinking they seem to share with the writers of the formal *artes*.

AUGUSTINE: LITERARY SPOLIATION IN *DE DOCTRINA CHRISTIANA*

The idea of reading as separation arises prominently in book 2 of Augustine's *De doctrina Christiana,* written in the late 390s.[95] Augustine in *De doctrina,* like Rufinus and Jerome, uses the decontextualizing and dislocating techniques of ancient grammatical writing in order to produce the opposing concepts of Christianity and paganism, and to locate the educated Christian subject in relation to them.[96] Although the *tractatio scripturarum* that forms the subject of *De doctrina* is often studied in relation to classical rhetorical *tractatio,*[97] the "treatment" of scripture in books 1–3 of *De doctrina* has much in common with late ancient grammatical textual analysis, also known as *tractatio.*[98] The reading practices that Augustine advocates for the resolution of verbal ambiguity, for example (language study, appropriate word division, and familiarity with a wide variety of word usages), obviously come out of the grammatical tradition.[99] Augustine explicitly compares his task in *De doctrina* to the work of the late Roman *litterator* or *grammaticus*:[100] "Whoever teaches how [the scriptures] should be understood is like the expositor of letters, who teaches how they ought to be read."[101] As I noted earlier, the grammarian Diomedes, Augustine's contemporary,[102] defines the task of grammar simply as "the understanding of the poets and the ready elucidation of writers and historians, and the logic of speaking and writing correctly."[103] Augustine similarly describes the program of *De doctrina* as covering first the correct method of understanding scripture and then the correct method of presenting it.[104] That *De doctrina* shares its basic approach with late ancient *artes grammaticae* should not come as a surprise: Augustine's discussions of language in other works also strongly recall the work of fourth- and fifth-century Latin grammarians, and Augustine's own early *De grammatica* was presumably a work in the same grammatical tradition.[105]

The particular placement of grammar in *De doctrina,* however, is significant. The *ars grammatica* proper, the discussion of verbal signs, does not begin until book 2. The discussion of signs in book 1 is cursory: after noting the difference between "things" (*res*) and "signs" (*signa*),[106] Augustine spends most of book 1 on "things" and the kinds of love the reader ought to have for them. The relationship between the reader and "things" is, famously, construed as a relationship based on love (*amor*), ultimately on the love of God, who is, for Augustine, the highest "thing": *una quaedam summa res.*[107] Augustine thus posits the dislocation of humanity from God[108] as paradigmatic for the relationship between readers and "things" more generally. This dislocation, for Augustine, underlies the *amor* that draws humanity to "things" and to God. In other words, in book 1 of *De doctrina* the reader is construed as a subject fundamentally desiring the enjoyment of God, since Augustine defines the relationship between humanity and "things," with God as the paradigmatic "thing," as a separation that engenders *amor* between the two.[109]

Grammar plays an important role in this amorous relationship. That Augustine conceives of the relationship between humanity and "things," particularly divine things, as based on separation and resulting in *amor* is clear, both in *De doctrina* and in other works.[110] Like Jerome's Israelite who marries a captive woman, Augustine's reader finds reading both a marker of separation and a means of overcoming that separation. In *De doctrina*, the mediator between readers and "things" is the sign: "All teaching is either of things or of signs, but things are learned through signs."[111] Moreover, the preeminent form that the sign takes, for Augustine, is the word, since words are signs "whose whole use is to signify. No one uses words except to signify."[112] Nouns, verbs, conjunctions, and the other parts of speech are the things that, as words, "have gained supremacy in signifying"; "all other signs are scant in comparison to words."[113] To the extent that it was the discipline of grammar, in antiquity, that concerned itself with the functioning of individual words,[114] the third part of Augustine's erotic triangle is grammar, the science of signs. Signs "come between" humanity and "things" both in the sense of mediating between them (since things are learned through signs) and in the sense of perpetuating their disjunction: not only does misunderstanding the signs of scripture lead the reader astray,[115] the mere existence of scriptural signs underscores the separation of the reader from the divine *res*.[116] Grammar occupies the space of dislocation.[117]

Dislocation, for Augustine, is mediated through language, in that language "moves" knowledge between things and people. It is, of course, this conception of knowledge, as something that can be transferred in discrete fragments from one context to another, that Augustine invokes in book 2 of *De doctrina*, on the spoiling of the Egyptians: "The Egyptians had not only idols and heavy burdens, which the people of Israel hated and fled, but also vessels, gold and silver ornaments, and clothes, which that people secretly claimed for a better use when they left Egypt."[118] The fourth-century equivalents of these spoils, according to Augustine, are the "liberal disciplines more fitting to be used for truth."[119] The transference of knowledge from one arena to another is not merely a matter of sharing methodology or philosophical assumptions; Augustine has in mind something rather more "literal," as his remarks immediately before the Exodus metaphor show: "I think it would be possible for someone who could, and who wanted to do some great and beneficial task for the use of the brothers, to commit to writing the geography, animals, plants and trees, stones and metals and whatever sorts of unknown things scripture mentions, discussing and explaining them."[120] The idea of compiling "sourcebooks" of knowledge that can be applied to the explication of scripture suggests a thoroughgoing dislocation and recontextualization of knowledge: Augustine, like his grammatical contemporaries, is interested in changing the signification of previously existing signs by "literally" removing them from their symbolic signifying contexts.[121] The *tractatio scripturarum*, following this method of reading, is simply another kind of spoliation; and Augustine's spoliating style is that of the late ancient grammarian. Language is both the means of movement and an object to be moved.

The configuration of scriptural *tractatio* as spoliation suggests the ways in which *De doctrina* addresses larger issues of cultural and religious identity. As spoliation, grammatical practice not only rejects "original" contexts, it simultaneously evokes them, in the same way that Jerome's captive woman evokes her "foreignness."[122] Thus, in Augustine's metaphor of spoliation, the gold and silver of the Egyptians may be used by the Israelites in Egypt, but they are first explicitly marked as "Egyptian." Hence Augustine's query: "Do we not see with how much gold and silver and clothing Cyprian, that sweetest teacher and blessed martyr, was laden when he left Egypt?"[123] The very visibility of Cyprian's "Egyptian" goods argues for the continuing "Egyptianness" of the liberal arts in Augustine's scheme. Here an originary context is invoked to mark the difference between "Egypt"/*gentes* and "Israel"/*fratres*. Moreover, by the proposed confinement of the liberal arts to the kinds of "sourcebooks" that Augustine imagines, their marking as "gentile," that is, not "Christian," is, at least in theory, perpetuated. This simultaneous recontextualization and decontextualization of knowledge is the grammatical matrix within which the *gentes* are produced in *De doctrina*. Here Augustine, like Jerome, uses the adjective *gentilis* and the noun *gentes* to describe those who possess "gentile" knowledge,[124] although this is again not a thoroughgoing creation of *gentilitas*. Like Jerome and Rufinus, however, Augustine uses a metaphorical substantive, "Egypt," to instantiate the conceptual unity that produces the knowledge that he then fragments. Augustine's excursus in book 2, the list of the branches of knowledge and what from them is to be either retained or rejected,[125] is as much a program of "gentile" education as it may be of Christian.[126] The *doctrina apud gentes*[127] both mediates and perpetuates the disjunctive relationship between reader and text.

At the same time, Augustine uses the desiring relationship between Christian reader and sacred text to reject the "original," "gentile" contexts of his spoils. Augustine refers to past authorities in the same homogenizing terms as the grammarians, but does so in order to highlight the need to assign them to a different place in the Christian scheme.[128] As spoil, the liberal arts are there precisely to be recontextualized, moved from a hypothetical "Egypt" to a hypothetical "Israel." Here again is a matrix within which Christianity can be imagined and invoked. If adherents to traditional Roman cult are the monolithic *gentes* from whom *doctrina* is taken, "Christians" are the equally monolithic *fratres* on whose behalf the *gentes* are despoiled.[129] Augustine's rhetorical flourishing of famous Christian names, Cyprian, Lactantius, Victorinus, Optatus, and Hilary, "passing over in silence those who are still alive, and innumerable Greeks,"[130] serves less to illustrate appropriate use of the liberal arts than to present the reader with an imagined crowd of "Israelites" who have left "Egypt." Augustine presents Cyprian and Lactantius as standing in for a large, undifferentiated, and anonymous body of "our many good faithful men."[131] In the same way that the grammarians' *antiqui* conjure a "classical world," Augustine's language here conjures a Christian one. The category "the people of God" stands as a structural parallel to "Egyptians" and, importantly, is presented as obviously separate: spoil, as such, must be transferred from one owner to another. The idea of spoil here invokes the two possible owners of the liberal arts in Augustine's scheme: Christians and *gentes*.

The production of Christianity as an abstraction is intimately related to the grammatical tasks of decontextualizing and recontextualizing knowledge for the explication of texts. The metaphor of spoiling the Egyptians implies not only an "Egypt" and "Israelites" but also a more general "Israel." Augustine ends his use of the metaphor in book 2 by claiming that "the wealth of gold, silver, and clothing that that people took with them out of Egypt" was small compared to "that of the riches which it had afterwards in Jerusalem, as was evident especially during the reign of Solomon."[132] Christianity is finally posited as a location and a separate political entity, parallel to "Egypt." Again, Augustine here uses not the abstract substantive *Christianitas* but the adjective *christianus*, like Rufinus and Jerome substantiating the constellation of "Christian" persons and objects into a metaphorical substantive, "Israel." The idea of spoliation allows Augustine to project an independent existence for Christianity, in a way that a more literal description of late ancient Christians as inhabitants, and products, of the Roman Empire might not.[133] While on one level Augustine's use of the story of Israel leaving Egypt is clearly secondary to the advent of Christianity, on another the story becomes a device for producing Christianity as a freestanding conceptual entity. It is the ultimate goal of the Israelites' departure, and thus the place of greatest "usefulness" in the larger goal of progress toward the divine.[134] The production of Christianity as such thus occurs through the metaphor of spoliation, inseparable from the simultaneous imagining, and appropriation, of *doctrina apud gentes*.[135]

Augustine's description of reading non-Christian literature as "spoiling the Egyptians" and Jerome's description of the same practice as marrying a "captive woman" are obviously similar, and both metaphors rely on the quotation of biblical fragments in order to position their authors as "Israelites." Yet these metaphors fundamentally involve the transgression of the boundaries that they create: the Israelites must enter Egypt before they can leave it; the captive woman represents the entry of the foreign into Israel. Augustine, Jerome, and Rufinus share the supposition that quotation collapses the distance between reader and text, although for Jerome and Augustine the existence of this distance is acknowledged and reproduced through the rhetoric of spoliation and capture. For all three writers, it is the act of reading, specifically the act of reading via fragmentation, that both demands and allows the creation of contexts in which reading takes place, and into which the reader can be inserted, in this case the religious contexts of the *gentes* and the *fratres*. These contexts become entities through the use of physical metaphors to delineate and unify different physical elements: for Rufinus, the *libri gentiles* become Jerome's "smoke"; for Jerome, the same books become a captive woman; and for Augustine they become Egypt. The entities of "Christianity" and "paganism" are thus indirectly posited through metaphors of physical unity. These metaphorical entities, however, take on a certain potency when interacting with the individual reader. As collectivities of texts, they are projected as prior to the reader who approaches them,[136] and thus as dictating identities to their readers: the lists of names that make up the inhabitants of "Egypt" or "Israel," the *saeculares* or the *fratres*, are given as the already existing bodies that the reader joins via reading. That is to say, by imagining entities that unify different existing books, the uses of the books become markers of particular identities. Rather than being preexistent or inherent, such entities and identities are the products of particular reading practices—dislocation and fragmentation—that enable the imposition of metaphorical unities upon the texts read.

Excess

The theorizing of grammar as an activity of displacement in the fourth century, along with the production of conceptual entities from and to which language can be displaced, extends to the more technical grammatical work of these writers as well, particularly Jerome and Augustine. Here the idea of displacement and productivity take the form of a concomitant decontextualization and multiplication of texts, so that in Christianizing authors at least the idea of Christianity takes shape in the form of linguistic excess. That is, given an originary text (in this case, a book or books of the Bible), Christianity comes into being as the linguistic multiplication surrounding that text, in the same way that "the classical" comes into being in the *artes* through the proliferation of language. Two of the Latin works in which this phenomenon occurs are Jerome's *Liber interpretationis Hebraicorum nominum* and Augustine's *Locutiones in Heptateuchum*. Both of these works come directly out of the etymological and text-critical tradition of ancient grammar, especially through its Christianizing form championed by Origen,[137] and like the grammatical *artes* these works are organized schematically, with a minimum of rhetorical flourish. It is possible that Augustine's work was influenced by Jerome's, as one of his preoccupations in the *Locutiones* is the question of textual variation in the Latin Heptateuch and its origins in Greek and Hebrew idiom; it is hard to imagine that this concern would not have been encouraged by Jerome's translation work, about which Jerome and Augustine famously corresponded.[138] There is, in the technical works of both men, a tendency to approach the biblical text via processes of disjunction and multiplication, processes in which both writers locate the substance of Christianity. To provide some of the disciplinary context for these works, I begin with a brief description of Origen's textual criticism in the *Hexapla* and then consider Jerome and Augustine in detail.

ORIGEN AND THE *HEXAPLA*

The *Hexapla* is the most obviously grammatical of Origen's works, coming out of the Alexandrian text-critical tradition. Despite the fragmentary nature of its present state the original format of the work seems clear:[139] a visual display in six columns, the first of which recorded, phrase by phrase, Origen's Hebrew text of the Hebrew Bible, and the successive columns of which provided a transliteration of the Hebrew into Greek characters, the LXX, and translations by Aquila, Symmachus, and Theodotion. Origen's project follows the contours of earlier Alexandrian text-critical projects, in that it is an overt collation and comparison of texts, with differences between the Hebrew and LXX marked with the critical signs (primarily the obelus and asterisk) introduced in Alexandria in the Hellenistic period by Zenodotus of Ephesus and expanded by Aristophanes of Byzantium.[140] It is not unreasonable to assume that Origen is in part attempting to establish a critical text of the LXX, in the same way that, for example, earlier Alexandrian grammarians attempted to establish critical texts of Homer and the comedians.[141] What is different about Origen's *Hexapla* is the sheer magnitude of the work. Origen does not, in fact, present his reader with a critical text but presents six texts, multiplying the words of his originary text to a remarkable degree, at the same time as the visual, columnar, component of the work requires repetitive, fragmented readings of each individual *locus*. That is, a "Hexaplar" reading of Genesis 1.1 ("In the beginning God created the heavens and the earth") would begin with the Hebrew, move to a transliteration of the Hebrew into Greek letters, and then go through four Greek translations of the verse before continuing on to Genesis 1.2. It would, of course, be possible for a reader to read any individual column continuously, but the presence of all six columns would encourage a discontinuous, comparative reading. Origen, in a sense, extends the text-critical principle of obelizing, rather than removing, questionable lines and presents the reader with a series of multiple readings that require the biblical text to become both fragmented and expansive.

The other, related, difference in Origen's grammatical work here is the fact that Origen is dealing with an originary text not in Greek and must confront issues of translation and transliteration. Questions regarding the meanings of words are found in both traditional Alexandrian scholarship, with its interest in obscure and difficult phrasings in early authors,[142] and in Stoic grammar, with its attention to the processes of linguistic signification,[143] but the comparison of translations and the attempt at full transliteration raise more difficult linguistic issues. As Greek words, of course, the collections of letters in the *Hexapla*'s column of transliterations make no "sense," nor are they precisely "Hebrew" words in their Greek alphabetic guise. Origen is appealing to a fundamentally vocal syllabic breakdown of language in order to generate a running column of "Hebraicizing" Greek sounds. The transliteration of the Hebrew Bible illustrates Origen's use of the proliferation of language in order to contain meaning:[144] the meaning of the Hebrew text is elusive, clearly not understandably resident in the phonetic elements that fail to become meaningful Greek words when transposed into Greek letters.[145] At the same time, the attempt to approximate that meaning leads Origen to produce a string of "nonsensical" words[146] as an intermediary between the Hebrew text and the following Greek translations. The presence of "meaningless" words (at least with respect to their Greekness) is in itself a significant gesture: although transliteration occurs in other contexts in antiquity to some degree, and usually where bilingualism cannot be assumed,[147] the transliteration of an entire literary work as long as the collected texts in the *Hexapla* is extraordinary. Beyond the practical issues of Origen's (and others') proficiency in Hebrew,[148] it raises the question of the symbolic nature of both the "unreadable" Hebrew text and the "nonsensical" Greek transliteration. The presence of the transliterated text indicates the opacity of the Hebrew text but also affirms the importance of reminding the Greek reader of that opacity, by gesturing toward the Hebrew letters and by generating syllables that are understood to negotiate that opacity, however meaninglessly. Transliteration thus functions as a double sign of opacity: it marks the opacity of the originary text and reaffirms the distance between meaning and text by inserting intermediary syllables between text and translations. The emphasis on opacity underlines the problem of signification and rhetorically justifies the multiplication of texts in the *Hexapla*. Origen deals with signification, as Jerome will do later on, by positing a method of expanding a target language through the conflation of that language with the language of the originary text.[149] Origen first presents the reader with simultaneous Hebrew and Greek texts and then transliterates the Hebrew into Greek letters; this introduces "new," but inaccessible, words into the Greek language and into Greek biblical reading. Having set up this rhetoric of meaninglessness, however, Origen goes on to generate multiple texts that signify the copious meaningfulness of the Hebrew text in the translations of Aquila, Symmachus, and Theodotion, as well as the LXX, which is Origen's primary concern. That is to say, a basic part of the project of the *Hexapla* is the overt representation of both inaccessible meaning and the proliferation of subsidiary meanings.

Origen's grammatical work illustrates one of the uses to which the movement from displacement to proliferation could be put. The Hebrew text of the Bible is here analogous to Jerome's "captive woman"; the movement of the Hebrew into a Greek context on the one hand indicates a dislocation of the Hebrew text but also generates a multiplicity of Greek words, even "new" Greek words, in the attempt to recontextualize it. Origen's work also resembles that which Jerome claims, in *Apology Against Rufinus* 1.16, is the point of grammarians' endeavors: where Jerome sees commentary as the locus for multiplication of textual interventions, Origen demonstrates the uses of multiplication in text-critical work. This process, as we will see, is overtly assimilated to the process of "Christianization" in the grammatical work of Jerome and Augustine.

JEROME'S *LIBER INTERPRETATIONIS HEBRAICORUM NOMINUM* AND THE IDEA OF CHRISTIAN LANGUAGE

Despite his self-styled status as a Ciceronian and Rufinus of Aquileia's description of him as *rhetor noster*, it is not difficult to place Jerome also into the more modest category of Christian grammarian. Certainly he was instructed in grammatical inquiry, as is clear from his references to Aelius Donatus, his teacher in Rome, the famous grammarian and commentator.[150] Several of the genres in which Jerome worked, moreover, particularly commentary, books of word lists, and *quaestiones* literature, were the traditional province of the grammarian rather than the rhetor, and among the charges that Rufinus lays at Jerome's feet is that of having "taken the grammarian's part" and taught grammar to boys at Bethlehem.[151] That Jerome's work, beyond theorizing the use of grammar, itself follows grammatical precedent is in itself not surprising, since, as we have seen, Origen was the most important of his models for biblical work, despite Jerome's disavowals of theological Origenism in the midst of the Origenist controversy. One of Jerome's most overtly philological works, the *Liber interpretationis Hebraicorum nominum*, which Jerome claims is a continuation of a work of Origen's,[152] reflects an ideological productivity similar to that of Origen's *Hexapla* in its use of multiplicity, but gives that multiplicity an explicitly Christian meaning. The work of the *Liber interpretationis* is not simply the translation of Hebrew names into Latin but the creation of another opportunity for Christianity to be articulated as an entity in its own right. In this case, the idea of excess meaning produced by the act of translation separates Christianity from the texts that are taken to found it, the Hebrew Bible and the New Testament. Where the metaphor of the captive woman creates a conceptual space for the removal and ideological marking of cultural goods, the more literal act of *translatio*, I suggest, attempts to fill and delineate that space with the idea of linguistic meaning. "Christianity" in turn denotes the idea of supplementary or excess meaning, and here comes into being as that which exceeds one-to-one verbal correspondence; hence, that which fills the newly created cultural space.

The *Liber interpretationis*, like Jerome's *Liber de situ et nominibus locorum*, is a list of proper names found in the Hebrew Bible and the Greek New Testament, along with short Latin translations of those names, such as *Adam homo sive terrenus aut indigena vel terra rubra. Abel luctus sive vanitas aut vapor vel miserabilis. Ada testimonium.*[153] The names are grouped alphabetically by initial letter according to their Latin transliteration, and are further grouped by biblical book: the first group of names in the *Liber interpretationis* is thus names in Genesis from A to Z, then names in Exodus from A to Z, and so on, through the book of Revelation and the Epistle of Barnabas. The work is formally similar to other of Jerome's philological works, such as the *Liber de situ et nominibus locorum* and the *Quaestiones Hebraicae in Genesim*, in that biblical knowledge is here broken down into individual units and arranged in list form, roughly following a given textual order, but without explicit narrative connection. The similarities between these three works are not coincidental. The *Liber interpretationis* was written probably around 392, shortly before Jerome published his *Quaestiones Hebraicae in Genesim*;[154] these two works, along with the *Liber de situ et nominibus locorum*, are presented in the preface of the *Liber interpretationis* as a kind of unit, designed to help the reader avoid "the belching and vomiting of the Jews."[155] That is, they are all recuperations of Hebrew for Christian use, and all configure "Jewish knowledge" as fundamentally linguistic.[156]

Jerome's technique for creating Christian space in these works is that which he advocates in letters 21 and 70: the fragmentation of previous knowledge and its literal and conceptual realignment into new texts. The most obvious target of fragmentation for all three works is the Hebrew Bible, passages and words from which appear in truncated and listlike form in all three works. In the *Liber interpretationis*, Jerome's "spoiling" of earlier authors is even more pronounced, as he opens the work by describing it as originally a project of Philo of Alexandria, "the most learned of the Jews" (*vir dissertissimus Iudaeorum*), taken over by Origen and rendered into Latin by himself.[157] Linguistic knowledge is thus presented as highly mobile: in the same way that Jerome can configure Latin and Greek grammatical knowledge as removable from its original contexts, he here configures "Jewish" knowledge as subject to the same despoiling maneuver. The *Quaestiones Hebraicae*, following this lead, opens with an apologia for the appropriation of the knowledge of others: it is not plagiarism, Jerome claims, to "wrench the club of Hercules from his hand."[158] What is fundamentally at issue is the configuration of certain types of knowledge, or units of knowledge, as transposable into new contexts. The nonnarrative, list format of all three works, like the lists of authors in the literature discussed earlier, accentuates the removal of the units of language from their original contexts and their reorganization into a new linguistic matrix. The simple act of removal creates the possibility of new space to be delineated.

The listing of names and definitions in the *Liber interpretationis*, however, has implications beyond those evident in letters 21 and 70. Where those texts articulate the possibility of Christian space in broad terms, the concrete philological work of the *Liber interpretationis* illustrates how that space comes to be filled and delineated by the concept of "Christianity." Hence, where Jerome's letters are governed by the metaphor of removal, the philological work seems dominated more by the idea of expansion. Jerome's etymological work suggests a movement beyond the brute syllables of the names themselves, and it is this expansive movement that provides Jerome with the ideological space in which to position a specifically Christian knowledge. The expansiveness of the work is evident at several levels. Take, for example, the following passage from Jerome's list of names in Genesis that begin with G: "Geon is 'breast' or 'rugged.' Gomer is 'acceptance' or 'completion' or 'perfection.' Gergesaeus is 'casting out a farmer' or 'approaching a foreigner.' Gerara is 'rumination' or 'an enclosure.' But note that [*sed sciendum quod*] gerara means 'lived in' and gedera means 'an enclosure' or 'hedge.' Gaza is 'his fortitude.'"[159] The first level of addition, both to the names and to the Latin language, is the presence of Latin transliteration of absent Hebrew names; there follow Latin definitions of these Latinate words, another layer of addition; for many, indeed most, of the names, there is more than one definition listed, a third layer of addition; finally there are the scattered comments introduced by *sciendum quod*, which introduce another level of possible knowledge. These levels intersect with each other at times: the alternate definitions can be seen as mutually exclusive, agglomerative, or hierarchical, though they need be none of these in particular.

The basic premise of the *Liber interpretationis*, moreover, itself entails a certain movement across linguistic boundaries, the most obvious of which is the divide between Hebrew, "a barbarian language,"[160] and Latin. In composing his work for the Latin reader, Jerome uses transliterated forms of Hebrew names, a decision that at the outset establishes one of the parameters of the Jerome's work: like Origen's transliteration of Hebrew into Greek, which establishes Greek as the new linguistic context for the Hebrew Bible, Jerome's transliteration is fundamentally about Latin and Latinity, with the distinction clearly marked between what is true *apud nos* and what is true *apud Hebraeos*.[161] Jerome's transliteration method is, perhaps inevitably, less sensitive to Hebrew than to Latin distinctions. Thus, although he notes in Genesis that there are three different Hebrew letters transliterated by the Latin *S*,[162] he does not afterward note this distinction in any of his translations; the Latin reader does not know which Hebrew letter is being used in any name beginning with *S*. On the other hand, Jerome does carefully note the different lengths of the vowels transliterated as *E* and *O*,[163] a distinction that can be maintained by using Latin linguistic categories.[164] Despite Jerome's fame for exploration of Hebrew texts, the movement of the project is fundamentally one of the expansion of the content of the Latin language, with a concomitant retention of Latinate form. By transliterating according to Latin conventions, Jerome can add words to the Latin language, as well as adding a Latin work to the corpus of Latin literature, without seeming to overturn that language's laws.

To a certain extent, as one might expect, the move from Hebrew to Latin can be mapped onto an ideological positioning of Judaism and Christianity, with Hebrew taking the place of Judaism and Latin, via Greek, representing Christianity. Jerome personifies the two religions in the persons of Philo, "the most learned of the Jews,"[165] and Origen, "whom no one except the ignorant would deny is the teacher of the churches after the apostles."[166] The chain of transmission that Jerome posits for the *Liber interpretationis*, from Philo to Origen to himself, and the chain of linguistic expansion from Hebrew to Greek to Latin thus come to stand in for the supersession of Judaism by Christianity. Jerome's Latin readers, for example, the *fratres* Lupulus and Valerianus, whom Jerome credits with persuading him to undertake the Latin translation,[167] are assumed to want to—and now to be able to—avoid interaction with Jews.[168] Grammatical work becomes a forum for the articulation of religious difference, as philology is taken to mark religious identity.[169] The chains of transmission that Jerome articulates for the *Liber interpretationis* are thus understood in the late fourth and early fifth centuries as shorthand narratives about the construction and (sometimes precarious) maintenance of religious positions.

Jerome, in turn, identifies Christianity as the end of those chains and hence the goal of his supplementary procedure, as he "establishes an old building with new care."[170] It is, indeed, the supplementarity of the work that establishes their Christian character, as Jerome claims that "what Philo, as a Jew, left out, [Origen, and by extension Jerome,] as a Christian, filled in."[171] Supplementarity, in Origen and in Jerome, is presented as the uniquely Christian aspect of the work.[172]

The movement from Hebrew to Latin, however, cannot be mapped absolutely onto a supposed movement from Judaism to Christianity. There are other expansions in the text of the *Liber interpretationis*, which complicate the narrative of supersession in its conventional form. Jerome's book does not stop with the Hebrew Bible;[173] it goes on to include the New Testament, analysis of which is the "consummation" of the etymological work begun by Philo.[174] The consummation, however, is of an unusual sort: new meanings are proposed for numerous names, phrases, and places, including many that are not at all linguistically related to Hebrew, such as "Tiberius" and "Caesar."[175] The *Liber interpretationis* offers "false" Hebrew etymologies for these non-Hebrew words, for example: "Areopagus: ancient solemnity," which, however, is followed by the comment, "but this is forced [*violentum*], since it is the name of the curia of Athens, which took its name from Mars."[176] The likeliest scenario for the production of these comments is simply that Jerome is copying (and commenting upon) a Greek *Vorlage* that itself assigns Hebrew meanings to non-Hebrew words.[177] Despite his appeal to Hebrew meanings for non-Hebrew words in other contexts,[178] it seems likely that these readings are not unproblematically endorsed by Jerome, as his frequent reminders that they are *violenta* suggests.[179] Indeed, at *Quaestiones Hebraicae in Genesim* 17.15 he argues that "no one who calls someone by a name in one language takes the etymology of that word from another language."[180] While Jerome may not have been consistent in his application of this principle, the obvious and persistent violation of it in the *Liber interpretationis* probably does not originate with Jerome; it may also be too much to claim that Jerome is here positing Hebrew as an originary language underlying or theologically informing secondary languages like Greek or Latin.[181] Nevertheless, I would like to suggest that this linguistic curiosity is in fact consonant with Jerome's narrative of supersession, and that Jerome's perpetuation of these "false" etymologies supports that narrative, although indirectly.

In the process of etymologizing in the *Liber interpretationis*, Hebrew and Greek texts are first of all collapsed into a single field of exploration;

that is, words from the Greek New Testament are considered to be as much in need of elucidation, and of the same kind of elucidation, as their counterparts in the Hebrew Bible. They are, further, and in line with the list format of the work, all construed as representing the same kind of and amount of knowledge—to the extent that all now represent Latin knowledge of Hebrew words, even when the original word to be etymologized is Greek or Latin. Theoretically "Christian" words are subjected to precisely the same procedure as theoretically "Jewish" words, which suggests the primacy of the procedure itself as Jerome's (or his predecessor's) main pursuit. The procedure of etymologizing produces additional meanings for the words examined, particularly clearly in the case of words that Jerome marks as wrongly etymologized: meaning is here overtly separated from the word itself, with Jerome's *sed et hoc violentum est* marking the supplementarity of meaning to word. This supplementary procedure is not, then, a strictly natural outgrowth of the presence of originally Hebrew words in the Latin Bible but is part of the process by which those Hebrew words, and indeed Greek and Latin words, are made to conform to the linguistic shift that is the basis of Jerome's "Christianizing." The process of Christianization occurs in the shift from Hebrew to Latin, and in the addition of the New Testament to the corpus of that which is to be analyzed, but also in the double shift from Latin to Hebrew and back to Latin, as when Jerome, apparently dutifully, translates "Tiberius" as "his appearance or his goodness" (*visio eius vel bonitas eius*).[182] In this sense, the sign of Christianization is not a change in the content of words from Jewish meaning to Christian meaning but is the process of linguistic supplementation itself, with the paradoxical result that even words from the New Testament can undergo Christianization. Jerome's introductory *hic ut Christianus inpleret*[183] itself carries a double meaning, so that Christianization is here equated with linguistic supplementation.

The repetitive movement from Hebrew to Latin is ultimately generative of more than just a dictionary; it is itself a statement about the possibility of linguistic shifts, and about their connotations. Jerome's acts of translating produce the concept of linguistic multiplicity, even, in the case of overtranslated words, an idea of linguistic excess, marked by *sed violentum est*. This multiplicity is partially contained by, and partly generative of, the idea of meaning: meaning is what connects the Latinized Hebrew words with the Latin words that follow them, but at the same time it is the presence of these sequences of words that projects the idea that the Hebrew words are meaningful. Notably, the *Liber interpretationis Hebraicorum nominum* is, as its title makes plain, a book of the translation of names—words that, in a formulation going back at least as far as Plato's *Cratylus*, can have either physical referents or linguistic ones. Jerome's work privileges the linguistic referents, adding the idea of supplemental linguistic meaning to the material referent. It is this idea of additional meaning that drives the project. Jerome claims that it is the idea of etymology's utility[184] that persuades him to undertake the translation;[185] that is, the supplementing of a material referent with a linguistic referent is configured as motivating the work, though it is also the case that this linguistic addition is only made visible through the sequences and juxtapositions of words that Jerome sets before his readers, and that he claims were originally set before him. The *Liber interpretationis* is, then, primarily about the production of additional meaning, and it is this additional meaning that, for Jerome's purposes, can come to be called the "Christian"[186] teaching of "the churches."[187]

AUGUSTINE'S *LOCUTIONES IN HEPTATEUCHUM*

While composing *De doctrina Christiana*, Augustine voiced the following wish, quoted earlier in this chapter: "I think it would be possible for someone who could, and who wanted to do some great and beneficial task for the use of the brothers, to commit to writing the geography, animals, plants and trees, stones and metals and whatever sorts of unknown things scripture mentions, discussing and explaining them."[188] Written some two decades later, in 419–420, Augustine's *Locutiones in Heptateuchum* is not the hoped-for work of 396. It, too, however, participates in Augustine's lifelong project of intellectually spoiling the Egyptians. The overt purpose of the *Locutiones in Heptateuchum*, as Augustine notes in his brief introduction to the work, is the explication of Greek or Hebrew idioms that have come through into the Latin text of the Heptateuch.[189] In the *Retractationes*, Augustine explains that this is for the benefit of those who might take offense at the Latin prose as it stands.[190] Where Augustine's suggested task in *De doctrina* is an explication of the content of unusual biblical words, the project of the *Locutiones* is an explication of their unusual form. The work consists, then, of lists of grammatically or rhetorically unusual passages from the Latin Heptateuch, together with Augustine's explanations of what these passages mean and how they might be rendered into more idiomatic Latin. One of the primary characteristics of the work, like that of Jerome's *Liber interpretationis*, is its nonnarrative form, in which words are given with explication but little connection is asserted between the listed items. These lists, in both works, objectify the linguistic units under consideration, removing them from their original contexts and arranging them as individual manipulatable units. Augustine's locutions from Genesis thus begin with Genesis 1.14, skipping then to 1.20, 1.28, and 2.5, taking short passages from each verse and coupling them with a brief editorial note before moving without overt transition to the next passage. Each passage, unconnected to the others, thus becomes an object in its own right, an individual unit of linguistic curiosity.[191]

The force of these disconnections in the biblical text is a certain destabilization. Instead of seeing a biblical text *in toto*, the reader is presented with multiple linguistic objects, each suggesting a broader biblical referent but not in fact supplying one. Augustine highlights the variability of the biblical text throughout the *Locutiones*, citing differences in the Latin texts to which he refers and comparing these to the multiple Greek texts of the Septuagint and Symmachus.[192] Augustine frequently introduces passages with the phrase "as many Latin codices have" or " as it is written in certain Latin codices," contrasting with "but the Greek [codices] have,"[193] and so on. While the actual variability in the text may simply be attributable to the vagaries of ancient book production,[194] what is notable here is the way in which Augustine overtly signals such vagaries. Rather than presenting the text as unified, Augustine breaks the Heptateuch into numerous unnamed Latin and Greek codices. By choosing a genre of work that configures words as discrete objects, Augustine transforms the Heptateuch into an almost accidental constellation of verbal singularities, compounding its fragmentation further by locating it within scattered physical objects. What emerges from this continual production and signaling of multiplicity is a highly unstable biblical text: there is, in a concrete sense, no single biblical text for Augustine, only fragments, copies, and translations to which the reader must constantly refer.[195]

The *Locutiones*, however, consist not only of Augustine's list of verbal objects but also of his glosses on such objects. These glosses provide Augustine with the opportunity to "correct" the number, gender, or case of certain problematic passages in the biblical texts he considers, as well as to provide the reader with what Augustine sees as clarifications of biblical wording. For example, in his gloss on Genesis 3.1, "the serpent was the most subtle of all the animals," Augustine prefers the translation *prudentissimus* to the common *sapientissimus*, arguing that this better represents the Greek *phronimôtatos*;[196] in his more curt gloss on Numbers 19.7, "And he will wash his body with water," Augustine says simply, "This would be understood even without the phrase 'with water.'"[197] Augustine can even speculate on multiple rewordings of scripture, as in his gloss on Genesis 22.16–17: *"per me ipsum iuravi: nisi benedicens benedicam te. It could also say: per me ipsum iuravi, quod benedicens benedicam te,* or simply, with no added word, *per me ipsum iuravi: benedicens benedicam te."*[198] These sorts of glosses may at first seem perfectly straightforward: Augustine proposes a wording for the text that more accurately, more concisely, or more conventionally expresses its meaning. Yet in combination with his concentration on the instability of the biblical text, Augustine's glosses take on greater importance: Augustine can use the actual text to project an ideality of words and meanings that exists beyond the confines of the text but is nonetheless based upon it—an ideality that is superimposed on the text by the act of reading. One of the effects, in other words, of Augustine's dissection of the Heptateuch is to suggest the possibility of another Heptateuch, one that could be free of grammatical difficulty or verbal redundancy, and in which the meaning and the words would be perfectly paired. On this account, Augustine's reading of the Heptateuch is in essence a doubling of the text: on the one hand the Heptateuch as its stands in the multiple Greek, Latin, and Hebrew codices to which Augustine refers, and on the other the Heptateuch as it can be imagined to stand, free of idiom or irregularity. The latter Heptateuch shadows the former in the *Locutions,* both providing justification for the work[199] and uniting the linguistic objects as they stand in an imagined text that would perfectly contain their meanings. Like Origen, Augustine is multiplying the biblical text.

Augustine is not here reverting to his early dislike for biblical prose;[200] rather, the process of reading as it is here practiced should be understood to be transformative, not merely of the reader[201] but of the text itself. When, for example, the grammarian Servius criticizes an irregularity in Virgil, he does not necessarily suggest that Virgil ought not to have written what he did; instead, he argues that Virgil is capable of breaking one rule of grammar or eloquence in order to follow other rules as established by the canon of ancient authors.[202] Late ancient grammatical criticism can thus preserve the authority of the original work while at the same time placing it in relation to a larger imagined canon, intertextually opening the original work to the insertion of other *corpora* precisely in order to project a much larger textual ideality through the reading of a single work.[203] The work in question thus becomes a repository of textual correctness, not only as exemplified in its own words but also in an abstract imagination of what linguistic propriety can be judged to be. Similarly, in Augustine's reading of the Heptateuch, the physical codices and verbal fragments become points of entry into a physically nonexistent but semiotically ideal text.[204]

The idealization of the Heptateuch in this sense, moreover, has further transformative effects on the content of the text. In positing his ideal text, Augustine of course refers to the rules of Latin grammar, but he refers also to numerous other texts, comparing the Heptateuch as it stands to texts with similar locutions, drawing these texts too into the purview of his ideal text.[205] It is perhaps not surprising that Augustine's imagined text in the *Locutiones* incorporates fragments from throughout the Old and New Testaments,[206] thereby conflating the writers of different biblical books into the same single imagined source of idealized language. What is more notable is that, in good grammarian's fashion, Augustine also includes quotations from Virgil[207] and references to Greek mythological figures[208] in his projection of what perfect biblical language might be. The perfect imagined text, the Heptateuch that Augustine's work projects out of the destabilized text of the Latin and Greek codices, is thus to be understood as singularly expansive, including the texts conventionally grouped together as scripture, as well as the authoritative texts of Roman literary culture. The individual textual objects that are the Heptateuch's locutions generate an imagined literary context for themselves that reaches beyond the bounds of the "actual" Heptateuch. The movement of reading here entails a movement of expansion not merely of the reader in relation to the text but of the text to be read, necessarily increased by its need to be "fixed" in the act of reading.[209] Augustine's dissection of the verbal irregularities of the Latin Heptateuch, then, creates an alternate, expanded text, potentially consisting of all the texts that can be imagined to bear favorable linguistic comparison. A perfect Heptateuch would be complete in the sense that it would contain all possible similar texts. Augustine's intention, stated in the *Retractationes*, of "opening" the text to the mind of the inquisitive reader[210] involves an opening of the text to include other bodies of literature as well.

The expansion of the ideal text is matched by the containment of the "real" Heptateuch in the *Locutiones*. In the *Retractationes*, Augustine suggests that "these sorts of locutions ought to be recognized where their meaning is clear, so that where they are unclear, this knowledge may assist in opening them to the inquiry of the reader."[211] The imaginary Heptateuch that Augustine projects thus has as one of its main functions the containment of meaning: by positing an ideal text in which idiom and meaning coincide, Augustine can project meaning back onto the fragmentary texts that are the concrete objects of his study. The standard grammarian's tactic of interpreting Homer *ex Homero*[212] requires as one of its conditions the postulating of a Homeric unity; Augustine likewise hypothesizes a unified, linguistically ideal text to stabilize the individual linguistic objects that are the realia at his disposal. One of the forms that this hypothesis takes is, of course, the term *scripture* itself. At numerous points throughout the *Locutiones*, *scriptura* is personified as "loving" this or that construction,[213] or as having particular linguistic habits.[214] By far the majority of the uses of the term *scriptura* in the *Locutiones* occur in context in which Augustine is arguing for the familiarity of a certain construction throughout the Bible as he projects it: most often, a locution is simply said to be "customary," "very familiar," or "very frequent" in the scriptures (*usitata, familiarissima, creberrima in scripturis*).[215] Augustine uses the term *codices* to talk about singularities in the text, but *scriptura* is used to delineate the imagined unity in which those singularities repeatedly occur. The *mos scripturarum*[216] is, on Augustine's reading, in control of the scriptural fragments; the postulated *scriptura* is in fact what "speaks" the fragments.[217] Faced with an unstable physical text of the Heptateuch, Augustine stabilizes his verbal objects by appealing to a much larger (indeed, infinitely expansive) imagined authority, scripture, that contains the Heptateuch and can even be supposed to generate it.

The control of the real text as found in the codices by the imagined text that is *scriptura* suggests a movement parallel to Augustine's proposed project in *De doctrina Christiana*. There, as we have seen, Augustine maintained that the explication of difficult words in the Hebrew Bible could be part of a broader Christianization of knowledge, a spoiling of Egyptian wisdom to build a Christian intellectual Jerusalem. In Augustine's proposed text in *De doctrina*, discrete units of pagan knowledge would be inserted into the edifice of scripture, the combination of pagan knowledge and Christian edifice superseding pagan knowledge and Hebrew scripture in their pre-Christian form.[218] The *Locutiones in Heptateuchum* is, in a similar sense, a text about supersession. The individual units of biblical text with which Augustine begins are repetitively juxtaposed with Augustine's ideal text, understood to control the smaller textual units first through the larger *mos scripturarum* and ultimately through the incorporation of the smaller units into the expansive combined textual world of scripture and literature. The repetition of this juxtaposition, necessitated by the list format of the *Locutiones*, drives home the continual consumption and supersession of the real by the ideal: at each textual point, the linguistic object of knowledge is "opened" into an idealized image of textuality and intertextuality.[219] The act of reading, following the *Locutiones*, thus becomes an exercise in moving from real to ideal; and the concrete biblical text becomes the sign of that movement: to return to the ideological plan of *De doctrina*, the meaning of a Christian text simply becomes the gesture of Christianization.

The ideological project of the *Locutiones in Heptateuchum* turns on the same gesture. In this case, it is the positing of an ideal text, the components of which are united under the rubric of scripture, and which is produced out of the variable and fragmented passages that make up the real Latin Heptateuch. Augustine's scripture, however, is not strictly coterminous with the biblical canon. The expansion of the ideal text to include intertexts from Virgil and Greek myth transforms the concrete Latin Heptateuch into a point of entry for a much larger textual universe. The reading of Heptateuchal fragments thus creates a physically unreal book that changes the Heptateuch into a matrix of semiotic purity and literary expansiveness. This production takes the Christianization advocated in *De doctrina* one step further: Augustine does not configure the Heptateuch as pre-Christian knowledge that is here being transformed, he configures it simply as the Latin property of the North African church.[220] It is, then, a Christian text that is being Christianized, as Augustine moves from *codices* to *scriptura*, and *scriptura* itself becomes in turn the repository of ideal expansive textuality. Like Jerome, who etymologizes New Testament names in his own Christianizing gesture, Augustine uses textual expansion to delineate the substance of Christianity.

Conclusion: Christianity, Grammar, and the Bible

Christianizing writing on grammar and in the grammatical discipline accomplishes two tasks: it theorizes the appropriation of linguistic elements from previous texts and thereby creates both *doctrina apud gentes* and *doctrina Christiana*, and it enacts the proliferation of this textual knowledge, thereby producing a substance for those *doctrinae*. Notably, although the theoretical discussions of grammar in Latin Christian authors tend to focus on the uses of traditional Roman and Greek literature, the grammatical work of the same authors concentrates not on Roman literature but on biblical texts—and in the examples I have discussed, specifically on the

Hebrew Bible. As I noted at the beginning of this chapter, this should not be taken to mean that no Christian grammarian studies Virgil: in fact, many late ancient grammarians appear to have been Christian, and the affiliations of many other Latin grammarians are unknown. Instead, the concentration on the Bible as the focus of grammatical study is, I think, an extension of the "Christianizing" gesture implied in the grammatical theory of these authors, for whom displacement and the multiplication of language become the hallmarks of Christian instantiation. One of the facts that Jerome and Augustine choose to bring to the reader's attention is that they are working with texts not originally in Latin. Hence Jerome's proffering of his linguistic credentials (*me putant aliquid in hebraeae linguae notitia profecisse*)[221] and Augustine's attribution of problematic Latin prose to the difficulties of translation (*secundum proprietates . . . linguae hebraicae vel graecae*).[222] While neither author would have agreed that the Christian use of the Old Testament was problematic in the same way that Christian use of Roman literature might be, both authors construed use of the Hebrew language as a similar kind of spoliation. For these Latin Christian writers, the Bible is the perfect object of linguistic spoliation: removed from its original languages, it here becomes subject to repeated multiplications, from Jerome's transliterations and false etymologies to Augustine's searching out of textual variants. Through the marking process that accompanies the dislocations and multiplications, that is, the fact that Augustine and Jerome locate Christianization in these reading practices, the Bible becomes visible as the quintessential "Christian" text.

The act of linguistic spoliation, as we have seen, and its concomitant textual proliferation, is one of the devices that makes Christianity visible as such, or that provides Christianizing writers with the space and substance to instantiate Christianity in multiplied texts and lists of authors. Like the literary past in the *artes grammaticae*, Christianity comes to the reader's imagination through a complex process of verbal signaling: the signaling of displacement and transferral in the act of quotation, the signaling of plenitude in the listing of authors, the signaling of meaningfulness in the acts of translation and transliteration, and the signaling of potential perfection or completeness in the listing of verbal infelicities. Christianizing writers are able to theorize the usefulness of this signaling by turning to the discipline of grammar. Thus, despite the importance of the Bible as a "Christianizable" text, the means by which this Christianizing could take place are articulated in terms of the traditional foci of Roman grammar, that is, the poets, rhetors, and dramatists of the grammatical schoolroom. Augustine, at *De doctrina* 3.1.1, suggests that decontexualized knowledge of the traditional disciplines is one of the "necessary things" for a Christian reading of scripture. Part of grammar's necessity may reside in its ability to generate Christianity as a thing that can be read at all.

5

Fear, Boredom, and Amusement
Emotion and Grammar

IF THE ACADEMIC PRACTICE of grammar construed Christianity and paganism as ideal entities manifested in physical texts, how, in turn, did grammatical schooling contribute to the construction of pagan and Christian *people* in late antiquity? How did late ancient authors' thoughts about grammatical education affect the way they or their readers might have imagined the manifestation of religious identity?[1] The affective language surrounding schooling and the learning of grammar reveals a great deal about how the learner is positioned with respect to these larger ideological questions. Three specific tropes of emotion surround grammar and contribute to the constitution of a historical subject as well as to a narrative of time passing, both of which are vital to late ancient Christianization.[2] Where the more technical works of the grammarians use the broad temporal categories of past and present to constitute subjects, however, these affective tropes provide moments in which subjects can be understood as experiencing the passage of time—although this is done, as we will see, in a fundamentally discontinuous manner. The three emotional tropes in question are, as the title of this chapter suggests, fear, boredom, and amusement.

Fear and boredom as emotions surrounding grammar occur in two slightly different contexts in Roman literature: fear is particularly evoked in accounts of children encountering, and being punished by, the grammarian or *magister* who instructs them, while boredom is generally reserved for the adult Roman interacting with a grammarian who reasserts (typically in some inappropriate fashion) his role as pedagogue. Both of these portrayals of grammarians are regularly written as occasions of amusement, and the pictures of children being afraid and adults being bored are themselves presented as entertaining. The accuracy of these emotional portraits is not at issue. What is remarkable is the consistency with which these tropes recur. Whether or not all students were afraid of grammarians or all adults were bored by them, grammarians were positioned within an affective field in which it made sense to speak of them as bullying or boring. The particular sense that these tropes made, I suggest, rearranged into a unitary developmental narrative the multiple, often conflicting, facets that produced the educated subject. Just as the ethical force of "past" and "present" could conjure a particular kind of pious subject, the description of affectively potent moments and their resolution into narratives of emotion formed unitary figures, figures who could carry with them certain kinds of cultural and religious markings. More expansively, the invocation of amusement implicated the reader, as a literate subject, into the narrative. I will begin by discussing fear and boredom separately, concentrating on specific textual instances from Jerome, John Chrysostom, Augustine, and Martianus Capella; the narrative and amusing aspects of the tropes will then be considered together.

Fear and the Breakdown of the Subject

It is well known that elementary education in antiquity involved a certain degree of physical danger.[3] Despite the advice of such figures as Seneca and Quintilian against the practice, corporal punishment of schoolchildren was standard procedure in the ancient world when either their behavior or their classroom performance was less than ideal.[4] Horace famously called his grammar teacher *Orbilius plagosus* (which Stanley Bonner translates as "Orbilius the Whacker"),[5] and Suetonius testifies to Orbilius' violent reputation in *De grammaticis et rhetoribus*.[6] Martial likewise assumes the commonality of the beating grammarian,[7] and in the later empire Ausonius' grammarian Ammonius is rebuked for his "savage" ways.[8]

The beatings received at the grammarian's hands served as a rite of passage for the educated classes, marking the boundaries between educated and uneducated, and between adult and child. As Ausonius tells his grandson, "Both your father and your mother underwent the same things. I hope . . . that you shall walk on the same path that I, and the proconsul your father and prefect your uncle, are on."[9] Beating allows the grouping of educated persons in the empire, and many of those undergoing the grammarian's punishment are spoken of as anonymized plurals: Suetonius, quoting Domitius Marsus, speaks of Orbilius' pupils simply as "those whom Orbilius felled with the cane and the lash."[10] To the same extent that actual beatings may have instilled a level of conformity with the grammarian's literary ideologies, descriptions of beatings suggested conformity between literate elites themselves.[11] At the same time, beatings could be used to mark lines of difference between competing groups. Cicero's reference to school-room beating in *epistulae ad familiares* 7.25 describes conflicts between his cohort and the followers of Caesar;[12] and Suetonius' Orbilius, after his habit of beating children is established, is shown verbally attacking prominent citizens.[13] Literary representations of beatings could thus represent social configurations, grouping some classes together and dividing others. The beating does not thereby lose its status as a physical event, but the representation of that event gives it social as well as corporal meaning. It posits an interaction between the physical body, the imagination of physical affect, and the social and ideological force that this imagination places on the physical subject. This interaction involves the evocation of narrative situations in which beating occurs, and the translation of the physical experience of beating into the emotional experience of fear.

The ideological usefulness of violent scenes is evident in the work of three different Christian writers: John Chrysostom, Jerome, and Augustine, all of whom invite their readers to imagine pedagogical situations in which, to borrow from Freud, a child is being beaten.[14] The violence that each of these patristic writers describes is, moreover, accompanied by an account of the beaten child's fear of being beaten. Two discrete moments are conjured: the moment of beating and the moment of anticipating the beating. The first moment involves the breaking down of the subject into localized bodily sensations, and the second moment involves a reconstitution of the subject in narrative. Beating is used in these texts to break down the educated subject into bodily fragments, which can then be reconstituted as a subject occupying a particular temporal and ideological position.

First, a brief description of each of the scenes: Augustine may be the most notorious beaten child of the late empire, as he presents his boyhood self in the *Confessions* as having begged God "with no little feeling, that I might not be beaten at school." Although, he concedes, "You did not listen to me," Augustine continues: "is there anyone, Lord, so greatsouled, attached to you with overwhelming love—is there, I ask, anyone . . . who, attached to you in devotion, is so greatly in love that he hardly notices racks and hooks and other tortures of that kind, which people everywhere beg you out of stark terror to let them avoid, who nonetheless loves those who fear them so, just as our parents laughed at the torture with which we children were punished by our teachers? We feared them no less, and begged you no less that we might escape them."[15] Here

Augustine imagines himself imagining a beating as a child. Fear plays a prominent role in the scene, as the motivating force behind Augustine's, and others', prayers, and as the test of one's devotion. It should be noted that a significant part of this passage is taken up with beating as a hypothetical situation ("is there anyone . . . ?"): Augustine offers his readers two possible narratives, one of childhood beating, and one of adult torture. The presence of both potential narratives does not invalidate either, since both judicial torture and classroom beating are presented as real possibilities, but the doubling of the narrative should alert the reader at the outset that the historicity of the account is not transparent.

Chrysostom, in describing the ideal education of the Christian child, considers it beneficial for the child to be able to imagine, as Augustine does, the pain of schoolroom punishment. In his sermon *On Vainglory and on the Raising of Children* he advocates instilling fear in one's child as a way of teaching him proper obedience to Christian instruction. In order to generate appropriate fear, Chrysostom recommends referring the child to schoolroom experience: in describing to the child the punishment of Cain, he suggests, "But say: 'Just like when you, standing before your teacher, are in agony over whether or not you are going to be whipped, and you tremble and are afraid, so he lived throughout his life.'"[16] Again, beating and the fear of beating are presented as protreptics to proper behavior, although, unlike Augustine, Chrysostom shows little discomfort at the prevalence of beating in schooling.[17] Chrysostom's account does match Augustine's in providing the reader with a doubled narrative, this time that of the child about to be beaten and the narrative of adult punishment in the story of Cain. Here, too, we should be alert to the hermeneutical function of the violent scenario, especially as Chrysostom asks that the child be told the scenario as part of his instruction in the biblical text. Beating here is very much a literary as well as physical phenomenon.

Finally Jerome, in his *Apology Against Rufinus*, inserts a description of himself about to be beaten as a child, in order to excuse his continuing use of classical authors in later life. They were, he explains, beaten into him: he invites Rufinus to picture the young Jerome being "dragged from my grandmother's lap like a captive, to savage Orbilius."[18] Jerome's childhood beating parallels another instance of pedagogical violence, described in his letter 22. Here Jerome relates to Eustochium his dream of Christ beating him for reading texts that make him unworthy of the name "Christian": "Asked as to my condition, I answered that I was a Christian. 'You lie,' he said, 'you are a Ciceronian, not a Christian; "where your treasure is, there

your heart will be also.'" At that I was struck dumb, and between blows—
since he had ordered me to be beaten—I was tormented more by the flames
of my conscience."[19] Jerome, having left the literal schoolroom, is beaten
for letting his unfortunately continuing status as "schoolboy" interfere with
his ascetic life. As in Chrysostom and Augustine, we note in Jerome the
elements of imagination and the doubled narrative of childhood and adult
punishment. Here, too, is the use of the violent scenario in a hortatory
context. Children in these Christianizing texts seem continually faced with
the threat of corporal punishment. The reader, in turn, is asked vividly to
imagine the beatings that the children are told to fear.

The emphasis in these texts, however, is not on punishment per se but
on the anticipation and trappings of it; the importance of the supposed
teacher/student conflict is exceeded by that of the fear attendant upon it.
In only one of the four passages described above does a beating actually
occur, in Jerome's dream beating of letter 22, and, whatever the experience of the dreamer, Jerome there writes that he was "tormented more
by the flames of conscience."[20] In Chrysostom, likewise, the usefulness in
beating a child is never in the beating but in the protreptic fear of beating, as he cautions: "But [the child] should always fear blows without
receiving them. . . . When you see him profiting from his fear, leave off."[21]
Indeed, Augustine's hypothetical figure who undergoes torment unfazed
seems to have reached an ideal state, not because he is not tortured but
because he is not afraid of torture. Passages that at first appear to be records
of simple violence instead substitute fear of violence to achieve their effect.
Pedagogical violence is a textual sleight of hand: although they may provide evidence for the commonality of beating in Roman education, these
passages do not record or describe such beatings as much as they invoke,
anticipate, and stage them. The dramatic tableaux before and after the beatings are what provide the atmosphere of childhood fear in the texts.[22]

That the beatings never in fact occur in the texts should also direct
attention away from actual beating and toward the structures that make
the emotional narrative of beating possible. The primary emphasis in each
of the accounts is the expectation of beating, that is, the suspense anticipating the bodily event—which may or may not eventually happen. This
suspense is, by definition, an interruption in the implied sequence of pedagogical events; indeed, it derives its importance from the possibility that
the beating might, but also might not, happen.[23] Augustine's urgent prayer
is not based on his knowledge that there will be a beating but on his not
knowing whether or not the beating will occur; it is predicated on the

possibility that the beating could be avoided ("we begged you no less that we might escape them"). Chrysostom wants the Christian child to be in continuous suspense about the possibility of beating ("in agony over whether or not you are to be beaten"). There is an empty space here in which not only is nothing happening but what will happen is still undetermined.[24] This interruption marks a kind of temporal rupture in the stereotypical state of affairs, in which the bad child is beaten after misbehaving. Here, on the imaginative plane, the torment of punishment is threatened before the child can misbehave, and informs the child's supposed fear of misbehavior and its consequences. In the exemplary scenario, however, the empty moment is resolved by the temporal momentum generated by the emotion of fear: fear implies that something will happen, whether or not it is a beating, and the child of the scenario is removed from the temporal problem by being understood as fearful.[25] The empty moment is thus narrated into fear; it is co-opted into the emotional language of fear by its apparent insertion into a narrative of disobedience followed by punishment.[26]

Fearfully anticipating and (at least imaginatively) witnessing a beating is made easier for the disobedient child and the reading audience by the presence of authenticating "props" in each of the scenes. Augustine, perhaps most dramatically, moves from suggested schoolroom beating to the concrete details of "racks, hooks, and torments" in judicial torture;[27] Chrysostom suggests that the Christian child be "threatened with the whip" and have Cain's "ten thousand" punishments described to him "not simply, but with vehemence."[28] The gestures toward realism, or perhaps hyperrealism,[29] reinforce the supposed reality of the imagined violence, a situation that Jerome's reaction to his dream beating explicitly acknowledges: "To the surprise of everyone, I opened my eyes, and they were so wet with tears that my pain convinced even the skeptics."[30] The believability of the dramatic violence must be supported by realistic proofs: details of real torture or pain. The dramatic context of the violent situation lends credibility to the fears of the children imagining punishment.[31] At the same time, the threat of violence lends believability to the larger dramatic context in which the violence is set. Jerome's tears persuade his earthly audience not only that the beating is real but that the dream encounter with Christ is real as well. Chrysostom's invocations of school violence are meant to persuade the Christian child that God's punishments are real;[32] and Augustine's fear of schoolroom violence persuades him to pray to a God who is "not evident to our senses."[33] Imagined violence both verifies and is verified by its dramatic surroundings.

The process whereby credibility must be produced in these scenarios calls attention to their constructed nature, and to the use of affectively charged situations to create new narratives. The violent disruption of the idealized pedagogical situation introduces a narrative that can contain that disruption. The disruption is not merely temporal or social, however: it extends to the constitution of the educated subject as well. At the moment of beating the beaten subject disappears in these texts, replaced at center stage by the fear-inducing mechanisms of beating.[34] As noted earlier, Augustine's prayer not to be beaten is followed not by a description of beating but by a reflection on the similarities between school violence and judicial violence;[35] Augustine muses on the terror experienced by unreal victims of judicial torture instead of describing any schoolroom incident. Jerome, similarly, as he is beaten, is "struck dumb" under the "blows of the whip" and the "fire of conscience."[36] Affective moments centered on violence again take the place of the subject, erasing the subject by the imagining (in this case, dreaming) of violence. Most overtly, the willfulness of Chrysostom's Christian child is replaced by a fear that is "like fire at full heat, consuming all the thorns around it, or like a long, sharp pick, digging into the depths."[37] The substitution of these fires, whips, and picks for the subject in the course of punishment highlights the charged moment of punishment as an apparatus of subjectivity, over and above the creation of the subject himself. The apparatus works through the substitution of affective intensities that take the place of the unified subject and break it into different objects used in the violent scene. The fearful subject exists only underneath the blows of the whip or the fires that are imagined, existing not as an autonomous individual but as an assemblage of imagined physical parts that are subjected to violence. The subject exists as a back under a whip, a thorn consumed by fire, or a body literally broken on a rack. The mechanisms of fear thus break the subject down into individual fragmented scenes or parts. Schoolroom violence serves to break down and erase complete subjects through the application of physical intensities.

The unity of the beaten subject is further broken down by the presence of spectators in the passages: Augustine inserts his parents into the scene as an audience for his dilemma; Jerome addresses Rufinus as the audience for his childhood beatings; and in Chrysostom the hypothetical Christian child is split into observer and observed, asked to be the audience for both Cain's and his own punishment.[38] More than the beatings of individual subjects are described in these texts, they are described as being watched by multiple subjects. The generative force of the violence thus also lies in its ability to create multiple figures surrounding the violence, or, more precisely, multiple figures anticipating and witnessing the violent scene. The authors do not dwell on the details of violence or on the behavior of the solitary victim undergoing punishment.[39] Instead, scenes of pedagogical violence are focused on the suspense of the victim as imaginative observer of his own punishment before the beating, and on the reactions of bystanders to the events. In Jerome's letter 22, the dream beating is relegated to a parenthetical few words ("he had ordered me to be beaten": *nam caedi me iusserat*),[40] amid the much more detailed treatment of the dream trial as a whole. Here the beating occurs before a group of dream bystanders who at the end of the beating return Jerome to a state of anticipation for the next: they suggest, claims Jerome, that he should be tortured even more terribly if he ever again reads pagan literature.[41] The beating and its aftermath are fragmented into the multiple blows of the whip, the multiple figures present, and the prospect of repetition.

All of the apparent schoolroom violence, then, is articulated in a set of connected, but not continuous, tableaux that are negotiated by the imposition of a unifying temporal line. There is the tableau of the child being punished, the tableau of the expectation of punishment, the tableau of the child being observed being punished. All of these involve temporal and subjective interruption, in that they require the decentering of sensations and viewpoints, and the rearrangement of narrative sequence (descriptions of punishment as a requirement for anticipation of punishment, experience of punishment as a means of avoiding punishment, and so on).[42] These positions are given coherence through the temporal implications of the emotion fear and its unification of the subject. Fear allows the conjured fearing subject to anticipate, witness, avoid, and experience the thing feared, as simultaneous imaginative phenomena.[43] At the same time, enclosing the multiplicity of sensations and temporalities in a single individual (understood as implicated in a narrative scenario) allows all of the factors to be presented as nonconflicting, since they can be presented as the result of individual actions or thoughts on the part of a subject moving through time. Thus Augustine can claim to have been beaten, pray not to be beaten, and conflate beating with judicial torture, yet not describe any of his own beatings, all in the same passage, a passage that ends with a narrative of individual volition: "We neither feared [punishment] less [than victims of torture do], nor did we pray to you less to avoid it, but we sinned all the same."[44] All of Augustine's imaginings of beating are condensed into a narrative of childish fear and individual action.

The imagination of beating thus suggests a fragmentation of the educated subject, while the imagination of fear sets the conditions under which
those diverse fragments can come together in a single narrative. Fear is
one of the emotional tropes surrounding literary education, an education
which involved the prospect of violence. The invocation of fear, moreover,
involves the writer in a breaking down of the beaten subject: on the one
hand the subject is reduced to the bodily affects of beating—with the
schoolmaster's rod fragmenting the subject—and on the other hand the
subject is split into both observer and observed in the anticipation of his
own punishment. Violence allows for the multiplication of the subject
into several split figures that surround the event of schoolroom punishment, and fear creates the structure in which that multiplication can be
contained. A similar splitting of the subject occurs in the trope of grammatically induced boredom, to which I will now turn.

Boredom and Passing Time

It is a time-honored trope that the study of grammar, while perhaps necessary for the young, is, in most of its forms, boring. An insistence on the
boringness of formal grammatical work dates from very early in the history
of the discipline. Seneca, for example, writing at a time when professional
grammarians were only beginning to establish themselves in the Roman
Empire,[45] describes one grammarian's work as follows: "The grammarian
Didymus wrote four thousand books. I would feel sorry for him if he had
merely read that many incredibly empty works. In these books is discussed the birthplace of Homer, the real mother of Aeneas, whether Anac-
reon was more lecherous than drunken, whether Sappho was a prostitute,
and other things that you should forget, if you knew them. Don't tell me
that life isn't long enough."[46] Aulus Gellius provides a similar complaint
against a man "of no mean reputation in the cultivation of *litteratura*,"
who provides him with a book of apparently random grammatical information, such as "who was the first to be called by the title 'grammarian,'
how many famous Pythagorases or Hippocrateses there have been . . . ,
what the names were of the companions of Ulysses who were snatched
and torn apart by Scylla," and the like. Gellius promptly returns the book.[47]
    The modern concept of boredom, it should be noted, is not precisely
analogous to ancient usages of *taedium* or *fastidium*, which denote irritation in a more general sense, nor is it exactly the same as the concept of

acedia, emergent in late ancient monastic literature to denote a range of experiences, from boredom to depression.[48] I use the term "boredom" here in a very specific sense, while recognizing that the textual and cultural production of any emotion is dependent on particular historical formations. Boredom, as it will be used here, will refer specifically to an irritation having to do with a lapse of time. For example, when Aulus Gellius concludes another story about grammarians, an account of two grammarians arguing over a technical matter (the correct vocative of *egregius*), he does so by saying, "I decided it was not worthwhile to listen to these same things for so long [*diutius*], and I left them shouting and arguing."[49] Gellius' attitude here exemplifies the type of boredom that grammarians engender: their work takes too long for its audience to enjoy. The situations they create are temporally problematic,[50] hence Seneca's insistence that the works of Didymus merely exhibit the human capacity for wasting time.

Boredom and grammar are explicitly joined in one treatise written by Didymus' intellectual kin, the introduction to grammar that is book 3 of Martianus Capella's *Marriage of Philology and Mercury*.[51] The references to boredom[52] throughout the nine books of this text, and especially in book 3 on grammar, serve a purpose similar to that found in the narratives of beating described above, namely, they break down individual subjects into bodily fragments, thereby also allowing, as we will see, for their reassemblage into new subjects of narrative.[53] Temporal irritation marks an interruption of temporal sequence, leaving the irritated party with, as it were, too many temporal options. To return to Gellius: from one temporal standpoint, the grammarians' argument ought to be over; it is not. Gellius is faced with a shift in flows of time.[54] On the one hand, there is the suggestion that the argument should end; on the other, there is the development of the argument that does not end. Gellius the observer exists in both flows at once, and his reaction is to walk away; that is, to move back into a narrative of his own agency and progress, leaving the temporal rupture and its protagonists behind.

The same pattern of temporal breakdown, submerging of a subject in grammar, and reemergence of the subject in narrative occurs in a much more complex manner in Martianus Capella's *Marriage of Philology and Mercury*, dating from the fifth century.[55] The work itself is in a mixed prose-and-verse genre, Menippean satire,[56] and relates, shifting between three different narrative planes, the joining of gods and mortals.[57] The allegorical tale is that of the divine ascent of the mortal woman Philology, chosen to be the bride of Mercury on account of her great learning. At the wedding, Philology's dowry is examined: it consists of seven female attendants who represent the seven traditional liberal arts. Each attendant is given a turn to speak in the divine assembly and summarize her discipline before the wedding can continue. The encyclopedic work of the speeches is, in other words, an interruption of the allegorical fable; and, indeed, in order to bring the wedding to its close, the gods decide in book 9 of the work to dispense with the speeches of two other liberal arts, Medicine and Architecture, as well as the speeches of the seven prophetic arts that Martianus also claims are part of Philology's dowry.[58] The canonical liberal arts—Grammar, Dialectic, Rhetoric, Geometry, Arithmetic, Astronomy, and Music—take precedence over the other arts for a place in the wedding ceremony, but are themselves interrupted so that the ceremony can end.

On one obvious level, were there no interruption in the ceremony, there would be no room for the display of the liberal arts, and the work would not accomplish its compendious purpose.[59] There are, however, enough overt episodes of disjunction and interruption in the work that interruption itself becomes a theme. The breaking up of textual flow continues to some degree in each of the books devoted to the liberal arts. All of the speeches end somewhat abruptly, when the speakers realize, or are told, that the gods are getting tired of listening to them. The arts are interrupted by the boredom of the gods. Grammar, however, is not allowed to finish her speech: she is simply told by Minerva to step down and is rebuked in no uncertain terms for inducing the irritation of the gods: "When Grammar, about to go on, had said all this as if it were merely a prologue, Minerva interrupted her on account of the irritation of the divine senate, and of Jove, saying: 'Unless I am mistaken, you are about to go back to the eight parts of speech and repeat the beginning, adding the causes of solecisms, the forms of barbarisms, and the other vices of speech. . . . If you bring these matters of elementary scholarship into the heavenly senate, you will lose any thanks you may have had from your previous learning.'"[60] The particular province of Grammar, as we have already seen, is the breaking up of texts and words.[61] Grammar's speech in book 3 is devoted first to the letters of the alphabet, then to the types of syllables, and then to the declension of nouns and the conjugation of verbs, all illustrated with material drawn from earlier Greek or Latin literature. Following the generic conventions of other late ancient grammar texts (from which he borrows freely),[62] Martianus construes the practice of grammar as an exercise in textual and linguistic fragmentation. The subjects of Grammar's analysis are, at their longest, single poetic lines; at their shortest, individual letters.

The effect of this fragmentation, however, is not to reduce the field over which Grammar holds sway but to enlarge it. In introducing herself Grammar claims that she is, like philosophy, the art of commenting intelligently on anything written or spoken,[63] and she claims to have a hand in anything produced by anyone literate.[64] Minerva's chastisement of Grammar at the end of book 3 includes the charge that, if she were allowed to continue, Grammar would preempt the speeches of the other arts, who are still waiting to be heard. The means by which this expansion of grammar takes place is, as with other ancient grammatical texts, the homogenization of verbal material that grammatical fragmentation allows. First, and most obviously, for Grammar all words are equally open to the same kind of analysis. All Latin is, as it were, equally Latinate, even when it originates in Greek.[65] More significantly, perhaps, all Latin literature comes under the aegis of "that which Grammar teaches," Grammar itself.[66] Grammar creates its own wide-ranging field of study, a body of literature all of whose words are, through grammar, interchangeable as objects of study. But the concrete examples of *litteratura* in book 3 are not drawn from just any texts. Virgil, Horace, Terence, Sallust, and Cicero are most prominent, and there are abundant references to mythic characters.[67] The expansion of Grammar's field of study, then, is twofold. First, Latinity is flattened into a single broad field; second, that field is persistently described by a select number of equally homogenized privileged writings. What we might call high literature is, in practice, made to represent all literature, and literature is made to be latent everywhere language is.[68] Ultimately, then, what shadows any act of reading informed by this grammar is an imagined (but not displayed) body of ideal texts that are continually suggested by the presence of Latin. In this sense, grammar may be exemplary for the project of the *Marriage* as a whole. Despite their clearly much abbreviated summaries of their fields, the seven liberal arts stand in for the idea of universal knowledge. Indeed, the truncated nature of the speeches invokes such knowledge, with its suggestion that much more is being left unsaid.[69]

Before this vast idealized concept of learning, the individual learner is faced with some difficulties. On the one hand, she (if we extrapolate her gender from that of Philology) participates in the idea of learning and, on the other, is persistently left out by the ideality and elusivity of that which is to be learned—there is always more, and better, material in what is left out. The reader, then, like the earlier beaten subject, is split in much the same way as the text is, as a result of the splitting of the text. The reader is partly taken into the projected ideal realm, and partly reminded of her exclusion from it.[70] This splitting of the reader is played out on several levels in the *Marriage*. The work opens with a poetic address to the god of marriage but soon shifts to Martianus' address to his son, who interrupts the poem. Martianus then offers to relate to his son a tale related to him by the personified goddess Satire. During the course of this tale are reported the speeches of the liberal arts during the divine wedding. The reader is constantly asked to assume a different listening position, listening first as Martianus' son, then as Martianus instructed by Satire, then as a member of the divine wedding party, instructed by the liberal arts. During Grammar's speech, in fact, the reader must both assume a facility with Latin and simultaneously an ignorance of it, as Grammar laboriously reminds her of, for example, the makeup of the Latin alphabet. Grammar ends her discussion of the pronunciation of the alphabet with the following shift in expected erudition: "*X* is the sibilant combination of *C* and *S*. *Y* is a breath with the lips close together. *Z* was abhorrent to Appius Claudius, because it resembles in its expression the teeth of a corpse."[71] It is of course unlikely that a reader of Martianus' time would be both unfamiliar with the pronunciation of the alphabet and yet versant in the opinions of Appius Claudius, the fourth-century B.C.E. Roman jurist.[72] But those appear to be the readerships that the reader must simultaneously imagine and inhabit. The individual reader is forced to reimagine herself as a composite of several projected readers, or several subjects, each adapted to a different kind of imagined text: one imagined reader knows ideal literature thoroughly and follows Martianus' Virgilian references with ease; another imagined reader must be taught the alphabet. These imagined readers are expected, moreover, to intersect. The actual reader of the *Marriage* is thus constituted as the point of intersection between different textual ideals and different projected readerships.[73]

If, as has been suggested, the theme of the *Marriage* is the ascent of humanity to divinity through learning,[74] represented in Philology's apotheosis, the disjunctions in the human reader are akin to those experienced by Philology. In one of the oddest passages of the work, Philology, preparing herself for marriage, meets the personification of Immortality, who tells her that unless she purges herself, she will never ascend to the heavens. Philology then proceeds to vomit out a stream of learned books and treatises, in fact all of the learning that had originally qualified her to be chosen as Mercury's bride. The books are then collected by the seven liberal arts, who are soon to become Philology's dowry. Lightened of her books, Philology ascends to heaven and is re-presented with her previous learning, now in the possession of the disciplines.[75] This series of events is disconcerting. Philology's persona is divided into at least three parts: learned mortal, potential immortal, and immortal proprietress of learning. The fact that Martianus does not mention her again in the narrative, moreover, turns her into an invisible cipher for the performance of multiple abstracted bodies of knowledge. She is, ultimately, an occasion for differentiated and idealized bodies of knowledge to exist and coexist.[76] If Philology stands in for a projected human reader—one who will participate in the divine through learning—this reader must be understood to be, like Philology, an occasion for the conjunction of different imagined bodies of knowledge. Like Philology, the reader must both contain these elements and disappear behind them.

The disappearance of Philology, subsumed in the multiple liberal arts, parallels the disappearance of the beaten children discussed earlier. In both cases the subject is replaced—overwhelmed—by pedagogical acts that, in overwhelming the subject, break it into multiple physical aspects. Philology "vomits" out the liberal arts, providing them physically to the seven personified attendants who replace her as the center of interest; less colorfully, Augustine, Jerome, and Chrysostom reduce the beaten child to a series of fearful or painful experiences: the grammarian's whips and rods are superimposed upon the subject in such a way as to make the subject invisible behind the graphic displays of violence. The work of teaching is here presented as involving the disappearance of physical subjects behind bodily fragments that are, in turn, subjected to a pedagogical order. During the course of grammatical instruction, no subjects are apparent: teachers and students alike are replaced by mechanisms of pedagogy.

Reconstitutions

Both beating and boredom, then, mark the breakdown and disappearance of subjects (the beaten child, the beating grammarian, Philology, the gods attending the wedding). The breakdowns are not, however, purely negative. As with the grammatical fragmentation of earlier texts, the breaking down of subjects plays a productive role in the late ancient imagination. Where fragmentation of texts spurs the production of the imaginative entities Christianity and paganism, the fragmentation of subjects promotes the production of imaginative narratives that attach to those entities. More specifically, these writers use the dissolution of subjects to narrate a chronological progression from (pagan, classical) past to (Christian, post-classical) present.

The affective moments under consideration up to this point have not been, strictly speaking, narratives: Augustine's list of torture instruments and Grammar's list of word functions do not in themselves order sequences of events. The emotional responses that they conjure, however, rely on narrative for their meaning; that is, the torture implements must be connected to a sequence involving a child being beaten; the word analyses must be placed in a wedding ceremony, for fear and boredom to be identifiable emotional responses.[77] Indeed, certain accounts of emotion in antiquity rely on narrative for emotion to be identified as such: Stoic definitions of emotion require both an external event to set off a chain of physical and intellectual responses and a subsequent event or act on the part of the emotional subject in order for emotion to be said to have occurred at all.[78] Emotion, then, requires narrative; and the use of emotional tropes in the texts under consideration may thus be seen as an imposition of narrative onto grammatical occasions. The expansion of grammatical experience to include chronological progression, rather than merely instantaneous or timeless ideological production, allows for the creation of different relationships between different subjects and grammatical texts: emotional tropes introduce pasts, presents, and futures for the reading subject.

The immediate narratives are, as we have seen, those offering the compression of diverse elements in the unifying emotional structures of fear and boredom. These structures allow the temporal disjunctions to be resolved on a small scale by their containment within conjured individuals existing in time and with individual autonomy: the child who fears punishment or the deity who is bored by long-windedness. On this level, the disjunction is portrayed as occurring within a specific subject, who resolves it by entering a temporally continuous scenario, so that the disjunctive effects of beating are ordered as a narrative of the misbehaving child afraid of punishment, and the disjunctive effects of primary education are resolved in the figure of the impatient goddess who calls for the next act.[79] The disjunctions that are created in the forum of grammatical education, however, are not wholly resolved by these individual narratives. All of the emotional figures must also be placed in a larger narrative, since their existence is predicated on their movement through time, as the means of resolving temporal multiplicity.

The larger narratives in question are, on one level, straightforward. Augustine, Chrysostom, and Jerome all embed their grammatical scenes in a larger narrative of growing up, so that the suspense surrounding beating is resolved less in the inevitable beating than in the presentation of the result of the beating, namely, the educated adult.[80] Fear, looking forward, finds its narrative closure in the adult of later years, as Augustine makes clear: "Or, indeed, some good judge of events might approve of my being beaten because I was playing ball as a boy, and in so playing I was kept from learning letters that much more quickly, with which as an adult I might play more dishonorably."[81] Introducing beating is one way of marking the passage of time from childhood to adulthood. What must be remembered, however, is that the narrative is not, as it were, organic—that is, although it may be reasonable to think of grammatical education as occurring at a certain point in a chronological continuum, in fact that continuum is here being created precisely to account for a multiplicity in adult identity: diachronicity is being invoked to explain synchronicity. Jerome's response to Rufinus is the most obvious example: in order to explain how he can both quote Virgil and be a Christian, Jerome reverts to a narrative of growing up. Chrysostom uses childhood education to deal with an apparent contradiction in his adult audience: they are both Christian and participants in "vain" civic life.[82] For Chrysostom, circumventing this contradiction involves creating a narrative of ideal childhood upbringing. Augustine, too, creates his childhood in order to account for multiple aspects of himself: his account of memory in *Confessions* 10 shows him negotiating and organizing the various multiple objects in his *aula memoriae*, of which childhood and grammar provide only a few.[83] None of these authors is constrained to use narrative; rather, narrative is exploited for the purposes of negotiating ideological multiplicity. To be two contradictory things at once ought to be impossible: narrative sequence allows the impossibility to be avoided.

The same kind of sequencing occurs even more overtly in the *Marriage of Philology and Mercury*. The splitting that the reader undergoes in the educative process is negotiated by appeals to temporality.[84] It is the juxtaposition of elementary and advanced knowledge that Minerva rebukes in Grammar: "You will complete your previous teachings in good form if you leave off the common and elementary trivialities from what you have already said."[85] This lapse in instructional linearity is the reason for the irritation of the gods in book 3 and for their tedium later on.[86] The issue is one of timeliness, or rather of temporal propriety. Minerva accuses Grammar on two fronts: first, that she has confused the appropriate temporal context for her teaching by behaving as if the divine senate were an elementary school and, second, simply that she threatens to speak for too long and take up the time allotted to other disciplines.[87] It is a call for sequence in time, rather than simultaneity. In other words, the disjunctions that Grammar introduces are to be dealt with by the imposition of a narrative sequence. The reader is being asked to exist on too many levels at once. If the multiple levels are arranged into a temporal order, the reader can go through them one at a time, from elementary school to advanced learning, or from Grammar through the other liberal arts. If this sequence is jumbled, as Minerva claims it is in Grammar's speech, the cry of temporal "foul"—that is, boredom—ensues.[88] The gods' *fastidium* is predicated on Grammar's failure to stick to a proper sequence of time.

More fundamentally, it is the imposition of narrative order that holds out hope for the consummation of the marriage. In the introduction to book 9, Venus asks the other gods, "When will there be an end? How long will learned exercises impede marital pleasure?" After describing the pallor and anxiety on the faces of Cupid and Pleasure, Venus blames their collective tedium on "these uncouth girls" and professes herself "hurt by the unusual delays."[89] The apparent inexhaustibility of each of the liberal arts (that is, the imagined field of knowledge that each of them represents) is constrained by the wedding's narrative timeframe. The Moon, in fact, complains that, day being nearly over, she will have to leave on her nightly course before the speeches end, if they do not end soon. Besides, she claims, the rest of the audience is far too tired to listen to any more.[90] Again, the invocation of tedium is at the service of temporal sequencing instead of simultaneity: the idealized, infinite, bodies of knowledge suggested in the speeches of the liberal arts must be made to coexist with the invoked presence of an audience in real time. One set of imaginings must give way to another. The objection that the speeches together or individually have taken "too long"[91] should then be understood as a means of regulating the splitting that the reader undergoes: multiplicity can be ordered sequentially. It is not, after all, that any gods are really being bored—in the *Marriage*, boredom is a device that allows the disjunctions involved in the vastness of the encyclopedic project to be made manageable. This is done by appealing to temporal order as an organizing principle. "Too much time" should be read as "too many times at once," which are then reduced to the one time of the narrative. In the interests of time, then, the gods decide to collapse the multiple arts into a single object of desire: Philology herself. Saturn appeals to an ancient Roman law indicating that after marriage, the wife herself can be called the dowry.[92] The single figure of Philology once again comes to stand in for the multiple, fragmentary, idealized, and elusive knowledges suggested by the liberal arts.[93] The gods' boredom, that is, the configuration of multiplicity as temporal in nature, both marks the splitting involved in conjuring the liberal arts and prompts the containment of that splitting through temporal and figural closure.

The use of narrative to contain multiplicity in a sequence of monolithic events, moreover, goes beyond the production of individual narratives of identity. It also expands into narratives of larger-scale ideological progression. The resolution of multiple subjects into subjects-over-time is accompanied by the introduction of time to the categories under which the subjects are presented as operating, namely, Christianity and paganism and the classical and postclassical worlds. These categories are introduced variously in the texts under consideration. Part of the backdrop to the scenes of violence is the supposed conflict between "Christianity" and "classical culture." Each of the patristic texts I have chosen to examine places its scene of pedagogical violence within a larger narrative of "Christian" resistance to "pagan" texts: Chrysostom is arguing for the replacement of mythological tales with biblical stories; Augustine is lamenting a youth wasted in learning Virgil; and Jerome is caught in a controversy over how familiar he really is with pre-Christian literature. Christianity and paganism, like the implements in Augustine's torture chamber, are part of the trappings of the violent situation. Unlike Augustine's "racks" and "hooks," however, Christianity and paganism are not immediately tangible physical objects—at least, not until the beating begins. In each of these texts, it is "Christianity" and "paganism" that are "beaten into" the misbehaving child. As Jerome tells Rufinus: "If you had ever learned letters, the vessel of your little genius would still have the scent of that with which it had once been filled."[94] Augustine similarly claims, "I do not blame the words, which are excellent and precious vessels, but the wine of error that was prepared for us in them. . . . If we boys refused to drink it we were beaten."[95] The "wine of error" takes on corporal power in the grammarian's beatings. Christianity, too, is embodied in the blows Jerome receives in his dream, and in the whip that Chrysostom's Christian child constantly fears. The anticipated beatings and beating implements thus become physical proofs for the real existence of the otherwise shadowy religious entities that Jerome labels "Christianity" and "Ciceronianism." Hovering uncertainly around the body of the educated child, they are instantiated in the punishments he is slated to undergo. Christianity and paganism here come into being as identical

techniques and tools of physical manipulation. Where grammatical techniques create Christianity and the classical as abstract bodies of knowledge,
the imagination of schooling conjures them as much more immediate pres-
ences. The process of educational punishment thus becomes one of the
means by which Christianity and paganism are produced as both instruments and objects of power and knowledge.[96]

The productivity of the violent situation also extends to the actors in
the pedagogical scene.[97] Since the point of pedagogy is not to erase the
subject but to fashion a particular kind of subject, the child reappears as
either a "Ciceronian" or a "Christian" after the beating or threat of beating has passed. So, after his digression on torture, Augustine returns to
the schoolroom and to his boyhood self with the remark, "Nonetheless,
we were at fault because we did less reading and writing and attending to
our studies than was demanded of us."[98] Augustine the future "Ciceronian"
rhetor would not have disagreed; Augustine the author here identifies with
the grammarian chastising his younger self. The mechanics of beating, moreover, also require the production of another subject, namely, the beating
magister. Augustine and Jerome correspondingly provide portraits of teachers as quintessentially pagan or Christian. Augustine's schoolmaster is portrayed as just as lost in error as his wayward students,[99] while Jerome's
punitive teachers are extremes at either end: Christ himself and Orbilius,
the pagan teacher of the pagan poet Horace. Permanently situated in the
pedagogical scene, the grammarian becomes an emblem of the classical
learning that that scene creates; he is, moreover, relegated to the individual
subject's past, and his subject matter, by extension, to a past era. By submitting their narratives to the logic of the violent situation, the putative
victims of the beatings, Jerome and Augustine the authors, are here able
to produce and control the material appearance of pagan and Christian
subjects, incarnate in the figures of the punishing authorities and their misbehaving students.[100]

The physical effects of education in Martianus Capella likewise sub-
stantiate the idea of a classical era. The most obvious mechanism of reification in the *Marriage* is the personification of the liberal arts, with Grammar
and her toolkit of pedagogical devices ready to practice upon the mouths
of her students:

She carried in her hands a polished box . . . from which like a skilled physician the
woman took out the emblems of wounds that need to be healed. Out of this box
she took first a pruning knife with a shining point, with which she said she could
prune the faults of pronunciation in children; then they could be restored to health

with a certain black powder. . . . She also cleaned the windpipes and the lungs by the application of a medicine. . . She also brought out a file fashioned with great skill . . . with which by gentle rubbing she gradually cleaned dirty teeth and ailments of the tongue and the filth which had been picked up in the town of Soloe.[101]

Here Grammar is conceived as a highly physical practice, focusing on the mouth, throat, and tongue, with applications to each under the medical supervision of the personified art herself. Correct Latin takes on a bodily aspect, both occurring in the body and influencing the ways in which the body is allowed to pronounce, breathe, and move its tongue. The physicality of correct Latin is, moreover, imagined to be imposed by a single authoritative entity, Grammar, the "skilled physician" who is synonymous with "literature." "Literature" is thereby made both unitary and substantial, manipulating bodies as a single overpowering agent in its own right.

The emotion of boredom, however, also has a role in making the classical substantial. First, it reinforces the physicality of the liberal arts' personification. Occurring in, indeed constituting, the framing narrative once the liberal arts begin to speak, the moments of divine tedium are reminders to the reader that the marriage ceremony is supposed to be taking place in a particular time and space. The benumbed countenances of Venus and Flora accentuate the physical effects of the liberal arts' speeches; the framing interruptions by the gods, demanding that the liberal arts step down, emphasize that the arts are individual entities with well-defined boundaries and agency. The boredom of the gods requires that Grammar stop before she can trespass on the province of Music;[102] she thereby becomes a distinct field of study and object of knowledge, as well as becoming a force with the ability to influence her audience and compete with reified rivals. Learning the accumulated wisdom of the past, in this scheme, is an interaction between a learner and a discrete authoritative individual, whose subject matter is circumscribed by boredom; only one such individual can occupy the learner's attention at any one time. Boredom, then, both physically manipulates the grammarian's audience and allows that audience to define the grammarian's province, making grammar both physically real and clearly bounded.

The second implication that boredom has for the liberal arts has more to do with its temporal aspect. Boredom, in defining the boundaries of grammar, also removes the boring object from the same temporal plane as its bored observers.[103] The specific charge that boredom generates against Grammar, as has already been noted, is that of temporal impropriety: Grammar treats the gods as elementary school students.[104] That this is inappropriate involves a retrojection of narrative: the gods "have done" grammar; they do not need to do it again. Minerva rebukes Grammar specifically for "getting set to repeat" elementary subjects.[105] The gods, then, exist in a flow of time different from that which Grammar's speech evokes; the overlapping of these flows creates the irritation that boredom signals. Repetition, in other words, is unnecessary; the gods by implication have had one grammatical education already and do not need another. Boredom thus retrojects a subject that has already studied *litteratura*. The gods, after all, are not young for Grammar; she is younger than they are, having been "found and brought up by Mercury himself."[106] She does not teach the gods anything they do not already know.

More paradoxically, the temporal confusion created by Grammar ensures that literature always belongs to an era different from that of its readers. If boredom suggests a subject that has already studied Grammar, it follows that boredom also retrojects literature as a past object of study. Literature must exist in a past even more remote than that of the personal narrative of learning: if one has studied grammar in the past, grammar must have existed prior to that past in order to be imagined as an object of study in it. Grammar/*litteratura*, following this scheme, is presented to the reader as an old woman, "who recalled her origins in Memphis during the reign of Osiris,"[107] in stark contrast to the youthful couple about to wed.[108] Grammar's appropriate charges, according to Minerva, are the young, so that literature is always "older" than its readers. The era of literature is inescapably that of the past. On the one hand, literature is ancient; on the other, it belongs to children.

Boredom, then, accomplishes two tasks: first, it reifies *litteratura*; second, it places *litteratura* in the past—either the cultural past (Grammar's birth during the reign of Osiris) or the past of the individual reader (childhood education in grammar). The constitution of Grammar/*litteratura* as an old woman, an autonomous agent capable of manipulating her charges and her listeners, entails the imagination of literature itself as authoritative and temporally separated from the learner. The mythological names and earlier Latin authors that form the content of Grammar's speech are contained within the figure of the elderly teacher as a unified ancient corpus, shaping, but fundamentally separate from, the reader's contemporary identity. Grammar in Martianus conforms to the grammarians' authorities in the *artes*, the *antiqui* and *maiores* that form the corpus of classical literature. Grammar is literally *antiqua* here, as the words, conjugations, and declensions of authoritative Latin are united to the figure of the old woman.

The boredom of the (youthful) gods thus creates two chronological sequences using the figure of the old woman: on the one hand, Grammar is the first and most elderly of the liberal arts and must give way to dialectic, as the first to the second of the arts; and on the other hand, the elderly Grammar must give way before the knowledge already possessed by her previously instructed hearers. The classical is thus placed in a chronological sequence whereby it is inevitably superseded—usable as a resource, but always left in the past.

In these emotional narratives one can begin to see the relations between the projection of larger cultural entities and the construction of individual cultured subjects. The disjunctions involved in grammatical education are resolved in narratives of emotion placed within specific subjects understood as experiencing that education. These subjects are then placed in a larger narrative scheme. The narrative movement involved in such a scheme, however, calls for subject entities much larger than individual figures, subject entities that are construed as historical and cultural movements. These are Christianity and classical culture, already suggested in the parallel narrative movement from the *antiqui* to *nos*. These entities are construed not as results of the disjunction but as anterior to it and producing it, much like Grammar is positioned as both prior to and subsequent to literature. Christianity and the classical, as the requisite subject entities, thereby also produce the subjects that are understood as experiencing the disjunctive education. This allows the narrative to close, with the end having become its own beginning, just as Grammar is both old and young. Both boredom and fear, in these contexts, help generate narratives of the historicity of Christianity and paganism, the classical and postclassical: these entities not only become real but also inhabit particular mutually exclusive historical moments—a before and after of religious and literary culture.

Amusement and Audience

Christianity and the classical are not alone in making this temporal transition: an addressed reader is called upon to join them and become a particular kind of subject as well. The interpellative mechanism propelling this reader through her subjective course is amusement. The texts under consideration rely on humor in different ways. Martianus is perhaps most overt, claiming that the frame story of the gods' boredom is dictated to him by the goddess Satire.[109] Augustine finds laughter impossible for the children receiving the beating but predictable in adult reactions to that beating, presumably including those adults reading the account of his childhood.[110] Jerome calls upon Rufinus to laugh at the picture of his childhood beatings;[111] and John Chrysostom expects that his audience will laugh at the apparent "trivialities" in his account of childhood.[112] Each of these authors appeals to the idea that basic education is amusing to watch.

The laughter that Augustine, Jerome, Martianus, and Chrysostom invoke follows earlier literary precedent. References to childhood education, especially to its accompanying beating, are frequently used to comic effect. Suetonius' references to Orbilius' savagery, for example, are coupled with a witty saying from Orbilius himself.[113] Likewise, Cicero's sketch of schoolroom beating parodies late republican political life.[114] Lucian satirizes the schoolboy's fear of beatings,[115] and Juvenal makes childhood beatings a prerequisite for writing satire.[116] The presence of laughter in the three patristic authors thus draws upon a connection between childhood beating and amusement established much earlier, while Martianus places the process of learning in the earlier tradition of Menippean satire. On the other hand, the more serious discussions of beating in, for example, Quintilian[117] preclude the assumption that childhood education was solely the province of amusement, much as the serious *artes grammaticae* preclude the assumption that childhood education was solely the province of satire. While it may be true, then, that Augustine's parents, or Chrysostom's audience, laughed at the thought of childhood education, the invocations of laughter here are equally serving a distinct rhetorical purpose.

The uses of comedy and satire in earlier writers rely on the apparent persuasive effects of humor: Orbilius' jibe is placed in the context of a courtroom, emphasizing the grammarian's propensity to attack both verbally and physically, as well as illustrating his use of humor to win over his audience.[118] Similarly, Juvenal's placement of the schoolteacher's cane in his satirical scheme forms part of his attempt to persuade his audience both of his credentials for writing satire and of their interest in reading it. Cicero's letter to his "Catonian" friend Gallus uses the trope of schoolroom beating to persuade Gallus to keep writing in the same vein as he has done earlier. The humor here connected with grammatical education is in a protreptic vein, urging the invoked reader or hearer to take a certain course, or more precisely, to be won over to the humorist's course, which is identified as the same as the imagined audience's. Cicero claims that only he and Gallus write in their particular style, and that they must keep to it;[119] Orbilius uses humor to sway his courtroom audience; and Juvenal asserts that satire should be the common interest of writer and audience in the times in which they live.[120] The humor of the pedagogical situation here helps to create an identity of causes between the writer fashioned by the text and the reader whom that writer invokes.[121]

Much of this humor is based on the display of incongruities, especially the "descent" into the bodily in what presumably ought to be a nonphysical situation.[122] Hence Juvenal's cultural credentials are his physical beatings and Cicero's political situation is like the threat of a schoolroom beating. The same incongruity marks the situation in the late ancient texts, as Augustine's parents see their son beaten while on the path to a lofty career, and Chrysostom's audience laughs at the predicaments of children in comparison to adult civic life. Incongruity is exposed through the doubling of narrative,[123] with Augustine, Jerome, and Chrysostom all providing narratives of adult punishment and of children being beaten, and with Martianus Capella framing Grammar's speech as a narrative within a larger narrative frame. Amusement, then, like fear and boredom, offers a response to incongruities, partly by acknowledging them, and partly by asserting the primacy of the nonbodily narrative: beating and boredom are eclipsed by education as an ideal, as Augustine notes: "My beatings were laughed at by those who were older, even my parents, who wanted nothing bad to happen to me."[124] Augustine's parents, in laughing, deny that anything bad is happening in the overall scheme of the young Augustine's education.

The assumption of amusement, then, involves a prospective audience in the writers' project. By suggesting humor to their projected readers, earlier authors implicate those readers in the narrative flow as a resolution to incongruity. Humor in the late ancient texts under consideration marks imagined narrative solidarities. The trope of amusement provides an opportunity for an implied audience to witness the educated subjects' fear or boredom, to assume the narrative that this fear or boredom implies, and to move on. Augustine's adults who laugh at children place themselves in a larger narrative of adult progress,[125] and Jerome attempts to convince Rufinus that the story of his "Ciceronianism" is finished by convincing Rufinus to laugh at it. Chrysostom's laughter-inducing account is likewise situated in the larger hortatory address of his sermon. Where Martianus frames his entire work in the genre of satire, assuming his audience's amusement, however, it is notable that each of the patristic authors concedes that his invoked audience might not, or perhaps ought not, to laugh: Augustine finds adult laughter at childish unhappiness heartless;[126] Chrysostom urges his audience to take the upbringing of children seriously, despite its comic appearance;[127] and Jerome suspects Rufinus of being humorless.[128] This signaling of possible nonidentification with the author highlights the ultimately consolidating effect of laughter. If only Rufinus will laugh, he will have to yield to Jerome's argument that use of "pagan" texts is still possible for a Christian; Augustine's adults, in laughing, accede to the scheme of education in "pagan" literature that the later Augustine calls into question; and Chrysostom's audience, laughing at the "trifles" of his topic, are embedded in Chrysostom's narrative of the growth of children into "vainglorious" citizens like the ones he is addressing, however problematic that growth is.[129] Laughter marks agreement with a hypothetical narrative of development, although this narrative may be problematized by the writer.

Yet it would be wrong to conclude that this laughter implies only assent in the sense of intellectual agreement. On the contrary, laughter is no less disruptive for the persona of the laugher than beating is for the persona of the learner, and both involve a restructuring of disrupted elements along narrative lines. The simultaneously disruptive and containing force of humor in the social realm has been the topic of much literary and theoretical discussion,[130] but it is also disruptive and containing on the level of the subject.[131] The audience figures who laugh are being shown the incongruity between an ideal and a bodily situation and are also participating in the incongruity themselves; their laughing is both a physical and an intellectual act. They should be seen as complicit in the rearranging of incongruity into narrative unity. In the same way that Augustine's parents actively prefer the ideal narrative of education to the disruptive bodily moment of beating, the reader, in laughing, is interpellated as a participant in the unifying narrative that eclipses physical affect with the progression of idealized entities.[132] In this way, it is not merely the subject constituted inside the text that is reconfigured; the subject constituted outside the text is reconfigured as well.

The mapping of Christianity and paganism, the classical and the post-classical, onto the grammatical narrative reinforces the idea that they, too, belong to a particular historical progression in which the audience also participates. The reality of Christianity and paganism as entities makes them players in the writer's narrative. In the narratives of violence, the physical presence of paganism conflicts with the physical presence of Christianity, so that the supposedly Christian child is beaten by the supposedly pagan *magister*, or the "Ciceronian" Jerome is beaten on the orders of Christ. The conflict, however, recedes in the narrative sequencing, so that it becomes part of the older adult's past. Likewise in the case of boredom, the classical corpus of Grammar, which has its effect in physical boredom, becomes an element of the past, not needing to be repeated to those who demonstrate, by their boredom, that they have already assimilated it. Amusement at the incorporation of the classical or pagan into these sequences implicates the audience in the sequencing. Thus the classical, pagan world is part of the audience's past once the audience laughs — and the laughter of the audience is here assumed. The placement of Christianity and paganism into this sort of narrative occurs through the suggestion of emotion: fear or boredom help reify them as entities, creating physical affects and suggesting a narrative sequence for those affects, and amusement, circumscribing these emotions, places the implied reader within a larger sequence, moving on from the "pastness" of paganism into a postpagan, postclassical world. The participation of the audience in this narrative scheme occurs in the laughter called upon by the writer; laughter places the audience within a particular historical setting, after the classical age, along with the educated subject with whom the audience identifies. Laughter verifies the pastness of the past.

Conclusion: *De futuro sponsio est*

The audience's assent to the temporal sequence suggested in the narratives of fear and boredom creates a new dimension in the scheme, one of mobility between the historical moments that the narratives suggest. Up to the point of laughter, the educated subject has been the one in the text, subject to its temporal vagaries. The introduction of an audience to the temporal progression projects an educated subject outside the text, one who identifies with the subject inside the text but is not wholly constrained by the narrative controls (fear, beating, boredom) that the text introduces.[133] This subject (no less a rhetorical creation of the text than the subject inside it)[134] is placed within the historical progression in the apparent postclassical present: it is this subject who is addressed by the authorial voice of the text. Augustine's putative addressee is, ambitiously, God;[135] Chrysostom's is his congregation in Antioch;[136] Martianus addresses his son;[137] Jerome addresses Rufinus and Eustochium.[138] The rhetorical audience is not necessarily synonymous with any actual reader or hearer of the text. The readers whom these writers coerce into laughter may stand in for actual readers, but they are themselves products of the epistolary, confessional, homiletic, educational, or apologetic texts in which they figure.

These audience figures denote a universe outside the text, one that can, as it were, independently verify the postulates of the text, just as the force of laughter verifies the historical progression that the text's narratives project. The separation from the text that these figures create enables the author to assume a certain independence on their part from the immediate temporality of the pedagogical scene: the audience figures, while serving to verify that the historical progression is correct, are also endowed with a certain mobility with respect to that progression. They can view it from their position of separateness. Thus Augustine can invoke a "long view" of the process of schoolroom beating: "The many [students] who had gone before us in this way had laid out those difficult paths on which we too were forced to walk, increasing the toil and pain of the sons of Adam."[139] Jerome projects a future for the beaten subject, taking him to Jerome's present day: in letter 22 his dream ends with the admonition that the divine judge "will exact tortures" from Jerome if Jerome ever reads pagan literature again; in his *Apology Against Rufinus* Jerome avers that his promise not to do so was "about the future," that is, his present state.[140] Rufinus, the educated subject implied outside the text, ought, on this account, to be able to see the past as well as the past's future, leading up to the current state of Jerome's literacy.

The function of the projected audience, then, is to allow for a certain temporal flexibility with regard to the historical scheme suggested in the narratives of fear and boredom. The audience, an implied educated subject, able to identify with the educated subject in the text, is also able to identify with the multiple temporal aspects of that subject, construed by the emotional narratives as existing at particular points. Perhaps the most obvious example of this is Augustine's disquisition on God's existence over and outside all time; God, Augustine's audience, is able to move in and out of Augustine's narrative of time passing.[141] On a more human scale, Jerome imputes the same ability to Rufinus, in terms of his ability to recall a childhood literary education in his adult years.[142] The projected audience, in other words, is split into multiple aspects in much the same way as the subject within the text, but is able to negotiate those multiplicities by accounting for them as existing in a temporal continuum belonging to a subject separate from themselves. The multiple subject in the text, placed on a temporal continuum, becomes a resource from which the multiple educated subject outside the text can draw different temporal moments from a vantage point of separateness, while still supporting the narrative plan of the pastness of the classical. The projected educated audience lives in the textual subject's future, having (it is implied) lived through the fear and boredom that the subject in the text perpetually undergoes. Jerome's Rufinus can imagine Jerome's beating, having himself learned to read Cicero; Chrysostom's adult audience can watch the progress of Chrysostom's hypothetical child from birth to adulthood, narrated throughout the second half of Chrysostom's sermon. The futurity in which the audience is imagined to live retains the pastness of the classical and creates a separateness from that text that turns the multiple moments in the text into a past over which the projected educated subject can demonstrate mastery.

This temporal flexibility in the implied shared universe of the author and the author's addressee is ultimately what gives the narratives of grammatical education their continued productive capacity. The implied reader identifies with the subject in the text, thereby gaining the education suggested in the text, but is also present as an observer of that education, thereby enabled to move away from it into that education's future, the postclassical world. The implied reader can move between classical and postclassical, using images from both to make up the projected universe in which she and the author are understood to live. Chrysostom, for example, appeals to his audience's knowledge of non-Christian narratives in order to oppose them to Christian stories: the story of Cain and Abel takes the place of "old wives' tales: 'This youth kissed that maiden. The king's son and the younger daughter have done this.'"[143] Classical myth is here relegated to the background of cultural knowledge; it continues to exist but is overshadowed by biblical narrative. Jerome suggests that Rufinus' knowledge of Cicero is likewise in the background of Rufinus' Christian work: "Where did you get such a wealth of words, the light of sentences, the variety in your translations. . . . ? Unless I am mistaken, you have secretly read Cicero, and have gotten so educated that way."[144] Rufinus here is understood to move between classical and postclassical in the creation of his "present-day" works. The introduction of temporal sequence in narratives of fear and boredom thus has a hand in the creation of the cultural background of "late" antiquity, first by projecting both the abstractions of the classical and postclassical, and then by introducing mobility through time as a means for postclassical readers to negotiate movement between those abstractions.

The splitting of the reader into observer and observed, along with the reification of abstract cultural and religious entities, ultimately allows the educated subject both to enter into the reified abstract and to watch its progress from a privileged vantage point. Paganism or the classical, and even Christianity, become resources on which the educated subject can draw, manipulating them as their variously stable and unstable natures allow. Chrysostom, for example, can play with classical and biblical narratives, substituting one for the other in his account of childrearing: in the middle of the story of Cain and Abel, which provides the occasion for the imagining of schoolroom beating, Chrysostom interrupts himself with the words, "Is it not a far better thing to relate this than fairy tales about sheep with golden fleeces?"[145] Chrysostom, in his aside, reasserts his mastery over both abstracts, Christian and pagan storytelling, and reiterates the progression from one to the other as an observer. Similarly, Jerome can claim to have control over classical literary culture and to use it while still outside it: though he remembers them, "I can swear that, after leaving school, I have never read ['pagan' texts] at all."[146] The educated subject, integrated into the narrative of progression, can thus exploit her multiplicity without apparent contradiction: Jerome or Augustine can place the classical in his past while still making use of it as a split subject. The continued invocation of abstracts, implied in the repetition of beating or boring scenarios, gains the split subject increased subjective mobility: the possibility of exploiting multiple aspects of the educated self in a realm of idealized abstractions.

The exploitation made possible by this configuration of reified abstracts and split subjects, in fact, opens to the educated subject the possibility of a partial apotheosis, not only observing or manipulating the entities in question but also entering them as part of the narrative herself. Philology, having under gone her splitting, enters the divine realm and (invisibly) watches the pageant of the liberal arts unfold in the company of what are now her fellow deities. Augustine, beaten at school, nonetheless admits to his love for stories of the gods; motivated by reward and the fear of beating (*praemio laudis et dedecoris vel plagarum metu*), he is celebrated for rhetorically impersonating a goddess, Juno, entering the emotional realm of myth.[147] Chrysostom's child, fearing a beating, uses that fear to enter into the story of Cain and Abel, with biblical narratives taking the place of traditional myths; Jerome's beating in letter 22 occurs before a divine tribunal. All of these texts bring their subjects, and by implication their readers, into contact with divinity. Through the mundane physical processes of grammatical education, the educated subject is narrated toward a perhaps unexpected divine end. The implication of the educated subject into the narrative of abstract historical progression, in other words, gives her a place among the gods.

6

Grammar and Utopia

GRAMMATICAL IMAGINATION changed the landscape of the Roman Empire. Classicizing and Christianizing writings about grammarians and the uses of the *ars grammatica* located religious and cultural difference in Roman places through the language of space and geography.[1] As we have already seen, patristic writers' use of the trope of spoiling the Egyptians, and their configuration of pagan learning as foreign, imply a spatial removal of Christianity from the classical, although they do not exploit the language of space fully: they neither claim that certain geographical locations are more Christian or pagan than others nor suggest that Christian removal from the classical necessitates a literal removal from one place to another.[2] Instead, the use of spatial and geographical language to describe both educational and religious difference occurs more prominently in writings of a more personal nature, in descriptions of individual persons and places, and especially in letter writing, itself a genre with concrete connections to space and removal. These texts allow their writers to explore the spatial aspects of literary and religious difference through appeal to specific locations and through the conflation of literal locations with symbolic places.[3]

More specifically, spatial language in texts about grammar constructs space for the classical world, imagined through the practices of textual fragmentation and expansion, and at the same time creates space for its Christian counterpart. These spaces serve two purposes: first, they reinforce the idea that the classical and the Christian are real entities, occupying space in the literal Roman Empire; and, second, they suggest the existence of classical and Christian utopian space—that is, they create ideal places of purely classical or purely Christian signification that are entered through particular reading and writing practices.[4] Allusions to, and quotations of, traditional Roman literature and the Bible are unified into territories that particular readers and writers can then be seen to inhabit or not to inhabit.[5] The use of grammatical techniques, and of grammarians themselves, to project landscapes in which all things are classical or Christian is one of the fundamental ways in which ideologies of the classical and the Christian are produced and set in opposition.

This productivity is suggested partly by the status of the *artes* themselves as products of cross-territorial movements. Few of the grammarians who wrote the surviving *artes* were native to the cities in which they taught, or to the later centers of the empire: Priscian, a "Caesarean,"[6] made his name in Constantinople, as, probably, did Charisius, although it may not have been his native city.[7] Pompeius was North African, and Donatus, although most renowned for his teaching at Rome, may also have been from Africa.[8] Augustine's attempts to further his career by leaving North Africa for Rome and Milan are well known; Jerome's first educational period in Rome was presumably paid for by his family in Stridon, in Dalmatia; and Rufinus, his fellow student in Rome, arrived there from Aquileia. That so many figures central to the understanding of grammar in the fourth and fifth centuries pursued Latin grammatical studies through changes of territory is revealing. It suggests the practical extent to which grammar homogenized literary and linguistic culture in the later Roman Empire;[9] it also suggests the configuration of the empire as a linguistically delineated space.[10] There are thus two productive acts involved in the meeting of grammar and territory: the turning of imagined space into physical space, and the turning of physical space into imagined space. These acts are not contradictory but complementary.

The conversion of real territory into imagined space is especially visible in the presence of homogenizing grammar and grammarians in the less central parts of the empire, like North Africa. From the number of easily recognizable names in grammatical writing who are thought to have hailed from the southern rim of the Mediterranean (Donatus, Pompeius, Priscian, Augustine, Martianus Capella, Fulgentius the Mythographer), it is clear that North Africa possessed a rich Latin grammatical culture in the late ancient period, but Augustine's worry over his accent[11] also suggests the persistent marking of provincial Latin as undesirable. The erasure of provenance in the *artes*, however, and the literal movement of grammarians away from Africa make possible the entry of what might otherwise be seen as "African" (and hence not "Roman") into a united Latin cultural space. This sort of cultural elision contributes to the noncontradictory inclusion of a series of potentially "non-Roman" places in Roman territory. Priscian, leaving Mauretania for Constantinople, can become the arbiter of Latinity in a Greek-dominated imperial center.[12] Geographic origins are thus transformed into imagined cultural positions. At the same time, the ideal of *latinitas* is instantiated in physical territories.[13] The presence and continuity of Latin grammatical culture in North Africa adds physical space to the imagined presence of Latinity; that is, Latinity becomes not only an abstract temporal relation but also a geographic, spatial reality. This unity is created by grammatical mobility (mobility both of textual units and of grammarians), so that space becomes both the mechanism and the proof of linguistic homogenization. The end of this process is the imagination of a unified Latin culture as existing within a unified geographic space.

We can gain a fuller picture of the process by examining two conversations about the uses of grammar in space, conversations that occur outside the *artes* but are clearly linked to them. The three sets of texts that I will examine in this chapter are Ausonius' set of poems on his teachers and colleagues, the grammarians and rhetors who make up the *Professors of Bordeaux*; Ausonius' correspondence with his former pupil Paulinus of Nola, on the relative Christianness or paganness of reading and writing practices; and the surviving letters of Jerome to Paulinus of Nola, which offer his own services as Paulinus' new *grammaticus*. These works are representative of a type of educational writing very different from both the *ars grammatica* and Christianizing grammatical work. They are concerned with more specific circumstances and relationships in which grammatical practices are learned and exercised, and with the ways in which these circumstances lend themselves to the textual gestures of Christianizing and classicizing. Ausonius' *Professors of Bordeaux*, for example, both localizes grammatical learning in Bordeaux and positions Bordeaux within a network of classical spaces, movement within which is tied to the circulation of classical literary knowledge, and which constitutes a utopian classicizing of Roman territory. Ausonius' correspondence with Paulinus of Nola, on the other hand, demonstrates the conversion of classical space into Christian space through Paulinus' configuration of Nola and the Spanish countryside as Christian space littered with classical landmarks. Finally, Jerome's letters from Bethlehem to Paulinus take the idea of spatiality to its logical conclusion by defining the "art of scripture" (*ars scripturarum*), in contrast to the *ars grammatica*, as the use of both classical and Christian texts to explore a utopian Christian Holy Land. In each case, the line between actual geographic locations and symbolic sites of religious and educational affiliation is blurred through the writers' configuration of traditional grammatical reading practices as spatial practices, a blurring that allows the cultural distinctions attendant upon fourth- and fifth-century literacy to be imposed on the landscape of the Roman Empire itself.

Classical Space:
Ausonius and the Geography of the Classical

The trajectory of Ausonius' career from grammarian in Bordeaux to consul under Gratian in 379 has, in most Ausonian scholarship, been attributed to the cultural authority of literary education in late antiquity; indeed, Ausonius' career is often invoked as the prime example of the social effects that such authority could produce.[14] Beyond the facts of Ausonius' rise to power, however, his poetic works on the subject of education and educators promote an ideology of cultural distinction based upon the notion of "learnedness"—a notion derived in large part from the practice of decontextualizing classical literature in order to produce the classical. Briefly, Ausonius' writing involves the creation of space in which fragments of "the classics" can circulate in a system of exchange; that is, Ausonius, like all late ancient grammarians, promotes the dominance of the classical as a form of cultural currency, and does so through the fragmentation and dislocation of earlier literary texts. The space in which the classics circulate is marked as "classical": by using images of classical knowledge as his authorities, Ausonius both creates a classical past and locates its remains in the possession of the learned.[15] Ausonius thus reinforces the ethical claims of grammar, in that he uses it to create figures as "learned" and applies these ethical claims to physical locations as well.

One of the texts in which Ausonius most clearly performs these double gestures is the *Commemoratio Professorum Burdigalensium*, or *Professors of Bordeaux*, in which the classicization of conceptual space is worked out in terms of literal space as well. Bordeaux, as the seat of the *professores*, becomes the terrain through which the classical circulates, and over which it asserts its dominance. Written around 388,[16] the *Professors* is a set of poems that describe the lives and careers of thirteen rhetors and nineteen grammarians, all linked by both their academic standing and their connection to the city of Bordeaux. The prosopographical information that can be deduced from the poems has been used in several studies of the social status of rhetors and grammarians in the western empire,[17] but for the most part, arguments concerning the status of Ausonius and his colleagues have ignored the poems' symbolic social and cultural purpose. Recent work in late ancient poetics and aesthetics suggests that, rather than merely cataloguing the names and positions of his former teachers, Ausonius' poems are engaged in a culturally significant system of display.[18]

The pictorial aspect of Ausonius' poetry has received important critical attention,[19] and the *Professors* may be placed within the same system of pictorial poetics. S. Georgia Nugent notes that much Ausonius scholarship has praised the poet's "realism," "literalness," or "attention to detail," when it has praised his poetry at all. The *Professors* has been mined for its sociological and demographic information based on a similar understanding of the work as usefully detailed.[20] Yet, as Nugent points out, this literalness may be more the result of an uncritical reading of Ausonius' poetic technique than of any realistic intentions on Ausonius' part.[21] Whether or not the scholars whom Ausonius describes in the *Professors* really had the characteristics he assigns to them is perhaps not Ausonius' final concern. Instead, it may help to consider the *Professors* as promoting a personal and cultural agenda for which the images of educators are particularly useful.[22] Rather than merely depicting persons, Ausonius is interested in depicting *personae*, figures who are imagined through a fragmentary, classicizing poetics.

That the *Professors* is not concerned primarily with conveying information about the *professores* themselves is made most clear at *Professors* 12, Ausonius' very short tribute to Thalassus, the Latin grammarian: "Young Thalassus, I heard of your position and name when I was a little boy, but I hardly remember them. This later era speaks little about you—either about what sort of person you were, in body or in *mores*, or about what family you came from. Rumor used to have it that you became a grammarian as a young man, but this reputation was even then so small that now nothing of it is left. But whoever you were, because you lived as a learned man in my lifetime, have this as my gift. Farewell."[23] The reason for Thalassus' inclusion in the *Professors* is clearly not to give the reader information about his life. Thalassus is instead a notation of late ancient learning. He serves two purposes: first, to incarnate the grammatical profession in an individual persona, however vacuous, and, second, to contribute to the totality of Ausonius' list. Something similar may be said of the three Greek grammarians of *Professors* 8, Corinthus, Spercheus, and Menestheus. The reader learns only that they were *seduli* and that neither Corinthus nor Spercheus could teach Ausonius Greek. By Ausonius' own admission they are "little spoken of."[24] The amount of information given about them in the poem is effectively nil, but like Thalassus they are commemorated because they held educational positions and were known to Ausonius.[25] The picture projected by the *Professors*, then, is of learning itself, represented in the solely iconic existence of these four grammarians in Ausonius' text. In the same way that the decontextualization of literary fragments allows for the construction of strictly literary knowledge, the decontextualization of these historical figures, and their reconfiguration as ciphers, allows for the construction of learning as an independent category.[26] The four figures mark the space occupied by learning: they enlarge the body of professors at Bordeaux, without, according to Ausonius, doing much more; in good grammatical style, they also expand Ausonius' poems about the place Bordeaux, inserting additional markers of learnedness without offering substantial information about either the persons or the positions involved. These grammarians are there to demonstrate that learning takes up space.

Ausonius underlines this spatial aspect of learning by recording the geographical movements of his *professores* in and out of Bordeaux. Minervius the rhetor is said to have spent time in Constantinople and Rome before coming to Bordeaux;[27] Concordius the grammarian, "leaving his native country, changed it for a chair in another city."[28] "Ambition" motivated the grammarian Anastasius to move from Bordeaux to Poitiers,[29] while Citarius, the Greek grammarian, "born in a city of Sicily, came to us as a stranger."[30] Other grammarians and rhetors whose changed locations Ausonius mentions include Ausonius' own uncle Arborius, the rhetor Exsuperius, the grammarian Marcellus, the rhetor Sedatus, and the "subdoctor" Victorius.[31] The movement in and around Bordeaux parallels the movement by the authors of the surviving *artes* and reinforces the centrality of physical mobility in the profession of grammar; more important, the representation of movement allows grammar to be thought explicitly in terms of territory. This strongly geographical component of the work maps the textual space taken up by the *professores* onto the actual spaces of the empire. Rome, Constantinople, and Sicily here stand as points of origin, or destinations, for the practice of grammar. Ausonius thus conflates learning with spatial practice: in order to do the work of learning, grammarians and rhetors must establish themselves within particular places; or rather, within the particular construction of space defined here by connection to Ausonius and Bordeaux.[32]

The "learning" of the learned space invoked in the *Professors* is, moreover, defined primarily by facility with, or comparability to, earlier authors, or authors who, like the grammarians, themselves promote "classical" scholarship. Hence the Latin grammarian Crispus is said to have been able, when drinking, to write poetry on a par with Virgil or Horace;[33] the rhetor Staphylius is said to know all of Livy, Herodotus, and Varro, and to rival Probus in grammatical erudition.[34] Victorius, the subdoctor,[35] is described as having had a particularly arcane store of knowledge, knowing more about Numa, Castor, Draco, or Solon than he does about Virgil or

Cicero.[36] Although Ausonius' portraits are not uniformly flattering, the use of the classical as the accepted and immediately recognizable form of cultural currency not only reinforces the *professores'* status as learned, it marks the space occupied by the *professores* as dominated by the classical. Virgil and Horace here stand in for an implied body of authoritative texts, facility with which is a form of cultural wealth. Ausonius does not need to catalogue all of the learning of each of his subjects; by appealing to the classics in their shortened form, as "Virgil" or "Horace," the image of a classical totality can be evoked. The image of that totality can then fill the space opened up by the professorial icons with the cultural authority of classical texts.[37] In the same way that the separate images of the *professores* combine to create a portrait of learnedness, the fragments of pagan Roman and Greek literature are combined, as in more formal grammatical literature, to form a picture of the classics in which the *professores* themselves can be located.[38] The *professores*, as ethical figures, are conjured as existing within classical space that is homogeneous and accessible via nonlinear reading. The geographical variability of the *professores'* careers contributes, analogously, to the transformation of different places in and around the empire into the single space of classical knowledge. All text fragments can be instantiations of the classical that is the object of knowledge; all spaces can be, and are, spaces in which this knowledge is physically located.

References to earlier authors in the text thus serve as what Foucault calls heterotopias,[39] that is, really existing places or objects that can both project and contain an imagined "placeless place,"[40] either utopian, dystopian, or simply inverted, as the case may be—and for which Foucault's primary example is the mirror.[41] In the *Professors*, allusions to the texts, or even the names, of the authors of the traditional curriculum open the poems into a utopian space of learnedness. Individual texts and authors are specific, real, instantiations of, and mirrors into, what occurs in this more general classical space. As in the *artes grammaticae*, specific texts and text fragments are homogenized as markers of the same classical corpus, but here the corpus is broadened into a territory that is full of the classical—in that everything that exists in that territory exists there only through its relationship to classical texts—though the classical space in question is opened only through the fragmentary references to those texts.[42] The classical textual objects that make up the learnedness of the *Professors* thus, by projection, fill the places that Ausonius' grammarians occupy, and translate those places into an ideal region of the classical.[43]

The *Professors*, then, invokes a system in which classical heterotopic objects can create a commonality of territory. The professors are presented as existing in a space in which individual classical fragments are both a means of both securing status within that space and a means of defining the existence of the learned body as such. In other words, the professors as a physical and conceptual group inhabit the space created by the idea of the classical; literary learning both justifies their existence as learned men and exists as a real entity in the space that they, in turn, occupy. Here the listlike form of the *Professors* also comes into play. The list on the one hand creates a generic, despatialized space, "learning," of which the professors mark the totality. On the other hand, the entries in the list reinsert these figures into physical spaces, thus moving the imagined space into ideological conjunction with experienced geography.[44] This conjunction is marked by rhetorics of unity similar to the reifying language of *latinitas* in the *artes*. In line 3 of the preface, Ausonius describes the professors as linked together by "bookish studiousness" (*studium in libris*), and several of the poems construe the relationships between the professors and Ausonius as variously those of fellow student, former teacher, or professional colleague.[45] The relationships are established and maintained through the replication of classical knowledge. Likewise, Ausonius refers to the persons in such relationships as forming a "number," a "column," and a "cohort" (*numerus, agmen, cohors*),[46] a whole for which each individual rhetor or grammarian can stand. The existence of this *cohors* again suggests an imaginative space dominated by the economy of the classical; that is, a conceptual landscape in which the *cohors* can function as a collective unit whose purpose is to perpetuate the display of the classical objects that justify the existence of the landscape.[47] In short, the *Professors* creates a space of classical knowledge in which the learned, insofar as they are possessors of this knowledge, become the inhabitants of a self-sustaining classical utopia.

That the classical space created in the *Professors* is mapped onto the actual geography of the later empire, and exists in conjunction with it, is equally clear. The *Professors* is, after all, about Bordeaux, and about the role Bordeaux plays in the educational landscape of the empire. Ausonius' insistence on the importance of his *patria* is clear throughout the poems: lines 1–3 of the preface set on an equal level a shared literary and educational culture and a common connection with Bordeaux.[48] The imaginative space occupied by the professors is matched by their occupation of the same geographical space, either from birth in or around Bordeaux or from travel to it in search of educational employment. Bordeaux becomes a hub of learning in the *Professors*, as educators move through it to and from such other centers as Rome and Constantinople, Athens and Sicily, and the rather nearer educational establishments of Toulouse, Narbonne, Poitiers, and parts of Spain. While one of the effects of these geographical details is to raise Bordeaux to the status of a later Roman metropolis,[49] the listing of places in which classical knowledge circulates also broadens the territory under the projected cultural dominance of the classical. It recontextualizes classical fragments into a classical space. Bordeaux, Athens, and Rome, according to Ausonius, participate in the same cultural economy: the rhetor Alethius is described as Bordeaux's "exemplar in those letters which learned Greece tended at Athens, and which Rome tends throughout Latium."[50] Any actual historical, geographical, or cultural difference between the three regions is here flattened into the sameness of the classical culture that the *Professors* valorizes. In short, the empire is here being claimed for the classical, as the space within which the classical occurs.

This "shared imaginative landscape"[51] is both the arena in which and the means by which Ausonius creates a system of distinction between his classicizing *cohors* and the "unlearned." It is not, after all, merely their status as possessors of cultural capital that gives Ausonius' grammarians and rhetors their importance. The act of circulating that capital, and the classical space in which that circulation takes place, is equally important.[52] Ausonius links place and learning as the boundaries of his *cohors* in the introduction and conclusion to his poems: "I will now commemorate you, whom no family tie joins to me, but rather fame, reverence for our dear country, bookish studiousness, and the busy task of teaching";[53] "my pious task makes offerings to famous and learned men, while it commemorates the beauties of my extraordinary native land."[54] The professors here function both as markers and as distributors of "learning" within a space that is at once highly symbolic (the space of the classical) and literally mapped onto Bordeaux and its environs. Those outside this symbolic and literal system are simply ignored. In the *Professors*, it is not simple knowledge of the classics that confers authority on the professors; what creates the system of authority is the allotment of imagined space to the classics, and the linguistic exchange of classical objects.[55] The *Professors* does not simply document the social power of classical education in late antiquity; rather, it invokes a network of spatial markers for utopian learnedness (the professors and their positions), and a cultural landscape (the Roman Empire itself) in which the classical can be seen as authoritative.

The meeting of utopian "placeless place" and physical geography is akin to the meeting of timelessness as historical narrative in the *artes*, in that it redirects spatiality to project and incorporate a particular ethos. Here the ethos is a spatialized one, represented in exemplary form in the professors themselves, who both inhabit real spaces and establish an imagined one. By implication, however, the ethos of the reader is also invoked as a spatial entity. The shades (*manes*) of the professors are addressed in the preface and conclusion of the *Professors*,[56] and the poems are addressed throughout to their individual subjects, a technique that clearly aids in the conflation of reader and professor. The simultaneous address to reader and defunct grammarian (line 1 of the preface begins strongly, with *vos*) gives this list, too, an appeal to readerly activity. The reader is asked to locate himself or herself within an imagined space and at the same time acknowledge its ties to physical space; the collapse of the reader into the professor also implicates the reader in the production and incarnation of classical space, since the reader, by reading, becomes another physical site for the marking of classical territory.[57] As with the interruption of narrative, however, the spatial implications of reading can also be resisted and redirected, and it is to an instance of such redirection that I will now turn.

Paulinus and Spatial Convers(at)ion

The geography of the classical is again invoked in another set of Ausonius' works, this time in a more troubled portrait of the classical world and its boundaries. Ausonius' correspondence with his former student and protégé Paulinus of Nola reflects the ways in which the production of classical space could be reconfigured in an interlocutory situation, and be used to ends very different from those of the *Professors*. Little is definitely known about Paulinus' education under Ausonius the *grammaticus*, although both men later acknowledged Ausonius' status as Paulinus' literary "father" and kept up a poetic correspondence through the 380s and early 390s.[58] The last of these letters are deservedly famous for their vivid depiction of the end of the friendship, which Paulinus attributes to his increasing Christian devotion and to the unsuitability of Ausonius' literary teaching to the Christian life.[59] Ausonius' letters to Paulinus, especially in the final exchange between the two men in 393 and 394, use the language of common and uncommon spaces in producing classical landscapes in which Ausonius and Paulinus can converse; Paulinus' responses, on the other hand, reconfigure the commonality of interlocutory space in such a way that Christianity emerges as a competing cartography in Ausonius' and Paulinus' epistolary world.

Catherine Conybeare's study of the letters of Paulinus suggests that Paulinus' correspondence was a means for Paulinus to explore the construction of Christian identity as relational; more broadly, in antiquity the genre of letter writing was fundamentally an exercise in the creation of shared ideological space.[60] It was also a spatial practice in a highly concrete sense, in that letters were the occasion for, and the means of representing textually, the traversal of space within the empire. The exchange of letters created a commonality of both the separate spaces of the writer and the recipient, or recipients, and the space within which it was conceivable for letters to be exchanged.[61] The correspondence between Ausonius and Paulinus is of particular note, since it reveals the construction of shared space as well as the language in which the transition is made to unshared space, represented finally in the rupture of communication between the two writers.

Ausonius' letters presume a commonality of educatedness between himself and Paulinus, a commonality that forms the basis of communication in many of the ways anticipated by the *Professors*: Ausonius claims to be Paulinus' father in the same way that Minervius was Ausonius' "father,"[62] and the "cohort" and "column" of scholars in the *Professors* are recalled in references to the *collegia* of the Muses and the "yoke" (*iugum*) of literary endeavor that Ausonius claims Paulinus no longer wishes to shoulder.[63] These reifications of literary relations act like, and are based on, the concept of Latinity in the *artes*; here the concept is converted into an intersubjective and, because epistolary, spatial unification instead of a temporal relation. More fundamentally, the letters of Ausonius reveal the heterotopic state of classical knowledge, the image of which constructs classical space in the *Professors*. The first surviving letter in the correspondence thanks Paulinus for his gift of a verse epitome of Suetonius' now-lost *De regibus*, and reciprocates with excerpts from Paulinus' poem and a bit of mock epic based on Virgil and Seneca.[64] Paulinus' reduction of Suetonius "opens" into an imagined (or remembered) classical text; the humor of Ausonius' poems relies on Paulinus' familiarity with the specific larger works to which he refers, and it gestures toward the epic as a genre far more broadly. Like the quotations of earlier texts in the *artes*, these gestures of fragmentation are homogenizing, collapsing Suetonius, Virgil, Seneca, and Paulinus into a single, broadly classicizing category. Similarly, letter 19 acknowledges another classicizing poem Paulinus has sent for comment and criticism, positioning the poem to be opened into classical space, and then offers iambic verses in return, using mythological figures and personifications to encourage

Paulinus to continue the correspondence. These literary movements are also imposed on physical objects of exchange that traverse geographic space. Not only the letters themselves but, for example, even the fish sauce sent by Paulinus as an accompanying gift with his poem are converted into an occasion for the evocation of a classical world: "You know that I do not usually, nor indeed can I, use the word *muria*, which is commonly used, since the most learned of the ancients . . . did not have a Latin name for *garum*."[65] The transformation of objects exchanged into classical objects to be located in classical space occurs again in letter 20, in which Ausonius, using the stock characters of Terence and Plautus as his models, describes his former land manager Philo and asks Paulinus' permission to let the man stay briefly on Paulinus' estates—thereby converting these estates into a classical theater: "You'll see him himself . . . the picture of his type: grey, hairy, prickly, grim, commanding, like Terence's Phormio, with bristly, rough hair like a sea-urchin or like my lines of verse."[66] In these exchanges, the decontextualized fragments of classical knowledge serve, as in the *Professors*, to create a utopian "collectivity"[67] of the classical: the deft interchange of pieces of Suetonius, Virgil, Seneca, Terence, and Plautus, to name only some of the authors used, argues for a literary system in which the yoke of learnedness is again constructed out of the common, and homogeneous, authority of decontextualized ancient texts. It is both reified and made physical in the exchange of objects.

In letters 21 and 24, the common space of classical exchange is projected onto the geography of the empire, much like the mapping that occurs in the *Professors*. The issue at stake, for Ausonius, is Paulinus' sojourn in Spain and failure to correspond with his former teacher and patron. The ethical appeal of grammar is configured as appearing in a spatialized body. Ausonius compares Paulinus' silence to that of Virgil's silent city of Amyclae, to the silence of the Egyptian god Horus, and to the laconic Spartans.[68] He blames the interruption of the friendship finally on the landscape of Spain itself: although, he says, caves, cliffs, and mountains echo, and winds and stream murmur,[69] the Pyrenees and rural villages of Spain have struck Paulinus dumb, and have left him wandering like Bellerophon in the wilderness.[70] The same tactic is used in letter 24. Here Ausonius claims that the failure of friendship is more suited to Persia or Arabia than to sons of Romulus;[71] he complains that "Punic Barcelona"[72] has caused the problem, and that the Alps and the Pyrenees are to blame for Paulinus' silence.[73] Ausonius further suggests that moving to a region closer to Bordeaux would reintroduce Paulinus to the common bond of classical conversation,[74] and he ends with the hope that the friendship will be renewed by a literal visit.[75] In applying the conditions of friendship to the circumstances of geographical space, Ausonius appeals to the notion that the classical, the ground of his relationship with Paulinus, occurs within specific spatial limits, and that readers represent spatialized learning. The presence of classical knowledge within this space reinforces the image of the classical as the dominant cultural currency of that space. The spatial projection of the classical, as in the *Professors*, allows Ausonius and his readers to imagine a Roman Empire that is culturally homogeneous; that is, an empire that is, or was, classical.

Paulinus, however, interrupts the process of classicizing space, and in so doing endangers the cultural homogeneity of the classical empire. Notably, "Christianity" of any kind does not make overt appearance in Ausonius' letters as the cause of Paulinus' silence. Rather, Ausonius configures the separation as between "culture" and "barbarism." The system of distinction to which Ausonius appeals is that produced by literary education: Ausonius' classicizing letters are contrasted to Paulinus' utter silence. Paulinus, once a member of the Muses' *collegium*, is in danger of losing his status as part of that elite cohort. The space in which he moves is, by virtue of his silence, not within the bounds of classical knowledge.[76] The ethical implication, of course, is that Paulinus himself is also lapsing into barbarism—hence the references to the wanderings of Bellerophon.[77] Ausonius suggests that the geographical wilderness in which Paulinus has purportedly settled is matched by a mental, or at least verbal, wilderness, perpetuated by silence and the avoidance of human company.[78] The interplay of the verbal and the geographical here again underscores Ausonius' means of creating a classical Roman Empire by appeal to common literary usage, embodied in persons located in specific places. Paulinus' unresponsiveness indicates the dependence of the projection of classical space on repeated physical movement, like the dependence of Latinity on repeated temporal narratives. Ausonius' correspondence requires regularity of response for the projection of common space to continue. Paulinus' silence, on the other hand, is characterized as "wandering," that is, as unprogrammatic movement, which fails to sustain the image of stable unified space.[79]

It is traditional to explain Paulinus' reluctance to answer Ausonius' letters with reference to Paulinus' gradual conversion to ascetic Christianity and an associated rejection of his former public and literary pursuits.[80] In the extant conversation of Ausonius and Paulinus, however, the gradual nature of the narrative is collapsed, and the emergence of Christianity in the vacuum of the classical is simultaneous with the reestablishment of

the classical economy. Christianity, in other words, serves here as a locution of separation, at the same time as Paulinus relies on the perpetuation
of the classical as space to articulate Christianity's reification as an "absence"
of classical knowledge. This double articulation of the classical and of its
absence occurs at several points in *carmina* 10 and 11, Paulinus' only surviving letters to Ausonius. Both letters are entirely in verse, allowing Paulinus to demonstrate his facility with traditional meters and providing a
generic initial response to Ausonius' charges of barbarity. In addition to
the metrical form of the letters, Paulinus signals his classical affiliation at
several points, especially in the lengthy *carmen* 10, which takes up the classical exchange at the outset, opening in elegiac couplets with an allusion
to Virgil's *Georgics*.[81] Similar Virgilian allusions occur throughout the poem,
along with tags from Ovid, Horace, Statius, Juvenal, Persius, Catullus, and
Terence.[82] Paulinus rejects Ausonius' characterization of his wandering as
akin to Bellerophon's, and he exchanges Ausonius' Tanaquil for Lucretia as
an appropriate description of his wife Therasia.[83] Paulinus has here reen-
tered the classical arena, offering in return for Ausonius' pieces of classical
language some classical language of his own, "sending reciprocal words"
(*referens mutua verba*).[84]

Paulinus' verbal reentry into the classical is matched by a geographical one. Spain, he claims, is not the wasteland Ausonius makes it out to
be: Paulinus lives near "proud cities"[85] that are "outstanding in lands and
edifices."[86] Rather than lying beyond the boundaries of civilization, Spain
itself sets those boundaries, "placing the limits of her territory at the edge
of the world."[87] If Ausonius' Bordeaux is part of classical territory, argues
Paulinus, and Ausonius' estates "vie with the houses of Romulus,"[88] then
it is equally reasonable to say the same of Spain. Paulinus' letters accept,
on one level, Ausonius' use of classical space: by responding in kind to
Ausonius' classicizing letters, Paulinus both reestablishes the spatial projection of the classical from classical heterotopias and establishes his own
"place" as a learned figure within classical space. He further accedes to the
construction of a classical landscape in which classical language can exercise
cultural authority. The extension of this landscape beyond the Pyrenees to
Spain implicates Paulinus in the creation of a classical literary empire. Again,
the stabilization of this imagined space depends on repeated movements.
By "returning" classical language to Ausonius, as well as (and by means
of) returning physical letters to him, Paulinus participates in a regularized
linguistic proliferation. This proliferation, and its regularity, are responsible, first, for Paulinus' movement out of the "wilderness" and back into the

territory deemed classical and, second, for the reimagining of this space as a viable entity in which actors can move.

There remains, however, the question of separation. The restoration of friendly ties is not Paulinus' object in writing, although the restoration of classical space may be one of its effects. Paulinus instead addresses the gap that Ausonius' letters have implied, the discontinuity in the classical conversation. Where Ausonius letters complain of silence, however, Paulinus suggests, on the contrary, that the interstices of the classical have already been filled: in *carmen* 10, he chastises Ausonius for believing "evil rumors" and "gossip";[89] in *carmen* 11, he asks, pointedly, "With what gossip has rumor so easily invaded your ears?"[90] The answer is not a mystery, as 10.278–85 reveals: "If perhaps . . . you hear that I have dedicated my heart to holy God, following the venerable command of Christ with obedient belief . . . I do not think that this would so displease my revered parent that he would think it intellectual wandering to live for Christ as Christ decreed."[91] Christianity is here the incarnation of the interstitial: where Ausonius accuses Paulinus only of an unclassical silence, Paulinus embodies that silence in Christian piety.[92] Much of the middle section of *carmen* 10 is dominated by images of absences or emptinesses filled by Christianity: the Muses, having left, are replaced by "another power";[93] the "emptinesses" (*vanis*) of business and leisure are better occupied by the divine laws;[94] poets, philosophers, and rhetors leave the heart "empty" (*vanis*);[95] God "empties" (*exhaurit*) the mind of its previous diversions in exchange for "chaste pleasure";[96] and so on. To Ausonius' charge that Paulinus lacks *pietas*, Paulinus responds that he is cultivating Christian *pietas* instead.[97] Christianity here arises as the locution of absence, that which fills the gaps created by the interruption of classical conversation. Classical textual heterotopias now open onto spaces filled with Christian meaning.[98] Where Ausonius uses fragmentation to produce a classical landscape, Paulinus exploits the idea of interruption to produce the anticlassical as itself a relational object.[99]

Paulinus fills other empty spaces of classical geography with Christianity as well. In *carmen* 10, Paulinus describes Christian ascetics who "live in deserted places . . . free from empty concerns."[100] While Paulinus does not claim to be of their number, he does insist on his "absence" from his literal native land,[101] and on forgetfulness of his "native heaven," as the occasion for his becoming mindful of his spiritual *patria*.[102] For all Paulinus' defense of Spain against Ausonius' charges of barbarism, in *carmen* 10 Paulinus carefully configures his Christianity as arising apart from Ausonius and the environs of Gaul. His absence from normal interchange with Ausonius thus becomes a means of inserting Christianity into the geography of the otherwise classical empire. Classical space, predicated on the fragmentation of ancient texts, opens up gaps that can be reified as "Christianity."[103] So thorough is the filling of classical gaps with Christianity, Paulinus claims in *carmen* 11, that in the absence of the classical, all space is effectively Christian. The *iugum* of classical interchange, the commonality of classical space, is here denied: "You accuse me of having shaken off a yoke by which I was joined to you in learned activity; I say that I never bore it, for only the equal are yoked."[104] The commonality of learned endeavor is replaced by the "common father" (*communis pater*) under whom all are joined, wherever they may be.[105] Gaps in Christian space exist: Cicero and Virgil have not disappeared, but they, too, are "unyoked": "Tully and Maro could hardly bear the yoke equally with you."[106] On one level, of course, this is a complimentary conceit; at the same time, it leaves Ausonius stripped of his system of classical collegiality. Cicero and Virgil, Ausonius' classical heterotopias, have been set loose from the system of utopian unification. They are now the "gaps" in Paulinus' image of Christian space.

It is important to note the different uses to which Latin literary fragments could be put. While Jerome and Augustine use biblical texts in grammatical works to give substance to Christianity, Paulinus here uses non-Christian texts to similar, although not identical, effect. This involves the dissolution of one spatial unity and its replacement with another, one that functions as the inverse of the first.[107] The difference between Paulinus' task in *carmina* 10 and 11 and Jerome's task in his book of Hebrew names lies not in the technique of dislocation but in the technique of relocation: Paulinus establishes Christian territory with objects overtly marked as discontinuous with that territory; Jerome establishes Christian substance with objects that are marked as continuous with that substance. This is not altogether different from the different narratives, of continuity and discontinuity, that are produced in the ethical appeal of Latinity. That is, spatial markers, like lines of time, can be redirected. The fragments of the classical provide Paulinus with the means of making space Christian; they are not erased, but are converted into discrete interruptions of the Christian totality.[108]

The creation of Christian space in the gaps between the fragments of the classical, moreover, introduces a different system for signaling access to utopia: where Ausonius creates an elite *cohors* out of the fragments of classical knowledge, Paulinus creates instead an ideal fraternity of Christian piety distilled from the interstices of those fragments. The more nonclassical the piety, the greater the value Paulinus assigns to it: the ascetic Christians in the "wilderness" have the greater "glory."[109] While Paulinus is certainly not alone in valorizing ascetic endeavor in this period,[110] it is notable that he configures the distinction here as between "the classical" and the "Christian," rather than between competing versions of Christianity, and makes these the embodied categories that determine the end of his correspondence with Ausonius.[111] Ausonius' powerful image of classical utopia in his correspondence with Paulinus has forced Paulinus' hand. The nature of the exchange requires Paulinus to accept Ausonius' classicizing premises in order to answer at all. Overt engagement with the classical qua classical calls for a reiteration of the classicism of the fragments in use. Paulinus accedes to this but demonstrates the use of classical objects to define the anticlassical. Paulinus' system of differentiation, a response to the differentiation of the classical from the barbaric, revalues the barbaric while demonstrating how the articulation of Christianity as a new, discrete cultural entity remained dependent on the continued existence of classical knowledge, even as an "absence" or "emptiness."[112]

Paulinus' and Ausonius' articulations of classical and Christian space occur within the "commonplaces" of Latin literature, transforming the fragmentary reading practices of the art of grammar, and indeed the sometimes peripatetic profession of grammarian itself, into occasions for classicizing and Christianizing the literal places of empire. Ausonius, on the one hand, uses the space implied in classical exchange to mark literal places as classical (or not), where Paulinus uses the same spaces to mark the gaps in classical knowledge, and to convert those gaps into real Christian places. Both, however, retain the classical qua classical, using literary textual units to signify the classical as in the contemporary *artes grammaticae*. The conversion of the art itself is, as we will see, another matter.

Jerome's Spatialization of Christian Literacy

The use of spatial metaphors to mark the "Christianization" of the Roman Empire recurs in Paulinus' correspondence with another figure whose ambivalence about classical culture is well documented: Jerome, the Ciceronian of his own worst nightmares. Jerome's letters to Paulinus (letters 53, 58, and 85, written in 394, 395, and 399)[113] have been studied primarily with respect to two separate themes; first, fourth-century attitudes toward pilgrimage[114] and, second, Jerome's invocation of an *ars scripturarum*, intended to supersede non-Christian *artes* of all kinds.[115] The confluence of these themes in the letters is not accidental; rather, Jerome uses the language of travel and of geography to achieve an effect similar to that created in Ausonius' and Paulinus' writings. While still referring to non-Christian Latin texts, however, Jerome turns to the landscape of Palestine, both literally and figuratively, in order to create an imagined Christian landscape, visible again through the mediations of fragmented literature. Reading practices, for Jerome, make Christianity conceivable and allow both real and imagined "Holy Lands" to be understood as Christian. Jerome is effectively competing with Ausonius to be Paulinus' *grammaticus*, and he takes on the task by using grammatical techniques to create a Christian utopia out of biblical texts. The intermediary "place" in which the imagined Christian landscape appears is, then, the textual commentary, Jerome's Christian "art" par excellence.

Jerome first establishes Christian reading as a spatial practice through metaphors of travel. Letter 53 is framed by the language of relocation, as Jerome begins by comparing Paulinus' course of scriptural study to travel undertaken by famous learned figures of Christian and pagan antiquity: Plato traveled to Sicily; Pythagoras to Egypt; and Apollonius to India;[116] Paul traveled to Jerusalem to be taught by the apostles.[117] The close of the letter returns to this theme by entreating Paulinus to "cut, rather than untying, the rope of your ship, dallying at sea."[118] This may be, on the one hand, a literal invitation to Paulinus to travel to Palestine,[119] but it is also a conflation of literal travel with the task of learning. Paulinus is advised to "live in the midst of" his studies, whether in Palestine or not; this figurative "place" is the "small earthly dwelling of the heavenly kingdom."[120] Notably, Jerome includes in his introduction the example of a man who had come to Rome to listen to Livy, but who, "although he had come to such a great city, sought something beyond the city."[121] Here the idea of pilgrimage is not itself the attraction of travel; literary learning is. The act of learning is further configured as a technique, applicable to heterogeneous contents. The combination of Christian and non-Christian examples in Jerome's exhortation reveals the flexibility of these markers of education, which here come to be synonymous with the practice of travel, rather than with specific content. There is a commonality in the act of learning when it is seen as a practical mechanism itself, rather than as the product of mechanisms.

Relocation involves Paulinus in a different verbal economy: Jerome inserts scriptural texts into the system of epistolary exchange, insisting that these shared texts will create a similarly shared space between himself and Paulinus. Jerome flourishes the names of biblical books and characters throughout letters 53 and 58, establishing a system of scriptural literacy that functions in the same way as the classical; indeed, the supplanting of classical fragments with scriptural ones is explicit, for example at 53.8, where Jerome calls David "our Simonides, Pindar and Alcaeus, and our Horace, Catullus and Serenus."[122] The figure of David functions both as a conceptual unification and as a superimposition on earlier, non-Christian, literary texts. At 53.1, Jerome suggests that what brings Paulinus and himself together is "fear of God and study of the divine scriptures";[123] later he offers to be Paulinus' "companion" and to "try to learn with [Paulinus] whatever [he] might ask."[124] In the same way that shared classical texts place Ausonius and Paulinus in the same classical landscape, shared biblical texts place Jerome and Paulinus within the same symbolic geographical system. Study of the same texts necessitates a shared location. Again, the goal of study is a unified space; here, however, the supplanting of classical places with Christian unification suggests that the imagined "placeless" utopian spaces (the classical and the Christian) are in a significant sense the same. Part of the character of Christian space, in this configuration, is its status as a superimposition.[125]

If the act of learning is configured as relocation, the material to be learned is in turn construed as the space into which and through which the learner moves. At 53.5, Jerome uses the story of the Ethiopian eunuch to indicate these multiple levels of spatial practice: the eunuch's reading of Isaiah in his chariot first establishes the simultaneity of learning and travel, but his baptism in transit allows Jerome to configure the eunuch's true object as "Jesus, who was hidden, concealed in the text."[126] Thus, says Jerome, the eunuch "found more in the desert font of the church than in the gilded temple of the synagogue."[127] The ultimate goal of traveling study, in this anecdote, is the space enclosed in the book. Such spatial metaphors recur throughout letters 53 and 58: Paul, for example, is called a "repository" of the scriptures,[128] becoming himself a space to be entered through study; Jerome also invokes the example of Crates of Thebes, who divested himself of his wealth while en route to study in Athens.[129] Jerome offers to "lead [Paulinus], not through Aonian mountains and the heights of Helicon . . . but through Zion and Tabor and Sinai, and the high places of scripture."[130] Paulinus is to learn "by what path [he] should walk in the holy scriptures";[131] and Paulinus' eloquence in scriptural matters is likened to "ascending to the rooftops of Zion" to declare "what [he] has learned in the inner rooms."[132] The mechanics of learnedness are uniform, as evidenced by the references to Crates, Aonia, and Helicon, along with biblical sites, but the sites produced by scriptural reading are construed as different to the extent that they superimpose themselves: Helicon and Zion are both mountains, but with different literary fragments attached to them.

The prominence of spatial language in these letters lends itself to a reading that concentrates on their significance for Christian attitudes toward pilgrimage, and certainly other letters of Jerome have pilgrimage as their main concern.[133] I would argue, however, that letters 53 and 58 use the language of travel instead to posit conceptual spaces for the activity of "being Christian," where Christianity is marked as that which can be superimposed on classical space. In the same way that philosophy is attached to the real, but also symbolic, city of Athens,[134] Paulinus' study of scripture is mapped onto the real, but also symbolic, sites of Palestine. Scriptural places are, in fact, used in the letters in a way that creates a very different "Palestine" from the one in which Jerome himself was living at the time of the correspondence. Letter 53.8 lists place after place in its rehearsal of the contents of biblical books: both still-existing places and those much transformed, or gone, by Jerome's time are invoked with little differentiation. Egypt, Judah, Israel, Assyria, Ephraim, Canaan, Edom, and Nineveh are placed side by side in Jerome's account of the density of scripture. The juxtaposition of accounts from vastly different time periods and his listing of varied geographical areas without distinction of location or history are far different from most late ancient narratives of Holy Land pilgrimage,[135] and they serve instead, like other lists, to collapse the geography of the Bible into a single vividly imagined country, in which notable places and events exist side by side.[136] This imagined country—simultaneously Egypt, Israel, and Judah—then becomes the homogenizing site of that which Jerome claims is enclosed in such scriptural *topoi*, namely, Christianity itself, since "[Christ], hidden in a mystery, . . . was predestined and prefigured in the law and the prophets."[137] All of Jerome's places are markers of an essential sameness, since all of them "figure" an iconic "Christianity." Or perhaps more accurately, they signify an iconic "Christianicity,"[138] since it is the elusive quality of "being Christian" that is evoked, rather than any specific set of Christian teachings or practices. Christianity is reified, as in Paulinus, as that which occupies the space produced by reading. "Jesus, hidden in the text," is the substance of scriptural travel. This instantiation occurs through a combination of ethical invocation (the figure of Jesus) and geography (scriptural place names).

In order for Jerome to project this spatial Christianity adequately, he must separate it from the literal Holy Land, while at the same time maintaining its connection to scriptural locations. Christianity is clearly abstracted from fourth-century Palestine in letter 58, in which the literal and imagined places are linked but are not coterminous. Here, famously, although Jerome claims that he has not "followed the example of Abraham in vain, leaving his family and country,"[139] nonetheless, "what is praiseworthy is not to have been in Jerusalem, but to have lived rightly in Jerusalem."[140] That is, Christian virtue is embodied in actors who locate themselves in specific places, thus idealizing actual space in the way that Ausonius' *professores* do. At the same time, the ideal is actualized in the real space of Jerusalem. Jerome maintains, of course, that "in saying this, [he] is not inconsistently refuting [him]self,"[141] and it may be useful to take him at his word. If Jerome is not merely caught in an either/or dilemma on the usefulness of pilgrimage, he can use the slippage between the literal terrain of Palestine and the conceptual space opened for Christianity in scriptural reading in two ways. First, by tying the metaphorical space of scriptural study to actual places, Jerome can naturalize the idea that Christianity does, indeed, occupy space, that is, that the ideal Christian place is a real entity.[142] For example, when Jerome claims that Paulinus is scaling the heights of Sinai through his study, the use of an actual location in the metaphor lends concreteness to the otherwise amorphous entity "Christianity," hypostatized as that which imposes meaning on literal space. Second, as the site in which this naturalizing occurs, Palestine itself takes on the mark of being Christian, that is, of being a place whose Christianicity is palpable. Letter 58.3 thus dramatizes the contestation of space by noting the practice of non-Christian (and non-Jewish) cult in Roman Palestine prior to Constantine. Late fourth-century Christianity exists in the Holy Land as an imposition on Roman cult sites, themselves understood as an imposition on sites made meaningful by biblical referents. The marking of reality and the reality of the marking are both produced by movement in the gap between literal and conceptual space.

The concomitant Christianizing of space and spatializing of Christianity is also played out in letter 58 through Jerome's rhetoric of "wilderness," akin to that used by Paulinus in his correspondence with Ausonius.[143] Jerome advises Paulinus to live "in a small field . . . in solitude" and to "leave behind cities and their crowds."[144] The empty spaces here envisaged are themselves conflated with biblical wildernesses: Jerome appeals to the examples of Elijah and Elisha as precedents, and to the "sons of the prophets, who lived in wilderness and solitude."[145] This solitary existence will allow Paulinus to "pray alone on the mount with Jesus."[146] The trope of "wilderness" allows Jerome both to emphasize the unity of imagined Christian space with the space described in biblical texts and, at the same time, to distance this imagined space from the literal environs of Palestine, particularly from the urban center of fourth-century Jerusalem, which he describes as full of "soldiers, prostitutes, mimes, and idlers."[147]

The ultimate effect of the language of travel and geography in letters 53 and 58, then, is to create a Christian utopia—a hypothetical space imperfectly mirrored in the actually existing sites of fourth-century Palestine. Christianity is configured as a conceptual place in which all textual sites meet, its ontological reality implied through the reality of the literal places that Jerome uses to create it.[148] This reality is reinforced by Christianity's instantiation in the actors assumed to inhabit its territory. Paulinus is invited to become one of these spatial figures, constantly moving through the landscape through his reading practices and thereby fulfilling the functions of an actual pilgrim. The conceptual place, clearly not accessible to literal pilgrimage, becomes in turn the "essential cipher of all possible" Christianities, the cipher "of the purest idea of" Christianity,[149] since it is marked as essentially the same no matter where it is entered. In a sense, letters 53 and 58 are both attempts by Jerome to persuade Paulinus to travel to the Holy Land. It is not, however, the literal Holy Land to which Jerome invites Paulinus; rather, it is the imagined country of Christianity, or the utopia of Christianicity, by virtue of whose fantastic existence earthly regions can be imagined as Christian.

Travel to this Christian utopia, like travel in and around Ausonius' classical space, requires textual facility. Where Ausonius' professors travel by means of the *ars grammatica*, in Jerome's letters the primary instrument for the production of Christian territory is the "art of scripture" (*ars scripturarum*), the exposition of scriptural text. The main theme of Jerome's correspondence with Paulinus, other than traveling, is the idea of scriptural interpretation. The biblical text provides both the occasion and the means for imagining Christianity as a utopian space: as discussed above, the geographical places of biblical narrative can be used to create a larger imagined space for the occupation of an ideal Christianity. The biblical text, then, functions heterotopically, much like Ausonius' references to classical authors in the *Professors*. Jerome's theory of textual exposition in these letters uses scriptural passages as "mirrors" through which to view, and in which to posit, ideal Christian space.

The *ars scripturarum* of letter 53.7 is, famously, introduced through quotation of Horace's *Ars poetica*, and certainly Paulinus' Christianizing poetry can be read as one attempt to realize a Christian literary ideal.[150] Jerome's art of scripture, however, is far more closely related generically to the techniques of the *ars grammatica*.[151] Moreover, letters 53 and 58 both encourage a grammatical approach to scriptural reading and perform one in miniature as a means of opening entrances to Christian space. Where standard commentarial practice in antiquity isolated the line, line segment, or individual part of speech and surrounded it with linguistic, historical, or cultural meaning,[152] Jerome isolates the names of biblical books and figures and uses them as textual anchors for specifically Christian meaning, filling the gaps created by textual fragmentation with generalized accounts of Christian significance.[153] Exodus is full of "mysterious and divine teachings";[154] elements of Leviticus "breathe holy heavenly things";[155] Zephaniah "knows the secrets of the Lord";[156] and David "sounds out Christ in his lyre."[157] Jerome's scriptural art, like ancient grammatical work, breaks down a complete text in order to suffuse it with extratextual meaning. Or, as Jerome says, quoting Plautus, "Whoever wants to eat the nut breaks the shell."[158]

Despite its usefulness as a reading technique, the textual heterotopia presents Jerome with a serious problem. The uses and meanings of textual fragments are very difficult to control, and the contours of the projected utopia may be mapped very differently by different readers. Hence Jerome's scathing remarks on scriptural commentators who use the same technique but with different results: "I pass over those like me, who come to the holy scriptures after learning worldly letters . . . , who juxtapose otherwise incongruous passages in order to make up their own meanings, as if this were some great thing, and not the faultiest teaching method of all, to distort the meaning and to force the reluctant scriptures to their bidding."[159] This is, says Jerome, an attack on the art of scripture itself.[160] Jerome is not in this case simply being insensitive or self-aggrandizing: in order to ensure both the accessibility of the Christian utopia and its credibility as a real place with definite boundaries, the art of scripture must plan specific interpretive paths, rather than claiming that all ways lie open.[161] In other words, in order for Jerome to configure Christianity as a place at which one can arrive, he must also configure it as a place at which one can *not* arrive. The concept of scriptural art, a matter of technical proficiency, allows Jerome to take the necessary exclusionary measures, in the same way that traditional grammarians construed the grammatical art as exclusionary.[162]

Jerome claims, then, that his look-alikes are simply not well enough versed in the art of scripture to plot the correct routes to meaning. "They teach it," he complains, "before they have learned it."[163]

In contrast, Jerome argues, "it is not possible to enter into the holy scriptures without a guide to show you the path."[164] Jerome here reasserts his own cartographic skills for the mapping of Christian space, offering himself as Paulinus' companion on his scriptural journey.[165] The metaphor of path and guide occurs again at 58.8 and 9: "If only it were possible for me to lead such a genius, not through the Aonian mountains and the heights of Helicon, as the poets say, but through Zion and Tabor and Sinai, and the high places of scripture."[166] Paulinus must in turn "listen to what path [he] ought to follow in the holy scriptures."[167] Jerome is effectively plotting Paulinus' route, configuring Christian space as territory difficult to chart, and himself as the explorer able to chart it. The "wilderness" that Jerome recommends to Paulinus is thus susceptible to taming and, in effect, to Christian civilization, as Jerome claims that, with his guidance through Zion and Sinai, "there would be born to us something which is lacking even in learned Greece."[168]

Jerome's competitors, on the other hand, are castigated primarily for leaving this utopian space undeveloped and underexplored. In Jerome's sarcastic account of wrong reading practices, the literal accounts of scripture are not examined more closely, since "Genesis is perfectly obvious. . . . Exodus is clear. . . . Leviticus is easy."[169] Where Jerome's art consists in opening these texts to the scriptural traveler, and in showing readers the appropriate paths into the Bible, his competition, he claims, leave the scriptures essentially closed to advanced interpretation. Quoting Revelation 3.7, Jerome exclaims: "How many people there are today who, thinking they know letters, [hold in their hands] a sealed book; nor can they open it unless he unlocks it, the one who has the key of David, who opens and no one closes, and who closes and no one opens."[170] Entry into the interpretive spaces of Christianity here is simply blocked for those without the right guidance; ultimately, it is Jerome's professional reading practice that controls the "opening" and "closing" of scriptural paths. This emphasis on opening is part of the more general practice of multiplication and proliferation in grammatical reading, here understood in spatial terms, so that reading also becomes a claim to, and production of, new territory.

The emphasis on "opening" and "entering" and the technique of surrounding textual fragments with interpretive "space" may also explain one of the more notorious elements of letter 53, Jerome's condemnation of Christian *centones*, in particular, apparently, the *Cento* of Proba.[171] At first sight, the centonist practice of breaking down texts for use in new texts may seem like a practice that Jerome would approve: it is not unlike the breaking of texts in his own reading practice. It is, moreover, an attempt to "move" classical texts into a Christian setting. What the centonist does not do, however, is leave the text open for interpretive entry: the joining together of passages from Homer or Virgil effectively closes off interpretive space in favor of creating a new, unbroken, text, "forc[ing] the reluctant scriptures to do [the centonist's] bidding." Jerome dismisses this practice as "childish" and "a game";[172] like the schoolroom practice of composing speeches on epic themes,[173] writing *centones* is, for Jerome, not representative of an interpretive art. The later history of Proba's *Cento* as a schoolroom text reflects not the rightness of Jerome's dismissal but the fact that the fragments of Virgil put together in the *Cento* are themselves ripe for refragmentation and opening into pedagogical interpretive space.[174] Jerome, for whom this fragmentation is the essential artistic act, will not allow the re-formation of fragments into "whole" texts to replace the commentary that makes fragments visible.

Jerome's own quotations of classical authors leave texts in fragmentary form, opening, instead of closing, gaps in the text. These fragments can then become entrances into the interpretive space of Christian meaning, under the guidance of the professional reader. When Jerome quotes Horace to introduce the concept of a scriptural art, the apparent meaning of Horace's words ("learned or unlearned, all of us write poetry") remains within the bounds of the author function as Jerome defines it,[175] but the line also becomes an opportunity to reinterpret this art as a specifically Christian practice. The reinterpretation takes place in the lines surrounding the fragment; that is, in the gap created in Horace's text. The art of scripture, then, as practiced by Jerome, is fundamentally a reading technique, not coterminous with the reading of scripture per se but defined primarily by the opening of texts onto Christian space. Jerome's use of classical fragments is not unlike Paulinus', in that he insists upon the fragments themselves as "non-Christian" ("nor . . . can we call Virgil a Christian without Christ"),[176] while still using them to mark Christian space. At the same time, however, his conversion of the *ars grammatica* into an *ars scripturarum* allows him to claim that the Christian art now completes the task of classical reading: as a technique of reading and composing, the art of scripture perfects the Latin linguistic arts; or, as Jerome puts it, "if you had this foundation . . . nothing would be more beautiful, nothing more learned, nothing more Latin than your works."[177] Where for Paulinus the separation of Christian and classical remains fundamental, Jerome's confidence in the art of scripture brings even Latinity into the art's compass. Christian space can ultimately take over the spaces of the classical, while still preserving their original status as non-Christian.

Jerome's transformation of the *ars* in his spatial writing thus preserves the functions of the *ars grammatica* in its more technical form. In construing the scripture artist as a figure ethically comparable to the grammarian, and employing pedagogical rhetoric to invite Paulinus to participate in grammatical practice, Jerome also construes scriptural reading as a practice invoking a specific ethos in the same way the traditional *artes* do, with the difference that Jerome's *pietas* is defined as specifically Christian. This ethical interpellation is also understood in spatial terms, so that the practitioner works out the relational aspect of Latinity not through movement in time but through movement in space, from the exterior to the interior of the textual universe. The temporal relation found in the *artes* is also here played out in the contestation and heterogeneity of textual space. Jerome constructs the literal Holy Land as alternately pagan and Christian, and he further links literal space to textual space, so that the act of reading can be simultaneously productive of pagan textual objects and Christian imagined space. The transformation of the *ars* represents a dislocation, the productivity of which should not at this point be surprising. Decontextualizing and recontextualizing the *ars* as a practice allows Jerome and his readers to create a Christianity both imaginatively pure and superimposed on apparently pagan material. It also allows them a place in which to read.

Conclusion: Jerome, Ausonius, and Paulinus at the Limits

Perhaps inevitably, Jerome's Christian utopia comes into sharp contrast with his experiences of day-to-day life in Palestine.[178] Letter 58, of course, contrasts the pristine wilderness of scriptural text with the raucous urban scene at Jerusalem, but the open space of Christianity created in letters 53 and 58 is altogether closed in letter 85, the last extant record of communication between Jerome and Paulinus.[179] Whereas in letter 53 Jerome's enthusiastic mapping of Christian space caused him to "exceed the bounds of a [single] letter,"[180] in letter 85 Jerome excuses himself from writing by citing the burdens of nonscriptural work: the translating of Origen's *On First Principles*[181] and the writing of more pressing letters, he says, make it impossible to keep up a correspondence with Paulinus.[182] In contrast to the perfect Latinity Jerome promises Paulinus as a result of scriptural travel, Jerome here claims that his own Latin style is at the mercy of the shipping schedule between Palestine and Rome: "When it is time for ships to sail west, so many letters are asked of me that if I wanted to reply to them all individually I would never be able to do it. Hence it happens that I dictate whatever comes to my mouth, leaving aside the arrangement of the words and a writer's care."[183] It is a commonplace in ancient letter writing that the writer has had to compose in haste,[184] but it is precisely the blunt banality of the excuse that contrasts so strikingly with Jerome's earlier picture of a perfect style that would result from an imagined journey east. Letter 85's depiction of the circumstances of writing is anything but fantastic.

The abrupt closing of the scriptural frontier[185] highlights two of the logical difficulties with the configuration of study as travel: first, the fundamental otherness separating the traveler and the landscape[186] and, second, the resultant ambiguity as to the identity or affiliation of the traveler.[187] It is clear from Jerome's absence from the Christian utopia in letter 85 that he is not, as it were, a permanent resident there. He has had, he complains, to postpone writing his Daniel commentary in order to oblige Pammachius and other connections at Rome;[188] moreover, his cursory answers to Paulinus' scriptural questions appeal more to other biblical "guides" than to Jerome's own expertise. Origen and Tertullian should provide Paulinus with what he needs.[189] The harried and overburdened Jerome of letter 85 is decidedly not "living among" the scriptural texts that form the "dwelling of the heavenly kingdom on earth," as he had urged Paulinus to do five years earlier. He moves instead more fitfully in and out of his ideal realm of Christianicity, and this movement is reflected in his reading and writing practices: his style, he claims, is unpolished, and he is engaged with projects very different from the scriptural commentaries that form his art. The ethical component of movement here becomes complicated. Although movement stabilizes the utopian territory into and out of which the reader moves, it also construes the reader as a mobile unit whose identity is not fixed. Latinity cannot occur in Jerome's letter because of literal movements west, and because of the resultant conceptual movement outside the utopia by virtue of which Latinity exists.

More dangerously, Jerome's movement out of Christianicity occurs in letter 85 in relation to Jerome's reading of Origen. As I noted in chapter 4, Jerome's relationship to Origen was at times complex: Origen was his model but was also repudiated during the Origenist controversy; it is nonetheless noteworthy that Jerome's own acceptance of Origen is based on Origen's position vis-à-vis the art of scripture. On the one hand, Jerome is willing, even in the midst of the controversy over Origen's orthodoxy, to credit Origen as an authority in a matter of scriptural commentary, referring Paulinus to Origen's exegesis of Romans 9.16; on the other hand, in letter 85 at least, he glosses Origen's unorthodoxies not as wrong scriptural practice but as wrong "doctrine."[190] Origen the scripture artist is, according to Jerome, within the bounds of Christianicity; Origen the theologian is not.[191] Jerome thus configures his own Christianicity with respect to Origenism as firmly grounded within the practice of scriptural commentary. Jerome claims to be "safe" in using Origen's scriptural practices but must strenuously distance himself from Origenist "dogma": "Do not think that I disapprove of everything that Origen has written, like some rustic fool would do . . . ; I only reject his bad doctrine."[192] Here the alterity of the commentator from the textual spaces he opens is evident: the potential mobility of both Jerome and Origen into and out of Christian space is predicated on the reading practices that Jerome claims they are pursuing. "Being Christian," then, is a tenuous matter, depending as it does on the use of literary practices which themselves indicate the gap between the practitioner and the practice.

Ausonius' professors have a similar difficulty. They, too, frequently fail to live up to the ideal that Ausonius' classical world demands. Delphidius the rhetorician, according to Ausonius, would have had a distinguished career "if [he] had kept attending to the work of the Muses, in tranquil letters";[193] some "think that [Iucundus] did not deserve the title of grammarian";[194] the grammarian Ammonius, "light in learning and rough in manners, hence had the modest fame that he deserved."[195] These lapses indicate the unclassical status of the professors, despite their usefulness in peopling the classical landscape from time to time. Delphidius, by pursuing nonliterary activities, absents himself from the *studium in libris* that constitutes classical space. Ammonius does the same with his unpolished manners. These inhabitants of the classical can slip out of the landscape that they help create, like Jerome and Origen, by failing to be coterminous with their art. Utopia here takes on more ideological force than the practices, and the practitioners, that create it.[196] In the *Professors*, it is frequently the individuating details of the professors (e.g., Ammonius' rough manners) that indicate their absence from the classical unity.[197] Like maintaining Christian identity, maintaining membership in the *collegium* of the Muses is difficult for individual learned figures, although the idea of their collective presence is the mechanism by which the utopia becomes visible.[198]

Invocations of the classical and the Christian as discrete yet competing spaces have further contributed to the difficulties Ausonius' poems as literary works present to the modern reader. Although Ausonius himself attributes his spectacular political career to his facility in using classical objects,[199] and thereby projecting the classical, Ausonius in the *Professors* is nonetheless performing two not quite compatible tasks: he first establishes himself, along with his professional colleagues, as a possessor and user of classical objects, and hence as a member of the educated elite. On the other hand, by writing as the possessor of these objects, Ausonius excludes himself from the group of authors who can thereby be seen to make up the corpus of such objects. For the late ancient reader, Ausonius becomes a repository of cultural wealth; for the modern reader, at a further remove, he becomes, touchstonelike, the means by which the wealth of the "classical" can be recognized, but by the same token not classical himself. Again, in the process of individuation, Ausonius leaves the collective realm of the classical, and his poetry is, "all in all, a perfectly artificial poetry, made of allusions, of metrical tours de force, and, at times, unsuitable erudition . . . a poetry that is a veritable Harlequin's coat, for which each classical author has supplied a patch."[200] It is, notably, the overt appeal to classical knowledge that is most problematic: the bulk of Ausonius' poetry is too classicizing to be classical.[201]

Paulinus also comes under suspicion here: his work, despite its impulse toward Christian literary space, also re-creates the classical territory of Ausonius' literary system. As I noted earlier, by using classical references and forms in *carmina* 10 and 11 Paulinus, conjures the same conceptual spaces, even while valorizing a different cartographical system. Using the fragments of the classical as landmarks around which Christianity can coalesce implicates Paulinus in a hybrid landscape at the outset. Christianity as the articulation of classical gaps requires the simultaneous presence and absence of the classical. Hence Paulinus' poems are described by Witke as achieving a purely Christian style only "intermittently";[202] *carmina* 10 and 11 in particular tend to be seen as "paradoxical,"[203] "ill-adjusted,"[204] or simply transitional.[205] Paulinus' use of the classical to create a system in which Christianity emerges as distinct has blurred the outlines of his own work. Paulinus' poetry thus suffers in the aftermath of the distinction of the purely classical from the purely Christian. In answering Ausonius' letters, he commits to a version of classical space, but in condemning the classical he writes himself out of both classical and Christian maps (especially Christian maps as imagined by Jerome) at the same time. His poetry, using traditional forms, is characterized as "old-fashioned";[206] the incorporation of both classical themes and Christian subject matter is undertaken "not always with the happiest results";[207] and the sum is frequently "an unfortunate contrast between promise and achievement."[208] The landscape that Paulinus charts, dependent on the idea of the classical and the Christian as two separate and opposing categories, forces Paulinus himself into an intermediate position, since the quality of his work is tied to the religious purity of his literary gestures.

By using the language of travel and geography, Ausonius, Paulinus, and Jerome create an image of reading and literacy as the exploration of utopian spaces, Christian and classical, contained within the bounds of individual textual heterotopias—real sites in real books that serve as springboards into an imagined world of pure signification. Moreover, by appealing to the status of reading as an art, established through professional grammatical practice, all three authors can claim to dominate the spaces to be discovered within the text: Jerome by celebrating his new profession of scriptural commentator; Ausonius by describing his own meteoric career and the prestige of Bordeaux; and Paulinus by configuring his "conversion" as an aristocratic "retreat" into Christian territory. The difficulty with these images, however, is that they simultaneously imply the closeness of the reader to the meaning of the text and the great distance between the reader's and the text's "native countries."[209] Jerome can venture into Christian space through his commentarial art, but he cannot stay there. Paulinus and Ausonius are likewise relegated to stylistic or religious limbo. The use of textual fragments to create an opposition between imagined "territories" is thus a highly problematic venture. Suggesting, as they do, the existence of ideal worlds in which the Christian or the classical exists in a pure state, they banish their users to the indeterminate realms of real geography. Ausonius, writing from Bordeaux after his political career was over, and after the center of imperial power had moved from Trier to Milan, could not persuade his former pupil to visit; Paulinus, though about to embark on an illustrious period at Nola,[210] never went to Palestine, nor did he become the scripture artist Jerome urged him to be; and Jerome, forging a Christian Holy Land from Bethlehem, was left to discourage literal pilgrimage.[211]

In the works here discussed, the *ars grammatica* functions heterotopically, like the works of classical authors and the names of biblical books: it is not the art itself that is the focal point of these three authors but the spaces generated in and around the art. Ausonius uses the grammarians and rhetors of Bordeaux to suggest the classical world that ought to be their home; Paulinus valorizes his own distance from his former *grammaticus* by marking the space between them as Christian; and Jerome, in construing himself as the ideal Christian grammarian, creates the Christian version of that art, by which Christian space may be entered. Approaching, and appropriating, the grammarian's art here becomes an exercise in a kind of literary exploration—an exploration not of texts themselves but of what a text can enclose and an act of reading reveal. For theorist Louis Marin, "utopia is the book in which the book has been deconstructed by showing the processes that constituted it. It is, in a manner of speaking, the book of the book where the act of reading encounters its accomplishment and end."[212] To apply this very literally, Jerome, Paulinus, and Ausonius each project a utopia precisely by writing about the constitution of grammar, the foundation of the late ancient act of reading. Ausonius does so by displaying the unity of teachers of grammar, Paulinus by rejecting that unity, and Jerome by theorizing an art of grammar intended to compete with Ausonius'. The idea of grammar, then, is what makes a text bigger on the inside than it is on the outside,[213] by allowing the reader to enter between and beneath the words of a text, and by positing a space in which the reader, however temporarily, can find utopia.

Epilogue
Christianization and Narration

GRAMMARIANS DO NOT ALWAYS TELL STORIES, but grammar does allow stories to be told. In this book I have attempted to use grammatical literature as a starting point for understanding how individuals were formed in relation to large-scale cultural stories: not only narratives like that found in the *Aeneid* but also the narratives implied by the very act of reading the *Aeneid*. This exploration has ranged across a very broad swath of intellectual territory, from learning the alphabet to the benefits of pilgrimage to the apotheosis of Philology herself. I cannot claim that this coverage has been exhaustive, and I hope to have provoked questions about the effects of late ancient grammar more than I have offered answers. Throughout this discussion, however, one theme has been consistent: the use of fragmented and repeated linguistic objects to construct narratives of movement from one imagined time, place, or community to another. It is with the broader implications of this theme that I would like to close.

The conceptual basis of my reading of grammar and its effects in Latin late antiquity is the movement from nonnarrative deployments of words to their narrative deployments. Perhaps more accurately, it is the movement from narrative to nonnarrative and again to (reconfigured) narrative, from text to grammar to history. The transformative potential of grammar lies in its capacity to break down existing texts and to reassemble their constituent parts into larger narratives of historical progression—narratives that ultimately conjure readers as actors in the movement from past to present. As a means of conceptualizing late ancient religious difference, grammatical techniques also allowed for the articulation of a temporal break that could then be construed as a break between preexistent religious entities, whose derived subjects necessarily occupied different cultural, religious, and physical spaces. Grammar's significance as a practice thus lies in its contribution to subjective disassembly and reconstitution.

I would like to emphasize the link between narrative and historical progression especially in the case of what is now commonly known as the Christianization of the Roman Empire, or the rise of Christianity. Traditional accounts of this process have focused to a high degree on the idea of conversion, either by individuals or by groups, and with varying definitions of "conversion" as a process or event.[1] Yet these accounts for the most part also rely on notions of religious identity in which such identity is derived from relation to a preexisting entity, such as Christianity. As we have seen, however, such entities are in a constant state of narrative production and enactment, based upon the decontextualization of cultural objects and their reinsertion into new narratives. To the extent that "Christianity" can "rise," then, its rising is not the force of an abstract entity on material bodies and practices but the result of the potential of such bodies and practices to create new narrative possibilities. One of the practices with this potential was the practice of grammar, and Christianization was one of grammar's narrative possibilities. Christianization is not the same as an accumulation of individual conversions, nor is it the same as the demise of paganism;[2] it is the addition of a new narrative of identity to the field of narratives being produced in late antiquity.

To consider Christianization as the creation of a narrative possibility, however, is also to redefine the parameters of "being a Christian," for the conjuring of a subject called, say, "Augustine," into (and out of) a narrative at one moment does not in any way preclude the conjuring of a similar subject called "Augustine" into another narrative at another moment—or, indeed, at the same moment.[3] "Augustine" is not limited to either narrative interpellation, even if each narrative construes its "Augustine" as existing as such only within its own parameters. To return, briefly, to the ambiguous status of Marius Victorinus and Ausonius: the success of Christianization is often gauged by the criterion of exclusivity, on the assumption that one figure must have only one religious identity, even if that identity can at times change through the process of conversion. In Augustine's account, Marius Victorinus is not a Christian until he is baptized;[4] likewise, for Paulinus and many of his later readers Ausonius is, by virtue of his participation in classicizing linguistic acts, not fully a Christian.[5] Yet both Victorinus and Ausonius also claimed to be Christian: Victorinus to the apparent skepticism of Simplicianus, and Ausonius to the skepticism of many of his later readers. If Christianization is not seen as the absolute conformity by a unitary individual to a preexistent entity, however, but rather as the existence of a narrative possibility into which a subject can be, in particular performative moments, imaginatively inserted (and thereby, in and for those moments, constituted as a different subject), there is no reason to take Victorinus' or Ausonius' professions of Christianity at anything but face value. That is to say, they exist as Christians in moments at which they are inserted into the same narratives that produce Christianity itself. That they can also exist in classicizing narratives is equally clear. The difference between Christian and pagan, then, is not fundamentally a difference between one person and another but the difference between two narrative options that conjure subjects as characters in their divergent stories of historical progression.

The idea that Christianization is the imaginative production of narratives of identity, that it is nonexclusive, and that it is not the irreversible stance of unified actors, should also lead to a reconsideration of how we can speak of the Christianization of the Roman Empire as a historical event.[6] Following this definition of Christianization, the Christianization of the Roman Empire did not happen in any straightforward sense. Rather, the idea of Christianization has always been a contestable and contingent interpretive paradigm through which evidence of piety in late antiquity might, or might not, be approached. The later Roman Empire was Christian for some late ancient writers and readers at some specific narrative moments, and not at others. For some, or possibly for many, inhabitants of the empire, Christianization may never have occurred at any particular moment. We cannot, then, speak of Christianization as if it were a historical event open to the scrutiny of all, as if, ineluctably, it happened. Removing Christianization from the category of historical events and placing it within the category of contingent identifying narratives, however, does not mean that Christianization cannot be studied historically, for history is obviously no stranger to narrative. Generating contemporary historical narratives of Christianization, in this model, would mean asking questions rather different from those traditionally asked. Rather than asking how or why Augustine became Christian, we might ask at what points, and under what conditions, might late ancient readers or writers have recognized a narrative or text as having Christianizing effects? At what points, and for what reasons, would late ancient narrators take up a Christianizing narrative, or refuse to do so? What were the media of Christianizing or classicizing narratives, and how did these media shape the senders' or the receivers' recognition of Christianizing or classicizing effects? More fundamentally, how did late ancient narrators understand religious "selves" as multiple or situational products of narratives, or identities as contingent temporal artifacts? These are questions in the history and technology of the imagination, and they are certainly historical, if not easy to answer.

By approaching late ancient narratives of identity through one of the mechanisms that produced them, grammatical education, I hope to move the discussion of Christianization in the later Roman Empire away from models of conversion and affiliation. Instead, I think it is profitable to examine the conditions under which it made sense to literate people living in the later empire to speak of themselves as pious individuals at all, and to insert themselves into narratives—literary, theological, grammatical, and historical—that they understood to be descriptive or constitutive of themselves as subjects. It is in this insertion, or as de Certeau might have it, this insinuation,[7] that I see the intersection of literary culture with religion in this period, and in such intersections that I would like to locate the variable productions of religious and educated subjects. Grammar, of course, is not the only technology of the imagination to produce such effects. Yet to the extent that narratives and narrative fragments circulated alongside texts and textual fragments in late antiquity, it is not necessary to posit broad access to the *grammatici* to speak of the basic gestures of grammar as having wide-ranging effects.[8] On the contrary, grammar itself is merely an institutionalization and perpetuation of the two fundamental acts of fragmentation and repetition. When these two acts are performed on or around any narrative, the opportunity arises for the entry of the ideologically new, even if it enters under the guise of the old.[9] The apparent conservatism of late ancient grammar, which Marrou describes as its abandonment of a living language for one that is dead,[10] should therefore not lead us to dismiss the discipline as historically unimportant. The fact that late ancient grammar may sometimes seem out of date should rather serve as a reminder that, with respect to the establishment of our own modernity, too, late ancient grammar continues to accomplish its narrative task.

Notes

Chapter 1. Introduction

1. See, for example, the Homeric Oracles in the Greek magical papyri, *Papyri Graecae Magicae* (PGM 7.1–148), tr. in Hans Dieter Betz, *The Greek Magical Papyri in Translation*, vol. 1 (Chicago: University of Chicago Press, 1997). The *Historia Augusta* records the use of Virgil for divination (*Hadrian* 2 and *Alexander Severus* 14); for examples of early Christian text-based magic, see Marvin Meyer and Richard Smith, eds., *Ancient Christian Magic* (Princeton: Princeton University Press, 1999), ch. 2; see also the discussion in Pierre Courcelle, "L'Enfant et les sorts bibliques," *Vigiliae Christianae* 7 (1953): 194–220, and William Klingshirn, "Defining the *Sortes Sanctorum*: Gibbon, Du Cange, and Early Christian Lot Divination," *Journal of Early Christian Studies* 10 (2002): 77–130.

2. Tr. George Lamb, *A History of Education in Antiquity* (Madison: University of Wisconsin Press, 1956; from the third French edition of 1948), 277. See also Marrou's *St. Augustin et la fin de la culture antique*, 4th ed. (Paris: E. de Boccard, 1958), 13–17.

3. Seminal work has included that of Robert Kaster, *Guardians of Language: The Grammarian and Society in Late Antiquity* (Berkeley: University of California Press, 1988); Louis Holtz, *Donat et la tradition de l'enseignement grammatical* (Paris: CNRS, 1981); Vivien Law, "Late Latin Grammars in the Early Middle Ages: A Typological History," in *The History of Linguistics in the Classical Period*, ed. Daniel Taylor (Amsterdam: John Benjamins, 1987), 191–206; the collected materials in Mario De Nonno et al., eds., *Manuscripts and Tradition of Grammatical Texts from Antiquity to the Renaissance* (Cassino: Università degli Studi di Cassino, 2000); and Raffaella Cribiore, *Writing, Teachers, and Students in Greco-Roman Egypt* (Atlanta: Scholars Press, 1996).

4. As Kaster, *Guardians*, 12, notes: "The grammarian's instruction and the effects of the literary education are to modern eyes appalling. Indictments are common. The scope was intolerably narrow. . . . Within its own domain, moreover, the education was suffocating. Merely pedantic (it is said) where not superficial, it first choked the spirit of literature with its rules, then hid the body under a rigid formalism."

5. Suetonius, *De grammaticis et rhetoribus* 2.1. I use the text and translation of Robert Kaster, *Suetonius: De grammaticis et rhetoribus* (Oxford: Oxford University Press, 1995).

6. Kaster's analysis in *Guardians*, chs. 1, 4, and 5, is fundamental for understanding the notion of "guardianship" attached to literary practice in late antiquity; see also Kim Haines-Eitzen's similarly titled *Guardians of Letters: Literacy, Power,*

and the Transmitters of Early Christian Literature (Oxford: Oxford University Press, 2000). Here I am particularly interested not in the "defensive" stance of grammatical practice but in the productivity that such a stance implies.

7. *Inst.* 1.6.45.

8. 1.6.44.

9. E.g., at 1.2, in which Quintilian argues for the benefit of public, rather than private, schooling; or in the preface to book 5, in which he suggests that both of the traditional definitions of oratory demand that it be an interaction between speaker and audience; in 7.9.14–15, he appeals to common notions of nature and equity as the means of deciding the intent of ambiguous laws. This dismissal of popular usage was a general practice in ancient grammatical work; see the useful discussion by Catherine Atherton, "What Every Grammarian Knows?" *Classical Quarterly* 46 (1996): 239–60.

10. See especially Amy Richlin, "Gender and Rhetoric: Producing Manhood in the Schools," and William Dominik, "The Style Is the Man: Seneca, Tacitus and Quintilian's Canon," in Dominik, ed., *Roman Eloquence* (London: Routledge, 1996).

11. *Inst.* 1.1.1; a gender assignment that Jerome would later change, in his *ep.* 107.

12. *Inst.* 1.2.6–8.

13. *Inst.* 1.5.14.

14. *Inst.* 1.5.8.

15. *Inst.* 1.5.29: *vetus lex sermonis.*

16. *Inst.* 1.4–5.

17. *De gram.* 5, 6, 10, 11, 12, 13, 15, 16, 17, 18, 19, 20, 21, and 23.

18. *De gram.* 22.

19. *De gram.* 24.

20. *De gram.* 8 and 9.

21. E.g., the standard account in Stanley Bonner, *Education in Ancient Rome* (Berkeley: University of California Press, 1977), 58. See also the more detailed study by Johannes Christes, *Sklaven und Freigelassene als Grammatiker und Philologen im antiken Rom* (Wiesbaden: Steiner, 1979).

22. *De gram.* 23.1, tr. Kaster.

23. Kaster, *Guardians*, 55.

24. The trope of the socially climbing grammarian appears in Aulus Gellius and Ausonius as well: Kaster, *Guardians*, 57, 131–32; Kaster argues that the grammarians in Ausonius' circle did not owe their rise to their profession per se, though their presence in Ausonius' *Professors of Bordeaux* indicates a certain prestige in itself. Ausonius' configuration of the grammarians of Bordeaux will be considered at greater length in Chapter 6.

25. Tr. Roland G. Kent, *Varro: On the Latin Language*, Loeb Classical Library 333 (Cambridge, Mass.: Harvard University Press, 1967).

26. *Conf.* 1.13.

27. *Ep.* 22.30.

28. The standard edition of these texts continues to be that of Keil, *Grammatici Latini*, 7 vols. (Leipzig: Teubner, 1855–1880), though more recent critical editions of some texts have also been published.

29. E.g., in Giulio Lepschy, ed., *History of Linguistics*, vol. 2 (London: Longman, 1994); or Daniel Taylor, ed., *History of Linguistics in the Classical Period*; or R. H. Robins, *Ancient and Medieval Grammatical Theory in Europe* (London: G. Bell, 1951).

30. At, e.g., GL 1.313.13.

31. I rely on a reading of schooling as an ideologically productive process: Althusser, "Ideology and Ideological State Apparatuses," tr. Ben Brewster, in *Lenin and Philosophy* (New York: Monthly Review Press, 1971), 127–86, although the historical specificity of late ancient schooling is kept in consideration throughout.

32. Pierre Bourdieu and Jean-Claude Passeron, *Reproduction in Education, Society, and Culture*, tr. Richard Nice (London: Sage, 1990); and Bourdieu, *Language and Symbolic Power*, tr. Gino Raymond and Matthew Adamson, ed. John B. Thompson (Cambridge, Mass.: Harvard University Press, 1991).

33. Especially Butler, *Gender Trouble*, 2nd ed. (London: Routledge, 1999), and *Excitable Speech* (London: Routledge, 1997).

34. Most fundamentally, Deleuze and Félix Guattari, *Anti-Oedipus*, tr. Robert Hurley et al. (Minneapolis: University of Minnesota Press, 1983); Deleuze, *Masochism: An Interpretation of Coldness and Cruelty*, tr. Jean McNeil (New York: Zone Books, 1991); Deleuze and Claire Parnet, *Dialogues*, tr. Hugh Tomlinson and Barbara Habberjam (New York: Columbia University Press, 1987); and Brian Massumi, *A User's Guide to Capitalism and Schizophrenia* (Cambridge, Mass.: MIT Press, 1992).

35. Marin, *Utopics: Spatial Play*, tr. Robert A. Vollrath (Atlantic Highlands, N.J.: Humanities Press, 1984).

36. See, e.g., Peter Brown, *Power and Persuasion in Late Antiquity* (Madison: University of Wisconsin Press, 1992), ch. 2.

37. Marrou, *History of Education*, 277–80; but see also his "Retractatio," part B, in *St. Augustin*, in which Marrou deals more fully with the question of "decadence" in late antique literary culture.

Chapter 2. Imagining Classics

1. The great exception to this is Henri-Irénée Marrou's consideration of grammar in the thought of Augustine in *St. Augustin et la fin de la culture antique*, 4th ed. (Paris: E. de Boccard, 1958). Marrou claims (15–16) that Augustine's thought remained primarily grammatical throughout his career. For the most part, however, analysis of grammar's influence on reading is richer in discussions of later periods: e.g., Martine Irvine, *The Making of Textual Culture: Grammatica and Literary Theory, 350–1100* (Cambridge: Cambridge University Press, 1994); Suzanne Reynolds, *Medieval Reading: Grammar, Rhetoric, and the Classical Text* (Cambridge: Cambridge University Press, 1996). More technical studies of grammatical literature and reading are common: on the role of grammarians in preserving earlier texts see, e.g., James E. G. Zetzel, *Latin Textual Criticism in Antiquity* (New York: Arno, 1981), esp. part 2, on grammarians as textual critics; Mario De Nonno, "Le citazioni dei grammatici," in *Lo Spazio Letterario di Roma Antica*, vol. 3: *La ricezione*

del testo, ed. Guglielmo Cavallo et al. (Rome: Salerno, 1990), 597–646; see also Rita Lizzi, "La memoria selettiva," 647–76, in the same volume. For a general introduction to the place of the Latin *artes* in the history of linguistics, see Peter Matthews, "Greek and Latin Linguistics," in *History of Linguistics*, vol. 2: *Classical and Medieval Linguistics*, ed. Giulio Lepschy (London: Longman, 1994), esp. sections 1.5 and 1.6; and Ineke Sluiter, *Ancient Grammar in Context* (Amsterdam: John Benjamins, 1990); more detailed studies of individual grammarians include Karl Barwick, *Remmius Palaemon und die römische Ars grammatica*, Philologus Supplementband 15, no. 2 (Leipzig: Dieter'sche Verlags-Buchhandlung, 1922); Louis Holtz, *Donat et la tradition de l'enseignement grammatical* (Paris: CNRS, 1981); Dirk Schenkeveld, *A Rhetorical Grammar* (Leiden: Brill, 2004); Anneli Luhtala, *Grammar and Philosophy in Late Antiquity: A Study of Priscian's Sources* (Amsterdam: John Benjamins, 2005).

2. On the social effects of grammatical training, see Robert Kaster, *Guardians of Language: The Grammarian and Society in Late Antiquity* (Berkeley: University of California Press, 1988), ch. 1; see also Peter Brown, *Power and Persuasion in Late Antiquity* (Madison: University of Wisconsin Press, 1992), ch. 2. The fundamental theoretical analysis of the relation between education and social recognition remains Pierre Bourdieu and Jean-Claude Passeron, *Reproduction in Education, Society, and Culture*, tr. Richard Nice (London: Sage, 1990; reprint of 1977 edition). Cf. Bourdieu, "The Production and Reproduction of Legitimate Language," and "Authorized Language: The Social Conditions for the Effectiveness of Ritual Discourse," in *Language and Symbolic Power*, tr. Gino Raymond and Matthew Adamson, ed. John B. Thompson (Cambridge, Mass.: Harvard University Press, 1994), 43–65 and 107–16. Benedict Anderson, *Imagined Communities* (London: Verso, 1991), 67–82, discusses the technologies of language circulation and distribution. Both Kaster and Anderson focus primarily on the social ramifications of unified language, rather than on its social production.

3. My debt to Paul Ricoeur, *Time and Narrative*, vol. 1, tr. Kathleen McLaughlin and David Pellauer (Chicago: University of Chicago Press, 1984), will be obvious throughout the chapter.

4. Vivien Law, drawing on Karl Barwick, has offered a helpful typology of grammatical writing, grouping together works that conform to a template for the *ars grammatica* proper, which analyzes each part of speech, as opposed to grammatical works that focus on individual parts of speech or elements of language: Law, "Late Latin Grammars in the Early Middle Ages: A Typological History," in *The History of Linguistics in the Classical Period*, ed. Daniel Taylor (Amsterdam: John Benjamins, 1987), 191–206, referring to Barwick, *Remmius Palaemon*, 89–90. The major surviving works in the former category, by Charisius, Donatus, Cledonius, Consentius, Probus, Diomedes, and Priscian, and including Servius' and Pompeius' commentaries on Donatus, form the basis of the discussion here. Law revisits the structure of the *ars grammatica* in two later essays, "The Mnemonic Structure of Ancient Grammatical Doctrine," in *Ancient Grammar: Content and Context*, ed. Pierre Swiggers and Alfonse Wouters (Leuven: Peeters, 1996), 37–52, and "Memory and the Structure of Grammars in Antiquity and the Middle Ages," in *Manuscripts and Tradition of Grammatical Texts from Antiquity to the Renaissance*, ed.

Mario De Nonno et al. (Cassino: Università degli Studi di Cassino, 2000), 9–57. Law, "Late Latin Grammars," 193–94, notes the newness of the genre of commentary on Donatus, unlike previous commentary on traditional literary texts. Since it is, however, "an offshoot of the *Schulgrammatik*" (194), I include it here. I am also constrained in part by the contours of Heinrich Keil, *Grammatici Latini*, 7 vols. (Leipzig: Teubner, 1855–1880), still the standard edition for most late ancient grammars. I use Keil's edition (abbreviated as GL) for all grammarians but Charisius, whom I cite by page and line number in Karl Barwick's Teubner edition, corrected by F. Kühnert (Leipzig: Teubner, 1964).

5. At the same time, it must be remembered that similarities are not spontaneous. Barwick's thorough reconstruction of textual dependence in the *artes* (*Remmius Palaemon*, part 1), may be "unduly complex," as Schenkeveld (*Rhetorical Grammar*, 20) suggests in his discussion of Barwick on Charisius, and may overattribute material to earlier sources (Schenkeveld, *Rhetorical Grammar*, 20–27), but it is undoubtedly true that grammarians were aware of, and deeply influenced by, their predecessors' work.

6. The technology of literary interruption is considered by George Landow, *Hypertext 2.0: The Convergence of Contemporary Critical Theory and Technology* (Baltimore: Johns Hopkins University Press, 1997); the productivity of interruption is posited by Roland Barthes, *S/Z*, tr. Richard Miller (New York: Hill & Wang, 1974). Barthes sets out some particularly germane principles of interruption at 12–16; a more radical insistence on this productivity is found in Gilles Deleuze, "On the Superiority of Anglo-American Literature," in *Dialogues*, with Claire Parnet, tr. Hugh Tomlinson and Barbara Habberjam (New York: Columbia University Press, 1987), 51–54; see also Vittorio Marchetti's interview with Deleuze and Félix Guattari, "Capitalism and Schizophrenia," tr. Jarred Becker, in Guattari, *Chaosophy*, ed. Sylvère Lotringer (New York: Semiotext(e), 1995), 76: "To desire consists of this: to make cuts. . . . And it was necessary to recognize production as being within desire itself."

7. To a certain extent the perception of words is implied in the history of punctuation and the physicality of book production. Jocelyn Penny Small attempts a reconstruction of how the physical realia of literacy may have shaped reading in antiquity in the somewhat impressionistic *Wax Tablets of the Mind: Cognitive Studies of Memory and Literacy in Classical Antiquity* (London: Routledge, 1997); Paul Saenger approaches the same topic for a later period in *Space Between Words: The Origins of Silent Reading* (Stanford: Stanford University Press, 1997); more technical, and less ambitious, is E. O. Wingo, *Latin Punctuation in the Classical Age* (The Hague: Mouton, 1972).

8. Sidonius Apollinaris, *ep.* 5.2.1, quoted also in Kaster, *Guardians*, 19.

9. GL 4.367–72.

10. For analysis of parallels in these sections between Donatus, (some of) Consentius, Charisius, Dositheus, and Diomedes, see Barwick, *Remmius Palaemon*, 3–52; Barwick, part 2, despite its admittedly speculative reconstructive nature, is still fundamental for the influence of Remmius Palaemon on later grammarians, although Barwick may claim too much for Palaemon's direct influence; cf. Schenkeveld, *Rhetorical Grammar*, 22–24. Barwick's concluding summary (215–68), interestingly, plays down Dionysius Thrax's influence on later Roman work.

11. GL 4.51.15–16: "But as for syllables, since this is no small topic, I will treat it elsewhere properly, together with meter." Another treatise on syllables has been conjectured to be by Probus: GL 4.219–64; but see Keil at GL 4.xxxi.

12. GL 4.75–76.

13. Barwick/Charisius, 233.2–3.

14. Barwick/Charisius, 234.22ff.

15. GL 1.322.6–10.

16. GL 3.461.15–22; Marrou, *A History of Education in Antiquity*, tr. George Lamb, 3rd ed. (Madison: University of Wisconsin Press, 1956), 279, quotes this passage, and describes it as an example of the "finicky and irritating" nature of grammatical education.

17. One assumes, for example, that rhetorical exercises in retelling narratives involved less attention to an original text; Augustine's prize-winning declamation (*Conf.* 1.17.27) on the rage of Juno, while obviously based on the *Aeneid*, does not seem to have involved detailed analysis of any one part of it. If the wide-ranging nature of the elder Seneca's *Controversiae* and *Suasoriae* can be trusted, students of rhetoric could embroider a given narrative very freely.

18. On the question-and-answer format, see Manfred Glück, "Priscians Partitiones und ihre Stellung in der Spätantiken Schule," *Spudasmata* 12 (1967): 25–29, who discusses both the format and its use outside grammatical literature. Horace, *Ars poetica* 326–30, famously describes a similar classroom scene, a question-and-answer arithmetic lesson; Teresa Morgan, *Literate Education in the Hellenistic and Roman World* (Cambridge: Cambridge University Press, 1998), 80, briefly describes "catechisms" of literary information.

19. *Inst. Or.* 1.1.25.

20. *Inst. Or.* 1.1.30; cf. Probus, *Catholica* 1 (GL 4.31.4), who includes the following comment on the syllable "xas": *xas: nullum repperi nomen hac syllaba terminatum*.

21. Raffaella Cribiore, *Writing, Teachers, and Students in Greco-Roman Egypt* (Atlanta: Scholars Press, 1996), 37–42, discusses the material evidence for this in Roman Egypt.

22. Cribiore, *Writing*, 131–37 and 148–52, argues that learning to write may have preceded learning to read (beyond the recognition of individual letters), and that the sequence of letters, syllables, texts in reading may have been changed to letters, texts, syllables in writing.

23. Quintilian, *Inst. Or.* 1.1.36 recommends using excerpts from poetry; Morgan, *Literate Education*, 100–119, considers the evidence of school papyri that quote Homer in the form of line fragments and lists of words or names; notably, the preponderance of quotations are from the early parts of the *Iliad*, suggesting a greater cultural currency for some "tag lines" than for others. Cribiore, *Writing*, 43–47, places the copying of maxims and quotations in the sequence of education between making word lists and copying long passages.

24. The discussion in Kaster, *Guardians*, 169–97, on the negotiation of *auctoritas* in Servius' Virgil commentary is fundamental to any treatment of this issue; cf. also his "Servius and *idonei auctores*," *American Journal of Philology* 99 (1978): 181–209, which responds to P. Wessner, "Lucan, Statius und Juvenal bei den römischen

Grammatikern," *Philologische Wochenschrift* 49 (1929): 296–303 and 328–35; Kaster's earlier discussion of the different levels of *auctoritas* in various authors will be discussed further below. For a theoretical analysis of the process of "authorization," see Bourdieu, "Production and Reproduction of Legitimate Language," 57–61; and more recently, Bourdieu, "Field of Power, Literary Field, and Habitus" and "Principles for a Sociology of Cultural Works," both tr. Claud du Verlie, in *The Field of Cultural Production*, ed. Randal Johnson (New York: Columbia University Press, 1993), 161–75 and 176–91.

25. Bourdieu, *Reproduction*, 26–27 and 38–39. At 38: "P[edagogic] W[ork] produces the legitimacy of the product and, inseparably from this, the legitimate need for this produce qua legitimate product, by producing the legitimate consumer."

26. See Kaster, *Guardians*, 174–79, on Servius "stand[ing] watch over *auctoritas* and *usus*" (178).

27. This imperative is used throughout the text, e.g. at GL 3.461.22, 469.20–21, 474.24, 478.14, and so on.

28. The voice of the grammarian as it appears in grammatical texts is easy to conflate with the "actual" grammarian, especially in a format like that of the *Partitiones*, but also in cases in which the dominant voice of the text seems markedly different from other such voices: e.g., in Pompeius' commentary on Donatus. Kaster, *Guardians*, 153, describes Pompeius (quite fairly) as "prolix." It is worth remembering, however, that the projection of the authorial figure is in most cases an effect of the *ars* itself, whenever there is no outside evidence for the grammarian. Thus for the reader of the *ars*, the status of the grammarian cannot be assumed *a priori*.

29. GL 3.465.37–466.10.

30. See Glück, *Priscians Partitiones*, 31–46, on the evidence for earlier Greek *epimerismoi*, in the tradition of which he places Priscian. Servius' Virgil commentary is similarly expansive, if not to the same degree as Priscian's, and the remnants of Tiberius Claudius Donatus' Virgil suggest a similar interest in drawing out grammatical and historical information. It is difficult (and possibly undesirable) to read ancient commentary without reference to Derrida's "chain of supplements" (*Of Grammatology*, tr. Gayatri Chakravorty Spivak, corrected edition [Baltimore: Johns Hopkins University Press, 1997], 152–57), in which the supplement "holds [the absent presence] at a distance and masters it" (155).

31. There are later examples: "Sergius" at one point even attributes a maxim to Symmachus (GL 4.488.31–32). There are, of course, far fewer quotations of later authors like Juvenal, Statius, and Lucan than there are of Virgil, and it is occasionally difficult to gauge how "quotable" these authors are. See De Nonno, "Citazioni," 643–46; and Kaster, "Servius and *idonei auctores*," on the shifting rhetorical uses of classifying certain authors as "more" or "less" authoritative in any given instance.

32. De Nonno, "Citazioni," 626–46, argues, in support of Law's generic division of grammars into *regulae* and *Schulgrammatik*, that quotation practices are to a great extent dependent on genre. The *regulae* type of grammar (focusing on individual parts of speech, or on figures or meter) uses far more exemplary quotations than the simpler *Schulgrammatik* (which covers all the parts of speech). It is certainly true that, for example, Donatus' *Ars Minor*, a classic *Schulgrammatik*, contains

very few quotations of exemplary texts, and that quotations abound in sections on the virtues and vices of speech, which De Nonno considers a conflation of the *regulae* and *Schulgrammatik* genres. On the basis of that conflation, though, I would argue that the generic divisions governing quotation may not be as firm as De Nonno suggests.

33. GL 5.136.3–25.

34. GL 2.268.7–269.24.

35. Kaster, "Servius and *idonei auctores*," 197–99; also Anne Uhl, *Servius als Sprachlehrer* (Göttingen: Vandenhoeck & Ruprecht, 1998), 220–24, on the different *auctoritates* in Servius, and their links to specific authors.

36. Kaster, "Servius and *idonei auctores*," 199–201; Raija Vainio, *Latinitas and Barbarisms According to the Roman Grammarians* (Turku: Painosalama Oy, 1999), 74–81, suggests two long-term reasons for the introduction of new examples: the use of new texts in schools, and linguistic evolution, so that formerly unexemplary texts become examples, particularly of error. I would add, however, that the symbolic function of quotation is not merely reflective but also productive of literary authority, as the conservatism of quotation practices (which Vainio notes at 62–65) indicates.

37. Kaster, *Guardians*, 175, suggests the useful idea of the linguistic "buffer zone," to indicate the dubious status of quoted texts that are authoritative but not imitable. De Nonno, "Citazioni," 628, also helpfully insists on the distinction between "lexical" and "paradigmatic" examples. As examples, however, both kinds of quotations possess a similar symbolic authority.

38. Cf. De Nonno, "Citazioni," 632–33.

39. GL 4.392.5–6.

40. GL 4.395.28–29.

41. Solecism, too, is to be avoided, although "in poetry, [solecism] is called a figure." GL 4.394.22–24.

42. Cf. Bourdieu, "Price Formation and the Anticipation of Profits," in *Language and Symbolic Power*, 76–85, on the use of "superfluous" language to mark bourgeois discourse. While Bourdieu is more concerned about basic conversational techniques, the use of superfluous or archaic language as a marker of "educated" discursive style is easily transposable to grammatical theory.

43. Discussed in Kaster, "Servius and *idonei auctores*," 197, following Wessner, "Lucan," 331.

44. For such shifts in meaning, see Barthes, "The Imagination of the Sign," in *Critical Essays*, tr. Richard Howard (Evanston: Northwestern University Press, 1972), 205–11; also Landow, *Hypertext*, 36–42, on the productivity of movement for the individual lexia.

45. Vainio, *Latinitas*, 62–65; De Nonno, 633, refers to repeatedly used exempla as "fossilized."

46. Quoted at Barwick/Charisius, 370.26; GL 3.492.25 (Priscian); GL 4.398.21 (Donatus).

47. Impersonal: GL 1.399.6 (Diomedes); 3.231.15 (Priscian); length: GL 5.106.20 (Pompeius); accusative: GL 4.390.26 (Donatus).

48. See Bourdieu, "Price Formation," 66: "Utterances . . . are also *signs of*

wealth, intended to be evaluated and appreciated, and *signs of authority*, intended to be believed and obeyed." Italics in original.

49. Barthes, "Imagination of the Sign," 209; Deleuze, "Anglo-American Literature," 36–39, on both the productivity of deterritorialization and its potential for reasserting static systems.

50. GL 1.441.1–443.4.

51. Landow, *Hypertext*, 49–89, "Reconfiguring the Text," provides a useful overview of some of the processes and ramifications of contemporary technologies of nonlinear reading.

52. GL 2.285.13–287.17.

53. De Nonno, "Citazioni," 643–44, attributes Priscian's expansiveness to his reliance on the earlier grammarian Caper, also an advocate of quotation, and to Priscian's incorporation of *regulae* characteristics into an *ars grammatica*.

54. Landow, *Hypertext*, 89, argues that nonlinear reading via hypertext "has a built-in bias against 'hypostatization,'" but he neglects, I think, to acknowledge the capacity of nonlinear organizations to be transposed into new linearities.

55. He is illustrating the uses of the noun: GL 5.136.3–25.

56. GL 5.76.11–77.9.

57. Nor are there signs in the grammarians' works that these texts are imagined to be already differentiated in the students' understanding; Augustine, in a comment that suggests the opposite, complains that "immoral" passages from Terence are used to teach basic vocabulary (*Conf*. 1.16.26). In other words, the fragmentary passages serve as the introductions to earlier works. It is certainly the case that any of Donatus', Priscian's, or Pompeius' "actual" readers would likely already be familiar with the texts, but in the idealized classroom that the grammarians' work conjures, that familiarity cannot be assumed. Cf. also Kaster, 206 at n. 29.

58. The unifying function of *auctoritas* is very briefly noted by Uhl, *Servius*, 231–32.

59. GL 1.439.16. Charisius (Barwick/Charisius 62.14–15) has the same criteria. Quintilian lists slightly different criteria: *ratio, vetustas, auctoritas,* and *consuetudo*. Vainio, *Latinitas*, 53–59, argues that for Quintilian the difference between *vetustas* and *auctoritas* lies in the difference between the meaning and form of words: *vetustas* refers to words that are, in meaning, archaic, while *auctoritas* refers to the use of archaic or archaizing forms of common words. Uhl, *Servius*, 27–32, seems to take Quintilian's criteria as the paradigm for late ancient grammar and defines *vetustas* more simply as the characteristic of words whose authority is based on their antiquity, with *auctoritas* as the characteristic of words whose authority is derived from attribution to a particular literary figure. Uhl's definition is more straightforward than Vainio's, but it leaves the distinction between the two criteria less clear in practice: if an "ancient" word is attributed to an author, say, Accius, it is difficult to tell which criteria it falls under. This does not mean that Uhl does not get closer to Quintilian's meaning than Vainio; the distinction may have been unclear in antiquity as well. Since, as Vainio (50) notes, the *artes* attributed to Augustine and Marius Victorinus use three of Quintilian's criteria but leave out *vetustas*, the confusion seems not to be new.

60. GL 1.439.28–29: *opinio secundum veterum lectionum*. At 29–30, he adds, "nor would they [the *veteres*] know how to explain it, if you asked them."

61. Barwick/Charisius, 63.6–7.

62. GL 5.161.22–25.

63. Cledonius: GL 5.45.7; 48.12; 48.25; 71.23; Consentius: GL 5.387.15; Servius: GL 4.435.31; see Kaster, *Guardians*, 174–96, and Uhl, *Servius*, 220–24, on Servius' construction of *auctoritas* in his Virgil commentaries.

64. GL 4.386.2–3; 388.25–26.

65. On the political uses and ramifications of creating a Roman literary tradition, see Thomas Habinek, *The Politics of Latin Literature* (Princeton: Princeton University Press, 1998), esp. ch. 2, "The Invention of Latin Literature"; the imagination of the Roman literary past in late antiquity is insightfully discussed in Charles Hedrick Jr., *History and Silence* (Austin: University of Texas Press, 2000), esp. chs. 3 and 7. More generally on the constructed nature of such unities, see Eric Hobsbawm's introduction, "Inventing Traditions," in *The Invention of Tradition*, ed. Eric Hobsbawm and Terence Ranger (Cambridge: Cambridge University Press, 1983); and Anderson, *Imagined Communities*, esp. ch. 11, "Memory and Forgetting."

66. E.g. GL 1.308.3, 406.33 (Diomedes); 2.82.10 (Priscian); cf. Uhl, *Servius*, 220–21.

67. Cf. Vainio's discussion of *auctoritas* and *vetustas* in Quintilian; on the overlap between *auctoritas* and *antiquitas* in Servius, see Uhl, *Servius*, 421–31. See also Habinek, *Politics*, 53–54, on the notion he finds in "writers as diverse as Cicero, Horace, Livy, Vergil, Seneca, and Tacitus" (54) that "not only preservation of tradition as a means of acculturation is one function of literature but that it is a function for which literature, or the literate man, is uniquely qualified."

68. The quotation thus functions much like Susan Stewart's "souvenir" in *On Longing: Narratives of the Miniature, the Gigantic, the Souvenir, the Collection* (Durham, N.C.: Duke University Press, 1993), 135: "We do not need or desire souvenirs of events that are repeatable. Rather we need and desire souvenirs of events that are reportable, events whose materiality has escaped us, events that thereby exist only through the invention of narrative." The linguistic event is here invoked through its attribution to a generic past. On early modern antiquarian uses of text fragments, see Marjorie Swann, *Curiosities and Texts: The Culture of Collecting in Early Modern England* (Philadelphia: University of Pennsylvania Press, 2001), ch. 4, "The Author as Collector"; and Peter Beal, "Notions in Garrison: The Seventeenth-Century Commonplace Book," in *New Ways of Looking at Old Texts*, ed. W. Speed Hill (Binghamton, N.Y.: Renaissance English Text Society, 1993), 131–47.

69. It is worth remembering here that Ricoeur locates Augustine's account of temporality precisely in the grammatical activities of repeating poems and measuring syllables: *Time and Narrative*, 19–22.

70. Stewart, *On Longing*, 135: "[The souvenir's] scandal is its removal from its 'natural' location." Cf. also Michel de Certeau, *The Writing of History*, tr. Tom Conley (New York: Columbia University Press, 1988), 72–73.

71. Stewart, *On Longing*, 151, thus differentiates the individual souvenir from the collection: "Whereas the souvenir lends authenticity to the past, the past lends authenticity to the collection." See also Krzysztof Pomian, *Collectors and Curiosities: Paris and Venice, 1500–1800*, tr. Elizabeth Wiles-Porter (Cambridge: Polity Press,

1990), 26–34, on the isolation of "meaningfulness" in archaic objects as a means of evoking an "invisible" past.

72. Pompeius and Servius, in their commentaries on Donatus, are the grammarians who seem to use *maiores* proportionately the most: e.g., at GL 5.98.20, 108.7, 110.6, 7, 141.11, 142.17, 172.24 (Pompeius); GL 4.409.17, 417.37, 419.27, 422.17, 422.35, 435.7, 441.25, 443.7 (Servius).

73. GL 4.391.14–15.

74. GL 4.363.4, 379.1, 379.14.

75. Plautus and Pacuvius: Barwick/Charisius 84.1–2; Terence, Lucilius, and Virgil: 123.17–124.3; Cicero and Lucilius: 139.22–24; Terence and Ennius: 257.3–8, following the lead of the grammarian Acron; Titinius, Terence, and Plautus: 276.21–28. Catullus is an ambiguous case: at 330.11–16, Charisius says *senesco autem nunc in usu est frequens, apud antiquos tamen et seneo dicebatur; unde et Catullus sic rettulit: "nunc recondita / senet quiete seque dedicat tibi, / <gemelle Castor et> gemelle Castoris." Unde et Catullus* could simply indicate that Catullus is archaizing.

76. Sallust and Terence: Barwick/Charisius 20.14–17; Varro: 83.24–25; Propertius and Virgil: 85.7–19; Ennius: 91.14–18; Terence and Plautus: 100.4–7; Cato and Pacuvius: 115.27–31; Lucretius: 116.7–8; Lucilius and Aemilius Macer: 127.28–128.6; Ennius and Accius: 376.12–20.

77. *Veteres*: e.g., at Barwick/Charisius 28.29–30; 48.5–7; 148.23–29; et passim; *antiquos*: 297.22; 325.8; 330.12.

78. At Barwick/Charisius 16.22–27: *Dicunt quidam veteres . . . item adhuc morem esse poetis . . . ut "aulai medio" Vergilius, "terrai frugiferai" Ennius in annalibus.*

79. See de Certeau, *Writing*, 42, on the rhetorical gestures that produce Barthes' "reality effect": "They seem to tell of facts, while, in effect, they express meanings which moreover refer what is *noted* (what historians hold to be relevant) to a conception of *whatever is notable*. The *signified* of historical discourse is made from ideological or imaginary structures; but they are affected by a referent outside of the discourse that is inaccessible in itself." Italics in original. Or at 120: "The vindication of facts indeed therefore 'illustrates' a doctrine, but a doctrine which is invisible and of which no more is given than the 'examples'—the 'facts.'"

80. R. B. Lloyd, "Republican Authors in Servius and the Scholia Danielis," *Harvard Studies in Classical Philology* 65 (1961): 291–341; Kaster, *Guardians*, 169–71; Uhl, *Servius*, 247–69. On *antiqui, veteres*, and *maiores*, see Uhl, *Servius*, 419–21.

81. Virgil: GL 4.409.17–20; Horace: 4.414.40–415.1; Juvenal and Cicero: *Comm. in Aen.* 6.612; Lucretius: *Comm. in Aen.* 12.87; Sallust: *Comm. in georg.* 1.208; Cato and Cicero: *Comm. in georg.* 2.412.

82. Cato and Terence: *Comm. in Aen.* 1.573; Cato and Juvenal: *Comm. in Aen.* 1.726; Pacuvius and Ennius: *Comm. in Aen.* 4.9; Plautus: *Comm. in Aen.* 4.301; Lucilius and Plautus: *Comm. in Aen.* 6.90; Livy, Sisenna, and Cato: *Comm. in Aen.* 11.316.

83. Virgil, Lucan, Statius: *Comm. in Aen.* praef.; Terence: *Comm. in Aen.* 1.657; Sallust: *Comm. in Aen.* 2.61; Ennius: *Comm. in Aen.* 2.355; Juvenal: *Comm. in Aen.* 2.445; Lucilius: *Comm. in Aen.* 3.119; Plautus: *Comm. in Aen.* 4.608; Calvus, Pacuvius, and Virgil: *Comm. in Aen.* 11.169; Titinius: *Comm. in Aen.* 11.457; Cicero: *Comm. in Aen.* 11.708; Coelius: *Comm. in georg.* 2.345.

84. For Servius' use of the terms *neoterici* (for poets after Virgil) and *recentes*, see Kaster, "Servius and *idonei auctores*"; and Zetzel, *Latin Textual Criticism*, 49–50.

85. Contra Kaster, *Guardians*, 180: "[Virgil's] words simply reflect the usage current *apud maiores*, of whom he is one."

86. *Comm. in buc.* 5.5: *secutus tam veterem quam nostram consuetudinem* . . . , *cum alibi secutus tantum antiquos*.

87. *Comm. in Aen.* 9.641: *quod autem "esto" non addidit, ab antiquitate descivit; nam veteres "macte esto" dicebant*.

88. See Kaster, *Guardians*, 180; also Uhl, *Servius*, 420–21, who notes that Virgil is the author most cited under the headings of *antiqui, veteres*, and *maiores*.

89. Cf. de Certeau, *Writing*, 35–49, on the work of history as a "labor of differentiation" (36). At 45: "Historical discourse makes a social identity explicit, not so much in the way it is 'given' or held as stable, as in the ways it is *differentiated* from a former period or another society." Italics in original.

90. Neither uses *maiores* with any specific earlier author. *Veteres* in Diomedes: Terence: GL 1.316.12–16; Cicero: 330.22–24; Sallust: 333.30–33 (he is said to be following Plautus, 333.33–36); Plautus and Naevius: 343.11–13; Plautus, Gnaeus Mattius, Caecilius, Laberius: 345.4–14; Virgil: 350.34–37; Cato and Virgil: 362.21–24; Plautus and Lucilius: 365.4–9; Ennius and Pomponius: 373.3–8; Virgil, Livy, and Cicero: 374.6–12; Naevius and Plautus: 380.15–20; M. Brutus, Claudius, and Caecilius: 383.7–14; Caesar, Naevius, Pacuvius, Ennius, Varro, and Plautus: 400.15–401.7. *Antiqui* in Diomedes: Catullus (cited, for the same reasons, and with the same passage, as in Charisius, *unde et Catullus*): GL 1.344.6–10; Sallust, Cato, and Seneca: 366.10–14; Terence and Virgil: 380.1–6; Sallust and Cicero: 399.20–26. *Veteres* in Priscian, *Institutiones*: Horace: GL 2.52.15–17 (who, however, is cited as *iunior* at 302.6–12); Varro, Marsus, and Novius: 168.15–169.1; Plautus: 205.23–206.6; Cicero, Cato, and Plautus: 226.8–15; Pacuvius and Accius: 254.6–11; Martial, Ovid, Cato: 257.10–18; Ennius: 259.5–8; Titinius, Afranius, Cato, Plautus, Licinius, Caelius, M. Cato, Caesar: 266.2–24; Accius, Cato, Cinna: 268.16–269.1; Virgil, Cicero, and Lucretius: 284.20–285.11; Virgil and Juvenal: 8–20; Sallust, Virgil, and Ovid: 366.9–18; Lucilius, Cassius, Varro, Lucius Caesar, Virgil, Cicero, G. Fannius, Fabius Maximus: 379.11–380.10; Ninnius Crasses and Turpilius: 478.11–17; Lucilius and Caecilius: 512.24–513.6. *Antiqui* in Priscian's *Institutiones*: Varro: GL 2.81.6–9; Plautus: 84.5–11; Terence: 6–7; Cicero: 95.18–96.2; Varro, Caelius, Sallust, Pliny the Elder: 98.8–17; Catullus and Plautus: 188.22–189.1; Ticidas: 189.2; Pacuvius, Cicero, Virgil, and Accius: 196.3–17; Plautus, Valerius, Caecilius, Pomponius, Laberius: 199.16–200.13; Naevius, Lucilius, Novius, Varro: 203.16–204.6; Cato, Ovid, Cicero, and Horace: 208.1–9; Livius Andronicus, Accius, and Ennius: 210.8–13; Lucan, Cicero, Accius, Ovid, Lucretius: 210.15–211.23; Plautus and Cornificius: 257.4–9; Terence, Lucan, Juvenal: 286.2–23; Gellius: 318.4–5; Cicero and Caesar: 351.1–5; Cato and Atta: 433.1–5; Afranius, Accius, Naevius, and Ennius (who are contrasted with Lucan, Statius, and Martial): 516.13–517.13; Plautus and Apuleius: 528.21.25; Virgil, Terence, and Statius: 574.8–19.

91. GL 1.343.11–13.

92. Also *mos vetus/vetustissimus/vetustatis*, *mos antiquus/antiquissimus*. GL 1.339.10; 400.14; 435.26 (where Virgil is cited as going against it); GL 2.18.16 (here

more antiquo Graecorum); 37.3; 39.8; 52.15; 268.11; 303.3; 517.3; in Servius, esp. *Comm. in Aen.*, *mos* describes both cultural and linguistic "custom," e.g., *Comm. in Aen.* 1.93; 1.233; 1.313; 1.446; 1.632; 1.706; 2.504; et passim. The combination will be discussed at greater length below.

93. Cf. Habinek, *Politics*, 53–54, on the invention of the *mos maiorum*.

94. GL 1.339.10–27.

95. The infinitude is especially strongly signaled by the lack of specificity about author and text: cf. de Certeau, *Writing*, 120; also Bourdieu, "Production and Reproduction," 58–59, on the normalization of specific examples of language usage.

96. GL 1.333.30–36.

97. E.g., at GL 2.66.1 and 76.26 (*poetica*); 82.10 and 97.7–8 (*veterum/ antiquissimorum*).

98. E.g., at GL 2.39.8; 268.11.

99. E.g., at GL 2.48.15; 133.24.

100. Barwick/Charisius, 148.29–30: *dixerunt veteres naviter [et] duriter humaniter, quae nos nave dure humane*; GL 5.47.3: *modo nos iugerorum debemus dicere; antiqui iugerum dicebant, sicut tuberum*; see also Uhl, *Servius*, 292–306, esp. on the use of the first person plural to construe a unified contemporary position; Kaster, *Guardians*, 179: "Freely paraphrased, these lessons would be understood to mean something like, 'Don't get it into your head that you should do what Vergil has done here.'"

101. De Certeau, *Writing*, 41–44; but esp. Stewart, *On Longing*, 19–20, on the double function of quotation, both to construe the present "authority of use" and to "lend the original an authenticity it itself has lost to a surrounding context."

102. Ancient and standard, e.g., at GL 1.435.22–26 (Diomedes); cf. Servius, *Comm. in Aen.* 4.598: *sane hic "subisse" iuxta praesentem usum accusativo iunxit, cum alibi antique dativo usus sit*; poetic, e.g., at GL 2.239.17 (Priscian).

103. E.g., at GL 1.349.30 (Diomedes); Servius, *Comm. in Aen.* 1.632.

104. Servius, *Comm. in Aen.* 9.641.

105. Ricoeur, *Time and Narrative*, 38–45, on the use of temporal plotting to create "concordance"; similarly de Certeau, *Writing*, 41–43 and 88–92, on the use of historical narrative in "making oppositions compatible."

106. Pompeius, at GL 5.277.2–6, is flexible on the use of *super*: *apud maiores nostros varie invenimus, et legimus sive accusativo sive ablativo iunctas. et hodie si vis dicere super tecto et super tectum, dabitur tibi facultas.* Elsewhere, e.g. at GL 5.303.16, he marks a clear division: *habebant hanc consuetudinem antiqui, modo nemo facit hoc.*

107. The reader as the consumer of quoted texts exists both as "inauthentic" or derivative with respect to the past and as gaining mastery over that past: Stewart, *On Longing*, 18–22.

108. Ricoeur, *Time and Narrative*, 58–59 and 70–82, on the "ethical" component of temporal narrative, on which more will be said below; but see also Bourdieu, *Reproduction*, 108–14, on the social compulsion that authoritative language produces.

109. GL 5.304.8–11.

110. Kaster, *Guardians*, 163–64, notes Pompeius' frequent vehemence concerning ancient usages that seem to him to defy grammatical norms.

111. Bourdieu, "Field of Cultural Production," 55–61, on the structuring of changes in authoritative language as temporal, indeed "epochal," concurrent with the need "to possess the whole history of the field" (61).

112. Bourdieu, *Reproduction*, 114–23, at 116: "no one acquires a language without thereby acquiring a *relation to language*." Italics in original.

113. Landow, *Hypertext*, 186–89; Barthes, *S/Z*, 156 and 181–82, on "fill[ing] in the chains of causality" (181).

114. Uhl, *Servius*, 292–308, configures the relation primarily in terms of "barriers" (307); and Kaster, *Guardians*, likewise as "a nearly closed door over which he stands guard" (175). I would instead like to see it as a reification of interaction; cf. Deleuze and Guattari, *Anti-Oedipus*, tr. Robert Hurley et al. (Minneapolis: University of Minnesota Press, 1983), 148–50 and 226–28.

115. Pompeius is fond of this locution, using it, e.g., at GL 5.98.20; 108.7; 110.6; 110.7; 141.11; 142.17; 172.24; 175.18; 175.25; and so on throughout his commentary.

116. Bourdieu, *Reproduction*, 20–22; de Certeau, *Writing*, 72–77, notes the need to decontextualize in order to produce historical facts.

117. Here I depart slightly from Landow, *Hypertext*, 186–87, who sees lists as primarily atemporal; as we will see, Charisius' lists, while overtly nonnarrative and atemporal, nonetheless introduce temporal and narrative elements that make claims on the reader. They thus reveal some of the tensions between temporal and atemporal modes of organizing units of knowledge.

118. Schenkeveld, *Rhetorical Grammar*, 5–8, on the structure of the work as a whole; Louis Holtz, "Sur les traces de Charisius," in *Varron, grammaire antique et stylistique latine*, ed. Jean Collart (Paris: Les Belles Lettres, 1978), 225–33, presents the textual and logical arguments against the inclusion of much of book 5 as Charisius' work, contra Barwick's edition.

119. Schenkeveld, *Rhetorical Grammar*, 30–38, on the possible relation of the material on analogy to the rest of Romanus' work.

120. Barwick/Charisius, 150.3–4: *quae exempli gratia Gaius Iulius Romanus sub eodem titulo exposuit*; cf. Schenkeveld, 39–42, on Romanus' own use of earlier sources.

121. In a questionable passage in book 4 (Barwick/Charisius 373.8–11, which Keil does not include), Charisius refers to *philosophi antiqui* and *grammatici antiqui*; Priscian once refers to *veteres scriptores artis grammaticae*: GL 2.195.6.

122. Note the difference between chronological and alphabetical organization in some early modern cataloguing, mentioned by Roger Chartier in *The Order of Books*, tr. Lydia G. Cochrane (Stanford: Stanford University Press, 1994), 71–72.

123. Adam and Abraham: Barwick/Charisius, 151.15–17. Some of the other persons include heroes of the Trojan War or characters in the *Aeneid*.

124. Barwick/Charisius, 160.8–19.

125. Schenkeveld, *Rhetorical Grammar*, 9–14, argues that Charisius is primarily a "compiler" and "editor" of previous grammarians' works, including the *liber de adverbio* of Romanus. This may be a fair characterization, as Charisius certainly attributes much of his material to others. The text of the *ars* as a whole, though, must be seen as a product of the fourth century and Charisius' hand.

126. Barwick/Charisius, 252.25–31.

127. Barwick/Charisius 253.1–14.

128. Barwick/Charisius 254.1–5.

129. Or "concordant," following Ricoeur, *Time and Narrative*, 42–45.

130. For the trope of "difference in times" in late ancient biblical exegesis, see Elizabeth A. Clark, *Reading Renunciation* (Princeton: Princeton University Press, 1999), 145–52.

131. For the notion that language and grammatical doctrine may be perfected over time, see Dirk M. Schenkeveld, "The Idea of Progress and the Art of Grammar: Charisius *Ars Grammatica* 1.15," *American Journal of Philology* 119 (1998): 443–59. Schenkeveld posits that this section in Charisius may originally be from Pliny the Elder.

132. Bourdieu, *Reproduction*, 113–14, on the imitation of "magisterial language" by students; but also "Production of Belief," 106–11, on the trope of differentiating oneself from one's antecedents. De Certeau, *The Practice of Everyday Life*, tr. Steven Rendall (Berkeley: University of California Press, 1984), 50–60, criticizes Bourdieu's early conception of the habitus; but more important, at 154–76 ("Quotations of Voices" and "Reading as Poaching") he argues that the line from text to readerly usage is not invariably straight.

133. Barwick/Charisius 325.3–14.

134. De Certeau, *Practice*, 162, on the potential transformations of authoritative language: "The literary text is modified by becoming the ambiguous depth in which sounds that cannot be reduced to a meaning move about." At 72, however, de Certeau notes that these transformations are subject to social hierarchies; cf. Bourdieu, *Reproduction*, 114, on the "propitiatory magic of a language in which the grandiloquence of magisterial discourse is reduced to the passwords or sacramental phrases of a ritual murmur."

135. Cf. Kaster, *Guardians*, 205, for the reader as an actor comparable to the grammarian, i.e., as a kind of replication of him: "The qualities and attainments that gave the grammarian his authority in the classroom, even if not directly transmissible, were nurtured in his pupils by his teaching, and, if he taught successfully, ceased to be distinctive to him."

136. Ricoeur, *Time and Narrative*, 76–82.

137. Ricoeur, *Time and Narrative*, 38–42.

138. Cf. De Nonno, "Citazioni," 628–29.

139. GL 4.355.2–3.

140. Pompeius, in his commentary on this list, offers some contextualization, which again leads to his imagining of several narrative scenarios. GL 5.96.32–97.3, for example, on the invention of the pronoun: "If someone says, 'Vergil wrote the bucolics,' he is using a noun; 'he [*ipse*] wrote the georgics,' he is using a pronoun. You could say, 'Vergil wrote the georgics.' But since the repetition of nouns would be irritating, this part of speech was invented."

141. GL 4.355.5–7.

142. The expectation of mastery is reinforced by the question-and-answer format but is not limited to it. See Bourdieu, *Reproduction*, 66–67, on the possibility of inculcation through the simple existence of pedagogical literature.

143. This narrative may or may not correspond to any actual sequence of learning; see Cribiore, *Writing*, 148–52, on the variable sequences of learning to read and write, which diverge significantly from the sequences set out in prescriptive literature like Quintilian.

144. Ricoeur, *Time and Narrative*, 39: "If succession can be subordinated in this way to some logical connection, it is because the ideas of beginning, middle, and end are not taken from experience. They are not features of some real action but the effects of the ordering of the poem."

145. Barwick/Charisius 1.8.

146. Irvine, *Textual Culture*, 79, sums up the "dual cultural function of the grammarian" by quoting a couplet from Suetonius, *De grammaticis et rhetoribus* 11: *Cato grammaticus, Latina Siren, / Qui solus legit ac facit poetas*. Irvine locates the functions in the combined *legit ac facit*; on an ideological level, I would argue that *solus* is equally important: it allows the two activities to be thought of as a single exercise, part of the unifying concept of the *grammaticus*, the intermediary, relational figure.

147. Charles N. Smiley, "*Latinitas* and *Hellenismos*," *Bulletin of the University of Wisconsin* 143 (1906): 211–18, traces the philosophical origins of the idea of Latinity to Stoic notions of pure language; Vainio, *Latinitas*, 47–49, discusses some of the later practical uses of the specific term; François Desbordes, "*Latinitas*: Constitution et évolution d'un modèle de l'identité linguistique," in *Hellenismos: Quelques jalons pour une histoire de l'identité Grecque*, ed. S. Said (Leiden: Brill, 1991), 33–47, considers *latinitas* as formulated primarily in opposition to images of the "barbarian" and the "Greek," but not in temporal terms; Uhl, *Servius*, 40–46, discusses *latinitas* and related locutions in Servius; Kees Versteegh, "Latinitas, Hellenismos, 'Arabiyya," in *The History of Linguistics in the Classical Period*, ed. Daniel J. Taylor (Amsterdam: John Benjamins, 1987), 251–74, considers the divide between normative and spoken languages, given the conservatism of notions of pure language in ancient literary culture.

148. See discussion, n. 59.

149. GL 1.439.15–17: *Latinitas est incorrupte loquendi observatio secundum Romanum linguam. constat autem, ut adserit Varro, his quattuor, natura analogia consuetudine auctoritate.*

150. Barwick/Charisius 1.7–12: *Latinae facundiae licentia regatur aut natura aut analogia aut ratione curiosae observationis aut consuetudine, quae multorum consensione convaluit, aut certe auctoritate, quae prudentissimorum opinione recepta est.*

151. GL 5.47.19–20.

152. GL 5.47.23–24.

153. GL 5. 48.4–16.

154. Kaster, *Guardians*, 18, suggests the complexity of the grammarian's cultural position when he portrays the grammarian as "pivotal in his own sphere, standing where linguistic, geographic, and social distinctions converged"; it would be accurate also to add "temporal distinctions" to the list. De Certeau, *Writing*, 69–72, outlines some of the mechanics of the creation of temporal differences through historical discourse, but also notes the problems in construing any relation between temporal entities as absolute.

155. Charisius here averages five or six quotations for every thirty lines of text in Barwick's Teubner edition.

156. Barwick/Charisius 357.19-30.

157. Especially to the extent that certain of these fragments eventually do become the only things known about their authors; cf. De Nonno, "Citazioni," 597–603.

158. Ricoeur, *Time and Narrative*, 7–12, dissects Augustine's account of time's division into past, present, and future, an account in which the present is indeed understood primarily in terms of memory and expectation.

159. GL 4.395.14–24.

160. De Certeau, *Practice*, 156–62, on the use of language that mimics familiar language; de Certeau focuses primarily on the oral quality of the "quotation-reminiscence" (156), but concedes (159) that an absolute distinction between auditory and written linguistic moments can rarely be made. Bourdieu, *Reproduction*, 110, less generously construes a lack of distinction between exempla as a product of the primary function of pedagogic language, namely, to reinforce "magisterial" authority.

161. GL 1.450.1–451.20.

162. In both senses, the probably late list of synonyms used by Cicero, which Barwick places in book 5 of Charisius' *ars*, is a perfect example of this tendency taken to its logical extreme (Barwick/Charisius 412.19–449.31); on its lateness, see Holtz, "Traces de Charisius," 231, relying on G. Brugnoli, *Studi sulle Differentiae verborum* (Rome: Signorelli, 1955), 27–37. The list both provides the reader with multiple units of knowledge (nearly forty Teubner pages' worth) and ties that knowledge to an imagined linguistic past, making that past, in de Certeau's term, "thinkable" as a linguistic period.

163. Law, "Late Latin Grammars," 194–96, suggests that one of the reasons for the later popularity of commentaries on Donatus was precisely the "economy" that precluded the inclusion of such sections. De Nonno, "Citazioni," 630–33, attributes the absence to a generic distinction between *Schulgrammatik* and *regulae*, but as Law, "Late Latin Grammars," 192, notes, the generic differences were not hard and fast.

164. GL 2.240.5–241.6.

165. Bourdieu, "Outline of a Sociological Theory of Art Perception," in *Field of Cultural Production*, 231: "The ability to go beyond school constraints is the privilege of those who have sufficiently assimilated school education to make their own the free attitude towards scholastic culture taught by a school so deeply impregnated with the values of the ruling classes that it accepts the fashionable depreciation of school instruction." Cf. Kaster's discussion, *Guardians*, 57–65, of Aulus Gellius' attitude toward grammarians who demonstrate pedantry rather than proper *mores*.

166. See, for example, Uhl, *Servius*, 440–62, for a good overview of Servius' conception of "archaism" and the relationship between earlier texts and their reception in later grammarians.

167. For some of the implications of configuring Latin as a "Roman" language, see the essays collected in *Becoming Roman, Writing Latin? Literacy and*

Epigraphy in the Roman West, ed. Alison Cooley, Journal of Roman Archaeology Supplements 48 (Portsmouth: Journal of Roman Archaeology, 2002). On contemporary analysis of Latin in the Roman Empire more generally, see Hannah Rosén, *Latine loqui: Trends and Directions in the Crystallization of Classical Latin* (Munich: W. Fink, 1999).

168. The significance of which is discussed in Saenger, *Space Between Words*.

169. Most famously considered in Derrida, *Of Grammatology*, esp. in part I, ch. 3, "Of Grammatology as a Positive Science," and part II, ch. 4, "From/Of the Supplement to the Source." But see also Judith Butler's discussion of Derrida and Bourdieu on the social dimension of repetition, in *Excitable Speech* (London: Routledge, 1997), 141–59.

170. The foundational essay is that of Walter Benjamin, "The Work of Art in the Age of Mechanical Reproduction," tr. Harry Zohn, in Benjamin, *Illuminations*, ed. Hannah Arendt (New York: Schocken Books, 1968), 217–51.

171. A useful comparison might be the way in which early modern collecting allowed collectors to become identifiable as belonging to a certain class: Swann, *Curiosities and Texts*, esp. 16–27. Swann notes the importance of ancient coins, "small, numerous, and relatively inexpensive" (22), to the burgeoning of the collecting class, but she might also have added that coins represent a form of mass production as well.

172. See Benjamin, "Work of Art," sections 5–7.

173. The ethical force of this reification will be discussed in the following chapter.

174. E.g., at GL 1.426.4–9 (Diomedes); 4.47.16–17 (Probus); 4.405.2–3 (Servius).

175. Cf. Foucault, "The Discourse on Language," tr. Rupert Swyer, in *The Archaeology of Knowledge*, tr. A. M. Sheridan Smith (New York: Pantheon, 1972), 223–27.

176. Cf. Brian Massumi, *A User's Guide to Capitalism and Schizophrenia* (Cambridge, Mass.: MIT Press, 1992), 68–80, on the stereotyping and fixing of narrative movement from past to present in the production of subjectivity.

177. Analogous to the social break between "authorized" and "unauthorized" language in Bourdieu, "Censorship and the Imposition of Form," in *Language and Symbolic Power*, 137–59; this analogy will be considered further in the following chapter.

178. With reference of course to Althusser, "Ideology and Ideological State Apparatuses (Notes Toward an Investigation)," in *Lenin and Philosophy*, tr. Ben Brewster (New York: Monthly Review Press, 1971), 127–86.

179. Althusser, "Ideology," 158–70; but cf. also Bourdieu's more specific discussion on misrecognition in the reproduction of ideological structures, *Reproduction*, 12–15 and 63–67.

180. Kaster, *Guardians*, chs. 3 and 6.

181. In many respects the fundamental consideration of this "lateness" is still Marrou's "Retractatio," part B, in the second edition of *St. Augustin et la fin de la culture antique*, in which Marrou addresses the second half of the work's title, the "end" of ancient culture, and the notion of "decadence."

182. See, for example, Rudolf Pfeiffer's magisterial *History of Classical Scholarship from the Beginnings to the End of the Hellenistic Age* (Oxford: Clarendon Press, 1968).

183. *De grammaticis et rhetoribus*, ed. and tr. Robert Kaster (Oxford: Oxford University Press, 1995).

184. GL 1.349.30 (Diomedes); Servius, *Comm. in Aen.* 1.632.

185. Cf. Barthes, "One Always Fails in Speaking of What One Loves," in *The Rustle of Language*, tr. Richard Howard (Berkeley: University of California Press, 1989), 296–305.

186. Massumi, *User's Guide*, 47–52, on the creation of these "stable formations" out of unstable elements.

Chapter 3. From Grammar to Piety

1. The difference is significant and will be discussed below. Both kinds of texts, however, form part of the discourse of grammar in late antiquity and should be viewed as complementary. Cf. Robert Kaster's admirable use of, e.g., Ausonius, Aulus Gellius, Libanius, and Macrobius, in addition to the more technical *artes*, in his *Guardians of Language: The Grammarian and Society in Late Antiquity* (Berkeley: University of California Press, 1988).

2. It is important here not to be distracted by the difficulty of dealing with the ancient concept of *pietas*, which is not strictly "religious," in the modern sense, but which can connote proper behavior toward gods as well as toward humans: cf. Carl Koch, "Pietas," in Pauly-Wissowa, *Realencyclopädie der classischen Altertumswissenschaft* (Stuttgart: J. B. Metzler, 1951). The late ancient authors whom I discuss here do use the concept of *pietas* in discussing dealings toward gods in terms that modern readers can, I think, easily describe as "religious." For a cautionary reminder of the problems involved in reading the modern category of "religion" into premodern texts, see esp. Talal Asad, *Genealogies of Religion* (Baltimore: Johns Hopkins University Press, 1993), introduction and ch.1. I would suggest only that the conflation that late ancient writers eventually create between *pietas* and "religion" in the literary sphere eventually contributes to the modern confusion between the two.

3. For Ausonius, I rely on the text of R. P. H. Green, *The Works of Ausonius* (Oxford: Oxford University Press, 1991), although I have also consulted the text and commentary of Massimo Lolli, *D. M. Ausonius, Parentalia* (Brussels: Latomus, 1997); for Macrobius, I use the text of James Willis, *Saturnalia* (Leipzig: Teubner, 1963); for Augustine, James J. O'Donnell, *Confessions*, vol. 1 (Oxford: Clarendon Press, 1992); for Julian, W. C. Wright, tr., *The Works of the Emperor Julian*, vol. 3, Loeb Classical Library 157 (London: William Heinemann, 1923).

4. See esp. Kaster, *Guardians*, 50–70. Kaster's work on the social status of grammarians (esp. in *Guardians*, ch. 3) has been groundbreaking; Teresa Morgan, *Literate Education in the Hellenistic and Roman World* (Cambridge: Cambridge University Press, 1998), ch. 5, pays more attention to the social formation of the grammarians' students, although the bulk of her chapter draws on Quintilian;

Martin Irvine, *The Making of Textual Culture: Grammatica and Literary Theory, 350–1100* (Cambridge: Cambridge University Press, 1994), 74–87, discusses some of the broader implications of grammatical training on social identity in late antiquity and the early Middle Ages. Most of the work on self-fashioning in Roman education, however, has focused on rhetoric and the figure of the orator, e.g., Maud Gleason, *Making Men: Sophists and Self-Presentation in Ancient Rome* (Princeton: Princeton University Press, 1995); Peter Brown, *Power and Persuasion in Late Antiquity* (Madison: University of Wisconsin Press, 1992); Richard Lim, *Public Disputation, Power, and Social Order in Late Antiquity* (Berkeley: University of California Press, 1995).

5. GL 1.299.19–23.

6. E.g., Phocas at GL 5.411.2–16; the status of Priscian's dedicatee Julianus is noted at GL 2.2.24–31. Ausonius' letter to his grandson, for example, calls official advancement the *praemia musarum* (*Protrepticus ad nepotem*, 42); cf. also Peter Brown's concise formulation, *Power and Persuasion*, 39: "What probably mattered more [than social mobility] at the time, however, was that *paideia* united potentially conflicting segments of the governing class. It joined imperial administrators and provincial notables in a shared sense of common excellence."

7. These tropes appear especially in depictions of "good" and "bad" grammarians, e.g. in Ausonius' *Professores*, in Aulus Gellius and in Macrobius: see discussion in Kaster, *Guardians*, 65–70; also Kaster, "Macrobius and Servius: *Verecundia* and the Grammarian's Function," *Harvard Studies in Classical Philology* 84 (1980): 219–62.

8. Cf. the famous statement of M. Cato that the orator must be "good"; and Quintilian's elaboration of this theme at *Inst. or.* 12.1.1–3. On the school texts, see Raffaella Cribiore, *Writing, Teaching, and Students in Greco-Roman Egypt* (Atlanta: Scholars Press, 1996), 43–47; Morgan, *Literate Education*, 120–51. The connection between literacy, virtue, and social status is perhaps made most clear by the high proportion of school papyri quoting maxims on the importance of seeking wealth, and on using wealth correctly, e.g., "Remember, being rich, to do good to the poor" (Morgan, *Literate Education*, 126).

9. GL 2.2.27–28.

10. The traditional picture is that of a small child being sent first to a *ludi magister* and then to a grammarian; this is the account in Stanley Bonner, *Education in Ancient Rome* (London: Methuen, 1977), 34–64; Kaster, "Notes on 'Primary' and 'Secondary' Schools in Late Antiquity," *Transactions and Proceedings of the American Philological Association* 113 (1983): 323–46, argues that this sequence was not always strictly followed, and that the grammarian might at times be the first of a child's teachers.

11. See Fannie J. LeMoine, "Parental Gifts: Father-Son Dedications in Roman Didactic Literature," *Illinois Classical Studies* 16 (1991): 337–66, on the trope.

12. Richard Klein, *Symmachus* (Darmstadt: Wissenschaftliche Gesellschaft, 1971), 57–58; cf. Jean Pierre Callu's introduction to his edition of Symmachus' letters, *Symmaque: Lettres* (Paris: Les Belles Lettres, 1972), 12.

13. Charles J. Hedrick, *History and Silence* (Austin: University of Texas Press, 2000), 183; James E. G. Zetzel, *Latin Textual Criticism in Late Antiquity* (New York, Arno, 1981), 217, gives the text of the subscription.

14. E.g., *epp.* 1.1–4, which are full of poetic exchanges.

15. *Ep.* 17.31–32 Green: *si erro, pater sum, fer me et noli exigere iudicium obstante pietate*; Ausonius' exchange with Paulinus will be discussed at greater length in Chapter 6. A happier example is Statius' tribute to his grammarian father in *Silvae* 5.3.

16. If one can extrapolate from Seneca, *ep.* 4.36.4, it is possible that learning outside this progression was frowned upon: *sed quemadmodum omnibus annis studere honestum est, ita non omnibus institui. Turpis et ridicula res est elementarius senex: iuveni parandum, seni utendum est;* cf. also Ausonius' reproach of Paulinus (mentioned above) for failing to show proper respect to Ausonius' age.

17. Which, of course, does not imply that the grammarians were not pious. Kaster's prosopography, *Guardians*, part 2, lists grammarians' religious affiliations where these are known.

18. Studies have tended to focus on the word "pagan" and its use: the classic discussion is Christine Mohrmann, "Encore une fois: Paganus," in Mohrmann, *Études sur le latine des Chrétiens*, vol. 3 (Rome: Edizioni di storia e letteraria, 1965), 277–89; James J. O'Donnell, "*Paganus,*" *Classical Folia* 31 (1977): 163–69, notes the scarcity of the term's use before the fifth century, "as the thing it described was dying out" (165). The notion, however, of a conceptual unity behind non-Christian, non-Jewish cults in the Roman Empire is often expressed in social or familial terms, as when Christians refer to others as *gentes, gentiles,* or *nationes*: O'Donnell, 164. O'Donnell, "The Demise of Paganism," *Traditio* 35 (1979): 49, astutely points out that "it may have been a Christian idiosyncracy to lump all non-Christians into one mass, but it was not necessarily mere paranoia." As I will argue below, it may not even have been a purely Christian idiosyncracy.

19. Herbert Bloch, "The Pagan Revival in the West at the End of the Fourth Century," in *The Conflict Between Paganism and Christianity in the Fourth Century*, ed. Arnaldo Momigliano (Oxford: Clarendon Press, 1963), 193–218, offers the basic argument for the revival; Alan Cameron, "Paganism and Literature in Late Fourth Century Rome," in *Christianisme et formes littéraires de l'antiquité tardive en occident*, ed. M. Fuhrmann (Geneva: Fondation Hardt, 1977), 1–30, is the now-standard rebuttal; Hedrick, *History and Silence*, takes issue with both accounts: "That Bloch is wrong and Cameron contradicts him does not make Cameron right" (201).

20. See Paul Ricoeur, *Time and Narrative*, vol. 1, tr. Kathleen McLaughlin and David Pellauer (Chicago: University of Chicago Press, 1984), 181, on the productive link between larger bodies and individual narratives.

21. Cf. Michel Foucault, "The Discourse on Language," tr. Rupert Swyer, as an appendix to Foucault, *The Archaeology of Knowledge*, tr. A. M. Sheridan Smith (New York: Pantheon, 1972), 220–21; also Pierre Bourdieu, *Reproduction in Education, Society, and Culture*, tr. Richard Nice, 2nd ed. (London: Sage, 1990), 118–19, on the problem of linguistic mimicry in education.

22. GL 5.304.8–11.

23. GL 5.304.7–8.

24. See discussion in Chapter 2.

25. It is also possible to argue for a fourth temporal level, in that Pompeius is arguing against, and thus specifically imagining, the statement's future use, as the formal use of the future *fecerit* might imply. The implication of temporal position

in "injurious" speech is discussed by Judith Butler, *Excitable Speech* (London: Routledge, 1997), 33–37, who argues that such speech interpellates its addressees and its speakers into historically specific situations. I would argue that the same interpellation occurs in the grammarian's attempt to define normative speech; it is also the case that Pompeius is describing a potentially "injurious" situation, although not in the sense addressed by Butler.

26. See Chapter 2, n. 27; the specific "force" of these imperatives will be discussed further in Chapter 6, on the trope of grammatical violence.

27. GL 4.355.5, 6.

28. On the production of knowledgeable subjects through generic performances of specialized language, see esp. Bourdieu, "Censorship and the Imposition of Form," in *Language and Symbolic Power*, tr. Gino Raymond and Matthew Adamson, ed. John B. Thompson (Cambridge, Mass.: Harvard University Press, 1991), 137–59, but also Bourdieu, *Reproduction*, 54–61, on the necessary "routinization" of academic knowledge. For an account of the equally necessary instabilities in this system of performances, see Butler, *Excitable Speech*, 147 and 152–59. More generally on speaking and interpellation, Butler, *Excitable Speech*, 24–28 and 153–54.

29. GL 5.97.20–24.

30. That is to say, here the speaker is overtly confronted with the demand to remain (literally) within the "speakable"—a demand that is predicated on the contemporary existence of authorized modes of speaking: see Foucault, "Discourse on Language," 219–24; Bourdieu, "Authorized Language: The Social Conditions for the Effectiveness of Ritual Discourse," in *Language and Symbolic Power*, 107–16; also Butler, *Excitable Speech*, 139, on the "risk" involved in speaking "at the border of the speakable."

31. Bourdieu, of course, suggests that this maintenance (of both correct speech and the social order) is in some sense inevitable, as is the central claim of *Reproduction*; Butler, among others, contests this claim, arguing for the possibility of reappropriating authorized language in contexts "without prior authorization" (*Excitable Speech*, 159–63). This contestation echoes that of de Certeau, *The Practice of Everyday Life*. tr. Steven Rendall (Berkeley: University of California Press, 1984). 50–60 and 98–108. I would argue that here, at least, Diomedes' interest is in establishing the social authorization of correct discourse; cf. Kaster, *Guardians of Language*, esp. ch. 3.

32. The projection of this "present" is not to be underestimated as an ideological task. While Ricoeur, *Time and Narrative*, focuses primarily on the imagining of, as it were, "forward" temporal movement in his discussion of time, he nonetheless notes (10) the need for "internal multiplicity" in the imagination of the present. To modify the spatial metaphor, with reference to de Certeau (see note above), I would call this projection of the present an equally necessary "lateral" movement of the imagination.

33. Robert Kaster, "Servius and *idonei auctores*," *American Journal of Philology* 99 (1978): 200; Mario De Nonno, "Le citazioni dei grammatici," in *Lo Spazio Letterario di Roma Antica*, vol. 3, *La ricezione del testo*, ed. Guglielmo Cavallo et al. (Rome: Salerno, 1990), 628.

34. On the idea of speech acts as fundamentally historical, see Butler, *Excitable*

Speech, 33–36; alternatively, for the idea of language as a constantly shifting constellation of pasts and futures, see Brian Massumi, *A User's Guide to Capitalism and Schizophrenia* (Cambridge, Mass.: MIT Press, 1992), 41–43. Deleuze, "A Conversation," in *Dialogues*, with Claire Parnet, tr. Hugh Tomlinson and Barbara Habberjam (New York: Columbia University Press, 1987), 13–14, notes the function of the European philosophical tradition to coerce conformity in the production of thought.

35. In this sense, the grammarian's "burden" (Kaster, *Guardians of Language*, ch. 1) remains social but is articulated in a historicized manner, so that the social and historical constitution of the speaker is simultaneous; cf. Butler, *Excitable Speech*, 27: "The responsibility of the speaker does not consist of remaking language ex nihilo, but rather of negotiating the legacies of usage that constrain and enable that speaker's speech."

36. GL 1.426.13–20; cf. Quintilian, *Inst. art.* 1.4.2.

37. See Irvine, *Textual Culture*, 2–4 on this definition; also Henri-Irénée Marrou, *St. Augustin et la fin de la culture antique*, 4th ed. (Paris: E. de Boccard, 1958), 11.

38. Bourdieu, "Censorship," 137–40, on the social field in which intellectual formulations are possible; Foucault, "Discourse," 219–20, on the "prodigious machinery of the will to truth." As I noted in Chapter 2, the use of these texts is largely a matter of posting linguistic boundaries.

39. It is important to bear in mind the distinction between the reader as "poacher" in de Certeau's formulation (*Practice of Everyday Life*, 165–76) and the reader here conjured by the text in individual textual moments (Judith Butler, *Gender Trouble* [London: Routledge, 1990], 173–85, and *Excitable Speech*, 46), although these are not mutually exclusive formulations. Here, however, I am emphasizing the reader as an effect of the discursive framework manifested in the *artes*.

40. Barwick/Charisius 2.224–25.

41. Barwick/Charisius 224.9–12.

42. Barwick/Charisius 224.16–19.

43. Barwick/Charisius 225.14–16.

44. Thus the "social" break between ordinary and specialized language imagined by Bourdieu ("Censorship," 140–51) is also articulated as a temporal break.

45. On the use of literary pasts to determine present obligations, see generally Thomas Habinek, *The Politics of Latin Literature* (Princeton: Princeton University Press, 1998), which rightly emphasizes that this temporal line should not be seen as naturally existing. Marrou's characterization of the grammars as "dominated by the idea of classicism" (*St. Augustin*, 13) is certainly true, but more accurate if taken to mean that the idea of "pastness" is construed as exerting force, rather than that an actual past necessarily exerted such force.

46. The requirement to copy exemplary texts in school (Cribiore, *Writing*, 43–47) is perhaps a clearer example of this combined obligation, on the one hand to a present authoritative figure (the grammarian) and on the other to the exemplary object. The double articulation of obligation in present and past tenses extends to the larger imagined pedagogical situation as well, so that it is not a specific pupil who is under obligation but any participant in learned discourse—who can only exist as such in a state of obligation. Butler, *Excitable Speech*, 46.

47. I do not mean to oversimplify these matrices by suggesting that they are only in concert with linear temporal progression or nonvariable forms of obligation: I would only suggest that the categories of time and obligation are large-scale categories in which more detailed and flexible formations continually occur. Cf. Deleuze, "Many Politics," in *Dialogues*, 124–34.

48. On the idea that different performatives create the effect of a stable interior core, see Butler, *Gender Trouble*, 173. To a certain extent, Butler's formulation can be usefully construed as similar to Bourdieu's *habitus* as the "core" of the social being, although in *Gender Trouble* Butler is more concerned with the idea of the persistent self as an effect, rather than sharing Bourdieu's emphasis on persistence itself as an effect.

49. GL 2.2.24–31.

50. The fundamental discussion of this practice is of course Foucault, "What Is an Author?" tr. Josué V. Harari, in *The Foucault Reader*, ed. Paul Rabinow (New York: Pantheon, 1984), 101–20.

51. GL 4.357.2–7.

52. Butler, *Gender Trouble*, 169–74, on the production of a supposedly stable "interiority" "through corporeal signs and other discursive means" (173). I take grammatical practice to be both discursive and corporeal; the imagination of its corporeal dimension will be discussed further in Chapter 5.

53. See Butler's discussion of J. L. Austin and the question of the "sovereignty" (as opposed to agency) of the subject, *Excitable Speech*, 15–17, esp. at 16: "The one who acts (who is not the same as the sovereign subject) acts precisely to the extent that he or she is constituted as an actor and, hence, operating within a linguistic field of enabling constraints from the outset."

54. See my discussion in Chapter 2.

55. The capacity for such formal repetition obviously extends beyond the bounds of the *artes*. So, for example, when Kaster (*Guardians of Language*, 23; more fully at "A Schoolboy's Burlesque from Cyrene," *Mnemosyne* 37 [1984]: 457–58) observes that graffiti in parodic imitation of the grammarian's discourse might cause the reader to "[recall] the jokes of his own school days," he rightly reveals the ways in which such discourse evokes a temporal continuity and narrative of selfhood, even outside its "normal" context. The question of iterability and its social demands and effects is discussed with reference to Derrida and Bourdieu in Butler, *Excitable Speech*, 148–55.

56. GL 1.449.18–21 and 450.19–24.

57. Again, the "break" that supports the structures that authorize language, which Bourdieu discusses primarily in social terms ("Censorship," 151–59), is here articulated in predominantly temporal terms. Foucault, to a certain extent, historicizes the formation of these structures in "Discourse on Language," 218–19.

58. Foucault, "Discourse on Language," 217: "The madman's speech did not strictly exist." This also explains the perilous closeness of "rustics" to "their flocks" in Diomedes' hierarchy of grammatical knowledge.

59. Or, to articulate the "meaningfulness" of the linguistic actor's existence via Massumi (*User's Guide*, 10–11): "The presence of the sign is not an identity but an envelopment of difference, of a multiplicity of actions, materials, and levels."

60. On the rise of a Roman "aristocracy" in Gaul, see Hagith Sivan, *Ausonius of Bordeaux: Genesis of a Gallic Aristocracy* (London: Routledge, 1993), esp. 6–27; on Ausonius' family and its social status more specifically, see M. Keith Hopkins, "Social Mobility in the Later Roman Empire: The Case of Ausonius," *Classical Quarterly* n.s. 11 (1961): 239–49. Alan D. Booth, "The Academic Career of Ausonius," *Phoenix* 36 (1982): 332.

61. Booth, "Academic Career," 339; on the idea of "promotion" from grammar to rhetoric, see Kaster, *Guardians*, 103–4. Hopkins, "Social Mobility," 243, on Ausonius as Gratian's tutor.

62. Sivan, *Ausonius*, 138–41.

63. For review of the debate, see R. P. H. Green, "The Christianity of Ausonius," *Studia Patristica* 28 (1993): 39–48; but cf. also J. Irmscher, "Heidnisches und Christliches bei Ausonius," *Studia Ephemerides "Augustinianum"* 42 (1993): 179–85, who argues that "[d]ie alternative Frage Christ oder Heide ist . . . a priori falsch gestellt" (184), since to make a stark distinction between the two is to ignore the important overlapping of the two in the context of fourth-century Gaul. Matthias Skeb comes to a similar conclusion in *Christo vivere: Studien zum literarishcen Christusbild des Paulinus von Nola* (Bonn: Borengässer, 1997), 57–60.

64. On the difference between *pietas* and *religio* in Roman thought generally, see Koch, "Pietas"; also Robert Wilken, *The Christians as the Roman Saw Them* (New Haven: Yale University Press, 1984), 54–62. Clearly, as Ausonius' use of *maestam religionem* makes clear, *pietas* and *religio* have a great deal of semantic overlap, although neither corresponds in any exact fashion to the modern notion of "religion."

65. *Praef. in prosa* 4–5 and 8–9.

66. *Praef. in prosa* 7–8; *praef. in vers.* 7.

67. Ovid, *Fasti*, 2.533–616; the continuing observance of this ritual in late antiquity, and its marking as specifically non-Christian, is attested in Augustine, *Conf.* 6.2.2 and *Quaest. in hept.* 5.47.

68. For a more extended discussion of Ausonius' Christianity, especially in the context of his relationship with Paulinus of Nola, see Chapter 6.

69. For the sake of convenience, I will identify this speaker as Ausonius, although I do not mean to deny the distinction between the historical figure of Ausonius and the literary figure imagined in the verses.

70. *Praef.* 1–4.

71. *Epicedion* 1.

72. For genealogy, see Sivan, *Ausonius*, 49–66; see also R. Etienne, "La démographie de la famille d'Ausone," in *Etudes et chronique de démographie historique* (Paris: Société de démographie historique, 1964), 15–25.

73. *Par.* 1.1–2.

74. *Par.* praef. in vers. 11–12. Note that this obligation is conveyed by writing.

75. *Par.* 3.1–4.

76. *Par.* 3.8.

77. *Par.* 3.9–10.

78. *Par.* 3.13.

79. *Par.* 3.15. Note, too, the portrayal of Arborius in the *Professors of Bordeaux* 16.1–4: *Inter cognatos iam fletus, avuncule, manes,/ inter rhetoricos nunc memorandus*

eris./ illud opus [viz., the *Parentalia*] *pietas, istud reverenda virorum/ nomina pro patriae religione habeant*. The use of pedagogical figures in the *Professors* is treated further in Chapter 6.

80. *Par.* 3.17–18.

81. *Par.* praef. in prosa 7–9; cf. *Epicedion* praef. 3–4, which also appeals to the title, *epicedion*, as being appropriate to the *religiosus* nature of the text.

82. *Par.* praef. in vers. 11–12.

83. Cf. Bourdieu, "Censorship," 137–40, and Deleuze, "Conversation," 13–14, on the use of specialized language to create objects of respect.

84. Roland Barthes, "The Discourse of History," in *The Rustle of Language*, tr. Richard Howard (Berkeley: University of California Press, 1989), 137–40; Hayden White, *The Content of the Form* (Baltimore: Johns Hopkins University Press, 1987), 1–25.

85. Praef. in vers. 9. Other examples of language suggesting tasks fulfilled are found at 26.7: *ergo commemorataque ave maestumque vocata/ pro genetrice vale*, or 5.11–12: *tranquillos aviae cineres praestate, quieti/ aeternum manes, si pia verba loquor*.

86. Cf. Barthes, "Discourse of History," 131–33; also Deleuze, "Many Politics," 143–44, more generally on the individual as such an assemblage.

87. Butler, *Excitable Speech*, 27–28.

88. Praef. in prosa 8–9.

89. More broadly on the need to shift Ausonius scholarship from an attempt to read Ausonius as a repository of information to a reading of Ausonius' works as poetic constructs, see S. Georgia Nugent, "Ausonius' 'Late-Antique' Poetics and 'Post-Modern' Literary Theory," *Ramus* 19 (1990): 26–50.

90. Foucault, "What Is an Author?" 105–8.

91. *Par.* 13.3–4: *minor iste natu me, sed ingenio prior / artes paternas imbibit*.

92. *Par.* 13.11–12: *germane carnis lege et ortu sanguinis, / amore paene filius*.

93. *Par.* 10.2: *meo nomine dicte puer*.

94. *Par.* 10.5: *tu gremio in proavi funus commune locatus*.

95. Barthes, "Discourse of History," 131–32; de Certeau, *The Writing of History*, tr. Tom Conley (New York: Columbia University Press, 1988), 312–16.

96. Praef. in vers. 3: *sufficit inferiis exsequialis honos*.

97. *Par.* 3.24.

98. *Par.* 4.1.

99. *Par.* 5.11–12.

100. *Par.* 8.17.

101. See Butler, *Excitable Speech*, 43–52, on the priority of speech-acts to subjects.

102. *Par.* 3.23–24.

103. *Par.* 5.11–12.

104. The other factor that contributes to a reading of the *Parentalia* as based on a conflation of literary and pious obligations is its continuation in the *Professors of Bordeaux*. While the two sets of poems were not begun at the same time, it seems likely (Green, *Works of Ausonius*, 298, 329) that the *Professors* were written shortly after much of the *Parentalia* and completed as Ausonius was working on additions to the *Parentalia*. The preface to the *Professors* both links the two sets of

poems and places the *Professors* in the same "religious" context as the *Parentalia*: *Vos etiam, quos nulla mihi congnatio iunxit, / sed fama et carae religio patriae / et studium in libris et sedula cura docendi, / commemorabo viros morte obita celebres. / fors erit ut nostros manes sic asserat olim exemplo cupiet qui pius esse meo.* The extension of the "pious" aspects of the *Parentalia* to include Ausonius' predecessors in grammar and rhetoric indicates the conflation of literary and pious obligation already noted in the prefaces to the *Parentalia*. The ideological functions of the *Professors* will be discussed further in Chapter 6.

105. Butler, *Excitable Speech*, 45–47.

106. In GL 5.595–655; cf. Jacques Flamant, *Macrobe et le Néoplatonisme Latin, à la fin du IVe Siècle* (Leiden: Brill, 1977), 244–52.

107. 1.7.8–9.

108. A cosmology which is not in itself incompatible with "Christian" self-identification: see Ekkehart Syska, *Studien zur Theologie des Macrobius* (Stuttgart: Teubner, 1993), who identifies Macrobius with adherence to solar cult; also Flamant, *Macrobe*, 652–80, who characterizes Macrobius as "hostile" to Christianity on the basis of solar cult.

109. Bloch, "Pagan Revival," 207–10; Alan Cameron, "The Date and Identity of Macrobius," *Journal of Roman Studies* 56 (1966): 25–38, argues, against Bloch, that "the pagan past is idealized on every page, but because it is *past*, not because it is pagan" (36); O'Donnell, "Demise," echoes Cameron to a certain extent when he says that "erudition" is the "hallmark" of the religion of the *Saturnalia*. Hedrick, *History and Silence*, 79–88, rightly argues, however, that the claim the *Saturnalia* makes on cultural memory is not negligible.

110. Much of the recent scholarship on the historical Praetextatus is usefully summarized in Maijastina Kahlos, *Vettius Agorius Praetextatus: A Senatorial Life in Between* (Rome: Institutum Romanum Finlandiae, 2002); J. H. W. G. Liebeschuetz, "The Significance of the Speech of Praetextatus," in *Pagan Monotheism in Late Antiquity*, ed. Polymnia Athanassiadi and Michael Frede (Oxford: Oxford University Press, 1999), 185–205, suggests the possibility that Macrobius' essay on solar cult in book 1 of the *Saturnalia* may be based on some of Praetextatus' own writings, but argues primarily that its "monotheism" is a conciliatory gesture aimed at making the senatorial aristocracy more comfortable with "their fairly recently acquired Christian religion" (202). On Nicomachus Flavianus, and the usurpation of Euguenius, see esp. James J. O'Donnell, "The Career of Virius Nicomachus Flavianus," *Phoenix* 32 (1978): 129–43; and Hedrick, *History and Silence*, chs. 2 and 3.

111. Cameron, "Date and Identity."

112. Hedrick, *History and Silence*, 82, responding to Cameron, "Date and Identity," 36: "Nostalgic idealization of the past"; Cameron, "Paganism and Literature," 26: Macrobius' "essentially nostalgic and literary paganism"; Cameron, "The Last Pagans of Rome," in *The Transformations of Urbs Roma in Late Antiquity*, ed. William V. Harris (Portsmouth: Journal of Roman Archaeology Supplements 33, 1999), 109–21. Susan Stewart, *On Longing: Narratives of the Miniature, the Gigantic, the Souvenir, the Collection* (Durham, N.C.: Duke University Press, 1993), 23, argues for the ideologically productive nature of nostalgia: nostalgia involves "the assumption that the mediated experience known through language

and the temporality of narrative can offer pattern and insight by virtue of its capacity for transcendence. . . . By the narrative process of nostalgic reconstruction the present is denied and the past takes on an authenticity of being, an authenticity which, ironically, it can achieve only through narrative."

113. *Sat.* 1.praef.3–4.

114. *Sat.* 1.praef.5.

115. *Sat.* 1.praef.1: *sed nulla nos magis quam eorum qui e nobis essent procreati caritate devinxit eamque nostram in his educandis atque erudiendis curam esse voluit.*

116. Book 3 is fragmentary, but it is likely that the topic preceding Praetextatus' discussion was Virgil's knowledge of augural law, as explained by Nicomachus Flavianus. For Praetextatus' offices, *CIL* 6.1779 is given in the appendix to Kahlos, *Praetextatus*, 216–18; the inscription is generally read as evidence for Praetextatus' devotion to a number of different non-Christian cults. Despite his otherwise minimalist reading of "pagan" religiosity in the fourth century, Cameron, "Last Pagans," 111, concedes that "it may well be that [Praetextatus] looked on his priesthoods as something more than status symbols."

117. *Sat.* 1.24.16.

118. *Sat.* 1.24.16.

119. *Sat.* 3.9.16.

120. *Sat.* 3.6.1. A similar consolidation of knowledge occurs in Flavianus' proposal to discuss Virgil's knowledge of augural law (1.24.17), which he calls a *scientia*. The discussion, however, is lost.

121. Venus: *Sat.* 3.8.1–3; purification: 3.1.1–8; animals: 3.5.1–11; sheep: 3.3.11–12.

122. On the necessary combination of linguistic and ritual facility, see Bourdieu, "Authorized Language."

123. See Barthes, "Discourse of History," 133–34, on the formulation of such collective entities as "shortcuts."

124. *Sat.* 1.praef.1.

125. Cameron, "Date and Identity," 34–37, takes the gap between writing and dramatic date to be indicative of a primarily antiquarian purpose to the work; Hedrick, *History and Silence*, 86, however, argues that such a dismissal "may conceal the continuing dangerous and disturbing connotations of the past."

126. See Ricoeur, *Time and Narrative*, 193, on the interdependence of narrated time and experienced time.

127. E.g., *Sat.* 3.3.1; 3.3.4; 3.3.9; 3.6.9; 3.4.6; 3.5.5.

128. Barwick/Charisius 13.29–32; the same passage in Diomedes, GL 1.435. 24–26; Servius, *Comm. in Aen.* 3.20; 3.119; 9.484; *Comm. in Buc.* 5.5. It is likely that Macrobius knew Servius' work: Cameron, "Date and Identity," 29–13; for a comparison of Virgilian criticism in Donatus, Servius, and Macrobius, see N. Marinone, *Elio Donato, Macrobio, e Servio commentatori di Vergilio* (Vercelli: Presso l'Autore, 1946).

129. *Sat.* 3.8.8–10.

130. Macrobius elsewhere (e.g., 3.3.1) uses it in a nonreligious sense.

131. *Sat.* 3.9.1.

132. Bourdieu, esp. "The Market of Symbolic Goods," in *The Field of Cultural Production*, 112–41, configures the relation of educated persons to cultural goods

as one in which possession of such goods is marked by a knowledge of when and how to display them, intimating a basic continuity in their transference; Ricoeur, *Time and Narrative*, 199, allows for greater leeway between continuity and discontinuity by asserting that the relation of individuals in narratives to larger entities in time is indirect.

133. Cameron, "Date and Identity," 33–37.

134. Kahlos, *Praetextatus*, 160–71 and 201–8 summarizes Christian and non-Christian responses to Praetextatus after his death.

135. Cf. *Sat.* 1.7.17, 1.11.1, 1.15.3, 1.17.1, 1.24.1.

136. *Sat.* 1.5.4

137. See discussion in Kaster, *Guardians*, 171–75, on the difference between the Servius defended by Praetextatus and the historical Servius.

138. See Roland Barthes, *S/Z*, tr. Richard Miller (New York: Hill & Wang, 1974), 94–95, on the unifying function of individual names. Cf. Massumi, *User's Guide*, 22–34, on subjects as interactions: "The subject is a transpersonal abstract machine" (26).

139. Ricoeur, *Time and Narrative*, 224, on the use of analogies between individuals and larger structures as a necessary feature of historical writing.

140. *Sat.* 3.10.1.

141. *Sat.* 3.10.2: *et nos, inquit, manum ferulae aliquando subduximus, et nos cepimus pontificii iuris auditum.*

142. Foucault, "Discourse on Language," 219–20.

143. The standard reference for Marius Victorinus is still Pierre Hadot, *Marius Victorinus: Recherches sur sa vie et ses oeuvres* (Paris: Études Augustiniennes, 1971); Hadot notes Jerome's and Augustine's accounts of the statue in the forum of Trajan at 13–14. Although Jerome places the erection of the statue in 354, Hadot suggests (28) that it may have been earlier, in 351.

144. Hadot, *Marius Victorinus*, discusses each of these at some length, and he provides a bibliography of modern editions at 403–4.

145. *Chron. ad* 363.

146. Julian is often dealt with as a "unique" case, not representative of "real" pagan sentiment because of his familial connection with Christianity: e.g., O'Donnell, "Demise," 52: "There was one thing about the young Julian that set him apart from the mass of his fellow non-Christians in the fourth century: he began life as a Christian." This is often asserted to be the cause of his exclusive formulation of Hellenism. O'Donnell again (53): "Julian took with him from Christianity in large measure that attitude toward religion which Christianity particularly fostered." This argument seems somewhat forced, especially given other instances of conversion to and away from Christianity in the period, which are often labeled ambiguous or insincere: cf. O'Donnell , 60–65, esp. 61, on converts away from Christianity who are not pictured as "zealots" for traditional worship. If Augustine, as O'Donnell (63) argues, "was more a typical pagan of his period than he has been given credit for being," it seems strange to deny Julian, who followed a similar course of conversion through reading, an equivalent consideration.

147. *Ep.* 36, 422a5–b3.

148. *Ep.* 36, 423d2–3.

149. *Ep.* 36, 423d3–5.

150. *Ep.* 36, 422c8–d2.

151. *Ep.* 36, 423a1–3.

152. *Ep.* 36, 423c6–d2.

153. See Ricoeur, *Time and Narrative*, 200, on the use of "characters" as "relay stations" in historical discourse.

154. *Ep.* 36, 424a1–5.

155. Interestingly, Augustine does not mention philosophers, nor does Rufinus in his account of the law in the *Ecclesiastical History* 1.32, referring only to the *ludi litterarum*; Ammianus 22.10.7 and 25.4.20 also omits philosophers, speaking only of *magistri, rhetorici,* and *grammatici.* It is possible that the edict was, in its Latin afterlife, understood to have applied primarily to teachers of reading and composition.

156. *Conf.* 8.5.10.

157. *Conf.* 8.2.3.

158. *Conf.* 8.2.3.

159. Ps. 143 (144).5, quoted at 8.2.4.

160. *Conf.* 8.2.4.

161. *Conf.* 8.2.4.

162. *Conf.* 8.2.4, paraphrasing Mt. 10.32–33.

163. Hadot, *Marius Victorinus*, 236–37, suggests that this reading may have been motivated by philosophical curiosity about the variety of paths, in Symmachus' words, *ad tam grande secretum.*

164. *Conf.* 8.2.3.

165. *Conf.* 8.2.3.

166. *Conf.* 8.2.4.

167. On the overlap between readers and texts in Augustine, see, esp. Brian Stock, *Augustine the Reader* (Cambridge, Mass.: Harvard University Press, 1996), ch. 3, "Reading and Conversion." As Stock notes, however (76–77), this is understood in Augustine as a retrospective process, or as a process given temporal structure from the viewpoint of eternity. Cf. Ricoeur, *Time and Narrative*, 22–30, on the importance of eternity for Augustine's structuring of time.

168. *Felicior: Conf.* 8.5.10.

169. *Conf.* 8.5.10.

170. See Bourdieu, *Reproduction*, 34–35; but also Butler, *Gender Trouble*, 174–76, on the ways in which imitation reveals the constructedness of "originals."

171. Butler, *Gender Trouble*, 185: "When the subject is said to be constituted, that means simply that the subject is a consequence of certain rule-governed discourses that govern the intelligible invocation of identity. . . . In a sense, all signification takes place within the orbit of the compulsion to repeat."

172. Robert Markus has argued for significant differences between Christian attitudes toward the classical past in the 350s and in Julian's period, the 380s and 390s (the dramatic date of the *Saturnalia* and the time of composition of Augustine's *Confessions*), and the 430s, the date of the *Saturnalia*'s composition: "Paganism, Christianity and the Latin Classics in the Fourth Century," in *Latin Literature of the Fourth Century*, ed. J. W. Binns (London: Routledge, 1974), 1–21.

173. See Hedrick, *History and Silence*, ch. 6, "Rehabilitating the Text," esp. 202–13.

174. Kaster, *Guardians*, 176, on the potential for "conflict" between ancient and contemporary language.

175. *Ep.* 36, 423a3–4.

176. E.g., at *ep.* 36, 423a2, 6.

177. *Sat.* 3.6.1–16.

178. Kaster, *Guardians*, 14.

179. Hedrick, *History and Silence*, 210, prudently reminds the reader that the late fourth to early fifth century "is a period of transition, and the problem to be explained . . . is ambivalence, the cohabitation of contradictions." Cf. O'Donnell, "Demise," 65, on "ambivalence and ambiguity" in religious identification. It should be noted, however, that this "ambivalence" is not necessarily conscious or psychological at all among late ancient readers: the Christians observing the Lupercalia in the late fifth century (O'Donnell, "Demise," 87) did not necessarily feel ambivalent about it. Perhaps "ambivalence" should be replaced with "multivalence" in the semiotic sense.

180. Markus, "Paganism," 10, notes that late ancient literate "pagans" "were all at least as interested in the books about the gods as in the gods themselves."

181. Barwick/Charisius 151.15–17.

182. Dirk M. Schenkeveld, *A Rhetorical Grammar* (Leiden: Brill, 2004), 3.

183. Hedrick, *History and Silence*, 202.

184. But see Stock, *Augustine the Reader*, 110–11, on both the "readerly character of conversion" and the uses of texts in "the creation of intersubjective thinking."

185. Markus, *End of Ancient Christianity*, argues that "secularity" was increasingly pushed aside by Christian thinking in this period.

186. These within the first few pages: Barwick/Charisius 150.15–17 (Cicero); 150.25–29 (Virgil); 151.1–3 (Terence); 151.8–9 (Varro); 151.15–17 are Adam and Abraham.

187. E.g., Hercules and Mars at Barwick/Charisius 168.33–169.9 and 173.20–24.

188. For a general account of principles of analogy in Dionysius Thrax, Quintilian, and Varro, see Matthews, "Greek and Latin Linguistics," 55–64; for a full account of analogy in Servius, with reference to both earlier and later grammarians, see Anne Uhl, *Servius als Sprachlehrer* (Göttingen: Vandenhoek & Rupracht, 1998), 130–94.

189. It is, of course, helpful to do so, as in, e.g., Markus, *End of Ancient Christianity*, 107–23; O'Donnell, "Demise," 48: "That such a spectrum of religious experiences should produce a single-minded population capable of forming itself into a single pagan movement with which Christianity could struggle is simply not probable."

190. See Butler, *Gender Trouble*, 185, on the "necessary failures" of imitation; but Ricoeur, *Time and Narrative*, 208–14, questions the possibility of historical inquiry that is free of narrative; and it is possible that in order to speak historically about late antiquity some hypostatization of "paganism" as part of a historical narrative is unavoidable. To extrapolate from this to a unitary "pagan" identity for

individual actors, however—that is, to suppress (in Ricoeur's terms) dissonance in favor of consonance—would be to "miss the properly dialectical character of [the] relationship" between the experience of time and the imagining of "plot" (72).

191. Schenkeveld, *Rhetorical Grammar*, 3.

192. *Conf.* 8.2.4: *omnesque christianas litteras.*

193. Cf. Augustine's correspondence with Volusianus, *epp.* 132 and 135–38, discussed in O'Donnell, "Demise," 62–63, and at greater length in A. Chastagnol, "Le sénateur Volusien et la conversion d'une famille de l'aristocratie romaine au Bas-Empire," *Revue des études anciennes* 58 (1956): 240–53.

194. *Conf.* 8.2.4: *quibus modis te insinuasti illi pectori? legebat.*

195. *Conf.* 8.2.4.

196. Recall the homogenization of Latin styles as different as those of Plautus and Juvenal in the *artes*. See Bourdieu, "Production of Belief," 80–81 and 106–11 ("Ritual Sacrilege" and "Being Different"), on the consistent nature of educatedness despite oppositional positions.

197. Note also Augustine's suppression of the time between Victorinus' conversion and his resignation of his teaching post in the wake of Julian's edict. Markus, "Paganism," 7, rightly observes that Augustine's account of Victorinus' conversion probably did not reflect Victorinus' understanding of that event.

198. As in, e.g., Cameron, "Paganism and Literature," 30: "On all sides we find this preoccupation with what was past rather than a realistic attempt to grapple with the present"; Markus, "Paganism," 8: "The real issues of the present seem, somehow, to elude these controversialists." Markus does, however, argue (8) that "archaism is more than a literary device: it provides a means of debating something which neither side in the debate has quite got into focus." I would suggest that archaism is rather the means of focusing.

199. As might be expected from the uses of the term *paganus* in Christian texts; cf. Mohrmann, "Encore une fois," 283–89; O'Donnell, "*Paganus,*" 168. Hedrick, *History and Silence,* 51–54, on the production of "the subjectivity of the pagan."

Chapter 4. Displacement and Excess

1. Besides Victorinus and possibly Charisius, the vehemently anti-Christian philosophers Celsus and Porphyry were familiar enough with the Christian Bible to launch detailed attacks on its veracity and consistency; Porphyry's critical discussion of the book of Daniel contains insights that, while rejected by ancient Christians, form a standard part of modern critical discussions of the book today. For general discussion, see Robert L. Wilken, *The Christians as the Romans Saw Them* (New Haven: Yale University Press, 1984), chs. 5 and 6.

2. See the prosopography of Robert Kaster, *Guardians of Language* (Berkeley: University of California Press, 1988), part 2, for information on individual grammarians.

3. For the text of the *Apologia contra Hieronymum*, I rely on the edition of Manlio Simonetti, *Tyrannii Rufini Scripta Apologetica, Corpus Scriptorum Ecclesiae Aquileiensis* 5.1 (Rome: Città Nuova, 1999); for the *Apologia contra Rufinum*, I rely

on the text of Pierre Lardet, *Saint Jérôme, Apologie contre Rufin, Sources Chrétiennes* 303 (Paris: Éditions du Cerf, 1983).

4. For these letters, I use the text of Jérôme Labourt, *Saint Jérôme, Lettres*, vols. 1 and 3 (Paris: Les Belles Lettres, 1949, 1953).

5. Text of R. P. H. Green, *De Doctrina Christiana* (Oxford: Oxford University Press, 1997); I have used the traditional numbering for ease of reference.

6. Ed. Frederick Field, *Origenis Hexaplorum quae supersunt* (Oxford: Clarendon, 1867–74).

7. Ed. Pierre de LaGarde, *Corpus Christianorum Series Latina* 72 (Turnhout: Brepols, 1959), 59–161. Since there are no chapter divisions, I have cited the text by page and line number.

8. Ed. J. Fraipont, *Corpus Christianorum Series Latina* 33 (Turnhout: Brepols, 1958), 381–465.

9. Wolfgang Iser, "Interaction Between Text and Reader," in Iser, *Prospecting: From Reader Response to Literary Anthropology* (Baltimore: Johns Hopkins University Press, 1989), 31–41. Compare also the tension between the actual selection of books in the early modern library and the idea of the library as the repository of universal knowledge, discussed by Roger Chartier, *The Order of Books*, tr. Lydia G. Cochrane (Stanford: Stanford University Press, 1994), ch. 3, "Libraries Without Walls." Although, as Chartier (64) notes, the idea of the library could be contrasted with that of the cabinet of curiosities, the selection of fragments in these collections could also be used to evoke universal knowledge: see especially Krzysztof Pomian, *Collectors and Curiosities: Paris and Venice, 1500–1800*, tr. Elizabeth Wiles-Portier (Cambridge: Polity Press, 1990), 26–34; and Marjorie Swann, *Curiosities and Texts: The Culture of Collecting in Early Modern England* (Philadelphia: University of Pennsylvania Press, 2001), 9–12, on the production of catalogues of collections as a textualization of material knowledge. For an exploration of how recontextualizations of linguistic fragments could be used both as practical aids to reading and as projections of a collector's persona, see Peter Beal, "Notions in Garrison: The Seventeenth-Century Commonplace Book," in *New Ways of Looking at Old Texts: Papers of the Renaissance English Text Society, 1985–1991*, ed. W. Speed Hill (Binghamton, N.Y.: Renaissance English Text Society, 1993), 131–47. On the significant historiographical differences between lists of events and narratives, see Hayden White, "The Value of Narrativity in the Representation of Reality," in idem, *The Content of the Form* (Baltimore: Johns Hopkins University Press, 1987), 1–25.

10. Cf. Jacques Derrida, *Of Grammatology*, tr. Gayatri Chakravorty Spivak (Baltimore: Johns Hopkins University Press, 1974, corrected edition, 1998), 18, on the idea of totality implied by the compilation of books.

11. There has been a great deal of literature produced on desire and reading, perhaps most famously the essays of Julia Kristeva, *Desire in Language: A Semiotic Approach to Literature and Art*, ed. Leon S. Roudiez, tr. Thomas Gora, Alice Jardine, and Leon S. Roudiez (New York: Columbia University Press, 1980); and Roland Barthes, *A Lover's Discourse*, tr. Richard Howard (New York: Hill and Wang, 1978); here, however, instead of assuming an inherent eroticism in reading, I focus on the overt language of *amor* and *desidio* used by patristic authors.

12. As Anne Carson, in her discussion of eros in Greek literature, remarks, with regard to Sappho's fragment 31: "Where eros is lack, its activation calls for three structural components: lover, beloved, and that which comes between them." *Eros the Bittersweet* (Normal: Dalkey Archive Press, 1998; originally published Princeton: Princeton University Press, 1986), 16. Carson cites Barthes, *A Lover's Discourse*, at 117.

13. *Ecclesiastical History* 6.2–3.

14. Neuschäfer, *Origenes als Philologe* (Basel: Friedrich Reinhardt, 1987), systematically outlines the ways in which the body of Origen's work fits into the traditional categories of grammatical work: textual criticism, in both the *Hexapla* and the biblical commentaries, is the grammarian's *diorthôsis* (122–40; explications of individual words are *glossêmatika* (140–55); explications of content are *historika* (155–202); explanations of grammar and rhetorical tropes are *technika* (202–40); and comments on meter and style are *metrika* (240–46). Neuschäfer also argues that Origen's use of scripture to explicate scripture follows the traditional practice of interpreting "Homer by Homer" (276–85).

15. On the meeting of Alexandrian literary criticism and Stoic grammatical thought in Dionysius, see Rudolf Pfeiffer, *History of Classical Scholarship from the Beginnings to the End of the Hellenistic Age* (Oxford: Clarendon Press, 1968), 261–72; for a detailed discussion of Origen's literary activity in relation to Alexandrian criticism, see the reasoned comments of Neuschäfer, *Origenes als Philologe*, 122–38; and John A. McGuckin, "Origen as Literary Critic in the Alexandrian Tradition," *Origeniana Octava*, ed. L. Perrone (Louvain: Peeters, 2003), 121–35.

16. Karen Jo Torjesen, *Hermeneutical Procedure and Theological Method in Origen's Exegesis* (Berlin: Walter De Gruyter, 1986), 3–12, reviews much of the theological literature on the subject. Neuschäfer, *Origenes als Philologe*, is basic for the grammatical nature of Origen's exegesis. On the relationship between earlier grammatical theory and the productivity of Origen's exegesis, see my "Origen and Christian Naming: Textual Exhaustion and the Boundaries of Gentility in *Commentary on John 1*," *Journal of Early Christian Studies* 14 (2006): 407–36.

17. The best recent discussion of Origen's exegetical theory, and the most pointed attempt to question the notion of substitution of meaning in Origen, is John David Dawson's *Christian Figural Reading and the Fashioning of Identity* (Berkeley: University of California Press, 2002), part 1.

18. *De princ.* 4.2.3.

19. *De princ.* 4.3.11.

20. *Hom. in Exod.* 1.1.1.

21. *Hom. in Lev.* 7.6.7.

22. *Hom. in Lev.* 7.6.5.

23. *De princ.* 4.2.4.

24. *De princ.* 4.3.4.

25. On the difficulty of maintaining a "threefold" approach to reading rather than a dualistic one, see Pierre Jay, "Saint Jérôme et le triple sens de l'Écriture," *Revue des études augustiniennes* 26 (1980): 214–27.

26. For a useful discussion of Origen's complex relationship with "corporal" meaning, see Dawson, *Christian Figural Reading*, ch. 1.

27. Groundwork for the twentieth-century study of relations between Jerome and Rufinus was laid by G. Grützmacher, *Hieronymus: Eine biographische Studie zur alten Kirchengeschichte*, 3 vols. (Leipzig: Dieterich'sche Verlag, 1901; and Berlin: Trowitzsch & Sohn, 1906, 1908), esp. 3:27–85; and F. Cavallera, *Saint Jérôme: Sa vie et son oeuvre*, 2 vols. (Louvain: Spicilegium Sacrum Lovaniense, 1922), 1:229–86. See also F. X. Murphy, *Rufinus of Aquileia (345–411): His Life and Works* (Washington, D.C.: Catholic University of America Press, 1945), 59–81 and 138–57, and J. N. D. Kelly, *Jerome: His Life, Writings, and Controversies* (London: Duckworth, 1975), 195–209 and 243–58; for a closer study of the numerous actors involved, see Stefan Rebenich, *Hieronymus und sein Kreis* (Stuttgart: Franz Steiner, 1992), 126–27, 138–39, and 198–208. On the influence of these networks of actors on the course of the controversy, see Elizabeth A. Clark, *The Origenist Controversy: The Social Construction of an Early Christian Debate* (Princeton: Princeton University Press, 1992). The dating of different stages of the controversy from 393 to 397 is covered by Pierre Nautin, "Études de chronologie hiéronymienne (393–97)," *Revue des études augustiniennes* 19 (1973): 69–86; for earlier reconstructions of the chronology of the entire controversy, see Grützmacher, *Hieronymus*, 1:65–90; and Cavallera, *Saint Jérôme*, 2:31–43 and 121–27.

28. A very useful discussion of the quotation of Origen in the controversy can be found in Ronald Heine, *The Commentaries of Origen and Jerome on St. Paul's Epistle to the Ephesians* (Oxford: Oxford University Press, 2002), 10–17.

29. Murphy, *Rufinus of Aquileia*, 8–9.

30. *Apol. c. Ruf.* 1.16. All translations, unless otherwise noted, are my own.

31. See esp. Mark Vessey, "Jerome's Origen: The Making of a Christian Literary Persona," *Studia Patristica* 28 (1993): 135–45. See also Cavallera, *Saint Jérôme*, 2:115–21, for a list of Jerome's references and tributes to Origen before the onset of the controversy, esp. 118–21, for Jerome's writings from 385 to 393: "Dans cette période de grande activité littéraire, Origène reste le grand inspirateur" (118).

32. Rufinus, in the preface to his own translation of Origen's *De Principiis* (pref. 2), reports that Jerome translated many of Origen's homilies and commentaries; Jerome, in his precontroversy phase, claims that Origen's commentaries on Galatians and Ephesians have been the chief source of his own, and it is likely that much more of Jerome's commentarial work is based on that of Origen, though without attribution. See esp. Caroline P. Bammel, "Die Pauluskommentare des Hieronymus: Die ersten wissenschaftlichen lateinischen Bibelkommentare?" in *Cristianesimo Latino e cultura Greca fino al sec. IV*, Studia Ephemeridis "Augustinianum" 42 (Rome: Institutum Patristicum Augustinianum, 1993), 187–207; and "Origen's Pauline Prefaces and the Chronology of His Pauline Commentaries," in *Origeniana Sexta*, ed. Gilles Dorival and Alain Le Boulluec (Louvain: Peeters, 1995), 495–513; also Ronald E. Heine, "In Search of Origen's Commentary on Philemon," *Harvard Theological Review* 93 (2000): 117–34.

33. Jerome, e.g. in his *ep.* 51, translates and endorses Epiphanius' letter to John of Jerusalem, in which Epiphanius lists his theological objections to Origen. As Kelly, *Jerome*, 198, notes, however, it is likely that neither Jerome nor Rufinus originally admired Origen for his doctrinal speculation but admired him for his exegetical method: "[Jerome's] veneration for him had been largely based on his

marvellous exegesis, not on his dogmatic writings, which up to [393] he does not seem to have studied closely." Admiration for Origen thus rested primarily on his activity as a grammarian rather than a philosopher or theologian, while objections to Origen tended to rest on his theological writing. Rufinus, in his translation of *On First Principles*, as Jerome pointed out, adjusted Origen's theological views to accord more closely to fourth-century orthodoxy: see Cavallera's discussion, *Saint Jérôme*, 1:229–48.

34. Cavallera, *Saint Jérôme*, 1:262–63; Murphy, *Rufinus of Aquileia*, 138–39. Jerome makes much of Rufinus' slowness at *Apol. c. Ruf.* 3.10.

35. *Apol. c. Hier.* 2.15–24.

36. *Ep.* 22.30.

37. *Praeceptor*: the same word that Jerome uses to describe Donatus at *Chron.* s. a. 354, and at *Apol. c. Ruf.* 1.16.

38. *Apol. c. Hier.* 2.11.

39. On Rufinus' care in assembling his charges throughout the *Apology*, see Cavallera, *Saint Jérôme*, 2:97–101: "Son exactitude au cours de cette polémique est incontextablement supérieure à celle de son adversaire" (101).

40. *Apol. c. Hier.* 2.7.

41. *Apol. c. Hier.* 2.7.

42. Note the imaginative productivity of lists of people in late antiquity itself, discussed by Patricia Cox Miller, "'Differential Networks': Relics and Other Fragments in Late Antiquity," *Journal of Early Christian Studies* 6 (1998): 113–38; and Miller, "Strategies of Representation in Collective Biography: Constructing the Subject as Holy," in *Greek Biography and Panegyric in Late Antiquity*, ed. Tomas Hägg and Philip Rousseau (Berkeley: University of California Press, 2000), 209–54.

43. Cf. Foucault's discussion of early modern constructions of fields of knowledge via taxonomy, in *The Order of Things* (New York: Random House, 1970, repr. 1994), 46–58.

44. I am not suggesting that these terms are in any way unique to Rufinus or Jerome, but I am interested in the fact that they are used here specifically to stand in for lists of names. As we will see, Augustine similarly uses the terms to stand in for lists of names. Note also that the term *saecularis* is not equivalent to the idea of "the secular" as a usable neutral category but carries here distinctly negative connotations as the antithesis of the "Christian." See esp. Robert A. Markus, *The End of Ancient Christianity* (Cambridge: Cambridge University Press, 1990), 107–23, on the question of defining "secular" events in the late fourth and fifth centuries.

45. *Apol. c. Hier.* 2.7.

46. *Apol. c. Ruf.* 1.16.

47. As the remainder of *Apol. c. Ruf.* 1.16–17 goes on to show, based as it is on slighting Rufinus' literary abilities.

48. On the use of the first person to indicate this temporal division, see the examples collected from Servius in Kaster, *Guardians*, 174–87.

49. *Apol. c. Hier.* 2.7.

50. *Apol. c. Hier.* 2.7.

51. *Apol. c. Hier.* 2.11.

52. *Apol. c. Hier.* 2.11.

53. *Apol. c. Hier.* 2.7.

54. Rufinus, *Apol. c. Hier.* 2.8, referring to Jerome, *ep.* 21.13, which in turn draws on 1 Cor. 8.9–11.

55. *Apol. c. Hier.* 2.8, quoting Jerome, *ep.* 22.30.

56. *Apol. c. Hier.* 2.7.

57. Referring to Jerome's claim to have read Porphyry in *ep.* 50.

58. Vessey, "Jerome's Origen," 135.

59. Cavallera, *Saint Jérôme*, 2:26; Rebenich, *Hieronymus und sein Kreis*, 145; but P. Nautin ("Le premier échange épistolaire entre Jérôme et Damase: Lettres réelles ou fictives?" *Freiburger Zeitschrift für Philosophie und Theologie* 30 [1983]: 331–43) suggests, as Rebenich notes, that the supposedly early letters between Damasus and Jerome are in fact Jerome's later creations.

60. Rebenich, *Hieronymus und sein Kreis*, 202.

61. The *Apol. c. Ruf.* was composed in part before the whole of Rufinus' *Apol. c. Hier.* was in circulation. Jerome appears to have obtained an earlier version of some of Rufinus' work through his brother Paulinian and other connections (*Apol. c. Ruf.* 1.1, 3; 1.21), so that the first two books of the *Apol. c. Ruf.* appeared before the *Apol. c. Hier.*, and the third book in 402, after Jerome had read the whole of Rufinus' work, sent to him by Rufinus himself (*Apol. c. Ruf.* 3.4). For the chronology, see Cavallera, *Saint Jérôme*, 2:40–42.

62. See discussion in Harald Hagendahl, *The Latin Fathers and the Classics* (Göteburg: Almquist & Wiksell, 1958), 108–9, 208–9.

63. *Ep.* 21.13.

64. *Ep.* 70.2.

65. *Ep.* 21.13.

66. *Ep.* 70.2.

67. *Ep.* 21.13.

68. *Ep.* 21.13: *libri . . . sapientiae saecularis . . . cura saecularium rerum*; *Ep.* 70.2: *saecularium litterarum . . . exempla . . . de gentilium libris . . . sapientiam saecularem*; 70.5: *gentilium litterarum. Gentes* at *ep.* 70.5, 6.

69. *Ep.* 70.2–5.

70. See Miller, "'Differential Networks,'" 133–34.

71. See Wolfgang Iser, "Indeterminacy and the Reader's Response in Prose Fiction," in Iser, *Prospecting*, 3–30; but see also Stanley Fish's critique of Iser's position, "Why No One's Afraid of Wolfgang Iser," *Diacritics* 11 (1981): 2–13. Fish faults Iser for configuring the text as possessing an existence independent of the reader's perception; following Fish, it may be more precise to say that the reader can use the text to insert himself or herself into a particular reading identity.

72. For the seminal modern configuration of lack in reading, see Jacques Lacan, "The Function and Field of Speech and Language in Psychoanalysis," in Lacan, *Écrits*, tr. Alan Sheridan (New York: W. W. Norton, 1977), 30–113.

73. See David M. Halperin's argument on the productivity of using female figures to delineate *sapientia* in "Why Is Diotima a Woman? Platonic *Eros* and the Figuration of Gender," in *Before Sexuality: The Construction of Erotic Experience in the Ancient Greek World*, ed. David M. Halperin, John J. Winkler, and Froma I. Zeitlin (Princeton: Princeton University Press, 1990), 257–308.

74. *Ep.* 21.13.

75. *Ep.* 70.2.

76. See Halperin, "Why Is Diotima a Woman?" 275–94, on Plato's use of ide-ologies of reproduction. I do not mean to suggest that this separation is inherent in some transhistorical sense in the act of reading, nor indeed that separation is transhistorically inherent in the production of desire; I merely wish to note that Jerome's metaphor of desire and reproduction rhetorically posits that separation. Rufinus, obviously, sets the act of reading in a different imaginative framework.

77. *Ep.* 21.13.

78. *Ep.* 21.13.

79. *Ep.* 21.13.

80. *Ep.* 70.2.

81. *Apol. c. Ruf.* 1.16.

82. On the career of Aristarchus, famous in antiquity for his commentaries on Homer, see R. Pfeiffer, *History of Classical Scholarship*, 210–33.

83. *Apol. c. Ruf.* 1.17: *occupatus in sensibus.*

84. *Apol. c. Ruf.* 1.17: *Illud miror quid, Aristarchus nostri temporis, puerilia ista nescieris.*

85. *Apol. c. Ruf.* 1.17: *uel si latina temptaueris, ante audire grammaticum, ferulae manum subtrahere et, inter parvulos athénogerón, artem loquendi discere.*

86. On ancient notions of the relationship between bodies as experienced in dreams and bodies as experienced in waking life, see Patricia Cox Miller, *Dreams in Late Antiquity* (Princeton: Princeton University Press, 1994), ch. 1, "Figurations of Dreams."

87. *Apol. c. Hier.* 2.8.

88. *Apol. c. Ruf.* 1.30.

89. *Ep.* 70.3.

90. *Apol c. Ruf.* 1.30.

91. *Apol. c. Ruf.* 1.31. Miller (*Dreams*, 41) cites Augustine, *De civitate Dei* 18.18, on late ancient beliefs on the independent existence of dream figures from their "real" counterparts. Here Augustine recounts the story of a philosopher who, in a dream, held a philosophical discussion that he had in waking life refused to hold.

92. *Apol. c. Ruf.* 1.31.

93. A reference to the treasonous Calpurnius Bestia in Sallust's *Jugurthine War* and to Calpurnius Lanarius, the traitor to whom Plutarch refers in his *Life of Sertorius*: Labourt, *Saint Jérôme, Lettres* 3:215 n. 1.

94. Cf. Iser, "Indeterminacy," 19–22. Iser suggests, in his reading of Thack-eray's *Vanity Fair*, that the presence of "gaps" in the text both leads the reader to participate in the construction of the novel and threatens to make the reader sub-ordinate to the authorial "management" of it. Note, however, that it is the imag-ined reader Magnus and Jerome's "persona" who are presented as destabilized here.

95. Some of the classic works on the subject of Augustine's relationship to traditional Roman literature include Henri-Irénée Marrou, *Saint Augustin et la fin de la culture antique* (Paris: E. de Boccard, 1938); Harald Hagendahl, *Augustine and the Latin Classics* (Göteburg: Almqvist & Wiksell, 1967), on Augustine's philosoph-ical education; Pierre Courcelle, *Les Confessions de Saint Augustin dans la tradition*

littéraire (Paris: Études Augustiniennes, 1963), part I; a recent reconsideration of classical themes in Augustine is Sabine MacCormack, *Shadows of Poetry: Virgil in the Mind of Augustine* (Berkeley: University of California Press, 1998).

96. Augustine, of course, knew of the famous quarrel between Jerome and Rufinus, as Jerome, *ep.* 110, shows, but was not influenced by them in the formulation of his own position on the uses of grammar, particularly as book 2 of *De doctrina* predates both *Apologies*, although postdating Jerome's *ep.* 21.

97. Gerald Press, "The Subject and Structure of Augustine's *De doctrina Christiana*," *Augustinian Studies* 11 (1980): 99–124; Kathy Eden, "The Rhetorical Tradition and Augustinian Hermeneutics in *De doctrina Christiana*," *Rhetorica* 8 (1990): 45–63; Michael Scanlon, "Augustine and Theology as Rhetoric," *Augustinian Studies* 25 (1994): 37–50; Carol Harrison, "The Rhetoric of Scripture and Preaching," in *Augustine and His Critics*, ed. Robert Dodaro and George Lawless (London: Routledge, 2000), 214–30.

98. Priscian, for example, analyzing the *Aeneid*, begins his detailed grammatical discussions of each line with the imperative *Tracta singulas partes. Partitiones duodecim versuum Aeneidos principalium*, ed. Keil in GL 3.457–515. Cf. Irvine, *Textual Culture*, 178–89.

99. *De doctrina* 3.1.1; cf. Irvine, *Textual Culture*, 179–83.

100. Robert Kaster has noted the considerable overlap between these two teaching professions in late antiquity: "Notes on 'Primary' and 'Secondary' Schools in Late Antiquity," *Transactions and Proceedings of the American Philological Association* 113 (1983): 323–46.

101. Praef.9.18.

102. On the dating of Diomedes, see Kaster, *Guardians*, 271.

103. GL 1.426.19–20. This is, clearly, a broad definition of grammar: Servius, in his commentary on Donatus, argues that grammar proper is concerned especially with the eight parts of speech (GL 4.405.10–11), but "Sergius" (on whom see Kaster, *Guardians*, 429–30), also commenting on Donatus, repeats Diomedes' assertion that the "*ars grammatica* consists principally in the understanding of the poets and in the logic of speaking or writing correctly" (GL 4.486.15–16).

104. 1.1.1.

105. Cf. G. Bellissima, "Sant' Agostino grammatico," *Augustinus Magister*, vol. 1 (Paris: Études Augustiniennes, 1954), 35–42; Jean Collart, "Saint Augustin grammairien dans le *De magistro*," *Revue des études augustiniennes* 17 (1971): 279–92; Vivien Law, "St. Augustine's 'De grammatica': Lost or Found?" *Recherches Augustiniennes* 19 (1984): 155–83; Irvine, *Textual Culture*, 169–78; at 178 Irvine calls *De doctrina* "a christian ars grammatica."

106. 1.2.2.

107. 1.4.4; 1.5.5: *Res igitur quibus fruendum est, pater et filius et spiritus sanctus, eademque trinitas, una quaedam summa res.*

108. Expressed, e.g., at 1.10.10.

109. H.-J. Sieben has argued that *caritas* in *De doctrina* is among the "things" at which scripture aims: "Die 'Res' der Bibel in 'Doctrina Christiana,'" *Revue des études augustiniennes* 21 (1975): 78–79. Although Augustine uses *caritas* more frequently than *amor* in book 1, it is, I think, significant that *amor* provides Augustine

with his definition of "enjoyment" at 1.4.4, and that this *amor* is directed toward the Trinity at 1.5.5. The conflation of *amor*, *caritas*, and other such terms (e.g., *dilectio* at 1.35.39) under the heading "love" may not be entirely out of order, as Augustine does not always use them as distinct technical terms: cf. Karla Pollman, *Doctrina Christiana: Untersuchungen zu den Anfängen der Christlichen Hermeneutik unter besonderer Berücksichtigung von Augustinus, De doctrina Christiana* (Freiburg: Universitätsverlag, 1996), 126–27. It is important here to note, however, that *caritas* and *amor* may not be completely synonymous for Augustine, since at *De doctrina* 3.10.16 Augustine describes *caritas* as movement toward "enjoyment," earlier defined as an instance of *amor*. In short, even if *caritas* is an Augustinian *res*, the relation between "things" and readers would still be based on *amor*. On the interpretive function of *caritas* in *De doctrina*, see esp. Pollman, 121–47, and William S. Babcock, "*Caritas* and Signification," in Duane W. H. Arnold and Pamela Bright, eds., *De doctrina Christiana: A Classic of Western Culture* (Notre Dame: University of Notre Dame Press, 1995), 154–57.

110. Most famously, perhaps, at *Confessions* 10.27.38.

111. 1.2.2. On the significance of Augustine's *per* in *res per signa*, see C. Mayer, "*'Res per signa*': Der Grundgedanke des Prologs in Augustins Schrift *De doctrina Christiana* und das Problem seiner Datierung," *Revue des études augustiniennes* 20 (1974): 104.

112. 1.2.2.

113. 2.3.4.

114. Grammatical *tractatio*, as illustrated most prominently in Priscian's *Partitiones*, tended to be either word-by-word analysis of written works or discussions of individual words in phrase-by-phrase reading; for discussion of one such analysis, see Kaster, *Guardians*, ch. 5, on Servius' Virgil commentary. On earlier uses of etymology in grammatical analysis, see Mark Amsler, *Etymology and Grammatical Discourse in Late Antiquity and the Early Middle Ages* (Amsterdam: John Benjamins, 1989), esp. 15–31.

115. 1.37.86–89.

116. 1.37.89–91.

117. See Martin Irvine's discussion of Augustine's theory of allegory for developments of this basic triangular scheme: Irvine, *Textual Culture*, 257–65.

118. 2.40.60.

119. 2.40.60. The trope of "spoiling the Egyptians" as a metaphor for Christian "use" of the liberal arts is not unique to Augustine; for discussion of the use of the Exodus metaphor from Marcion on, see Christian Gnilka, *Chrêsis: Die Methode der Kirchenväter im Umgang mit der Antiken Kultur*, vol. 1, *Der Begriff des "Rechten Gebrauchs"* (Basel: Schwabe, 1984), 57 n. 120. Gnilka, 102–33, also notes the prevalence in early Christian and other ancient writers of the trope of the bee as a similar metaphor (the student, beelike, is to take the "nectar" of literature and put it to proper, usually philosophical, use), but Gnilka does not connect this decontextualizing trope with the work of ancient grammarians.

120. 2.39.59. Augustine may here have in mind the sort of project more commonly associated with Roman antiquarianism, as for example the second-century dictionary of Festus. In 419, Augustine himself compiled a list, not of geographical

or botanical terms from the Bible but of unidiomatic Latin phrases in the Hepta-teuch, as a similar kind of reading aid, the *Locutiones in Heptateuchum*, which will be discussed further below.

121. This disjunctive procedure is applied even to the signs of scripture, which must be brought into the context of the "rule of faith" in order to be under-stood properly; 3.2.2.

122. Cf. Lacan, "Function and Field," 86: "For the function of language is not to inform but to evoke."

123. 2.40.61.

124. 2.40.60: *doctrinae omnes gentilium . . . de societate gentilium*; 2.40.61: *superstitiosa gentium consuetudo*; 2.42.63: *de libri gentium*.

125. 2.19–42. The role of this list in *De doctrina* has long been debated; Poll-man, *Doctrina Christiana*, 89–108, places it within the overall structure of the work by reading *De doctrina* as fundamentally dihairetic in structure; on book 2, 149–55. L. M. J. Verheijen, however, has argued that the list of pagan studies is a "digres-sion" from the primary argument of book 2: "Le *De doctrina christiana* de Saint Augustin: Un manuel d'herméneutique et d'expression chrétienne avec, en II. 19.29–42.63, une charte fondamentale pour une culture chrétienne," *Augustiniana* 24 (1974): 10–20. While I would not argue that the discussion at 2.19–42 is merely tangential to the rest of book 2, I agree with Christoph Schäublin that Augustine here "abruptly shifts his viewpoint": "*De doctrina christiana*: A Classic of Western Culture?" in Arnold and Bright, *De doctrina*, 50. The thoroughness of the "review" of learning in the passage allows Augustine to conjure "paganism" precisely by means of the mass of detail not directly pertinent to his argument (e.g., the list of differ-ent kinds of superstition at 2.20.31); cf. Lacan, "Function and Field," 86: "What is redundant as far as information is concerned is precisely that which does duty as resonance in speech."

126. For discussion of the historiographical controversy over whether or not *De doctrina* is a programmatic guide to Christian "education" or "culture," see esp. Eugene Kevane, "Augustine's *De doctrina christiana*: A Treatise on Christian Edu-cation," *Recherches Augustiniennes* 4 (1966): 97–133; and Verheijen, "Le *De doctrina*," 10–20; more recently, Gerald Press, "*Doctrina* in Augustine's *De doctrina christiana*," *Philosophy and Rhetoric* 17, no. 2 (1984): 98–120; and Schäublin, "*De doctrina chris-tiana*," 47–52.

127. 2.39.58.

128. Cf. Amsler, *Etymology*, 102–3.

129. 2.39.59.

130. 2.40.61.

131. 2.40.61.

132. 2.42.63.

133. The use of geographical metaphors to create religious identity will be discussed in Chapter 6.

134. 2.42.63.

135. Interestingly, of the only twenty-four times that Augustine uses the word *christianus* in *De doctrina*, fourteen occur in book 2, in the course of Augus-tine's description of the branches of learning and how they are to be despoiled for

the *tractatio scripturarum*: 2.12.17; 2.16.24; 2.18.28; 2.23.36; 2.25.38; 2.25.40; 2.29.45; 2.35.53; 2.39.59 (twice); 2.40.60 (twice); 2.40.61; and 2.41.62. The other occurrences are at praef. 4 and 5 (twice); 1.14.13; 1.30.32; 3.8.12; 4.1.1; 4.7.11; 4.14.31; and 4.31.64.

136. See Fish, "Why No One's Afraid of Wolfgang Iser," 10–13.

137. On the place of Jerome and Augustine in this tradition, see Amsler, *Etymology*, 82–118; see also Louis Holtz, *Donat et la tradition de l'enseignement grammatical* (Paris: CNRS, 1981), 40–46.

138. Jerome, *ep.* 112; Augustine, *ep.* 71.

139. For a brief discussion of the transmission of the *Hexapla*, see O. Munnich, "Les *Hexaples* d'Origène à la lumière de la tradition manuscrite de la Bible grecque," in *Origeniana Sexta: Origène et la Bible*, ed. Gilles Dorival and Alain Le Boulluec (Louvain: University Press, 1995), 167–85; and J.-N. Guinot, "La fortune des *Hexaples* d'Origène aux IVe et Ve siècles au milieu antiochien," 215–25, in the same volume. For a more thorough introduction to the fragments and testimonia, see P. Nautin, *Origène: Sa vie et son oeuvre* (Paris: Beauchesne, 1977), 303–61.

140. On Zenodotus, see esp. Pfeiffer, *History of Classical Scholarship*, 105–22; on Aristophanes, 171–209.

141. See Neuschäfer, *Origenes als Philologe*, 86–103, on Origen's need to establish a critical text of the LXX.

142. On the *Lexeis* of Aristophanes, see Pfeiffer, *History of Classical Scholarship*, 197–202.

143. See esp. Michael Frede, "Principles of Stoic grammar," in *The Stoics*, ed. John Rist (Berkeley: University of California Press, 1978), 59–73; and Urs Egli, "Stoic Syntax and Semantics," in *The History of Linguistics in the Classical Period*, ed. Daniel J. Taylor (Amsterdam: John Benjamins, 1987), 107–32.

144. More commonly discussed in relation to Origen's allegorical reading of scripture: Irvine, *Textual Culture*, 265–71; see also Patricia Cox Miller, "Origen and the Witch of Endor: Toward an Iconoclastic Typology," *Anglican Theological Review* 66 (1984): 137–47.

145. On Stoic approaches to the problem of the existence of multiple languages, see Frede, "Principles," 68–69; on Origen's syllabic approach to Hebrew names, see R. P. C. Hanson, "Interpretations of Hebrew Names in Origen," *Vigiliae Christianae* 10 (1956): 103–23.

146. This ought not to suggest that the words do not evoke meaning, despite the fact that they are, properly, not meaningful words. Patricia Cox Miller has eloquently discussed the possibilities of meaningful evocation in other kinds of phonetic writing in late antiquity: "In Praise of Nonsense: A Piety of the Alphabet in Ancient Magic," in Miller, *The Poetry of Thought in Late Antiquity* (Aldershot: Ashgate, 2001), 221–45.

147. Though multilingual writings, such as inscriptions, seem to have been more common in the Eastern parts of the empire than in the Western; see Ralph Häussler, "Writing Latin—From Resistance to Assimilation: Language, Culture, and Society in N. Italy and S. Gaul," in *Becoming Roman, Writing Latin?* ed. Alison E. Cooley, Journal of Roman Archaeology Supplements 48 (Portsmouth: Journal of Roman Archaeology, 2002), 61–76.

148. For a discussion of the possible purposes of the transliteration, see Nautin, *Origène*, 336–39, who summarizes earlier literature on the topic and concludes that Origen is working from a tradition of Jewish synoptic biblical texts, compiled for Jews without knowledge of Hebrew.

149. I do not mean to suggest that Origen's project with regard to the recuperation of Hebrew for Christian use is precisely the same as Jerome's; for a discussion of the differences, see Andrew S. Jacobs, *Remains of the Jews: The Holy Land and Christian Empire in Late Antiquity* (Stanford: Stanford University Press, 2003), 60–67.

150. E.g., at *Apol. c. Ruf.* 1.16.

151. *Apol. c. Hier.* 2.11.

152. Though this is questionable; on the problem of assigning Origen authorship of the *Vorlage* of the *Liber interpretationis*, see the work of F. Wutz, *Onomastica Sacra*, Texte und Untersuchungen zur Geschichte der altchristlichen Literatur 41.1–2 (Leipzig: Hinrichs, 1914–15), 30–43.

153. *Lib. int.* 60.17–19.

154. On the dating of the *Liber interpretationis* and *Quaestiones*, see Wutz, *Onomastica Sacra*, 259ff.; also C. T. R. Hayward's introduction to his *Saint Jerome's Hebrew Questions on Genesis* (Oxford: Clarendon, 1995).

155. *Lib. int.* praef.59.20–23.

156. This is not, of course, the only possible configuration of Jewish knowledge, even for Jerome, though his exploration of Hebrew is that for which he is most famous. For Jerome's reliance on Jewish "local knowledge" for projects that are partly linguistic and partly geographical or cultural (i.e., having to do with the geography or customs of Palestine), see Jacobs, *Remains of the Jews*, ch. 3, "'Captive Judaea': The Production of Jewish Knowledge," 67–83. Even here, however, Jerome's conflation of actual Jews with "biblical" Jews is ultimately based on questions arising out of the biblical text, so that the basis of Jewish knowledge in language is simply assumed.

157. *Lib. int.* praef.59.1–5, 59.25–60.3. The existence of a Jewish *Liber nominum*, probably not Philonic, taken up by Christian readers, seems indisputable; see Wutz, *Onomastica Sacra*, 14–24; N. de Lange, *Origen and the Jews* (Cambridge: Cambridge University Press, 1976), 117–18, for Origen's interest in Hebrew etymologies, despite the fact that the author of Jerome's *Vorlage* was probably not Origen; see Adam Kamesar, *Jerome, Greek Scholarship and the Hebrew Bible* (Oxford: Clarendon Press, 1993), 103–26, on the presence of the originally Jewish *Liber nominum* in Jerome's *Liber* and *Quaestiones Hebraicae in Genesim*.

158. *Quaestiones Hebraicae in Genesim* praef., *Corpus Christianorum Series Latina* 72 (Turnhout: Brepols, 1959); on the question of plagiarism and Jerome's metaphor here, see Richard Layton, "Plagiarism and Lay Patronage of Ascetic Scholarship: Jerome, Ambrose and Rufinus," *Journal of Early Christian Studies* 10 (2002): 489–522.

159. *Lib. int.* 66.23–27: *Geon pectus sive praeruptum. Gomer adsumptio sive consummatio vel perfectio. Gergesaeus colonum eiciens sive advenam propinquantem. Gerara ruminationem vidit seu maceria. Sed sciendum quod gerara interpretatur incolatus, gedera vero maceria sive saepes. Gaza fortitudo eius.*

160. *Quaestiones* 21.14, on the age of Ishmael: "Nor should we be amazed that a barbarian language has its own distinctive characteristics, when even in Rome today all sons are called infants" (tr. Hayward).

161. 60.10–11.

162. Samech, sin, and sade, 71.1–10. Cf. James Barr, "St. Jerome and the Sounds of Hebrew," *Journal of Semitic Studies* 12 (1967): 1–36.

163. E.g., at 65.28–29 and 70.14–15.

164. Jerome also notes, for some consonants, the presence or absence of aspirates in transliteration, appealing, e.g. at 63.9–10, to the difference between *C* and the Greek chi, transliterated into Latin as *Ch*.

165. 59.2.

166. 59.25–60.1.

167. 59.9–10.

168. 59.20–23.

169. Indeed, so strongly is language connected to religious identity that Rufinus will later rebuke Jerome for his apparent willingness to bring the biblical text too much under the control of Jewish interpreters, through his work on the *hebraica veritas* (*Apol. c. Hier.* 2.12). Augustine, famously, voices the same complaint at *ep.* 71.2–3.

170. 59.12–13.

171. 60.2–3.

172. See the classic discussion of the place of supplementarity in linguistic work in Derrida, *Of Grammatology*, part II.2, "That Dangerous Supplement."

173. Unfortunately Adam Kamesar's and C. T. R. Hayward's discussions of the *Liber interpretationis* are focused primarily on its etymologizing of names in Genesis, as their primary concern is the work's relation to the *Quaestiones Hebraicae in Genesim*.

174. 59.23–24.

175. 139.28–29 and 139.9.

176. 143.12–14. Wutz considers in some detail the etymological routes by which many of Jerome's non-Hebrew words could be assigned Hebrew meanings (Wutz, *Onomastica Sacra*, 424–31).

177. Wutz, *Onomastica Sacra*, 259ff.

178. Often in more commentarial contexts: for discussion, see Amsler, *Etymology*, 109–18.

179. Cf. 148.26–28: *Haec omnia graeca nomina vel latina quam violenter secundum linguam hebraicam interpretata sint, perspicuum puto esse lectori.*

180. Tr. Hayward.

181. Here I disagree slightly with Amsler on the function of false Hebrew etymologies in the *Liber interpretationis*; where he reads these as theologically motivated and deliberate, I see them as less overtly theological for Jerome in this context, though I would not deny that Jerome's Greek *Vorlage* may have had a definite theological interest in such "Hebrew" etymologizing of New Testament names, as Amsler describes in earlier Alexandrian grammatical work. Nor would I suggest that Jerome never etymologizes with theological intent, but his repeated comments of *violentum est*, especially for Hebrew etymologizing of words in the book of Acts, seems to indicate a certain hesitancy in his endorsement of them.

182. 139.28–29.

183. 60.3.

184. 59.4,11.

185. See Amsler, *Etymology*, 109–11, on some of the possible theological motivations for Jerome's etymological work.

186. 60.3.

187. 59.26.

188. *De doctr.* 2.39.59.

189. *Loc. in Hept.* 1.praef.2–4. On the particular biblical texts that Augustine had at his disposal see the work of A.-M. La Bonnardière, *Biblia Augustiniana* (Paris: Études Augustiniennes, 1960–).

190. *Retr.* 2.54.5–9.

191. An ancient example of similar "curiosity-hunting" would be Phlegon of Tralles' *Book of Marvels* (*De Mirabilibus*, ed. A. Westerman. in *Paradoxographoi: Scriptores Rerum Mirabilium Graeci* [Amsterdam: A. Hakkert, 1963]; English translation and commentary in William Hansen, *Phlegon of Tralles' Book of Marvels* [Exeter: University of Exeter Press, 1996]) in which odd events or objects are likewise presented in list form.

192. Symmachus is explicitly mentioned at 1.20.88–94 and 6.10.68.

193. E.g., at 1.36.145–46; 1.124.453–54; 1.178.666–67; 2.3.20–21; 2.69.290–91, *et passim*; *latini* at 1.6.18–22; 1.7.23; 1.8.29–31; 1.10.40–44; 1.13.58–62 *et passim*; *graeci* at 1.52.218; 1.53.223–24; 1.54.225–29; 1.60.245–46; 1.75.284–86 *et passim*.

194. On Christian book production, see esp. Harry Y. Gamble, *Books and Readers in the Early Church* (New Haven: Yale University Press, 1995), ch. 2, "The Early Christian Book."

195. Cf. James J. O'Donnell's brilliantly brief statement: "Augustine never saw a Bible," in his entry on the Bible in *Augustine Through the Ages: An Encyclopedia*, ed. Allan D. Fitzgerald (Grand Rapids: Eerdmans, 1999), 99.

196. *Loc. in Hept.* 1.8.29–31.

197. *Loc. in Hept.* 4.61.232–33.

198. *Loc. in Hept.* 1.71.271–74.

199. *Retr.* 2. 54.1–14, on the use of linguistic clarity to contain linguistic irregularity; cf. *De doctrina* 3.1.1, on the use of similar principles in biblical interpretation more generally.

200. For which the *locus classicus* is *Conf.* 3.5.9.

201. Brian Stock, *Augustine the Reader* (Cambridge, Mass.: Belknap, 1996), esp. ch. 3, on the transformative power of reading for the reader in Augustine's thought.

202. For discussion, see Kaster, *Guardians*, esp. 179–90.

203. See Roland Barthes, "From Work to Text," in *Image-Music-Text*, tr. Stephen Heath (New York: Hill and Wang, 1977), 157, on the productivity of texts.

204. Cf. Augustine's comments on the necessity of reading "spiritually" rather than "carnally" at *De doctrina* 3.5.9–3.6.11.

205. See Mark Vessey's discussion of the "all-encompassing" nature of Mallarmé's ideal book, and its relation to late antique reading, in "Theory, or the

Dream of the Book (Mallarmé to Blanchot)," in *The Early Christian Book*, ed. William Klingshirn and Linda Safran (Washington, D.C.: Catholic University of America Press, 2007), 241–73.

206. E.g., at 1.19.15; 1.133.506–9; 1.136.518; 1.147.549; 1.22.98–100; 2.38.166; 2.51.228–29, *et passim*.

207. At 1.94.348; 3.47.142–45; 4.28.104–5; and 6.10.72–73.

208. At 2.133.574–76.

209. On intertexuality as the transformation of texts, see the seminal work of Julia Kristeva, "Word, Dialogue, and Novel," tr. Thomas Gora et al., in *Desire in Language*, ed. Leon S. Roudiez (New York: Columbia University Press, 1980), 64–91; cf. also Barthes, "From Work to Text," 155–64. For discussion of how Kristeva's work may be applied to the reading of Roman texts, see Lowell Edmunds, *Intertextuality and the Reading of Roman Poetry* (Baltimore: Johns Hopkins University Press, 2001), esp. ch. 1; for intertextuality and biblical exegesis in antiquity, see Daniel Boyarin, *Intertextuality and the Reading of Midrash* (Bloomington: Indiana University Press, 1990).

210. *Retr.* 2.54.13.

211. *Retr.* 2.54.11–13.

212. See esp. Christoph Schäublin, "Zur paganen Prägung der christlichen Exegese," in *Christliche Exegese zwischen Nicaea und Chalcedon*, ed. J. Van Oort and Ulrich Wickert (Kampen: Kok Pharos, 1992), 148–73.

213. E.g., at 1.97.354–55; 1.152.559–60; and 2.130.569.

214. E.g., at 1.12.52–53; 1.23.105; 1.25.115–16; 1.50.213; *et passim*.

215. E.g., at 1.12.52–53 (*frequens in scripturis*); 1.23.105 (*usitata in scripturis*); 1.25.116 (*familiarissima in scripturis*); 1.50.213 (*locutio quidem scripturarum est usitatissima*); *et passim*.

216. 1.40.160; 1.43.175; and 2.67.313.

217. E.g., *quod ait scriptura* at 1.39.155 and 1.44.181.

218. *De doctrina* 2.40.60–2.42.63; on Augustine and Jews, see esp. the ongoing work of Paula Fredriksen, e.g.: "*Excaecati Occulta Justitia Dei*: Augustine on Jews and Judaism," *Journal of Early Christian Studies* 3 (1995): 299–324; "*Secundem carnem*: History and Israel in the Theology of St. Augustine," in *The Limits of Ancient Christianity*, ed. William Klingshirn and Mark Vessey (Ann Arbor: University of Michigan Press, 1999), 26–41; "Allegory and Reading God's Book: Paul and Augustine on the Destiny of Israel," in *Interpretation and Allegory: Antiquity to the Modern Period*, ed. J. Whitman (Leiden: Brill, 2001), 125–49; and "Augustine and Israel: *Interpretatio ad litteram*, Jews, and Judaism in Augustine's Theology of History," *Studia Patristica* 38 (2001): 119–35.

219. Cf. Barthes, "From Work to Text," 159: "The Text is plural. . . . The Text is not a co-existence of meanings but a passage, an overcrossing; thus it answers not to an interpretation, even a liberal one, but to an explosion, a dissemination."

220. I find no overt reference to "Jews" or "Hebrews" in the *Locutions*, beyond the occasional reference to "Hebrew idiom" (e.g., at 1.praef.3); indeed, in the *Quaestiones in Heptateuchum*, Augustine simply groups the Heptateuch together with "the holy scriptures that are called canonical" (1.praef.2). In his correspondence with Jerome (*ep.* 71.2.3–71.3.5), it is specifically the Hebrew Bible that is coded

as "Jewish"; here Augustine's concern is primarily with the Greek and Latin text that he takes to be unproblematically available for Christian use.

221. *Lib. int.* 59.10–11.

222. *Loc. in Hept.* praef.

Chapter 5. Fear, Boredom, and Amusement

1. Discussion of children in antiquity has generally been grouped under the heading of the ancient family, on which much work has recently been done. See, e.g., Beryl Rawson, ed., *Marriage, Divorce, and Children in Ancient Rome* (Oxford: Clarendon Press, 1991); Keith R. Bradley, *Discovering the Roman Family: Studies in Roman Social History* (New York: Oxford University Press, 1991); Suzanne Dixon, *The Roman Family* (Baltimore: Johns Hopkins University Press, 1992); Beryl Rawson and Paul Weaver, eds., *The Roman Family in Italy: Status, Sentiment, Space* (Oxford: Clarendon Press, 1997); Thomas Wiedemann, *Adults and Children in the Roman Empire* (New Haven: Yale University Press, 1989).

2. I rely on the senses of the terms "emotion" and "affect" articulated by Brian Massumi, "The Autonomy of Affect," in *Deleuze: A Critical Reader*, ed. Paul Patton (Oxford: Blackwell, 1996), 217–39. Massumi argues for the primacy of a bodily reaction (which he labels "intensity" and equates with affect) to events or images, a reaction that is then narrated into emotion: "Emotion is qualified intensity [that is, affect], the conventional consensual point of insertion of intensity into semantically and semiotically formed progressions, into narrativizable action-reaction circuits, into function and meaning. It is intensity owned and recognized. It is crucial to theorize the difference between affect and emotion."

3. Henri-Irénée Marrou, *A History of Education in Antiquity*, tr. George Lamb from the 3rd French ed., 1948 (Madison: University of Wisconsin Press, 1956), 158–59 and 272–73, cites many of the classical references to schoolroom beatings in ancient Greece and Rome. On punishments of schoolchildren in Rome in particular, Stanley Bonner, *Education in Ancient Rome* (Berkeley: University of California Press, 1977), 142–45, is standard; more recent work on the corporal punishment of children in Roman society has tended to focus on beatings administered at home: e.g., Richard Saller, "Corporal Punishment, Authority, and Obedience in the Roman Household," in Rawson, ed., *Marriage, Divorce, and Children in Ancient Rome*, 144–65; see also Theodore de Bruyn, "Flogging a Son: The Emergence of the *pater flagellans* in Latin Christian Discourse," *Journal of Early Christian Studies* 7, no. 2 (1999): 249–90. For a theoretical discussion of the classroom as a site of symbolic violence, see Pierre Bourdieu and Jean-Claude Passeron, *Reproduction in Education, Society, and Culture*, tr. Richard Nice, 2nd ed. (London: Sage, 1990), esp. book 1: "Foundations of a Theory of Symbolic Violence"; cf. also Michel Foucault, *Discipline and Punish*, tr. Alan Sheridan (New York: Vintage Books, 1979), part 3, ch. 2, "The Means of Correct Training."

4. Seneca, *De clementia* 1.16; Quintilian, *Institutio oratoria* 1.3.13–17.

5. *Ep.* 2.1.70; Bonner, *Education in Ancient Rome*, 144.

6. *De gram. et rhet.* 9.4.

7. Martial, *Epig.* 10.62.8–9.

8. *Prof.* 10.18: *moribus inplacidis.* Examples could be multiplied: see, e.g., Ovid, *Am.* 1.13.17; Juvenal, *Sat.* 1.15; Cicero *ep. ad. fam.* 7.25.1.

9. *Ep.* 22.33–44.

10. *De gram. et rhet.* 9.4: *quos Orbilius ferula scuticasque cecidit.*

11. Cf. Bourdieu and Passeron, *Reproduction*, 46–47.

12. The letter, to M. Fabius Gallus, written in 45 B.C.E, urges Gallus to continue to write against Caesar, and identifies both Cicero and Gallus as "Catonians," i.e., supporters of the republican cause backed by M. Porcius Cato until his death in 46 B.C.E. Speaking of possible repercussions to them from Caesar's followers, Cicero takes the rhetorical stance of a schoolboy about to be caught misbehaving: "Attention now! No more writing! Here comes the beak, sooner than expected! It's the cat [*catomus*, a form of beating] for the Catonians, I fear" (tr. D. R. Shackleton Bailey, in *Cicero's Letters to His Friends* [Atlanta: Scholar's Press, 1988]).

13. 9.5: *ac ne principus quidem virorum insectatione abstinuit.*

14. For analysis of Freud's famous essay, see Ethel Spector Person, ed., *On Freud's "A Child Is Being Beaten"* (New Haven: Yale University Press, 1997). Person, 1–28, provides the Standard Edition version of the essay from James J. Strachey, *The Standard Edition of the Complete Psychological Works of Sigmund Freud*, vol 17 (London: Hogarth Press, 1955), 179–204.

15. *Conf.* 1.9.14–15.

16. *De inani gloria et de liberis educandis* 39. A.-M. Malingrey discusses the authenticity and date (393 or 394) of the sermon in her introduction to the *Sources Chrétiennes* edition, *Sur la vaine gloire et l'éducation des enfants* (Paris: Cerf, 1972), 13–47. For discussion of Chrysostom's writing about children more generally, see Blake Leyerle, "Appealing to Children," *Journal of Early Christian Studies* 5, no. 2 (1997): 243–70.

17. Which is not to suggest, however, that Chrysostom was unaware of arguments against beating; he elsewhere (30) admonishes parents not to beat their children in actuality, as this will prove counterproductive to the generation of fear; I discuss this attitude further below.

18. *Apol. c. Ruf.* 1.30.

19. *Ep.* 22.30.

20. *Ep.* 22.30.

21. *De inan. glor.* 30, tr. M. L. W. Laistner, *Christianity and Pagan Culture in the Later Roman Empire* (Ithaca: Cornell University Press, 1951).

22. Cf. Gilles Deleuze's discussion of the dramatic qualities of masochistic literature and practice, in which he suggests that "formally speaking, masochism is a state of waiting; the masochist experiences waiting in its pure form," and that "in Masoch's novels, it is the moments of suspense that are the climactic moments": *Masochism: An Interpretation of Coldness and Cruelty*, tr. Jean McNeil (New York: Zone Books, 1991), 71 and 33.

23. See Massumi on the separation of affect from event, and from subsequent narratives of emotional response: "Autonomy of Affect," 217–19.

24. Massumi, "Autonomy of Affect," 218, and Massumi, *A User's Guide to*

Capitalism and Schizophrenia: Deviations from Deleuze and Guattari (Cambridge, Mass.: MIT Press, 1992), 10, on the "envelop[ment] of potential."

25. Deleuze, *Masochism*, 71: "Pure waiting divides naturally into two simultaneous currents, the first representing what is awaited, something essentially tardy . . . the second representing something that is expected and on which depends the speeding up of the awaited object."

26. See Massumi, "Autonomy of Affect," 221.

27. *Conf.* 1.9.15. A similar move occurs in *De civitate Dei* 22.14 (tr. Henry Bettenson [London: Penguin, 1972]), when, after listing "the stick, the strap, the birch, and all the means of [school] discipline," Augustine continues with the judicial threat of being "chained and imprisoned, exiled and tortured, [having] limbs . . . cut off and organs of sense destroyed, bodies . . . brutally misused to gratify the obscene lust of the oppressor, and many such horrors."

28. *De inan. glor.* 30, 39.

29. On the use of "hyperrealism" in late ancient art and poetry, see esp. S. Georgia Nugent, "Ausonius' 'Late-Antique' Poetics and 'Post-Modern' Literary Theory," *Ramus* 19 (1990): 26–50; and Patricia Cox Miller, "'Differential Networks': Relics and Other Fragments in Late Antiquity," *Journal of Early Christian Studies* 6 (1998): 113–38. For the narrative uses of detail to create a "reality effect," see Roland Barthes, "The Reality Effect," tr. R. Carter, in *French Literary Theory Today*, ed. T. Todorov (Cambridge: Cambridge University Press, 1982), 11–17.

30. *Ep.* 22.30.

31. For discussion of the uses to which "real" props can be put in the heightening of violent drama, see John K. Noyes, *The Mastery of Submission: Inventions of Masochism* (Ithaca: Cornell University Press, 1997), 1–4, on the purchase of KGB interrogation equipment by a sadomasochistic establishment.

32. *De inan. glor.* 39.

33. *Conf.* 1.9.14.

34. Noyes, *Mastery of Submission*, 219: "[The masochistic game] mobilizes subjective disappearance as a productive force, a kind of identity machine."

35. *Conf.* 1.9.15.

36. *Ep.* 22.30.

37. *De inan. glor.* 30.

38. *Conf.* 1.9.14, 15; *Apol. c. Ruf.* 1.30; *De inan. glor.* 39.

39. In this sense the passages differ from the Foucaultian premodern "spectacle of the scaffold": *Discipline and Punish*, part 1, ch. 2; for discussion of Chrysostom's use of "the gaze" in the context of Christian asceticism, see Blake Leyerle, "John Chrysostom on the Gaze," *Journal of Early Christian Studies* 1 (1993): 159–74, and Leyerle, *Theatrical Shows and Ascetic Lives* (Berkeley: University of California Press, 2001), esp. ch. 3, "John Chrysostom's View of the Theater."

40. *Ep.* 22.30.

41. *Ep.* 22.30.

42. On the depiction of varying flows of time, see Deleuze, *Cinema 2: The Time-Image*, tr. Hugh Tomlinson and Robert Galeta (Minneapolis: University of Minnesota Press, 1989), 16–18.

43. Massumi, *User's Guide*, 12–14; Deleuze, *Masochism*, 70–72.

44. *Conf.* 1.9.15.

45. For a brief history of grammar in early Rome, see esp. ch. 5 of Bonner's *Education in Ancient Rome*, 47–64; the main primary source for this history is the *De grammaticis et rhetoribus* of Suetonius. On the composition and transmission of this text, see Robert Kaster's *Suetonius: De Grammaticis et Rhetoribus* (Oxford: Clarendon Press, 1995), xxi–lvii.

46. Seneca, *Ep.* 88.

47. *Noc. Att.* 14.6.

48. See Peter Toohey, "Some Ancient Notions of Boredom," *Illinois Classical Studies* 13 (1988): 151–64; Toohey, "Acedia in Late Classical Antiquity," *Illinois Classical Studies* 15 (1990): 339–52; the standard account of boredom from antiquity to the present is Reinhard Kuhn, *The Demon of Noontide: Ennui in Western Literature* (Princeton: Princeton University Press, 1976); Edward Peters sketches out a history of boredom from the twelfth century on in his "Notes Toward an Archaeology of Boredom," *Social Research* 42 (1975): 493–511; Martin Wangh helpfully follows this with his "Boredom in Psychoanalytic Perspective," *Social Research* 42 (1975): 538–50; on boredom more generally in the history and philosophy of Christianity, see Michael L. Raposa, *Boredom and the Religious Imagination* (Charlottesville: University of Virginia Press, 1999), whose first chapter briefly deals with the emergence of acedia; although see also Siegfried Wenzel, who defines acedia somewhat differently in his *The Sin of Sloth: Acedia in Medieval Thought and Literature* (Chapel Hill: University of North Carolina Press, 1967).

49. *Noc. Att.* 14.5.

50. On the temporal implications of boredom, cf. Jeff Nunokawa, "The Importance of Being Bored: The Dividends of Ennui in *The Picture of Dorian Gray*," in *Novel Gazing: Queer Readings in Fiction*, ed. Eve Kosofsky Sedgwick (Durham: Duke University Press, 1997), 153–55.

51. Martianus Capella, *De nuptiis Philologiae et Mercurii*, ed. James Willis (Leipzig: Teubner, 1983); references throughout will be to Willis' text. I have also consulted the translations and commentaries by William H. Stahl and Richard Johnson, *Martianus Capella and the Seven Liberal Arts*, 2 vols. (New York: Columbia University Press, 1971), and Ilaria Ramelli, *Marziano Capella: Le Nozze di Filologia e Mercurio* (Milan: Bompiani, 2001).

52. *Taedium* and *fastidium*, used, e.g., at 3.326.4, 6.704.12, 8.809.1, 8.897.20, and 9.888.8.

53. On the use of narrative to "get out" of boredom, see the useful study of Patricia Meyer Spacks, *Boredom: The Literary History of a State of Mind* (Chicago: University of Chicago Press, 1995), esp. ch. 3, "The Consciousness of the Dull: Eighteenth-Century Women, Boredom, and Narrative."

54. On individuals as made up of differing flows of time, see esp. Deleuze, *Cinema 2*, chs. 4 and 5. Also helpful is Claire Colbrook's discussion of Deleuze's work on the cinema, "Cinema: Perception, Time, and Becoming," ch. 2 of her *Gilles Deleuze* (London: Routledge, 2002).

55. Little is known of Martianus the author; he seems to have been from Carthage. For a summary of the debate over the dating of the work, see Sabine Grebe, *Martianus Capella "De Nuptiis Philologiae et Mercurii": Darstellung der Sieben*

Freien Künste und ihrer Beziehungen Zueinander (Leipzig: Teubner, 1999), 10–22; Alan Cameron, "Martianus and His First Editor," *Classical Philology* 81 (1986): 320–28, argues for a date some time in the first third of the fifth century; Danuta Shanzer, *A Philosophical and Literary Commentary on Martianus Capella's De Nuptiis Philologiae et Mercurii Book 1* (Berkeley: University of California Press, 1986), 1–28, argues for a date near the end of the fifth century; and Grebe, "Gedanken zur Datierung von *De Nuptiis Philologiae et Mercurii* des Martianus Capella," *Hermes* 128 (2000): 353–68, suggests that it may be as late as the close of the fifth or beginning of the sixth century. There is also debate as to Martianus' religious inclinations: Shanzer, *Commentary*, 26, argues on the basis of Martianus' interest in theurgy and divination that the work is "latter-day pagan propaganda," but S. J. B. Barnish cautions that "sentimental pagan nostalgia" in the *Marriage* does not preclude a Christian writer or audience: Barnish, "Martianus Capella and Rome in the Late Fifth Century," *Hermes* 114 (1986): 108.

56. On the history of the genre as a whole, see Joel Relihan, *Ancient Menippean Satire* (Baltimore: Johns Hopkins University Press, 1993); ch. 9 (137–51) discusses Martianus specifically.

57. For discussion, see Fannie J. LeMoine, *Martianus Capella: A Literary Reevaluation* (Munich: Arbeo-Gesellschaft, 1972), 14–43.

58. 9.888–99. Much work has been done on the history of the canonical liberal arts in antiquity; most fundamental perhaps is that of Ilsetraut Hadot, *Arts libéraux et philosophie dans la pensée antique* (Paris: CNRS, 1984). Martianus, with his comments on Medicine and Architecture, clearly knows a tradition of nine liberal arts, stemming, at least in the Latin tradition, from Varro: see Stahl and Johnson, *Martianus Capella*, 1:42–44, and Shanzer, *Commentary*, 14–17.

59. Relihan, *Ancient Menippean Satire*, 149–51, argues that Martianus intends to parodize and subvert the tradition of encyclopedic learning; if so, the joke is perhaps on Martianus, given the later tradition of using his work precisely to celebrate compendious knowledge. Even in satirizing the encyclopedia, Martianus gives it a highly usable form. Cf. Stahl and Johnson, *Martianus Capella*, 1:55–79, on the transmission of Martianus.

60. 3.326.3–12.

61. The same is true to a certain extent of the other arts of the trivium, Dialectic and Rhetoric, at least in their analytical mode. Dialectic, too, is interrupted in her speech, but she is allowed a rejoinder to Minerva, on the importance of what is being left out: 4.424. Generally speaking, as Relihan, *Ancient Menippean Satire*, 149, notes, the verbal arts of the trivium are treated more brusquely than the mathematical arts of the quadrivium. While this may be in part due to the "greater importance" of the latter, it may also be due to the traditional use of the former in textual analysis—that is, because the literary arts specialize in textual fragmentation, they are themselves more fragmented.

62. Cf. Stahl and Johnson, *Martianus Capella*, 1:101–2, and Grebe, *Martianus Capella*, 53–59.

63. 3.230.4–6.

64. 3.231.15–17.

65. E.g., Grammar's explication of Latin letters and names that have been

taken over from Greek, at 3.234–35, in which these terms are noted as originally Greek but now Latin.

66. 2.231.16: *litterae sunt, quas doceo, litteratura ipsa, quae doceo.*

67. E.g., at 3.278, for multiple passages of Virgil, or 3.300, for the declension of Greek names transliterated into Latin.

68. For a theoretical discussion of "school literature's" effect on the standardization of language, see Pierre Bourdieu, "The Production and Reproduction of Legitimate Language," in *Language and Symbolic Power*, tr. Gino Raymond and Matthew Adamson, ed. John B. Thompson (Cambridge, Mass.: Harvard University Press, 1991), 57–61: "The struggles among writers over the legitimate art of writing contribute, through their very existence, to producing both the legitimate language, defined by its distance from the 'common' language, and belief in its legitimacy." Quote at 58.

69. Cf. n. 61 above, on Dialectic's retort to Minerva as to the importance of the material left out: the effect is that "many of the gods, who had previously laughed, were terrified" (4.424.10–11). Wolfgang Iser, discussing the "cutting techniques" of the modern serial novel, argues that "the reader is forced by the pauses imposed on him to imagine more than he could have done if his reading were continuous": Iser, "Indeterminacy and the Reader's Response in Prose Fiction," in *Prospecting: From Reader Response to Literary Anthropology* (Baltimore: Johns Hopkins University Press, 1989), 11; Iser (21) quotes Thackeray as saying: "I have said somewhere it is the unwritten part of books that would be the most interesting."

70. Iser (23) remarks, on reading *Ulysses*: "The density of allusions and the continual segmentation of style involve an incessant changing of perspectives, which seem to go out of control whenever the reader tries to pin them down."

71. 2.261.17–20, tr. Stahl and Johnson.

72. On Martianus' own knowledge of Appius Claudius, see Ramelli, *Marziano*, 838.

73. Iser's discussion of the effects of "cutting techniques" on the reader recalls Gilles Deleuze's observations on the constitution of individuals as "segments" and "molecules": Deleuze, "Many Politics," in Gilles Deleuze and Claire Parnet, *Dialogues*, tr. Hugh Tomlinson and Barbara Habberjam (New York: Columbia University Press, 1987), 124–34; 125: "We have as many tangled lines as a hand."

74. LeMoine, *Martianus Capella*, 70–106, provides a detailed analysis of the structure of book 2, arguing that Philology's ascent must be read in terms of Platonic movement toward the Good. On the theme of "heavenly voyage" in Menippean satire more generally, see Shanzer, *Commentary*, 33–34.

75. LeMoine, *Martianus Capella*, 87–88, suggests that the vomiting represents the imperfection of earthly as opposed to heavenly knowledge, gained after the ascent.

76. Cf. Deleuze, "Many Politics," 127: "There is now only an abstract line, a pure movement which is difficult to discover, he never begins, he takes things by the middle, he is always in the middle—in the middle of two lines?"

77. Cf. Massumi, "Autonomy of Affect," 217–21.

78. For Stoic accounts of emotion, see Richard Sorabji, *Emotions and Peace of Mind from Stoic Agitation to Christian Temptation* (Oxford: Oxford University Press, 2001), esp. chs. 1–4.

79. Deleuze, *Cinema 2*, 36–37, on the way in which representations of time (different flows of time) de-center movement, and on the "subordination" of time by "normal movement."

80. Notably, the framing account in Martianus' work (1.2.5–16) is that of father-son discourse implying the education of the younger man. That is, like the other *artes* dedicated to sons, Martianus' work participates in the production of a larger temporal and ethical framework, on which see my discussion in Chapter 3. On the trope of father-son dedications in Roman literature, see Fannie J. LeMoine, "Parental Gifts: Father-Son Dedications and Dialogues in Roman Didactic Literature," *Illinois Classical Studies* 16 (1991): 337–66.

81. *Conf.* 1.9.15.

82. For discussion of the place of education in the moralizing context of this sermon, see especially Leyerle, "Appealing to Children," 245–46, 266. J. N. D. Kelly briefly summarizes and contextualizes the sermon in his *Golden Mouth: The Story of John Chrysostom: Ascetic, Preacher, Bishop* (London: Duckworth, 1995), 85–87; for a schematic summary, see Malingrey, *Sur la vaine gloire*, 8–9.

83. On the position of grammar in the memory, see Catherine M. Chin, "Christians and the Roman Classroom: Memory, Grammar, and Rhetoric in *Confessions X*," *Augustinian Studies* 33 (2002): 161–82.

84. Deleuze, "Many Politics," 125, on F. Scott Fitzgerald: "Fitzgerald explains . . . that a life always goes at several rhythms, at several speeds." But Deleuze also notes (128–30) that it is precisely this multiplicity that is unstable and that both depends on and requires mechanisms of control.

85. 3.326.14–15.

86. *Fastidium* at 3.326.4 and 8.897.20; *taedium* at 6.704.12, 8.809.1, and 9.888.8.

87. 3.326.3–14.

88. Cf. Nunokawa, "Importance of Being Bored," 159. Nunokawa argues that the "proliferation of passions" promoted in the novel resolves itself in the boredom of pleasures taken *seriatim*.

89. 9.888.

90. 9.897.10–898.3.

91. As Martianus himself suggests in the introduction to his work: 1.2.15–16.

92. 9.898.5–8.

93. Cf. Brian Massumi's analysis of Deleuze and Guattari's fragmentary individuals likened to fractals: "In spite of its infinite fissuring, it *looks like* and *can function as* a unified figure if we adopt a certain ontological posture toward it: monism as produced meaning, optical effect" (emphasis in Massumi): Massumi, *User's Guide*, 22.

94. *Apol. c. Ruf.* 1.30.41–42.

95. *Conf.* 1.16.26.

96. See Foucault, "Truth and Power," in *Power/Knowledge*, ed. Colin Gordon (New York: Pantheon, 1980); reprinted in *The Foucault Reader*, ed. Paul Rabinow (New York: Pantheon, 1984), 51–75.

97. On the productivity of masochistic violence, see Leo Bersani, *The Freudian Body* (New York: Columbia University Press, 1986), 39: "I wish to propose that, most

significantly, *masochism serves life*. It is perhaps only because sexuality is ontologically grounded in masochism that the human organism survives the gap between the shattering stimuli and the development of resistant or defensive ego structures" (emphasis in original). Suzanne Stewart (*Sublime Surrender: Male Masochism at the Fin-de-Siècle* [Ithaca: Cornell University Press, 1998], 13) notes, however, that Bersani's unqualified acceptance of masochistic productivity ignores the historical situations by which that production is governed, and the uses to which it is put: "[M]asochism establishes a new normativity in the name of anti-normativity, and . . this new normativity has questionable political effects." More generally on the productive nature of power, cf. Foucault, "Truth and Power," 61: "What makes power hold good, what makes it accepted, is simply the fact that it doesn't only weigh on us as a force that says no, but that it traverses and produces things, it induces pleasure, forms knowledge, produces discourse."

98. *Conf.* 1.9.15.

99. *Conf.* 1.9.15.

100. Cf. Deleuze, *Masochism*, 22: "The masochistic hero appears to be educated and fashioned by the authoritarian woman whereas basically it is he who forms her, dresses her for the part and prompts the harsh words she addresses to him."

101. I.e., soloecisms; 3.223–26.

102. 3.326.12–15.

103. For discussion of how the description of a work as "boring" marks temporal shifts, see Spacks, *Boredom*, esp. ch. 5, "A Dull Book is Easily Renounced"; Spacks considers boredom here a response to historical "shifts of taste" (140), but it is equally the case that they rhetorically mark differences in taste as part of historical change. Boredom, in this sense, creates temporal difference as much as it responds to it.

104. 3.326.10–11.

105. 3.326.5–6: *ni fallor, octo partes orationis velut incunabula repetitura intimare disponis.*

106. 3.223.28: *repertam educatamque Cyllenio*, tr. Stahl and Johnson.

107. 3.223.26–27: *quae se in Memphide ortam rege adhuc Osire memorabat.*

108. On Mercury's youth, 1.5.19–22.

109. *De nupt.* 1.2.15.

110. *Conf.* 1.9.14–15.

111. *Apol. c. Ruf.* 1.30.31–33.

112. *De inan. glor.* 17.1.

113. *De gram. et rhet.* 9.5: "Indeed, he did not forbear to attack even the leading men of the city: thus, when he happened to be testifying in a crowded courtroom, back in the days before he became well known, he was asked by Varro Murena, an advocate for the other side, what line of work he was in and what craft he pursued—and (because Murena was a hunchback) he answered that he 'put hunchbacks in the shade'" (tr. Kaster).

114. *Ep. ad fam.* 7.25 makes the supporters of Cato into misbehaving schoolchildren afraid of Caesar: "Attention now! No more writing! Here comes the beak, sooner than expected! It's the cat for the Catonians, I fear" (tr. Shackleton Bailey).

115. *De parasito* 13.

116. *Sat.* 1.15: *et nos ergo manum ferulae subduximus.*

117. *Inst.* 1.3.13–17.

118. On the uses of aggression in Roman humor, see especially Amy Richlin, *The Garden of Priapus: Sexuality and Aggression in Roman Humor*, rev. ed. (New York: Oxford University Press, 1992), chs. 4 and 5.

119. *Ep. ad fam.* 7.25: "Nobody but us two talks in this style—good or bad, that's another question; but whatever it is, it's *ours.* So press on and don't budge a nail's breadth, as they say, from your pen" (tr. Shackleton Bailey; emphasis Shackleton Bailey's).

120. *Sat.* 1, esp. 30–36.

121. Henri Bergson, in his seminal study of humor, *Le Rire*, argued that laughter is primarily a group activity; laughter places those who laugh within the same group while excluding the laughed-at object. Bergson, *Le Rire*, translated as *Laughter* by Cloudesley Brereton and Fred Rothwell (New York: Macmillan, 1928), 5–8. Similarly, in his study *Semantic Mechanisms of Humor* (Dordrecht: D. Reidel, 1985), Victor Rankin notes the difficulty of defining humor per se and suggests that a more helpful method of describing humor may be through defining the necessary conditions for what Rankin calls the "humor act." The most important of these conditions is the presence of an audience that laughs. "It is the perceiver's presence, of course, which makes a humor act a humor act, simply because it is the perceiver who laughs" (3).

122. On the concept of the bodily in humor, and descent toward it, the standard work is Bakhtin's on Rabelais, *Rabelais and His World*, tr. Helene Iswolsky (Bloomington: Indiana University Press, 1984).

123. Gilles Deleuze, *The Logic of Sense*, tr. Mark Lester and Charles Stivale, ed. Constantin V. Boundas (New York: Columbia University Press, 1990), 136–37.

124. *Conf.* 1.9.14.

125. *Conf.* 1.10.16.

126. *Conf.* 1.9.15.

127. *De inan. glor.* 17.2.

128. *Apol. c. Ruf.* 1.30.31–33.

129. On Chrysostom's use of children to problematize adult morality, see Leyerle, "Appealing to Children," 258–66.

130. See Bakhtin's discussion of the disruption and restoration of social order in *The Dialogic Imagination* (Austin: University of Texas Press, 1981), 99–105; for a discussion of this phenomenon in New Comedy, see Paul Shaner Dunkin, *Post-Aristophanic Comedy: Studies in the Social Outlook of Middle and New Comedy at Both Athens and Rome*, Illinois Studies in Language and Literature 31, nos. 3–4 (Urbana: University of Illinois Press, 1946), esp. chs. 1 and 3.

131. See Judith Butler's discussion of both the disruptive possibilities of drag and the use of performatives to insist on the continuity of the gendered subject, *Gender Trouble*, 2nd ed. (London: Routledge, 1999), 174–80.

132. Deleuze, *Logic of Sense*, 134–35.

133. That is, the invoked audience is not coterminous with the educated subjects presented as being frightened or bored within the text, though it is presented

as participating in these emotional moments. On the invocation of a reader by a text, the classic work is Wolfgang Iser's *The Implied Reader* (Baltimore: Johns Hopkins University Press, 1974), which takes a phenomenological view of reading; but Stanley Fish criticizes Iser for maintaining the determinacy of the text: "Why No One's Afraid of Wolfgang Iser," in *Doing What Comes Naturally* (Durham: Duke University Press, 1989), 68–86; for discussion of the debate, see Elizabeth Freund, *The Return of the Reader* (London: Methuen, 1987), 148–51. I here take a "lower" view of the invocation of the reader, with the "implied reader" the ostensible addressee of the works in question. This allows for the indeterminacy of the text on a larger scale while not disregarding the useful notion of readerly "implication."

134. See Freund, *Return of the Reader*, 143–45.

135. *Conf.* 1.6.7.

136. See Kelly, *Golden Mouth*, 83–103, on Chrysostom in Antioch.

137. *De nupt.* 1.2.11–16; cf. LeMoine, "Parental Gifts."

138. *Ep.* 22.1; *Apol. c. Ruf.* 1.30.31.

139. *Conf.* 1.9.14.

140. *Ep.* 22.30; *Apol c. Ruf.* 1.30.23.

141. *Conf.* 11.12.14–11.14.17.

142. *Apol. c. Ruf.* 1.30.41–43 and 1.30.57–61.

143. *De inan. glor.* 38.

144. *Apol. c. Ruf.* 1.30.57–61.

145. *De inan. glor.* 39.

146. *Apol. c. Ruf.* 1.30.50–52.

147. *Conf.* 1.17.27.

Chapter 6. Grammar and Utopia

1. I will not link this language with the important work being done on spatiality in more material settings, or in ritual studies; instead I focus on the ways in which metaphors of space are used to articulate particular relationships to grammatical learning. While these articulations undoubtedly did have physical settings and repercussions—and relied on physical settings for some of their effect— I would like to argue that the projection of Christian and classical onto particular places is also a literary phenomenon, here tied to the acts of reading and writing. For a consideration of the production of "real" holy spaces, see Jonathan Z. Smith's now-classic *To Take Place: Toward Theory in Ritual* (Chicago: University of Chicago Press, 1987); on spaces more generally, see Edward W. Soja, *Postmodern Geographies: The Reassertion of Space in Critical Social Theory* (London: Verso, 1989); various approaches to premodern productions of space can be found in *Medieval Practices of Space*, ed. Barbara A. Hanawalt and Michael Kobialka (Minneapolis: University of Minnesota Press, 2000).

2. Both of these arguments were made, in other contexts, during the course of the fourth and fifth centuries, particularly with the concomitant developments of Christian pilgrimage and asceticism. On the increasing importance of pilgrimage in the period, see, e.g., E. D. Hunt, *Holy Land Pilgrimage in the Later Roman*

Empire A.D. 312–460 (Oxford: Clarendon Press, 1982); P. W. L. Walker, *Holy City, Holy Places?* (Oxford: Oxford University Press, 1990); Robert Ousterhout, ed., *The Blessings of Pilgrimage* (Urbana: University of Illinois Press, 1990); Georgia Frank, *The Memory of the Eyes* (Berkeley: University of California Press, 2000); on asceticism and removal, see, e.g., Derwas Chitty, *The Desert a City* (Oxford: Blackwell, 1966); William Deal, "Toward a Politics of Asceticism," in *Asceticism*, ed. Vincent Wimbush and Richard Valantasis (New York: Oxford University Press, 1995); and the essays of James Goehring, *Ascetics, Society, and the Desert* (Harrisburg: Trinity Press International, 1999).

3. See Michel de Certeau, *The Writing of History*, tr. Tom Conley (New York: Columbia University Press, 1988; French original 1975), 312ff.

4. Here I draw primarily on two theoretical texts: Louis Marin's *Utopics: Spatial Play*, tr. Robert A. Vollrath (Atlantic Highlands, N.J.: Humanities Press, 1984; French original 1973), with its trenchant observation (61) that "Utopia is a discourse"; and Michel Foucault's essay "Of Other Spaces," tr. Jay Miskowiec, *Diacritics* 16 (1986): 22–27 (French original 1984, from a lecture given in 1967). For a reading of Marin, see Fredric Jameson's "Of Islands and Trenches: Naturalization and the Production of Utopian Discourse," *Diacritics* 7 (1977): 2–21; see also Jameson's own argument "that the effectively ideological is also, at the same time, necessarily Utopian," in the concluding chapter of his *The Political Unconscious* (Ithaca: Cornell University Press, 1981), "The Dialectic of Utopia and Ideology," quotation at 286. On utopia more generally, see Ruth Levitas, *The Concept of Utopia* (New York: Philip Allan, 1990); for a more classically Marxist discussion, see Karl Mannheim, *Ideology and Utopia*, tr. Louis Wirth and Edward Shils (New York: Harcourt Brace, 1954; German original 1936), reconsidered by Paul Ricoeur, *Lectures on Ideology and Utopia* (New York: Columbia University Press, 1986). On utopian writing in antiquity, see Doyne Dawson, *Cities of the Gods* (New York: Oxford University Press, 1992), who argues (284–87) that the tropes of classical utopian theory are taken up by patristic authors in writing about monastic life. I am grateful to Jeremy M. Schott for this reference.

5. See Jameson, *Political Unconscious*, 290–91.

6. Possibly from Caesarea in Mauretania: Robert Kaster, *Guardians of Language* (Berkeley: University of California Press, 1988), 346.

7. See Dirk M. Schenkeveld, *A Rhetorical Grammar* (Leiden: Brill, 2004), 1–4, on the various possibilities for Charisius' origin.

8. See Kaster, *Guardians*, 343–44 and 275.

9. Noted in, e.g., Peter Brown, *Power and Persuasion in Late Antiquity* (Madison: University of Wisconsin Press, 1992), ch. 2; but perhaps more obvious in Benedict Anderson's description of nineteenth-century uses of language, *Imagined Communities* (London: Verso, 1991), chs. 5 and 6. See also my discussion in Chapter 2.

10. See Anderson, *Imagined Communities*, ch. 6; also Pierre Bourdieu, *Language and Symbolic Power*, tr. Gino Raymond and Matthew Adamson, ed. John B. Thompson (Cambridge, Mass.: Harvard University Press, 1991), 44–52; and Homi K. Bhabha, "Signs Taken for Wonders: Questions of Ambivalence and Authority Under a Tree outside Delhi, May 1817," in Bhabha, *The Location of Culture* (London: Routledge, 1994), 102–22.

11. *Conf.* 1.18.29, perhaps echoing Catullus 84.

12. See Bhabha, "Signs," 105–11, on the importance of displacement to the production of unified cultures.

13. Bhabha, "DissemiNation: Time, Narrative, and the Margins of the Modern Nation," in Bhabha, *Location of Culture*, 146–52.

14. Hagith Sivan, *Ausonius of Bordeaux: Genesis of a Gallic Aristocracy* (London: Routledge, 1993), 85–91; Alan D. Booth, "The Academic Career of Ausonius," *Phoenix* 36 (1982): 332–33; Kaster, *Guardians*, 201–30, on grammarians' social status; on competition for municipal academic chairs at Bordeaux, see R. P. H. Green, "Still Waters Run Deep: A New Study of the *Professores* of Bordeaux," *Classical Quarterly* 35 (1985): 491–506.

15. On the spatial nature implicit in systems of cultural distinction, see Michel de Certeau, *The Practice of Everyday Life*, tr. Steven Rendall (Berkeley: University of California Press, 1984), 91–110.

16. R. P. H. Green, *The Works of Ausonius* (Oxford: Clarendon Press, 1991), 328–29.

17. Perhaps the most influential of these studies has been that of M. Keith Hopkins, "Social Mobility in the Later Roman Empire: The Evidence of Ausonius," *Classical Quarterly* 11 (1961): 239–49; Alan D. Booth, "Notes on Ausonius' *Professores*," *Phoenix* 32 (1978): 235–49, contains a similar survey of the lives and status of Ausonius' subjects, as does Green, "Still Waters." Kaster's *Guardians*, the most thorough study of late ancient grammarians, also derives prosopographical information from the *Professores*: section II, "Prosopography," entries 9, 11, 21, 28, 35, 36, 40, 70, 86, 89, 93, 94, 99, 105, 139, 140, 148, 162, and 165; and in appendix 4, "The Number of Grammarians at Bordeaux," 455–62.

18. See esp. Michael Roberts, *The Jeweled Style: Poetry and Poetics in Late Antiquity* (Ithaca: Cornell University Press, 1989); S. Georgia Nugent, "Ausonius' 'Late-Antique' Poetics and 'Post-Modern' Literary Theory," *Ramus* 19 (1990): 26–50; and Patricia Cox Miller, "'Differential Networks': Relics and Other Fragments in Late Antiquity," *Journal of Early Christian Studies* 6 (1998): 113–38.

19. E.g., Nugent, "Ausonius' 'Late-Antique' Poetics," 31–33, on *Cupido cruciatus*; Roberts, *Jeweled Style*, 77–78, on the *Moselle*.

20. Nugent, "Ausonius' 'Late-Ancient' Poetics," 33–37.

21. Nugent, "Ausonius' 'Late-Ancient' Poetics," 35–36.

22. Cf. Miller, "'Differential Networks,'" 134, on the uses of collective biography: "The individualizing details invite the reader to linger—but not for long, since the real interest in such collections is in the network of relationships that represent the theological [or, in Ausonius' case, cultural] vision of the collection as a whole."

23. *Officium nomenque tuum, primaeve Thalasse, / parvulus audivi. vix etiam memini / qua fama aut merito fueris, qua stirpe parentum; / aetas nil de te posterior celebrat. / grammaticum iuvenum tantum te fama ferebat, / tum quoque tam tenuis, quam modo nulla manet. / sed quicumque tamen, nostro quia doctor in aevo / vixisti, hoc nostrum munus habeto: vale.* Unless otherwise noted, all translations from Ausonius are my own; for his works I have used the Latin text of Green, *Works of Ausonius*.

24. *Prof.* 8.6: *tenuisque sermo.*

25. *Prof.* 8.7: *quia nostro docuere in aevo.*

26. Cf. Pierre Bourdieu, "The Historical Genesis of a Pure Aesthetic," tr. Charles Newman, in *The Field of Cultural Production*, ed. Randal Johnson (New York: Columbia University Press, 1993), 254–66.

27. *Prof.* 1.4–5.

28. *Prof.* 10.19–21: *qui profugus patria / mutasti sterilem / urbe alia cathedrem.*

29. *Prof.* 10.47: *transtulit ambitio.*

30. *Prof.* 13.7: *urbe satus Sicula nostram peregrinus adisti.*

31. *Prof.* 16, 17, 18, 19, and 22.

32. On the professional mobility of grammarians more generally, see Kaster, *Guardians*, 125–26.

33. *Prof.* 21.7–9.

34. *Prof.* 20.1–10.

35. *Prof.* 22, *titulus*, reads: *Victorio subdoctori sive proscholo.* On the position, which "gave him a taste of being a grammarian," see Kaster, *Guardians*, 373; Green, *Works of Ausonius*, 359.

36. *Prof.* 2.6–14.

37. On synecdoche and systems of cultural authority, see de Certeau, *Practice of Everyday Life*, 101.

38. Cf. Miller's note on Ausonius' *Technopaegnion*, which provides "a succinct statement of the late ancient aesthetic embrace of narrative forms that convey intimate relatedness precisely by advertising disjunction." Miller, "Differential Networks," 127.

39. Foucault, "Of Other Spaces," 24.

40. Foucault, "Of Other Spaces," 24.

41. Foucault, "Of Other Spaces," 24: "The mirror is, after all, a utopia, since it is a placeless place. . . . But it is also a heterotopia in so far as the mirror does exist in reality, where it exerts a sort of counteraction on the position that I occupy."

42. See Carol Thomas Neely, "Woman/Fetish/Utopia," in *Heterotopias*, ed. Tobin Siebers (Ann Arbor: University of Michigan Press, 1994), 58–95, on the creation of utopian completeness through mechanisms surrounding absence.

43. The prominence of apparently descriptive detail in the *Professors* fits in with Marin's observation (*Utopics*, 50) that "the mode of discourse proper to Utopia is description."

44. De Certeau, *Practice of Everyday Life*, 93–95.

45. Cf. *Prof.* 1.9–11; 3.1–2; 7.13; 8.9–11; 9.3; 10.11–13; 11.3; 15.14–15; and 24.5.

46. *Prof.* 7.11; 22.21; and 6.23.

47. Marin, *Utopics*, 61: "[Utopia] stages [historical narrative] as a representation by articulating in the form of a structure of harmonious and immobile equilibrium." Cf. de Certeau, *Practice of Everyday Life*, 117: "Thus space is composed of intersections of mobile elements. It is in a sense actuated by the ensemble of movements deployed within it. Space occurs as the effect produced by the operations that orient it, situate it, temporalize it, and make it function in a polyvalent unity of conflictual programs or contractual proximities." The collectivity of the *cohors* in the *Professors*, a collectivity that makes such proximities possible, replaces the individuality of the professors, who in reality would likely have held chairs either in succession or in different locations. On the question of professorial chairs

at Bordeaux itself, see Green, "Still Waters"; Booth, "Academic Career," 329–43; Kaster, *Guardians*, 455–62.

48. *Prof.* praef.1–3: *Vos etiam, quos nulla mihi cognatio iunxit, / sed fama et carae religio patriae / et studium in libris et sedula cura docendi.*

49. See Sivan, *Ausonius*, 31–48, on the status of Bordeaux as a city in the Roman Empire.

50. *Prof.* 2.8–10: *exemplar unum in litteris, / quas aut Athenis docta couit Graecia / aut Roma per Latium colit.*

51. The phrase is Brown's, *Power and Persuasion*, 41. Brown uses it to discuss *paideia* primarily in the eastern parts of the empire, but Ausonius clearly intends both Greek and Latin parts of the empire to fall under the same cultural purview.

52. Bourdieu has helpfully analyzed educational communication as a language of power: "Magisterial language derives its full significance from the situation in which the relation of pedagogic communication is accomplished, with its social space, its invisible constraints which constitute pedagogic action as the action of imposing and inculcating a legitimate culture." In turn, this "language can ultimately cease to be an instrument of communication and serve instead as an instrument of incantation whose principal function is to attest and impose the pedagogic authority of the communication and the content communicated." Pierre Bourdieu and Jean-Claude Passeron, *Reproduction in Education, Society, and Culture*, tr. Richard Nice, 2nd ed. (London: Sage, 1990; 1st ed. 1977), 108–10. I do not mean to ignore the significant differences between de Certeau and Bourdieu; de Certeau's critique of the inflexibility in Bourdieu's concept of the *habitus* is important to his definition of space as the location of exchanges; however, de Certeau, *Practice of Everyday Life*, 50–60, primarily contests Bourdieu's insistence on the objectivity of authoritative structures and the inability of subjects to respond to them in any but officially sanctioned ways. The production of distinction through authoritative structures is not what de Certeau contests; cf. de Certeau, *Practice of Everyday Life*, 94–95, on the production of "the city" as authoritative space.

53. Praef.1–4: *Vos etiam, quos nulla mihi cognatio iunxit, / sed fama et carae relligio patriae, / et studium in libris et sedula cura docendi, / commemorabo.*

54. 25.9–10: *claris doctisque viris pia cura parentat, / dum decora egregiae commeminit patriae.*

55. It must be stressed, of course, that the *Professors* is not a sociological survey of education at Bordeaux, and that it does not capture the conditions of "actual" teaching of classical literature in the later empire; rather, it is Ausonius' imaginative portrait of that teaching, and the ideological conditions created in that portrait, that are under discussion here.

56. Praef.5; and 26.1.

57. De Certeau, *Practice of Everyday Life*, 99–103; but see also Gilles Deleuze and Félix Guattari, *Anti-Oedipus*, tr. Robert Hurley et al. (Minneapolis: University of Minnesota Press, 1983), 281–83, on movement and the production of "full bodies."

58. For discussion, see Dennis E. Trout, *Paulinus of Nola: Life, Letters, and Poems* (Berkeley: University of California Press, 1999), 28–30.

59. It is commonly accepted that seven letters from Ausonius to Paulinus

survive, although Green, in his critical edition of Ausonius, prints one of the letters, Schenkel 25/Peiper 27, as two, Green 23 and 24, arguing that 24 is a second, revised version of 23: Green, *Works of Ausonius*, 654–55. I follow Green's numbering for ease of reference. The dating and order of the letters, in particular the last few, written in 393 and 394, has also been a matter of some disagreement. Since I am not here interested in reconstructing the course of the friendship or of the exchange, I will not attempt to survey the extremely complex textual issues involved; for detailed discussion, see Green, *Works of Ausonius*, 647–49 and 654–55; Serafino Prete, "The Textual Tradition of the Correspondence Between Ausonius and Paulinus," in *Collectanea Vaticana in honorem Anselmi M. Card. Albareda* (Vatican City: Biblioteca Apostolica Vaticana, 1962): 309–30; Pierre de Labriolle, *Un épisode de la fin du paganisme: La correspondence d'Ausone et de Paulin de Nole* (Paris: Librairie Bloud, 1910): 51–52; and Trout, *Paulinus*, appendix B, on the chronology of Paulinus' life as a whole.

60. *Paulinus Noster: Self and Symbols in the Letters of Paulinus of Nola* (Oxford: Oxford University Press, 2000), esp. chs. 3 and 6 on the relational aspect of the letters. Conybeare's excellent discussion in ch. 2 of "letters as sacraments" explores the epistolary genre primarily in a Christian context. Her discussion (ch. 1) of letter carrying, however, is of course equally applicable to correspondence in the Roman Empire writ large.

61. For an overview of late ancient letter exchange, see Denys Gorce, *Les voyages, l'hospitalité, et le port des lettres dans le monde chrétien des IVe et Ve siècles* (Paris: A. Picard, 1925).

62. Ausonius as Paulinus' father, e.g., at *ep.* 17.31. Minervius: *Prof.* 1.38.

63. *Collegia: ep.* 22.35; *iugum: epp.* 23.1 and 24.1.

64. *Ep.* 17; for literary analysis of the letter, and of the correspondence as a whole, see Charles Witke, *Numen Litterarum: The Old and the New in Latin Poetry from Constantine to Gregory the Great* (Leiden: Brill, 1971): 6–10 on *ep.* 17; 3–65 on the correspondence.

65. *Ep.* 19.4–7: *scis autem me id nomen muriae, quod in usu vulgi est, nec solere nec posse dicere, cum scientissimi veterum . . . Latinum in gari appellatione non habeant.*

66. 20b.7–12: *videbis ipsum, . . . / imago fartunae suae, canus comosus hispidus trux atribux, / Terentianus Phormio, / horrens capillis ut marinus asperis / echinus aut versus mei.* Cf. Witke, *Numen Litterarum*, 17.

67. Jameson, *Political Unconscious*, 291.

68. 21.26–27 and 36–37; see Green, *Works of Ausonius*, 351, on *Prof.* 15.6 and its reference to Amyclae.

69. *Ep.* 22.9–25.

70. *Ep.* 21.50–72. On the image of Bellerophon as a reference to Christian asceticism, see Trout, *Paulinus*, 70–75. Interestingly, whether Ausonius was accusing Paulinus of fanatical asceticism, or of Priscillianism, or neither, he does not couch his accusation in overtly Christian language, remaining instead firmly within the confines of classical exchange.

71. 24.50–52.

72. 24.60–61.

73. 24.79–80. Note the recurrence of the trope of Africa.

74. 24.67–78.

75. 24.115–24.

76. See Witke, *Numen Litterarum*, 42, on Paulinus *carm.* 11, in which Paulinus claims that the friendship with Ausonius continues despite his silence: "[Paulinus] makes no undertaking to supply what will nourish the friendship in this world: namely, letters."

77. See Trout, *Paulinus*, 70–72.

78. *Ep.* 21.69–72.

79. Cf. Deleuze and Guattari, *Anti-Oedipus*, 283.

80. Paulinus, *carm.* 10, claims not to have received some of Ausonius' letters, but most commentators relate the apparent break in the friendship to more than just the peccadilloes of the late Roman postal system. See, e.g., de Labriolle, *Épisode de la fin du paganisme*, 17–20; Pierre Fabre, *Saint Paulin de Nole et l'amitié Chrétienne* (Paris: E. de Boccard, 1949), 161, on Paulinus' conversion: "Voilà donc la raison qui a motivé son silence"; Nora Chadwick, *Poetry and Letters in Early Christian Gaul* (London: Bowes & Bowes, 1955), 63–69; cf. Conybeare, *Paulinus Noster*, 149–51; W. H. C. Frend, "The Two Worlds of Paulinus of Nola," in J. Binns, ed., *Latin Literature of the Fourth Century*, 108, concedes, "Maybe part of the fault was simply communications." Trout, *Paulinus*, 76–78, seems to give more credence to Paulinus' claim but sees the intervening years of silence as also significant, as only Ausonius' accusations "drove Paulinus finally to renew contact" (77).

81. Noted by P. G. Walsh, *The Poems of St. Paulinus of Nola*, Ancient Christian Writers 40 (New York: Newman Press, 1975), 364 n. 2.

82. See R. P. H. Green, *The Poetry of Paulinus of Nola: A Study of His Latinity*, Collection Latomus 120 (Brussels: Latomus, 1971), 41–60.

83. 10.191–92. I use the text of Paulinus *carm.* 10 and 11 that is found in appendix B of Green, *Works of Ausonius*, 708–19.

84. 10.16.

85. 10.216–17: *superbis / urbibus.*

86. 10.234: *egregias terris et moenibus urbes.*

87. 10.238: *orbe suo finem ponens in limite mundi.*

88. 10.257: *aemula Romuleis habitans fastigia tectis*, tr. Walsh.

89. 10.265–66: *mala . . . / fama*; 10.268: *scaevo rumore.*

90. 11. 21–22: *quo rumore pium facilis tibi fama per aures irrupit . . . ?*

91. *at si forte . . . , quod legi et quod seqor, audis / corda pio vovisse deo, venerabile Christi / imperium docili pro credulitate sequentem / . . . on reor id sancto sic displicuisse parenti / mentis ut errorem credat sic vivere Christo / ut Christus sanxit.*

92. Cf. de Certeau's comment (*Practice of Everyday Life*, 127) on Christian Morgenstern's poem "Der Lattenzaun" as a depiction of the "transformation of the void into a plenitude, of the in-between into an established place." De Certeau, oddly, suggests that the architect of Morgenstern's poem wishes to "cement up" the fence, but the reification of space requires nothing so prosaic; the spaces between the pickets of the fence are exploited despite their immateriality.

93. 10.29: *alia . . . vis.*

94. 10.33.

95. 10.39.

96. 10.61: *castae voluptatis*.

97. 10.85–88.

98. Recall Foucault's remark ("Of Other Spaces," 24) that heterotopias can also open onto dystopian or inverted spaces.

99. De Certeau, *Practice of Everyday Life*, 127–28.

100. 10.163–66: *desertis habitare locis . . . / . . . de vanis libera curis / otia amant*.

101. 10.103.

102. 10.193–95: *nec mihi nunc patrii est, ut vis, oblivio caeli, / qui summum suspecto patrem, quem qui colit unum / hic vere memor est caeli*.

103. See de Certeau, *Practice of Everyday Life*, 95–101, on the strategies of resistance to authoritative space implied in the act of walking, i.e., of exploiting the interstitial spaces of maps, an act that both perpetuates the authority of the map and resists it.

104. 11.30–32: *discussisse iugum quereris me, quo tibi doctis / iunctus eram studiis. hoc ne gestasse quidem me / assero*.

105. 11.59.

106. 11.38–39: *vix Tullius et Maro tecum / sustineant aequale iugum*.

107. De Certeau, *Practice of Everyday Life*, 107–8.

108. Paulinus' conversion of classical into Christian space illustrates the versatility of the heterotopia: the space into which it opens does not necessarily have a fixed meaning or value. See Foucault, "Of Other Spaces," 25: "A society, as its history unfolds, can make an existing heterotopia function in a very different fashion." I would suggest that the different functions of the heterotopia are, however, not so much products of an "unfolding history" as they are a means of creating a spatialization of history, as Paulinus does here, using his alternative reading of classical space to mark his own "conversion." The possibility of such shifts should instead be seen as part of the "mixed, joint experience" (24) of heterotopic gazing.

109. 10.181.

110. On the general trend of "asceticization" in this period, see esp. Robert A. Markus, *The End of Ancient Christianity* (Cambridge: Cambridge University Press, 1990), ch. 3, "Conversion and Uncertainty."

111. See Trout, *Paulinus*, 79: "Oppositions of old and new, false and true, foolishness and wisdom, visible and invisible, transient and eternal polarize [*carm.* 10's] message, demanding that the reader, Ausonius, locate himself in only one set of categories." One might add that the same constraint applies to the writer.

112. Cf. Homi Bhabha, "How Newness Enters the World," in Bhabha, *Location of Culture*, 216–17; de Certeau, *Practice of Everyday Life*, 154: "A lapse insinuates itself into language. The territory of appropriation is altered by the mark of something which is not there and does not happen (like myth)."

113. For an overview of Jerome's relations with Paulinus, see Stefan Rebenich, *Hieronymus und Sein Kreis* (Stuttgart: Franz Steiner, 1992), 220–39; a briefer statement of the place of these letters in Jerome's life is in J. N. D. Kelly, *Jerome: His Life, Writings, and Controversies* (London: Duckworth, 1975), 192–94; P. Nautin, "Études de chronologie hiéronymienne (393–397): III. Les premières relations entre Jérome et Paulin de Nole," *Revue des études augustiniennes* 19 (1973): 213–39, is standard for the dating of the letters; cf. Dennis Trout, "The Dates of the Ordination of Paulinus

of Bordeaux and of His Departure for Nola," *Revue des études augustiniennes* 37 (1991): 237–60, and Trout, *Paulinus*, 90–101. On Paulinus as Jerome's correspondent, see also Conybeare, *Paulinus Noster*, 128–30.

114. For discussion, see esp. Hillel I. Newman, "Between Jerusalem and Bethlehem: Jerome and the Holy Places of Palestine," in *Sanctity of Time and Space in Tradition and Modernity*, ed. A. Houtman et al. (Leiden: Brill, 1998), 215–27; see also Blake Leyerle, "Landscape as Cartography in Early Christian Pilgrimage Narratives," *Journal of the American Academy of Religion* 64 (1996): 130–32, which concentrates primarily on Jerome, *epp.* 46 and 108; Leyerle does note (132), however, that in *ep.* 58 to Paulinus, "the real city to visit is, apparently, the city of the book." E. D. Hunt, *Holy Land Pilgrimage in the Later Roman Empire, A.D. 312–460* (Oxford: Clarendon Press, 1982), 192–94, uses the exchange to describe the theological politics of pilgrimage during the Origenist controversy, which I discuss further below.

115. See esp. Mark Vessey, "Conference and Confession: Literary Pragmatics in Augustine's '*Apologia contra Hieronymum*,'" *Journal of Early Christian Studies* 1 (1993): 179–85, on Jerome's "professionalizing" of Christian reading; cf. Vessey, "Ideas of Christian Writing in Late Roman Gaul" (unpublished D.Phil. thesis, University of Oxford, 1988), 49–56.

116. 53.1.

117. 53.2.

118. 53.11: *et haerentis in salo nauiculae funem magis praecide quam solue*. I use the Latin text of Jérôme Labourt, *Saint Jérôme: Lettres*, 8. vols. (Paris: Belles Lettres, 1949–1963). Translations are my own.

119. This is the standard reading of *ep.* 53, with *ep.* 58 as Jerome's "change of mind" in the midst of the Origenist controversy: Nautin, "Chronologie," 224–39; cf. Rebenich, *Hieronymus*, 228–35. I would not argue that *ep.* 53 does not contain an invitation, but I would like to read that invitation as applying primarily to joint scriptural study, possibly, but not necessarily, undertaken with both parties at Bethlehem. Certainly the language of *ep.* 53 is very different from that of *ep.* 46, which is a clear exhortation to travel in Palestine.

120. 53.10: *inter haec vivere . . . nonne tibi videtur iam hic in terris regni caelestis habitaculum?*

121. 53.1: *ut urbem tantam ingressus alium extra urbem quaereret.*

122. *Dauid, Simonides noster, Pindarus et Alcaeus, Flaccus quoque, Catullus et Serenus.*

123. *Timor Domini et diuinarum scripturarum studia conciliant.*

124. 53.10: *comitem*; 53.11: *quidquid quaesieris tecum scire conabor.*

125. See de Certeau, *Writing of History*, 312, on superimposed places; also *Practice of Everyday Life*, 91.

126. 53.5: *Iesum qui clausus latebat in littera*. Cf. Origen's use of the language of concealment at *De princ.* 4.3.11, discussed in Chapter 4.

127. 53.5: *plus in deserto fonte ecclesiae quam in aurato templo repperit synagogae.*

128. 53.3: *armarium.*

129. 58.2.

130. 58.8: *non per Aonios montes et Heliconis vertices . . . sed per Sion et Itabyrium et Sina et excelsa ducere scripturarum.*

131. 58.9: *quo in scripturis sanctis calle gradiaris*.

132. 58.11: *et ascendentem . . . tecta Sion, canere in domatibus quod in cubiculis cognouisses*.

133. E.g., *ep*. 46.

134. 58.2; cf. Ausonius' use of Athens at *Prof*. 2.9 and 14.9.

135. See, e.g., Jas Elsner's reading of the Bordeaux pilgrim's travel account, "The *Itinerarium Burdigalense*: Politics and Salvation in the Geography of Constantine's Empire," *Journal of Roman Studies* 90 (2000): 181–95, in which the text's careful attention to details of location "most potently characterizes the Christian transformation of the Empire" (189).

136. Cf. de Certeau, *Writing of History*, 312, on Freud's *Moses and Monotheism*: "Through metaphor, a rhetorical means, and through ambivalence, a theoretical instrument, many things are in play in the same spot, transforming each spatial element into a volume where they intersect, and introducing the movement of a quid pro quo (what comes in place of what?) everywhere." Foucault, "Of Other Spaces," 25, argues that "the heterotopia is capable of juxtaposing in a single real place several spaces, several sites that are in themselves incompatible."

137. 53.4: *qui, in mysterio absconditus . . . praedestinatus autem et praefiguratus in lege et prophetis*.

138. I base the word "Christianicity" on Roland Barthes' use of the term "Italianicity," "the condensed essence of everything that could be Italian," in "The Rhetoric of the Image," in Barthes, *Image-Music-Text*, tr. Stephen Heath (New York: Hill and Wang, 1977), 48. For discussion of Barthes' own uses of "utopia," see Diana Knight, *Barthes and Utopia: Space, Travel, Writing* (Oxford: Clarendon Press, 1997).

139. 58.3: *Neque . . . ut frustra videar ad exemplum Abraham et meos et patria reliquisse*.

140. 58.2: *Non Hierosolymis fuisse, sed Hierosolymis bene vixisse laudandum est*.

141. 58.3: *Neque vero hoc dicens memet ipsum inconstantiae redarguo*.

142. Barthes, "Rhetoric," 51.

143. On Jerome's use of "the desert" as a symbolic site in other work, see Patricia Cox Miller, "Jerome's Centaur: A Hyper-Icon of the Desert," *Journal of Early Christian Studies* 4 (1996): 209–33; for the symbolism of the desert in other ascetic literature, see esp. James Goehring, "The Encroaching Desert: Literary Production and Ascetic Space in Early Christian Egypt," *Journal of Early Christian Studies* 1 (1993): 218–96.

144. 58.4: *si urbibus et frequentia urbium derelicta in agello habites, et Christum quaeras in solitudine*.

145. 58.5: *filii prophetarum, qui habitabant in agris et solitudine*.

146. 58.4: *ores solus in monte cum Iesu*.

147. 58.4.

148. Cf. Louis Marin, "The Frontiers of Utopia: Past and Present," *Critical Inquiry* 19 (1993): 412: "[Utopia offers] the synthetic unity of the same and the other, of past and future, of this world and the beyond (and the frontier would be in this case the place where conflicting forces are reconciled)."

149. Barthes, "Rhetoric," 48.

150. On the doubtfulness of Jerome's influence on Paulinus' later work, see Vessey, "Ideas of Christian Writing," 57.

151. Adam Kamesar, *Jerome, Greek Scholarship and the Hebrew Bible* (Oxford: Clarendon Press, 1993), emphasizes Jerome's dependence on Origen, Antiochene exegetes, and rabbinic method. Y.-M. Duval, "Les premiers rapports de Paulin de Nole avec Jérôme," *Studi Tardoantichi* 7 (1989): 177–216, considers the different valences of "poetry" and "exegesis" in *ep.* 53; cf. Vessey, "Ideas of Christian Writing," 51–54.

152. For a detailed analysis of one such commentary, and its social and ideological location, see Kaster, *Guardians*, ch. 5, on Servius' commentary on the *Aeneid*.

153. Barthes, "Rhetoric," 38–41.

154. 53.8: *mysticis divinisque praeceptis*.

155. 53.8: *spirant caelestia sacramenta*.

156. 53.8: *arcanorum Domini cognitor*.

157. 53.8: *Christum lyra personat*.

158. 58.9: *Qui esse vult nuculeum frangit nucem*.

159. 53.7: *Taceo de meis similibus, qui si forte ad scriptural sanctas post seculares litteras uenerint . . . , sed ad sensum suum incongrua aptant testimonia, quasi grande sit et non uitiosissimum dicendi genus depravere sententias, et ad uoluntatem suam scripturam trahere repugnantem*.

160. 53.7.

161. Foucault, "Of Other Spaces," 26: "In general, the heterotopic site is not freely accessible like a public place." See Kaster, *Guardians*, 17–31, on the exclusionary uses of grammatical training.

162. Vessey, "Conference and Confession," 182, on Jerome's "exclusive . . . claim for interpretive expertise"; cf. Servius, *Commentarium in artem Donati*, GL 4.405.3–4: *vel certe ideo ars dicitur, quod artis praeceptis cuncta concludat, id est angustis et brevibus*.

163. 53.8: *docent, antequam discant*.

164. 53.6: *in scripturis sanctis sine praevio et monstrante semitam non posse ingredi*.

165. 53.10–11.

166. *O si mihi liceret istius modi ingenium non per Aonios montes et Heliconis vertices, ut poetae canunt, sed per Sion et Itabyrium et Sina et excelsa ducere scripturarum*.

167. 58.9: *ausculta paulisper quo in scripturis sanctis calle gradiaris*.

168. 53.8: *nasceretur nobis aliquid quod docta Graecia non haberet!*

169. 53.8: *Videlicet manifestissima est Genesis. . . Patet Exodus. . . In promptu est Leviticus liber*.

170. 53.5: *Quanti hodie putantes se nosse litteras tenent signatum librum nec aperire possunt, nisi ille reseruauerit "qui habet clauem Dauid, qui aperit et nemo claudit, qui claudit et nemo aperit"!* Cf. Origen, *De princ.* 4.2.3.

171. For discussion of the literature on Proba in relation to Jerome, see Carl P. E. Springer, "Jerome and the *Cento* of Proba," *Studia Patristica* 28 (1993): 96–105; on Proba and the *Cento* more generally, Elizabeth A. Clark and Diane F. Hatch, *The Golden Bough, the Oaken Cross* (Chico: Scholars Press, 1981), remains fundamental.

172. 53.7: *puerilia . . . ludo*.

173. As Quintilian recommends and describes in *Institutio Oratoria* 1–2.

174. See Clark and Hatch, *Golden Bough*, 98–100.

175. This is the limit Jerome suggests that centonists exceed: 53.7.

176. 53.7: *ac non sic etiam Maronem sine Christo possimus dicere Christianum*, despite the fact that many of Jerome's contemporaries, and certainly later Latin tradition, did grant Virgil special "Christian" status.

177. 58.9: *Si haberes hoc fundamentum. . . . nihil pulchrius, nihil doctius, nihilque latinius tuis haberemus voluminibus.*

178. On the problem of utopias and their implied dystopias, see Anthony Stephens, "The Sun State and Its Shadow: On the Condition of Utopian Writing," in *Utopias*, ed. Eugene Kamenka (Melbourne: Oxford University Press, 1987), 1–19.

179. Cf. Trout, *Paulinus*, 223, who describes the letter as "formal and curt."

180. 53.9: *excessisse modum epistulae.*

181. 85.3.

182. 85.1.

183. 85.1: *uno ad Occidentem navigandi tempore, tantae a me simul epistulae flagitantur, ut si cuncta ad singulos velim rescribere, occurrer nequeam. Vnde accidit ut omissa compositione verborum et scribentium sollicitudine, dictem quicquid in buccam uenerit.*

184. Conybeare, *Paulinus Noster*, 22–24.

185. Marin, "Frontiers of Utopia," 416–17, describes utopian spaces as "constantly, unceasingly displaced, about to be inscribed at the very moment when [they are] about to be erased amidst all the real islands that travellers register."

186. Cf. Tzvetan Todorov, "The Journey and Its Narratives," tr. Alyson Waters, in *Transports*, ed. Chloe Chard and Helen Langdon (New Haven: Yale University Press, 1996), 293: "The first important feature of the travel narrative as it is unconsciously imagined by today's reader seems to be to be a certain tension (or a certain balance) between the observing subject and the observed object." Or Foucault, "Of Other Spaces," 24, on the heterotopic mirror: "It exerts a sort of counteraction on the position that I occupy. From the standpoint of the mirror I discover my absence from the place where I am since I see myself over there."

187. See Foucault, "Of Other Spaces," 24–25, on the uses of heterotopias to mark transitions or deviances in identities.

188. 85.3 and 6. On Jerome's connection from Bethlehem to Pammachius and Rome, see Rebenich, *Hieronymus*, 193–207; on Jerome's use of this connection during the Origenist controversy, see Elizabeth A. Clark, *The Origenist Controversy* (Princeton: Princeton University Press, 1992), 11–42.

189. 85.3: Origen; 85.5: Tertullian.

190. 85.4: *praua dogmata.*

191. Cf. also *ep.* 84.8, which praises Origen's scriptural learning, and 84.3, which several times condemns Origen's "dogma": e.g., *uenenata sunt illius dogmata, aliena a scripturis sanctis.*

192. 85.4: *ne me putes in modum rustici balatronis cuncta Origenis reprobare quae scripsit . . ., sed tantum praua dogmata repudiare.*

193. *Prof.* 5.19–20: *felix, quietis si maneres litteris / opus Camenarum colens.*

194. *Prof.* 9.2: *nomen grammatici nec meruisse putant.*

195. *Prof.* 10.38–41: *doctrina exiguus / moribus inplacidis: / proinde, ut erat meritum, / famam habuit tenuem.*

196. Marin, *Utopics*, 197: "Utopic practice is the productive force that the product (as a final, achieved figure) masks." Cf. also the prominence of travel in utopian narratives: it is typical for utopian narrative to be attributed to one who has moved both into, and out of, utopia. Marin, *Utopics*, 42–48.

197. Marcellus is ranked among grammarians of little merit because of his "wicked nature" (*pravi . . . ingenii*: 18.10); Ausonius' nephew Herculanus the grammarian is ranked low because of youthful folly (11.4); Anastasius' poverty causes him to lose the "little glory" he had (*gloriolam*: 8.51).

198. Jameson, *Political Unconscious*, 293–94.

199. Esp. in the *Gratiarum actio* of 379. For discussion, see Martin Irvine, *The Making of Textual Culture: Grammatica and Literary Theory, 350–1100* (Cambridge: Cambridge University Press, 1994), 84–87.

200. Labriolle, *Épisode de la fin du paganisme*, 16–17. Even a sympathetic reader of Ausonius has concluded that "it is not enough to define and then condemn the comparative inadequacies of that period's taste, as Gibbon did. It is more proper to observe the incredible limitations placed on life and leisure and then assess the product in the light of its very narrowed resources": H. Isbell, "Decimus Magnus Ausonius: The Poet and His World," in J. W. Binns, ed., *Latin Literature of the Fourth Century* (London: Routledge & Kegan Paul, 1974), 56. Isbell also provides a brief introduction to some of the earlier, less sympathetic readers of Ausonius.

201. See Bourdieu on the trope of "natural" giftedness: *Distinction*, tr. Richard Nice (Cambridge, Mass.: Harvard University Press, 1984), 67–68.

202. Witke, *Numen Litterarum*, 101.

203. Trout, *Paulinus*, 78.

204. Witke, *Numen Litterarum*, 54.

205. Chadwick, *Poetry and Letters*, 66: Paulinus "is gently withdrawing from the early intimate relationship, and passing to a new world of emotions."

206. Witke, *Numen Litterarum*, 101.

207. Chadwick, *Poetry and Letters*, 84.

208. Green, *Poetry of Paulinus of Nola*, 129.

209. Cf. Todorov, "Journey and Its Narratives," 293–96.

210. On Paulinus as the host of other travelers, see Sigrid Mratschek, "*Multis enim notissima est sanctitas loci*: Paulinus and the Gradual Rise of Nola as a Center of Christian Hospitality," *Journal of Early Christian Studies* 9 (2001): 511–53.

211. *Ep. 58*.

212. *Utopics*, 65.

213. A concept not unknown to utopian geography, as in C. S. Lewis' Narnia. Lewis, *The Last Battle* (London: William Collins, 1989; first published 1956), 169: "The further up and the further in you go, the bigger everything gets. The inside is larger than the outside."

Epilogue

1. For some representative English-language accounts of Christianization, see, e.g., E. R. Dodds, *Pagan and Christian in an Age of Anxiety* (Cambridge:

Cambridge University Press, 1965); Ramsey MacMullen, *Christianizing the Roman Empire* (New Haven: Yale University Press, 1984); Rodney Stark, *The Rise of Christianity* (Princeton: Princeton University Press, 1996); more nuanced, and not relying on the idea of individual conversion motivated by "belief," is Michele R. Salzman, *The Making of a Christian Aristocracy* (Cambridge, Mass.: Harvard University Press, 2002).

2. I borrow the phrase from James J. O'Donnell's article of the same title in *Traditio* 35 (1979): 45–88.

3. See Judith Butler, *Gender Trouble*, 2nd ed. (London: Routledge: 1999), 186–87, on the potential for acts and narratives of gender identity to repeat and proliferate.

4. *Conf.* 8.2; see my discussion in Chapter 3.

5. See my discussion in Chapter 6.

6. The literature on the relationship between history and narrative is vast; for a useful overview of twentieth-century debates, see Elizabeth A. Clark, *History, Theory, Text: Historians and the Linguistic Turn* (Cambridge, Mass.: Harvard University Press, 2004); for this epilogue I have found most useful Paul Ricoeur, "Imagination in Discourse and in Action," tr. Kathleen Blamey, in Ricoeur, *From Text to Action: Essays in Hermeneutics II* (Evanston: Northwestern University Press, 1991), 168–87; Barbara Herrnstein Smith, "Narrative Versions, Narrative Theories," in W. J. T. Mitchell, ed., *On Narrative* (Chicago: University of Chicago Press, 1981), 209–32; and Paul J. Hopper, "The Category 'Event' in Natural Discourse and Logic," in *Discourse, Grammar and Typology: Papers in Honor of John W. M. Verhaar*, ed. Werner Abraham, T. Givón, and Sandra A. Thompson (Amsterdam: John Benjamins, 1995), 139–50.

7. *The Practice of Everyday Life* (Berkeley: University of California Press, 1984), 154.

8. Averil Cameron, *Christianity and the Rhetoric of Empire* (Berkeley: University of California Press, 1991), ch. 3, "Stories People Want."

9. Homi K. Bhabha, "How Newness Enters the World," in Bhabha, *The Location of Culture* (London: Routledge, 1994), 227–28.

10. Henri-Irénée Marrou, *St. Augustin et la fin de la culture antique*, 4th ed. (Paris: E. de Boccard, 1958), 13–14.

Works Cited

PRIMARY SOURCES

Augustine of Hippo. *Confessiones*. Ed. James J. O'Donnell, *Augustine: Confessions*. Vol. 1. Oxford: Clarendon Press, 1992.

——. *De civitate Dei*. Ed. B. Dombert and A. Kalb. Leipzig: Teubner, 1928.

——. *De civitate Dei*. Tr. Henry Bettenson, *The City of God*. London: Penguin, 1972.

——. *De Doctrina Christiana*. Ed. R. P. H. Green, *De Doctrina Christiana*. Oxford: Oxford University Press, 1997.

——. *Locutiones in Heptateuchum*. Ed. J. Fraipont. Corpus Christianorum Series Latina 33. Turnhout: Brepols, 1958, 381–465.

Aulus Gellius. *Noctes Atticae*. Ed. P. K. Marshall. Oxford: Clarendon, 1968.

Ausonius. *Opera*. Ed. R. P. H. Green, *The Works of Ausonius*. Oxford: Oxford University Press, 1991.

——. *Parentalia*. Ed. Massimo Lolli, *D. M. Ausonius: Parentalia*. Brussels: Latomus, 1997.

Charisius. *Ars grammatica*. Ed. Karl Barwick, corrected by F. Kühnert. Leipzig: Teubner, 1964.

Cicero. *Epistulae ad familiares*. Tr. D. R. Shackleton Bailey, *Cicero's Letters to His Friends*. Atlanta: Scholar's Press, 1988.

Grammatici Latini. Ed. Heinrich Keil. Leipzig: Teubner, 1855–1880.

Horace, *Ars poetica*. Ed. and tr. Léon Herrmann, *Horace: Art poétique*. Brussels: Latomus, 1951.

Jerome. *Epistulae*. Ed. Jérôme Labourt, *Saint Jérôme: Lettres*. Paris: Les Belles Lettres, 1949–1963.

——. *Apologia contra Rufinum*. Ed. Pierre Lardet, *Saint Jérôme: Apologie contre Rufin*. Sources Chrétiennes 303. Paris: Cerf, 1983.

——. *Liber Interpretationis Hebraicorum Nominum*. Ed. Pierre de LaGarde. Corpus Christianorum Series Latina 72. Turnhout: Brepols, 1959, 59–161.

John Chrysostom. *De inani gloria et de liberis educandis*. Ed. and tr. A.-M. Malingrey, *Sur la vaine gloire et L'éducation des enfants*. Sources Chrétiennes 188. Paris: Cerf, 1972.

Julian. *Epistulae*. Tr. Wilbur C. Wright, *The Works of the Emperor Julian*. Vol. 3. Loeb Classical Library 157. London: William Heinemann, 1923.

Juvenal. *Saturae*. Ed. W. V. Clausen. Oxford: Clarendon Press, 1966.

Macrobius. *Saturnalia*. Ed. James Willis. Leipzig: Teubner, 1963.

——. *Saturnalia*. Tr. Percival Vaughan Davies. New York: Columbia University Press, 1969.

Martianus Capella. *De nuptiis Philologiae et Mercurii*. Ed. James Willis. Leipzig: Teubner, 1983.

——. *De nuptiis Philologiae et Mercurii*. Tr. William H. Stahl and Richard Johnson, *Martianus Capella and the Seven Liberal Arts*. Vol. 2. New York: Columbia University Press, 1977.

——. *De nuptiis Philologiae et Mercurii*. Tr. Ilaria Ramelli, *Marziano Capella: Le Nozze di Filologia e Mercurio*. Milan: Bompiani, 2001.

Origen. *De principiis*. Ed. Henri Crouzel and Manlio Simonetti, *Origène: Traité des Principes*. 5 vols. Sources Chrétiennes 252, 253, 268, 269, 312. Paris: Cerf, 1978–1984.

——. *Hexapla*. Ed. Frederick Field, *Origenis Hexaplorum quae supersunt*. Oxford: Clarendon Press, 1867–1874.

——. *Homelia in Exodum*. Ed. Marcel Borret, *Origène: Homélies sur l'Exode*. Sources Chrétiennes 321. Paris: Cerf, 1985.

——. *Homelia in Leviticum*. Ed. Marcel Borret. *Origène: Homélies sur le Lévitique*. 2 vols. Sources Chrétiennes 286, 287. Paris: Cerf, 1981.

Ovid. *Amores*. Ed. E. J. Kenney. Oxford: Clarendon Press, 1968.

——. *Fasti*. Tr. Sir James George Frazer, revised by J. P. Goold. Loeb Classical Library 253. London: William Heinemann, 1989.

Phlegon of Tralles. *De mirabilibus*. Ed. A. Westerman, *Paradoxographoi: Scriptores Rerum Mirabilium Graeci*. Amsterdam: A. Hakkert, 1963.

——. *De mirabilibus*. Tr. William Hansen, *Phlegon of Tralles' Book of Marvels*. Exeter: University of Exeter Press, 1996.

Quintilian. *Institutio Oratoria*. Tr. H. E. Butler. Loeb Classical Library 124–127. London: William Heinemann, 1920–1922.

Rufinus of Aquileia. *Apologia contra Hieronymum*. Ed. Manlio Simonetti, *Tyrannii Rufini Scripta Apologetica*. Corpus Scriptorum Ecclesiae Aquileiensis 5.1. Rome: Città Nuova, 1999.

Seneca. *De clementia*. Tr. John W. Basore, *Seneca: Moral Essays*. Loeb Classical Library 214. London: William Heinemann, 1928.

Suetonius. *De grammaticis et rhetoribus*. Ed. and tr. Robert Kaster, *Suetonius: De grammaticis et rhetoribus*. Oxford: Oxford University Press, 1995.

Symmachus. *Epistulae*. Ed. Jean Pierre Callu, *Symmaque: Lettres*. Paris: Les Belles Lettres, 1972.

Varro. *De lingua Latina*. Tr. Roland G. Kent, *Varro: On the Latin Language*. Loeb Classical Library 333. Cambridge, Mass.: Harvard University Press, 1967.

SECONDARY SOURCES

Althusser, Louis. "Ideology and Ideological State Apparatuses." Tr. Ben Brewster. In *Lenin and Philosophy*. New York: Monthly Review Press, 1971.

Amsler, Mark. *Etymology and Grammatical Discourse in Late Antiquity and the Early Middle Ages*. Amsterdam: John Benjamins, 1989.

Anderson, Benedict. *Imagined Communities*. London: Verso, 1991.

Asad, Talal. *Genealogies of Religion*. Baltimore: Johns Hopkins University Press, 1993.

Atherton, Catherine. "What Every Grammarian Knows?" *Classical Quarterly* 46 (1996): 239–60.

Babcock, William S. "*Caritas* and Signification." In *De doctrina Christiana: A Classic of Western Culture*, ed. Duane W. H. Arnold and Pamela Bright. Notre Dame: University of Notre Dame Press, 1995.

Bakhtin, Mikhail. *The Dialogic Imagination*. Ed. Michael Holquist, tr. Caryl Emerson and Michael Holquist. Austin: University of Texas Press, 1981.

———. *Rabelais and His World*. Tr. Helene Iswolsky. Bloomington: Indiana University Press, 1984.

Bammel, Caroline Hammond. "Origen's Pauline Prefaces and the Chronology of His Pauline Commentaries." In *Origeniana Sexta*, ed. Gilles Dorival and Alain Le Boulluec. Louvain: Peeters, 1995.

———. "Die Pauluskommentare des Hieronymus: Die ersten wissenschaftlichen lateinischen Bibelkommentare?" In *Cristianesimo Latino e cultura Greca fino al sec. IV*. Studia Ephemeridis "Augustinianum" 42. Rome: Institutum Patristicum Augustinianum, 1993.

Barnish, S. J. B. "Martianus Capella and Rome in the Late Fifth Century." *Hermes* 114 (1986): 98–111.

Barthes, Roland. *Critical Essays*. Tr. Richard Howard. Evanston: Northwestern University Press, 1972.

———. *Image-Music-Text*. Tr. Stephen Heath. New York: Hill and Wang, 1977.

———. *A Lover's Discourse*. Tr. Richard Howard. New York: Hill and Wang, 1978.

———. "The Reality Effect." Tr. R. Carter. In *French Literary Theory Today*, ed. T. Todorov. Cambridge: Cambridge University Press, 1982.

———. *The Rustle of Language*. Tr. Richard Howard. Berkeley: University of California Press, 1989.

———. *S/Z*. Tr. Richard Miller. New York: Hill and Wang, 1974.

Barwick, Karl. *Remmius Palaemon und die römische Ars grammatica*. Philologus Supplementband 15.2. Leipzig: Dieter'sche Verlags-Buchhandlung, 1922.

Beal, Peter. "Notions in Garrison: The Seventeenth-Century Commonplace Book." In *New Ways of Looking at Old Texts*, ed. W. Speed Hill. Binghamton, N.Y.: Renaissance English Text Society, 1993.

Bellissima, G. "Sant' Agostino grammatico." *Augustinus Magister* I. Paris: Études Augustiniennes, 1954.

Benjamin, Walter. "The Work of Art in the Age of Mechanical Reproduction." Tr. Harry Zohn. In Benjamin, *Illuminations*, ed. Hannah Arendt. New York: Schocken Books, 1968.

Bergson, Henri. *Laughter*. Tr. Cloudesley Brereton and Fred Rothwell. New York: Macmillan, 1928.

Bersani, Leo. *The Freudian Body*. New York: Columbia University Press, 1986.

Bhabha, Homi K. *The Location of Culture*. London: Routledge, 1994.

Bloch, Herbert. "The Pagan Revival in the West at the End of the Fourth Century." In *The Conflict Between Paganism and Christianity in the Fourth Century*, ed. Arnaldo Momigliano. Oxford: Clarendon Press, 1963.

Bonner, Stanley. *Education in Ancient Rome*. London: Methuen, 1977.

La Bonnardière, A.-M. *Biblia Augustiniana*. Paris: Études Augustiniennes, 1960–.

Booth, Alan. D. "The Academic Career of Ausonius." *Phoenix* 36 (1982): 329–43.

Bourdieu, Pierre. *Distinction*. Tr. Richard Nice. Cambridge, Mass.: Harvard University Press, 1984.

——. *The Field of Cultural Production*. Ed. Randal Johnson, tr. Claud du Verlie. New York: Columbia University Press, 1993.

——. *Language and Symbolic Power*. Tr. Matthew Adamson and Gino Raymond, ed. John B. Thompson. Cambridge, Mass.: Harvard University Press, 1991.

Bourdieu, Pierre, and Jean-Claude Passeron. *Reproduction in Education, Society, and Culture*. Tr. Richard Nice. 2nd ed. London: Sage, 1990.

Boyarin, Daniel. *Intertextuality and the Reading of Midrash*. Bloomington: Indiana University Press, 1990.

Bradley, Keith R. *Discovering the Roman Family: Studies in Roman Social History*. New York: Oxford University Press, 1991.

Brown, Peter. *Power and Persuasion in Late Antiquity*. Madison: University of Wisconsin Press, 1992.

Brugnoli, G. *Studi sulle Differentiae verborum*. Rome: Signorelli, 1955.

de Bruyn, Theodore. "Flogging a Son: The Emergence of the *pater flagellans* in Latin Christian Discourse." *Journal of Early Christian Studies* 7 (1999): 249–90.

Butler, Judith. *Excitable Speech*. London: Routledge, 1997.

——. *Gender Trouble*. 2nd ed. London: Routledge, 1990.

Cameron, Alan. "The Date and Identity of Macrobius." *Journal of Roman Studies* 56 (1966): 25–38.

——. "The Last Pagans of Rome." In *The Transformations of Urbs Roma in Late Antiquity*, ed. William V. Harris. Journal of Roman Archaeology Supplements 33. Portsmouth: Journal of Roman Archaeology, 1999.

——. "Martianus and His First Editor." *Classical Philology* 81 (1986): 320–28.

——. "Paganism and Literature in Late Fourth Century Rome." In *Christianisme et formes littéraires de l'antiquité tardive en occident*, ed. M. Fuhrmann. Geneva: Fondation Hardt, 1977.

Cameron, Averil. *Christianity and the Rhetoric of Empire*. Berkeley: University of California Press, 1991.

Carson, Anne. *Eros the Bittersweet*. Princeton: Princeton University Press, 1986; Normal: Dalkey Archive Press, 1998.

Cavallera, F. *Saint Jérôme: Sa vie et son oeuvre*. 2 vols. Louvain: Spicilegium Sacrum Lovaniense, 1922.

de Certeau, Michel. *The Practice of Everyday Life*. Tr. Steven Rendall. Berkeley: University of California Press, 1984.

——. *The Writing of History*. Tr. Tom Conley. New York: Columbia, 1988.

Chadwick, Nora. *Poetry and Letters in Early Christian Gaul*. London: Bowes & Bowes, 1955.

Chartier, Roger. *The Order of Books*. Tr. Lydia G. Cochrane. Stanford: Stanford University Press, 1994.

Chastagnol, A. "Le sénateur Volusien et la conversion d'une famille de l'aristocratie romaine au Bas-Empire." *Revue des études anciennes* 58 (1956): 240–53.

Chin, Catherine M. "Christians and the Roman Classroom: Memory, Grammar, and Rhetoric in *Confessions X*." *Augustinian Studies* 33 (2002): 161–82.

——. "Origen and Christian Naming: Textual Exhaustion and the Boundaries of Gentility." *Journal of Early Christian Studies* 14 (2007): 407–36.

Chitty, Derwas. *The Desert a City*. Oxford: Blackwell, 1966.

Christes, Johannes. *Sklaven und Freigelassene als Grammatiker und Philologen im antiken Rom*. Wiesbaden: Steiner, 1979.

Clark, Elizabeth A. *History, Theory, Text: Historians and the Linguistic Turn*. Cambridge, Mass.: Harvard University Press, 2004.

——. *Jerome, Chrysostom, and Friends*. Lewiston: Edwin Mellen Press, 1979.

——. *The Origenist Controversy: The Social Construction of an Early Christian Debate*. Princeton: Princeton University Press, 1992.

——. *Reading Renunciation*. Princeton: Princeton University Press, 1999.

Clark, Elizabeth A., and Diane F. Hatch. *The Golden Bough, the Oaken Cross*. Chico: Scholars Press, 1981.

Colbrook, Claire. *Gilles Deleuze*. London: Routledge, 2002.

Collart, Jean. "Saint Augustin grammairien dans le *De magistro*." *Revue des études augustiniennes* 17 (1971): 279–92.

——, ed. *Varron: Grammaire antique et stylistique latine*. Paris: Les Belles Lettres, 1978.

Cooley, Alison, ed. *Becoming Roman, Writing Latin? Literacy and Epigraphy in the Roman West*. Journal of Roman Archaeology Supplements 48. Portsmouth: Journal of Roman Archaeology, 2002.

Conybeare, Catherine. *Paulinus Noster: Self and Symbols in the Letters of Paulinus of Nola*. Oxford: Oxford University Press, 2000.

Courcelle, Pierre. *Les Confessions de Saint Augustin dans la Tradition Littéraire*. Paris: Études Augustiniennes, 1963.

——. "L'Enfant et les 'sorts bibliques.'" *Vigiliae Christianae* 7 (1953): 194–220.

Cribiore, Raffaella. *Writing, Teachers, and Students in Greco-Roman Egypt*. Atlanta: Scholars Press, 1996.

Dawson, Doyne. *Cities of the Gods*. New York: Oxford University Press, 1992.

Deal, William. "Toward a Politics of Asceticism." In *Asceticism*, ed. Vincent Wimbush and Richard Valantasis. New York: Oxford University Press, 1995.

Deleuze, Gilles. *Cinema 2: The Time-Image*. Tr. Hugh Tomlinson and Robert Galeta. Minneapolis: University of Minnesota Press, 1989.

——. *The Logic of Sense*. Ed. Constantin V. Boundas, tr. Mark Lester and Charles Stivale. New York: Columbia University Press, 1990.

——. *Masochism: An Interpretation of Coldness and Cruelty*. Tr. Jean McNeil. New York: George Braziller, 1971.

Deleuze, Gilles, and Félix Guattari. *Anti-Oedipus*. Tr. Robert Hurley et al. Minneapolis: University of Minnesota Press, 1983.

Deleuze, Gilles, and Claire Parnet. *Dialogues*. Tr. Hugh Tomlinson and Barbara Habberjam. New York: Columbia University Press, 1987.

Derrida, Jacques. *Of Grammatology*. Tr. Gayatri Chakravorty Spivak. Corrected edition. Baltimore: Johns Hopkins University Press, 1997.

Desbordes, François. "*Latinitas*: Constitution et évolution d'un modèle de l'identité linguistique." In *Hellenismos: Quelques jalons pour une histoire de l'identité Grecque*, ed. Suzanne Said. Leiden: Brill, 1991.

Dixon, Suzanne. *The Roman Family*. Baltimore: Johns Hopkins University Press, 1992.

Dodds, E. R. *Pagan and Christian in an Age of Anxiety*. Cambridge: Cambridge University Press, 1965.

Dominik, William, ed. *Roman Eloquence*. London: Routledge, 1996.

Dunkin, Paul Shaner. *Post-Aristophanic Comedy: Studies in the Social Outlook of Middle and New Comedy at Both Athens and Rome*, Illinois Studies in Language and Literature 31.3–4. Urbana: University of Illinois Press, 1946.

Duval, Y.-M. "Les premiers rapports de Paulin de Nole avec Jérôme." *Studi Tardoantichi* 7 (1989): 177–216.

Eden, Kathy. "The Rhetorical Tradition and Augustinian Hermeneutics in *De doctrina Christiana*." *Rhetorica* 8 (1990): 45–63.

Edmunds, Lowell. *Intertextuality and the Reading of Roman Poetry*. Baltimore: Johns Hopkins University Press, 2001.

Egli, Urs. "Stoic Syntax and Semantics." In *The History of Linguistics in the Classical eriod*, ed. Daniel J. Taylor. Amsterdam: John Benjamins, 1987.

Elsner, Jas. "The *Itinerarium Burdigalense*: Politics and Salvation in the Geography of Constantine's Empire." *Journal of Roman Studies* 90 (2000): 181–95.

Etienne, R. "La démographie de la famille d'Ausone." In *Études et chronique de démographie historique*. Paris: Société de démographie historique, 1964.

Fabre, Pierre. *Saint Paulin de Nole et l'amitié Chrétienne*. Paris: E. de Boccard, 1949.

Fish, Stanley. "Why No One's Afraid of Wolfgang Iser." *Diacritics* 11 (1981): 2–13.

——. *Doing What Comes Naturally*. Durham, N.C.: Duke University Press, 1989.

Flamant, Jacques. *Macrobe et le Néoplatonisme Latin, à la fin du IVe Siècle*. Leiden: Brill, 1977.

Foucault, Michel. *The Archaeology of Knowledge and The Discourse on Language*. Tr. A. M. Sheridan Smith. New York: Pantheon, 1972.

——. *Discipline and Punish*. Tr. Alan Sheridan. New York: Vintage Books, 1979.

——. *The Order of Things*. New York: Random House, 1970.

——. "Of Other Spaces." Tr. Jay Miskowiec. *Diacritics* 16 (1986): 22–27.

——. "Truth and Power." In *Power/Knowledge*, ed. Colin Gordon. New York: Pantheon, 1980. Reprinted in *The Foucault Reader*, ed. Paul Rabinow. New York: Pantheon, 1984.

——. "What Is an Author?" Tr. Josué V. Harari. In *The Foucault Reader*, ed. Paul Rabinow. New York: Pantheon, 1984.

Frank, Georgia. *The Memory of the Eyes*. Berkeley: University of California Press, 2000.

Frede, Michael. "Principles of Stoic Grammar." In *The Stoics*, ed. John Rist. Berkeley: University of California Press, 1978.

Fredriksen, Paula. "Allegory and Reading God's Book: Paul and Augustine on the Destiny of Israel." In *Interpretation and Allegory: Antiquity to the Modern Period*, ed. J. Whitman. Leiden: Brill, 2001.

——. "Augustine and Israel: *Interpretatio ad litteram*, Jews, and Judaism in Augustine's Theology of History." *Studia Patristica* 38 (2001): 119–35.

——. "*Excaecati Occulta Justitia Dei*: Augustine on Jews and Judaism." *Journal of Early Christian Studies* 3 (1995): 299–324.

———. "*Secundem carnem*: History and Israel in the Theology of St. Augustine." In *The Limits of Ancient Christianity*, ed. William Klingshirn and Mark Vessey. Ann Arbor: University of Michigan Press, 1999.

Frend, W. H. C. "The Two Worlds of Paulinus of Nola." In *Latin Literature of the Fourth Century*, ed. J. W. Binns. London: Routledge & Kegan Paul, 1974.

Freund, Elizabeth. *The Return of the Reader*. London: Methuen, 1987.

Gamble, Harry Y. *Books and Readers in the Early Church*. New Haven: Yale University Press, 1995.

Gleason, Maud. *Making Men: Sophists and Self-Presentation in Ancient Rome*. Princeton: Princeton University Press, 1995.

Glück, Manfred. *Priscians Partitiones und ihre Stellung in der Spätantiken Schule*. Spudasmata 12. Hildesheim: G. Olms, 1967.

Gnilka, Christian. *Chrêsis: Die Methode der Kirchenväter im Umgang mit der Antiken Kultur*. Vol. 1, *Der Begriff des "Rechten Gebrauchs."* Basel: Schwabe, 1984.

Goehring, James. *Ascetics, Society, and the Desert*. Harrisburg: Trinity Press International, 1999.

———. "The Encroaching Desert: Literary Production and Ascetic Space in Early Christian Egypt." *Journal of Early Christian Studies* 1 (1993): 281–96.

Gorce, Denys. *Les voyages, l'hospitalité, et le port des lettres dans le monde chrétien des IVe et Ve siècles*. Paris: A. Picard, 1925.

Grebe, Sabine. "Gedanken zur Datierung von *De Nuptiis Philologiae et Mercurii* des Martianus Capella." *Hermes* 128 (2000): 353–68.

———. *Martianus Capella "De Nuptiis Philologiae et Mercurii": Darstellung der Sieben Freien Künste und ihrer Beziehungen Zueinander*. Leipzig: Teubner, 1999.

Green, R. P. H. "The Christianity of Ausonius." *Studia Patristica* 28 (1993): 39–48.

———. *The Poetry of Paulinus of Nola: A Study of His Latinity*. Collection Latomus 120. Brussels: Latomus, 1971.

———. "Still Waters Run Deep: A New Study of the *Professores* of Bordeaux." *Classical Quarterly* 35 (1985): 491–506.

———. *The Works of Ausonius*. Oxford: Clarendon Press, 1999.

Grützmacher, G. *Hieronymus: Eine biographische Studie zur alten Kirchengeschichte*. 3 vols. Leipzig: Dieterich'sche Verlag, 1901; Berlin: Trowitzsch & Sohn, 1906, 1908.

Guattari, Félix. *Chaosophy*, ed. Sylvère Lotringer. New York: Semiotext(e), 1995.

Guinot, J.-N. "La fortune des *Hexaples* d'Origène aux IVe et Ve siècles au milieu antiochien." In *Origeniana Sexta: Origène et la Bible*, ed. Gilles Dorival and Alain Le Boulluec. Louvain: University Press, 1995.

Habinek, Thomas. *The Politics of Latin Literature*. Princeton: Princeton University Press, 1998.

Hadot, Ilsetraut. *Arts libéraux et philosophie dans la pensée antique*. Paris: CNRS, 1984.

Hadot, Pierre. *Marius Victorinus: Recherches sur sa vie et ses oeuvres*. Paris: Études Augustiniennes, 1971.

Hagendahl, Harald. *Augustine and the Latin Classics*. Göteburg: Almqvist & Wiksell, 1967.

———. *The Latin Fathers and the Classics*. Göteborg: Almqvist & Wiksell, 1958.

Halperin, David M. "Why Is Diotima a Woman? Platonic *Eros* and the Figuration of Gender." In *Before Sexuality: The Construction of Erotic Experience in the Ancient Greek World*, ed. David M. Halperin, John J. Winkler, and Froma I. Zeitlin. Princeton: Princeton University Press, 1990.

Hanawalt, Barbara A., and Michael Kobialka, eds. *Medieval Practices of Space*. Minneapolis: University of Minnesota Press, 2000.

Harris, William V. *Ancient Literacy*. Cambridge, Mass.: Harvard University Press, 1989.

Harrison, Carol. "The Rhetoric of Scripture and Preaching." In *Augustine and His Critics*, ed. Robert Dodaro and George Lawless. London: Routledge, 2000.

Häussler, Ralph. "Writing Latin—From Resistance to Assimilation: Language, Culture and Society in N. Italy and S. Gaul." In *Becoming Roman, Writing Latin?* ed. Alison E. Cooley, Journal of Roman Archaeology Supplements 48. Portsmouth: Journal of Roman Archaeology, 2002.

Hayward, C. T. R. *Saint Jerome's Hebrew Questions on Genesis*. Oxford: Clarendon, 1995.

Hedrick, Charles Jr. *History and Silence*. Austin: University of Texas Press, 2000.

Heine, Ronald E. "In Search of Origen's Commentary on Philemon." *Harvard Theological Review* 93 (2000): 117–33.

Hobsbawm, Eric, and Terence Ranger, eds. *The Invention of Tradition*. Cambridge: Cambridge University Press, 1983.

Holtz, Louis. *Donat et la tradition de l'enseignement grammatical*. Paris: CNRS, 1981.

——. "Sur les traces de Charisius." In *Varron: Grammaire antique et stylistique latine*, ed. Jean Collart. Paris: Les Belles Lettres, 1978.

Hopkins, M. Keith. "Social Mobility in the Later Roman Empire: The Evidence of Ausonius." *Classical Quarterly* 11 (1961): 239–49.

Hopper, Paul J. "The Category 'Event' in Natural Discourse and Logic." In *Discourse, Grammar and Typology: Papers in Honor of John W. M. Verhaar*, ed. Werner Abraham, T. Givón, and Sandra A. Thompson. Amsterdam: John Benjamins, 1995.

Hunt, E. D. *Holy Land Pilgrimage in the Later Roman Empire, A.D. 312–460*. Oxford: Clarendon Press, 1982.

Irmscher, J. "Heidnisches und Christliches bei Ausonius." *Studia Ephemerides "Augustinianum"* 42 (1993): 179–85.

Irvine, Martine. *The Making of Textual Culture: Grammatica and Literary Theory, 350–1100*. Cambridge: Cambridge University Press, 1994.

Isbell, H. "Decimus Magnus Ausonius: The Poet and His World." In *Latin Literature of the Fourth Century*, ed. J. W. Binns. London: Routledge & Kegan Paul, 1974.

Iser, Wolfgang. *The Implied Reader*. Baltimore: Johns Hopkins University Press, 1974.

——. *Prospecting: From Reader Response to Literary Anthropology*. Baltimore: Johns Hopkins University Press, 1989.

Jacobs, Andrew S. *Remains of the Jews: The Holy Land and Christian Empire in Late Antiquity*. Stanford: Stanford University Press, 2003.

Jameson, Fredric. "Of Islands and Trenches: Naturalization and the Production of Utopian Discourse." *Diacritics* 7 (1977): 2–21.

———. *The Political Unconscious*. Ithaca: Cornell University Press, 1981.

Kahlos, Maijastina. *Vettius Agorius Praetextatus: A Senatorial Life in Between*. Rome: Institutum Romanum Finlandiae, 2002.

Kamesar, Adam. *Jerome, Greek Scholarship and the Hebrew Bible*. Oxford: Clarendon Press, 1993.

Kaster, Robert. "A Schoolboy's Burlesque from Cyrene?" *Mnemosyne* 37 (1984): 457–58.

———. *Guardians of Language: The Grammarian and Society in Late Antiquity*. Berkeley: University of California Press, 1988.

———. "Macrobius and Servius: *Verecundia* and the Grammarian's Function." *Harvard Studies in Classical Philology* 84 (1980): 219–62.

———. "Notes on 'Primary' and 'Secondary' Schools in Late Antiquity." *Transactions and Proceedings of the American Philological Association* 113 (1983): 323–46.

———. "Servius and *idonei auctores*." *American Journal of Philology* 99 (1978): 181–209.

———. *Suetonius: De Grammaticis et Rhetoribus*. Oxford: Clarendon Press, 1995.

Kavanaugh, James. "Ideology." In *Critical Terms for Literary Study*, ed. Frank Lentricchia and Thomas McLaughlin. 2nd ed. Chicago: University of Chicago Press, 1995.

Kelly, J. N. D. *Golden Mouth: The Story of John Chrysostom—Ascetic, Preacher, Bishop*. London: Duckworth, 1995.

———. *Jerome: His Life, Writings, and Controversies*. London: Duckworth, 1975.

Kevane, Eugene. "Augustine's *De doctrina christiana*: A Treatise on Christian Education." *Recherches Augustiniennes* 4 (1966): 97–133.

Klein, Richard. *Symmachus*. Darmstadt: Wissenschaftliche Gesellschaft, 1971.

Klingshirn, William. "Defining the *Sortes Sanctorum*: Gibbon, Du Cange, and Early Christian Lot Divination." *Journal of Early Christian Studies* 10 (2002): 77–130.

Knight, Diana. *Barthes and Utopia: Space, Travel, Writing*. Oxford: Clarendon Press, 1997.

Koch, Carl. "Pietas." In Pauly-Wissowa, *Realencyclopädie der classischen Altertumswissenschaft*. Stuttgart: J. B. Metzler, 1951.

Kristeva, Julia. *Desire in Language: A Semiotic Approach to Literature and Art*. Ed. Leon S. Roudiez, tr. Thomas Gora, Alice Jardine, and Leon S. Roudiez. New York: Columbia University Press, 1980.

Kuhn, Reinhard. *The Demon of Noontide: Ennui in Western Literature*. Princeton: Princeton University Press, 1976.

de Labriolle, Pierre. *Un épisode de la fin du paganisme: La correspondence d'Ausone et de Paulin de Nole*. Paris: Librairie Bloud, 1910.

Lacan, Jacques. "The Function and Field of Speech and Language in Psychoanalysis." In *Écrits*, tr. Alan Sheridan. New York: W. W. Norton, 1977.

Laistner, M. L. W. *Christianity and Pagan Culture in the Later Roman Empire*. Ithaca: Cornell University Press, 1951.

Landow, George. *Hypertext 2.0: The Convergence of Contemporary Critical Theory and Technology*. Baltimore: Johns Hopkins University Press, 1997.

de Lange, Nicholas. *Origen and the Jews*. Cambridge: Cambridge University Press, 1976.

Law, Vivien. "Late Latin Grammars in the Early Middle Ages: A Typological

History." In *The History of Linguistics in the Classical Period*, ed. Daniel Taylor. Amsterdam: John Benjamins, 1987.

——. "Memory and the Structure of Grammars in Antiquity and the Middle Ages." In *Manuscripts and Tradition of Grammatical Texts from Antiquity to the Renaissance*, ed. Mario De Nonno et al. Cassino: Università degli Studi di Cassino, 2000.

——. "The Mnemonic Structure of Ancient Grammatical Doctrine." In *Ancient Grammar: Content and Context*, ed. Pierre Swiggers and Alfonse Wouters. Louvain: Peeters, 1996.

——. "St. Augustine's 'De grammatica': Lost or Found?" *Recherches Augustiniennes* 19 (1984): 155–83.

Layton, Richard. "Plagiarism and Lay Patronage of Ascetic Scholarship: Jerome, Ambrose and Rufinus." *Journal of Early Christian Studies* 10 (2002): 489–522.

LeMoine, Fannie J. *Martianus Capella: A Literary Re-evaluation*. Munich: Arbeo-Gesellschaft, 1972.

——. "Parental Gifts: Father-Son Dedications in Roman Didactic Literature." *Illinois Classical Studies* 16 (1991): 337–66.

Lepschy, Giulio, ed. *History of Linguistics*. Vol. 2. London: Longman, 1994.

Levitas, Ruth. *The Concept of Utopia*. New York: Philip Allan, 1990.

Lewis, C. S. *The Last Battle*. London: William Collins, 1989. First published 1956.

Leyerle, Blake. "Appealing to Children." *Journal of Early Christian Studies* 5 (1997): 243–70.

——. "John Chrysostom on the Gaze." *Journal of Early Christian Studies* 1 (1993): 159–74.

——. "Landscape as Cartography in Early Christian Pilgrimage Narratives." *Journal of the American Academy of Religion* 64 (1996): 119–43.

——. *Theatrical Shows and Ascetic Lives*. Berkeley: University of California Press, 2001.

Liebeschuetz, J. H. W. G. "The Significance of the Speech of Praetextatus." In *Pagan Monotheism in Late Antiquity*, ed. Polymnia Athanassiadi and Michael Frede. Oxford: Oxford University Press, 1999.

Lim, Richard. *Public Disputation, Power, and Social Order in Late Antiquity*. Berkeley: University of California Press, 1995.

Lizzi, Rita. "La memoria selettiva." In *Lo Spazio Letterario di Roma Antica*. Vol. 3: *La ricezione del testo*, ed. Guglielmo Cavallo et al. Rome: Salerno, 1990.

Lloyd, R. B. "Republican Authors in Servius and the Scholia Danielis." *Harvard Studies in Classical Philology* 65 (1961): 291–341.

Luhtala, Anneli. *Grammar and Philosophy in Late Antiquity: A Study of Priscian's Sources*. Amsterdam: John Benjamins, 2005.

MacCormack, Sabine. *Shadows of Poetry: Virgil in the Mind of Augustine*. Berkeley: University of California Press, 1998.

MacMullen, Ramsay. *Christianizing the Roman Empire*. New Haven: Yale University Press, 1984.

Mannheim, Karl. *Ideology and Utopia*. Tr. Louis Wirth and Edward Shils. New York: Harcourt Brace, 1954.

Marchetti, Vittorio. Interview with Gilles Deleuze and Félix Guattari. "Capitalism and Schizophrenia." Tr. Jarred Becker. In Guattari, *Chaosophy*, ed. Sylvère Lotringer. New York: Semiotext(e), 1995.

Marin, Louis. "The Frontiers of Utopia." *Critical Inquiry* 19 (1993): 397–420.

——. *Utopics: Spatial Play*. Tr. Robert A. Vollrath. Atlantic Highlands, N.J.: Humanities Press, 1984.

Marinone, N. *Elio Donato, Macrobio, e Servio commentatori di Vergilio*. Vercelli: Presso l'Autore, 1946.

Markus, Robert A. *The End of Ancient Christianity*. Cambridge: Cambridge University Press, 1990.

——. "Paganism, Christianity and the Latin Classics in the Fourth Century." In *Latin Literature of the Fourth Century*, edited by J. W. Binns. London: Routledge & Kegan Paul, 1974.

Marrou, Henri-Irénée. *A History of Education in Antiquity*. Tr. George Lamb. 3rd ed. Madison: University of Wisconsin Press, 1956.

——. *Saint Augustin et la fin de la culture antique*. 4th ed. Paris: E. de Boccard, 1958.

Massumi, Brian. "The Autonomy of Affect." In *Deleuze: A Critical Reader*, ed. Paul Patton. Oxford: Blackwell, 1996.

——. *A User's Guide to Capitalism and Schizophrenia*. Cambridge, Mass.: MIT Press, 1992.

Matthews, Peter. "Greek and Latin Linguistics." In *History of Linguistics*. Vol. 2: *Classical and Medieval Linguistics*, ed. Giulio Lepschy. London: Longman, 1994.

Mayer, C. "'*Res per signa*': Der Grundgedanke des Prologs in Augustins Schrift *De doctrina Christiana* und das Problem seiner Datierung." *Revue des études augustiniennes* 20 (1974): 100–112.

Miller, J. Hillis. "Narrative." In *Critical Terms for Literary Study*, ed. Frank Lentricchia and Thomas McLaughlin. 2nd ed. Chicago: University of Chicago Press, 1995.

Miller, Patricia Cox. "'Differential Networks': Relics and Other Fragments in Late Antiquity." *Journal of Early Christian Studies* 6 (1998): 113–38.

——. *Dreams in Late Antiquity*. Princeton: Princeton University Press, 1994.

——. "In Praise of Nonsense: A Piety of the Alphabet in Ancient Magic." In Miller, *The Poetry of Thought in Late Antiquity*. Aldershot: Ashgate, 2001.

——. "Jerome's Centaur: A Hyper-Icon of the Desert." *Journal of Early Christian Studies* 4 (1996): 209–33.

——. "Origen and the Witch of Endor: Toward an Iconoclastic Typology." *Anglican Theological Review* 66 (1984): 137–47.

——. "Strategies of Representation in Collective Biography: Constructing the Subject as Holy." In *Greek Biography and Panegyric in Late Antiquity*, ed. Tomas Hägg and Philip Rousseau. Berkeley: University of California Press, 2000.

Mohrmann, Christine. "Encore une fois: paganus." In *Études sur le latine des Chrétiens*. Vol. 3. Rome: Edizioni di storia e letteraria, 1965.

Morgan, Teresa. *Literate Education in the Hellenistic and Roman World*. Cambridge: Cambridge University Press, 1998.

Mratschek, Sigrid. "*Multis enim notissima est sanctitas loci*: Paulinus and the Gradual

Rise of Nola as a Center of Christian Hospitality." *Journal of Early Christian Studies* 9 (2001): 511–53.

Munnich, O. "Les *Hexaples* d'Origène à la lumière de la tradition manuscrite de la Bible grecque." In *Origeniana Sexta: Origène et la Bible*, ed. G. Dorival and A. Le Boulluec. Louvain: University Press, 1995.

Murphy, F. X. *Rufinus of Aquileia (345–411): His Life and Works*. Washington, D.C.: Catholic University of America Press, 1945.

Nautin, P. "Études de chronologie hiéronymienne (393–397)." *Revue des études augustiniennes* 19 (1973): 69–86.

——. *Origène: Sa vie et son oeuvre*. Paris: Beauchesne, 1977.

——. "Le premier échange épistolaire entre Jérôme et Damase: lettres réelles ou fictives?" *Freiburger Zeitschrift für Philosophie und Theologie* 30 (1983): 331–43.

Neely, Carol Thomas. "Woman/Fetish/Utopia." In *Heterotopias*, ed. Tobin Siebers. Ann Arbor: University of Michigan Press, 1994.

Neuschäfer, Bernhard. *Origenes als Philologe*. Basel: Friedrich Reinhardt, 1987.

Newman, Hillel I. "Between Jerusalem and Bethlehem: Jerome and the Holy Places of Palestine." In *Sanctity of Time and Space in Tradition and Modernity*, ed. A. Houtman et al. Leiden: Brill, 1998.

De Nonno, Mario. "Le citazioni dei grammatici." In *Lo Spazio Letterario di Roma Antica*. Vol. 3: *La ricezione del testo*, ed. Guglielmo Cavallo et al. Rome: Salerno, 1990.

De Nonno, Mario, et al., eds. *Manuscripts and Tradition of Grammatical Texts from Antiquity to the Renaissance*. Cassino: Università degli Studi di Cassino, 2000.

Noyes, John K. *The Mastery of Submission: Inventions of Masochism*. Ithaca: Cornell University Press, 1997.

Nugent, S. Georgia. "Ausonius' 'Late-Antique' Poetics and 'Post-Modern' Literary Theory." *Ramus* 19 (1990): 26–50.

Nunokawa, Jeff. "The Importance of Being Bored: The Dividends of Ennui in *The Picture of Dorian Gray*." In *Novel Gazing: Queer Readings in Fiction*, ed. Eve Kosofsky Sedgwick. Durham, N.C.: Duke University Press, 1997.

O'Donnell, James J. "Bible." In *Augustine Through the Ages: An Encyclopedia*, ed. Allan D. Fitzgerald. Grand Rapids: Eerdmans, 1999.

——. "The Career of Virius Nicomachus Flavianus." *Phoenix* 32 (1978): 129–43.

——. "The Demise of Paganism." *Traditio* 35 (1979): 45–88.

——. "Paganus." *Classical Folia* 31 (1977): 163–69.

Ousterhout, Robert, ed. *The Blessings of Pilgrimage*. Urbana: University of Illinois Press, 1990.

Passeron, Jean-Claude. "Theories of Socio-Cultural Reproduction." *International Social Science Journal* 110 (1986): 619–29.

Person, Ethel Spector, ed. *On Freud's "A Child is Being Beaten."* New Haven: Yale University Press, 1997.

Peters, Edward. "Notes Toward an Archaeology of Boredom." *Social Research* 42 (1975): 493–511.

Pfeiffer, Rudolf. *History of Classical Scholarship from the Beginnings to the End of the Hellenistic Age*. Oxford: Clarendon Press, 1968.

Pollman, Karla. *Doctrina Christiana: Untersuchungen zu den Anfängen der Christlichen*

Hermeneutik unter besonderer Berücksichtigung von Augustinus, De doctrina Christiana. Freiburg: Universitätsverlag, 1996.

Pomian, Krzysztof. *Collectors and Curiosities: Paris and Venice, 1500–1800*. Tr. Elizabeth Wiles-Porter. Cambridge: Polity Press, 1990.

Press, Gerald. "*Doctrina* in Augustine's *De doctrina Christiana*." *Philosophy and Rhetoric* 17, no. 2 (1984): 98–120.

———. "The Subject and Structure of Augustine's *De Doctrina Christiana*." *Augustinian Studies* 11 (1980): 99–124.

Prete, Serafino. "The Textual Tradition of the Correspondence between Ausonius and Paulinus." In *Collectanea Vaticana in honorem Anselmi M. Card. Albareda*. Vatican City: Biblioteca Apostolica Vaticana, 1962.

Ramelli, Ilaria. *Marziano Capella: Le Nozze di Filologia e Mercurio*. Milan: Bompiani, 2001.

Rankin, Victor. *Semantic Mechanisms of Humor*. Dordrecht: D. Reidel, 1985.

Raposa, Michael L. *Boredom and the Religious Imagination*. Charlottesville: University of Virginia Press, 1999.

Rawson, Beryl, ed. *Marriage, Divorce, and Children in Ancient Rome*. Oxford: Clarendon Press, 1991.

Rawson, Beryl, and Paul Weaver, eds. *The Roman Family in Italy: Status, Sentiment, Space*. Oxford: Clarendon Press, 1997.

Rebenich, Stefan. *Hieronymus und sein Kreis*. Stuttgart: Franz Steiner, 1992.

Relihan, Joel. *Ancient Menippean Satire*. Baltimore: Johns Hopkins University Press, 1993.

Reynolds, Suzanne. *Medieval Reading: Grammar, Rhetoric, and the Classical Text*. Cambridge: Cambridge University Press, 1996.

Richlin, Amy. *The Garden of Priapus: Sexuality and Aggression in Roman Humor*. Rev. ed. New York: Oxford University Press, 1992.

Ricoeur, Paul. "Imagination in Discourse and in Action." Tr. Kathleen Blamey. In Ricoeur, *From Text to Action: Essays in Hermeneutics II*. Evanston: Northwestern University Press, 1991.

———. *Lectures on Ideology and Utopia*. New York: Columbia University Press, 1986.

———. *Time and Narrative*. Vol. 1. Tr. Kathleen McLaughlin and David Pellauer. Chicago: University of Chicago Press, 1984.

Roberts, Michael. *The Jeweled Style: Poetry and Poetics in Late Antiquity*. Ithaca: Cornell University Press, 1989.

Robins, R. H. *Ancient and Medieval Grammatical Theory in Europe*. London: G. Bell, 1951.

Rosén, Hannah. *Latine loqui: Trends and Directions in the Crystallization of Classical Latin*. Munich: W. Fink, 1999.

Saenger, Paul. *Space Between Words: The Origins of Silent Reading*. Stanford: Stanford University Press, 1997.

Said, Suzanne, ed. *Hellenismos: Quelques jalons pour une histoire de l'identité Grecque*. Leiden: Brill, 1991.

Saller, Richard. "Corporal Punishment, Authority and Obedience in the Roman Household." In *Marriage, Divorce, and Children in Ancient Rome*, ed. Beryl Rawson. Oxford: Clarendon Press, 1991.

Salzman, Michele R. *The Making of a Christian Aristocracy*. Cambridge, Mass.: Harvard University Press, 2002.

Scanlon, Michael. "Augustine and Theology as Rhetoric," *Augustinian Studies* 25 (1994): 37–50.

Schäublin, Christoph. "*De doctrina christiana:* A Classic of Western Culture?" In *De Doctrina Christiana: A Classic of Western Culture*, ed. Duane W.H. Arnold and Pamela Bright. Notre Dame: University of Notre Dame Press, 1995.

———. *Untersuchungen zur Methode und Herkunft der antiochenischen Exegese*. Cologne: P. Hanstein, 1974.

———. "Zur paganen Prägung der christlichen Exegese." In *Christliche Exegese zwischen Nicaea und Chalcedon*, ed. J. Van Oort. Kampen: Kok Pharos, 1992.

Schenkeveld, Dirk M. "The Idea of Progress and the Art of Grammar: Charisius *Ars Grammatica* 1.15." *American Journal of Philology* 119 (1998): 443–59.

———. *A Rhetorical Grammar*. Leiden: Brill, 2004.

Shanzer, Danuta. *A Philosophical and Literary Commentary on Martianus Capella's De Nuptiis Philologiae et Mercurii Book 1*. Berkeley: University of California Press, 1986.

Sieben, H.-J. "Die 'Res' der Bibel in 'Doctrina Christiana.'" *Revue des études augustiniennes* 21 (1975): 72–90.

Sivan, Hagith. *Ausonius of Bordeaux: Genesis of a Gallic Aristocracy*. London: Routledge, 1993.

Skeb, Matthias. *Christo vivere: Studien zum literarishcen Christusbild des Paulinus von Nola*. Bonn: Borengässer, 1997.

Sluiter, Ineke. *Ancient Grammar in Context*. Amsterdam: John Benjamins, 1990.

Small, Jocelyn Penny. *Wax Tablets of the Mind: Cognitive Studies of Memory and Literacy in Classical Antiquity*. London: Routledge, 1997.

Smiley, Charles N. "*Latinitas* and *Hellenismos*." *Bulletin of the University of Wisconsin* 143 (1906): 211–71.

Smith, Barbara Herrnstein. "Narrative Versions, Narrative Theories." In *On Narrative*, ed. W. J. T. Mitchell. Chicago: University of Chicago Press, 1981.

Smith, Jonathan Z. *To Take Place: Toward Theory in Ritual*. Chicago: University of Chicago Press, 1987.

Soja, Edward W. *Postmodern Geographies: The Reassertion of Space in Critical Social Theory*. London: Verso, 1989.

Sorabji, Richard. *Emotions and Peace of Mind from Stoic Agitation to Christian Temptation*. Oxford: Oxford University Press, 2001.

Spacks, Patricia Meyer. *Boredom: The Literary History of a State of Mind*. Chicago: University of Chicago Press, 1995.

Springer, Carl P. E. "Jerome and the *Cento* of Proba." *Studia Patristica* 28 (1993): 96–105.

Stahl, William H., and Richard Johnson. *Martianus Capella and the Seven Liberal Arts*. 2 vols. New York: Columbia University Press, 1971.

Stark, Rodney. *The Rise of Christianity*. Princeton: Princeton University Press, 1996.

Stephens, Anthony. "The Sun State and Its Shadow: On the Condition of Utopian Writing." In *Utopias*, ed. Eugene Kamenka. Melbourne: Oxford University Press, 1987.

Stewart, Susan. *On Longing: Narratives of the Miniature, the Gigantic, the Souvenir, the Collection*. Durham, N.C.: Duke University Press, 1993.

Stewart, Suzanne. *Sublime Surrender: Male Masochism at the Fin-de-Siècle*. Ithaca: Cornell University Press, 1998.

Stock, Brian. *Augustine the Reader*. Cambridge, Mass.: Harvard University Press, 1996.

Swann, Marjorie. *Curiosities and Texts: The Culture of Collecting in Early Modern England*. Philadelphia: University of Pennsylvania Press, 2001.

Swiggers, Pierre, and Alfonse Wouters, eds. *Ancient Grammar: Content and Context*. Louvain: Peeters, 1996.

Syska, Ekkehart. *Studien zur Theologie des Macrobius*. Stuttgart: Teubner, 1993.

Taylor, Daniel, ed. *The History of Linguistics in the Classical Period*. Amsterdam: John Benjamins, 1987.

Todorov, Tzvetan. "The Journey and Its Narratives." Tr. Alyson Waters. In *Transports*, ed. Chloe Chard and Helen Langdon. New Haven: Yale University Press, 1996.

Toohey, Peter. "Acedia in Late Classical Antiquity." *Illinois Classical Studies* 15 (1990): 339–52.

——. "Some Ancient Notions of Boredom." *Illinois Classical Studies* 13 (1988): 151–64.

Trout, Dennis. "The Dates of the Ordination of Paulinus of Bordeaux and of His Departure for Nola." *Revue des études augustiniennes* 37 (1991): 237–60.

——. *Paulinus of Nola: Life, Letters, and Poems*. Berkeley: University of California Press, 1999.

Uhl, Anne. *Servius als Sprachlehrer*. Göttingen: Vandenhoeck & Ruprecht, 1998.

Vainio, Raija. *Latinitas and Barbarisms According to the Roman Grammarians*. Turku: Painosalama Oy, 1999.

Verheijen, L. M. J. "Le *De doctrina christiana* de Saint Augustin: Un manuel d'herméneutique et d'expression chrétienne avec, en II. 19.29–42.63, une charte fondamentale pour une culture chrétienne." *Augustiniana* 24 (1974): 10–20.

Versteegh, Kees. "Latinitas, Hellenismos, 'Arabiyya." In *The History of Linguistics in the Classical Period*, ed. Daniel J. Taylor. Amsterdam: John Benjamins, 1987.

Vessey, Mark. "Conference and Confession: Literary Pragmatics in Augustine's '*Apologia contra Hieronymum*.'" *Journal of Early Christian Studies* 1 (1993): 175–213.

——. "Theory, or the Dream of the Book (Mallarmé to Blanchot)." In *The Early Christian Book*, ed. William Klingshirn and Linda Safran. Washington, D.C.: Catholic University of America Press, 2007, 241–73.

——. "Ideas of Christian Writing in Late Roman Gaul." D.Phil. thesis, University of Oxford, 1988.

——. "Jerome's Origen: The Making of a Christian Literary Persona." *Studia Patristica* 28 (1993): 135–45.

Walker, P. W. L. *Holy City, Holy Places?* Oxford: Oxford University Press, 1990.

Walsh, P. G. *The Poems of St. Paulinus of Nola*. Ancient Christian Writers 40. New York: Newman Press, 1975.

Wangh, Martin. "Boredom in Psychoanalytic Perspective." *Social Research* 42 (1975): 538–50.

Wenzel, Siegfried. *The Sin of Sloth: Acedia in Medieval Thought and Literature*. Chapel Hill: University of North Carolina Press, 1967.

Wessner, P. "Lucan, Statius und Juvenal bei den römischen Grammatikern." *Philologische Wochenschrift* 49 (1929): 296–335.

White, Hayden. *The Content of the Form: Narrative Discourse and Historical Representation*. Baltimore: Johns Hopkins University Press, 1987.

Whitman, Jon, ed. *Interpretation and Allegory: Antiquity to the Modern Period*. Leiden: Brill, 2001.

Wiedemann, Thomas. *Adults and Children in the Roman Empire*. New Haven: Yale University Press, 1989.

Wilken, Robert. *The Christians as the Roman Saw Them*. New Haven: Yale University Press, 1984.

Wingo, E. O. *Latin Punctuation in the Classical Age*. The Hague: Mouton, 1972.

Witke, Charles. *Numen Litterarum: The Old and the New in Latin Poetry from Constantine to Gregory the Great*. Leiden: Brill, 1971.

Wutz, F. *Onomastica Sacra*. Texte und Untersuchungen zur Geschichte der altchristlichen Literatur 41.1–2. Leipzig: Hinrichs, 1914–15.

Young, Frances. *Biblical Exegesis and the Formation of Christian Culture*. Cambridge: Cambridge University Press, 1997.

Zeiller, J. *Paganus: Étude de terminologie historique*. Paris: E. de Boccard, 1917.

Zetzel, James E. G. *Latin Textual Criticism in Antiquity*. New York: Arno, 1981.

Index

Acknowledgments

This project began its life some time ago as a series of loosely connected thoughts on early Christianity and Roman education, and with help from a number of friends and colleagues, these thoughts have settled into a book. It is a pleasure to acknowledge the people who have done most to shape and encourage this process. Very little of what is useful in this book would have been written without Elizabeth Clark, my deeply admired mentor. Kalman Bland, Mary T. Boatwright, Kent Rigsby, and Warren Smith were all extraordinarily generous with their time and insight. Other friends, colleagues, and teachers have formed an invaluable conversational network through the process of writing and revising; they deserve much more credit in individual ways than this list of their names can convey: Lewis Ayres, Vahni Capildeo, Stephanie Cobb, Rebecca L. Gibson, Andrew S. Jacobs, Diane Lipsett, Deborah Marcuse, Meaghan O'Keefe, Michael Penn, Jeremy Schott, Caroline T. Schroeder, Tina Shepardson, Mark Vessey, Medi Volpe, and Sarah Willburn. Patricia Cox Miller's 1997 presidential address to the North American Patristics Society, "'Differential Networks': Relics and Other Fragments in Late Antiquity" (subsequently published in the *Journal of Early Christian Studies* 6 [1998]: 113–38), provided the intellectual stimulus for most of this project; this book might easily be read as a commentary on, and tribute to, that text.

I was fortunate enough to spend 2003–2004 at the American Academy in Rome, and I would like to thank that year's Fellows and Residents, in particular Mary H. Doyno, Victoria Morse, William North, and Emma Scioli, for their constant company and encouragement. Colleagues at the Catholic University of America, especially Philip Rousseau and Leonora Neville at the Center for Early Christian Studies, likewise offered much support. I am very grateful to Virginia Burrus, who encouraged me to send the manuscript to the University of Pennsylvania Press.

Parts of this book have appeared elsewhere. Part of Chapter 4 appeared in an earlier form as "The Grammarian's Spoils: *De doctrina Christiana* and the Contexts of Literary Education," in *Augustine and the Disciplines: From Cassiciacum to Confessions*, edited by Karla Pollmann and Mark Vessey

(Oxford: Oxford University Press, 2005); part of Chapter 6 appeared in an earlier form as "Through the Looking-Glass Darkly: Jerome Inside the Book," in *The Early Christian Book*, edited by William Klingshirn and Linda Safran (Washington, D.C.: Catholic University of America Press, 2007). I thank those presses for permission to republish that work here.

Finally, and most personally, I would like to thank my parents, although my mother did not live to see this project to its completion. To them this book is dedicated.